ABOLISHING
ONE MAN'S AT·I·

A BRIGHT IDEA.
The Peace Recruiting Sergeant trying to enlist the Duke.

Abolishing War: One Man's Attempt

by
Nicholas Gillett

William Sessions Limited
York, England

ISBN 1 85072 321 4

Printed in 11 point Plantin Typeface
from Author's Disk
by Sessions of York
The Ebor Press
York, England

Table of Contents

List of Illustrations

Foreword

NICHOLAS GILLETT HAS led an active life in steady pursuit of the aims and principles that spring from his Quaker beliefs. Coming from a family with a tradition of devotion to serious causes he has characterized his own objective as "a quest for peace, the abolition of war, and what is now termed the establishment of a culture of peace." These are certainly important, not to say ambitious, objectives. In pursuing them, Nicholas Gillett has at various times been a social worker in the 1930s work camps for the unemployed and later for refugees from Hitler; a farm worker (as a conscientious objector in World War II; a teacher; an international civil servant (with UNESCO); a director in a charitable trust; and a peace worker in Belfast. While in the Quaker office in Geneva, he wrote an invaluable small book, *The Swiss Constitution: Can It Be Exported?* Gillett's experiences in various parts of the world inclined him to think that on the whole it could not.

It is refreshing to read a memoir based on a respected but largely unfashionable point of view, and on an approach that maximises the cause and the philosophy and minimizes the kind of ill-concealed bragging and pretension that characterize so many memoirs. Gillett believes, I think, that we shall only transform the world through changing the way people think and by thus building a culture of peace. This is an enormous task that can best be tackled at what the Americans call the 'grass roots level.' Nicholas Gillett's memoir gives a splendid account of one man's attempt to do this.

Sir Brian Urquhart
Formerly Under-Secretary General
of the United Nations.

Introduction

AS YOU, THE READER, open a new book, you are, so to say entering the front door of the house of a hospitable author. The word 'WELCOME' is woven into the doormat. If you have decided to read the whole book you hang up your coat and settle down to it. If you have any doubts about it, you may first want to read the page of contents, the chapter headings. They correspond with the rooms in the house. Each room or chapter contains different things to suit its purpose. Even the most weary cook will not want a bed in the kitchen.

In choosing to mix a treatise on the desirable conditions of peace with an autobiography I knew I was taking a risk of confusing the reader and making the meal difficult to digest. Yet I believe the autobiography can be understood as a continuous search and the search can be more personal and therefore more interesting. The untidy rooms of busy persons provide insights into their characters and their concerns.

It might have been possible to produce a better, more authoritative, more useful book by securing the cooperation of a number of people each from a different academic discipline, from law, history, mathematics, science, sociology, economics, philosophy, psychology and then attempting to weld the parts into a whole.

On the other hand an attempt has been made to gather the oracular wisdom of sages and proverbs together with the farsightedness of the futurists and to spice the resulting mixture with my own anecdotes, so that no one may accuse me of plagiarism.

This book's format has been largely determined by the varied sequence of my activities arranged roughly in date order. Stress is rightfully laid on the apparent need to know a little of many subjects and to defy the frequent criticism of being master of none. At the early stages or chapters I was assuming that my wish to do something useful for the general public could best be satisfied by improving the educational system, as far as any single person can reasonably hope to do so, while leaving higher ambitions to others. For the most part Quakers can best work for peace when the violence comes to an end.

The next stage began with the proverbial unsolicited letter on the breakfast table. It took the form of an invitation to join UNESCO's technical assistance programme in developing countries. At the same period, I was invited to join the Joseph Rowntree Charitable Trust and shortly afterwards to manage my parents' Charitable Trust, which though small at the time was due to grow considerably. Together the three events formed a turning point in my life, which diverted me towards a wider task involving a quest for peace, the abolition of war and what is now termed the establishment of a culture of peace. Although money by itself achieves little, if it is used to strengthen the arms of talented people who have vision, it can achieve a great deal.

Since that time I have kept in touch by acquainting myself more systematically with the numerous conditions in which peace and justice can be manifested. These include the practical experience of United Nations Technical Assistance and working in Belfast and Geneva, but also fundraising for a permanent post at the United Nations Association. They also includes reading books and periodicals, attending conferences and seminars so as to know who and what to support with grants. If there were more of us holding similar views about solving disputes and conflict non-violently rather than by military force, the ridiculous disparity between the funds allotted would be changed. Redirecting one percent of military expenditure each year could well make a start, to develop alternative forms of defence such as a stronger United Nations.

Already, under Kofi Annan's leadership a valuable boost to the UN's morale has been given by the record breaking donation of a billion dollars from Ted Turner and the award of the Nobel Peace Prize to Kofi Annan himself and to the staff. Whether he can call in some of the wiser big firms and Non-Governmental Organisations to keep the more short-sighted sovereign states in order, remains to be seen but the process has started well. This is the drama, which is taking place in our lifetimes and in which everyone has a part to play. The stakes are high. It is not just a matter of life and death but a question of widespread genocide through the destruction of the environment as well as through nuclear weapons. It is said of the dinosaurs: 'Too much armour, too little brain, died out.' It could be that this will be the more aptly written epitaph for the human race, if there is anyone left to write it. This was in my mind at a meeting in Geneva, which was addressed by the Vice-President of the USA when he had two armed bodyguards facing the meeting. The two leading experts on nuclear winters from USSR, and the USA were taking part and luckily I was able to provide them with copies of Byron's grim poem about the summer which never happened, when in some parts of Europe no one was left to bury the dead because the harvest failed due, as we now know, to such a huge volcanic explosion that the atmospheric dust obstructed the sun, causing crops to fail and famine to spread. By good fortune I had the Russian translation with me.

The inclusion of an anecdote in the introductory pages is intended to indicate that I believe in keeping autobiographies as personal and interesting as possible, hoping that the reader will appreciate the leaven.

Acknowledgments

THIS BOOK WOULD have never been written but for the continual encouragement and editing of Dean Rees-Evans and to the countless people in the peace movement from whom I have learned step by step. I would also like to thank Kerry Channing for assistance in preparing the book for publication, and in setting up the web site accompanying this book, http://www.insearchofpeace.net

Finally I wish to give very special thanks to Sir Brian Urquhart, formerly Under Secretary-General to the United Nations, who has interrupted an exceedingly busy retirement to commend the book. Having had practical experience of peacekeeping, there is no one in a better position to do so.

CHAPTER 1

The Coming of the Quakers: An Active Inheritance

THE KING OF NEPAL was standing in UNESCO House in Paris speaking to a large audience gathered from all over the world to do with thirty-one less developed countries. It was 1982 and already hopes of finding good ways to help such countries were fading. 'Do you know,' he asked 'how it feels to be a poor man. It means to go to bed hungry, to look into the children's eyes and be sad for them, to be afraid what the next day will bring.' He looked so sincere, one felt as though he himself must have been fasting. Thoughts flashed through my mind. I wondered how many people in the audience were laughing to themselves to think that a King could tell them anything about hunger. Yet he was wishing to speak for the 'South,' people from the 'North' were not yet ready to believe that a rich 'North' and a poor 'South' cannot exist together without leading to disaster. Violent conflict lies ahead. No one at that time could possibly have foreseen the events of September 11th 2001 or the dangers of anthrax in the post, or the bombing of nuclear power stations. To be sure the King used no threats. He did not need to do so. The situation posed the threats. A few people began to comment that development was not working as expected.

My life has been a long search for peace and my love of books has been an integral part of that search. Anyone seeking the implications of a culture of peace does well to consult John Ferguson's book *The Politics of Love*.[1] For the first two centuries after Jesus' death, it was assumed that any Roman soldiers who wished to join the Christians would first leave the army. This high standard of ethics, based on Jesus' teachings, was only changed when the

1

Emperor Constantine brought about a fusion of church and state. In *The Politics of Love* Ferguson quotes from very numerous early Christian writers of whom two are especially relevant: Minucius Felix in the second or third century wrote, 'It is not right for us even to see or hear of a man being killed.' He was following Tertullian 160 - 220 CE, who also wrote assuming Christians would be pacifists. The second, Lactantius wrote, 'of friends even to their enemies ... who know how to restrain their anger.' This is a very strong message to those who control the media today, even too strong for most parents. It stands in stark contrast with the Crusaders and with the British Army, which claims when advertising itself that 'Peace is our business'. This brings the culture of peace into practical terms to be kept in mind especially when looking after children, what a comment on violence on television and the daily newspapers! I am glad to have given up both, and that my children are inclined the same way.

The pacifist element in Christianity was upheld here and there among the monasteries during the Middle Ages, but there was no appeal to ordinary people until the aftermath of the seventeenth century's religious wars. At that time in Britain, after the Civil War between Catholics and Protestants, war weariness prevailed, and there was a strong move for democratic ways of living. Meanwhile the loyalty to Crown and Church was weakened and a consequent belief followed that the individual's conscience and insight were better guides to understanding the meaning of the New Testament than the preaching of priests or ministers.

Such were the bases on which the Society of Friends was founded. Early on, the famous Peace Testimony was worded, to inform King Charles II that he had no need to fear the growing movement since 'we do utterly deny all outward wars and strife, and fighting with outward weapons for any end [...] and this is our testimony to the whole world'.[2]

It may have originated as a plea that there was no need for the government to fear a peaceful people, but it became much more than this. It was accepted as the principal statement of the Quakers' non-violence and their culture of peace, which has grown into the basis for new approaches to war, slavery, mental breakdown, race relations, imprisonment, capital punishment, and education in all of which the Friends have played a leading role. All of the implications of the belief that there is 'that of God in everyone', were not at once apparent but have been more widely appreciated by many, and by some understood, as grounds for a more equal treatment of all individuals, as the centuries passed.

This extension has been facilitated in two ways: firstly in the form of the silent meeting for worship on Sundays. A Methodist minister in Belfast once remarked to me about silent worship: 'You Friends have got the right idea. You do listen to what the Lord has to say. You don't keep telling him what he should do.' He further endeared himself to us by adding: 'if I did not like talking so much, I think I would become a Quaker myself.' Many a young person in the Friends has been influenced by the thoughts which came to them as a result of those deep silences. Some favourite quotations within the Society of Friends include: 'let your lives speak,' and, 'by their fruits ye shall know them.' They imply a combination of meditation and social activity unfamiliar to many other Christian Sects.

In depicting what is intended to happen during a period of worship, it is easy to get carried away. It is not always as straightforward as it first appears. One well-known Quaker used to tell the story against himself in old age, that as a young student at a theological college, delighted with his newly acquired knowledge, he came home to his humble little meeting of simple folk and 'ministered' theologically at length. After the meeting was over, an elderly woman Friend chatted to him but then added the warning: Jesus said, "feed my lambs, not giraffes." To those who are puzzled by the story, he added that the implication was that having a higher education did not necessarily give a greater understanding of worship.

The updated volume *Quaker Faith and Practice*,[3] in addition to such documents as the Peace Testimony, also contains brief passages from the writings of individual Friends. Every generation revives these by adding new ones and dropping others. Many of them are drawn from the early years of Quakerism, from such people as George Fox and William Penn and some are taken from the writers of today. This results in an essential measure of flexibility, which is particularly welcome to the young and can open their eyes to visions of the future.

3

Accepting guidance of this kind, about right and wrong, and the importance of the individual's conscience is never very popular with Church, State, or the representatives of society, because conscience is sometimes a challenge to established authority and Quakers have been a small minority, being both persecuted and ridiculed. They often assumed the habits of minorities, feeling unjustly treated, failing to understand the difficulties of others, sometimes developing an undue sense of superiority, drawing close together to reassure themselves, and making much of family relationships; of 'marrying in', in other words marrying another Quaker. This practice only ended in about 1850, alongside the wearing of Quaker dress. It is little wonder that many emigrated to the colonies in America where there was more freedom in religion.

In the first two centuries, until Victorian times, many Quaker families lived apart, alienated from society at large. On their farms and in their meetings they never suffered from anomie, the loss of guiding values, which is an obvious social problem at the start of the new millennium. It is very unlikely that anyone could join the Friends as a 'member' without a strong sense of right and wrong formed in the silences of the Quaker meetings for worship. There may be some differences, even the 'Peace Testimony' has not made pacifists of us all, but we have all tried to follow the guidance of our consciences, based on our Quaker principles and ethics. My father, for example, volunteered to join the army in the First World War, expecting to fight the Germans in Africa. He was rejected on account of his ill health. This did not prevent him from being an elder in the growing Oxford Meeting of Friends.

Friends have never expected all members to be active pacifists. They do maintain an atmosphere in which active pacifism can flourish by listening in the silence of the meeting or to the ministry of those who speak. In this way, they keep in training for standing out from the crowd - to the point of eccentricity. If perplexed, such Friends can ask the meeting for a committee for 'clearance' to advise him or her whether the career or course of action being considered is right for them to undertake or whether they should give more time for reflection.

It was in such conditions that all my ancestors lived, right back to the founding of the Society in the 1650's. Apart from the Cornish fisherman, my namesake, Nicholas Jose, said by George Fox to be like Peter the Apostle, little is known about who they were and what they did before 1750. The 18th century was a very quiet period for Friends and I suspect they had not kept in training for what needed to be done. One exception to this was Isaac and Rachel Wilson, my great-grandmother's great-grandparents. Isaac moved from High Wray to Kendal on marriage to set up as a wool trader in 1740. The southern part of the Lake District and its neighbourhood are known as the birthplace of Quakerism and other relatives lived at Firbank and Brigflatts. As soon as the family's children were old enough, Rachel felt called to 'travel in the Ministry' in the British colonies, in what is now part of the USA. The account of her travels conveys the earnest way in which Friends worked in those days under a sense of 'concern' for more people to live a peaceful way of life.

It was not until John Bright (1811-1889) that there was a pacifist activist in the family, my mother's, mother's father. He was in Parliament from 1843 until his death, with a short gap, created by his pacifism. Having made a great name during the campaign against the Corn Laws, people came in their thousands to hear him, possibly more than to any other speaker. It must be realised that before 1832 the government was controlled by so few people that there was little reason for public meetings, comparable with our times, when the media including radio and television have made meetings, in a sense, superfluous. Between these two dates roughly 1832-1950 the role of the orator was crucial. It was before the days of pop stars and famous footballers and people would hang on to their every word, quoting them to each other after the event, and accepting their guidance up to a point, since there were few other ways of obtaining information.

For John Bright it was over the Crimean war against Czarist Russia that he sacrificed his popularity. It is easy for demagogues to stir up a crowd to rioting, and in Manchester an effigy of John Bright was burned and he lost the next election. His friends in Birmingham welcomed him to that city and he represented it for the next 30 years. One of those friends was Joseph Sturge, an uncle by marriage of my grandfather William Clark of Millfield at Street. He visited the Czar to urge him to free the serfs in Russia in 1860.

5

John Bright's daughter, Helen Priestman Bright Clark made it her work to invite speakers and arrange meetings on what might be termed 'good causes' in Street; and after her death when I ventured into her closet, through the mysterious door on the stairs, I found a mass of pamphlets and papers, mostly arranged in pigeon holes marked with such subjects as 'peace', 'free trade', 'women's causes', and 'slavery'. Her daughters shared her interests; Aunt Hilda worked for the forerunner of Quaker Peace and Service. She helped war victims and refugees from war zones with food and medical care, as she was a doctor. She was strongly supported by her sister Aunt Alice. I recall the letters which arrived from Germany during the inflation with millions and later billions of Marks in stamps on them, welcome prizes for a small boy of eight years old, but I knew there was a terrible story behind them, so terrible I did not dare to ask questions, about the suffering of the refugees and others.

I was also aware that the very large portraits of Wilberforce, Gladstone and Bright hanging in the dining room, were in some way connected. In an alcove on the stairs was a very memorable scene moulded in clay which represented the story of the 'underground railway' as it was called, to help slaves escaping from a slave state in the south of the USA. Little did I guess that fifty years later my wife Ruth and I would be setting up a similar organisation in Belfast for those whose lives were in danger.

Millfield was the house which William and Helen Clark had built to be both a farm and a home. I saw it have a profound influence on those who rested there after working abroad, on the speakers who came for a night, and on us children who came on many holidays and especially for me staying for some months at the age of four to five while my parents were in South Africa.

There was only one dissonant feature and that was the crossed swords on the wall of the hall, which had been found on the site of the Battle of Sedgemoor in Somerset, the last battle to be fought on English soil (1685), some six miles away. It was after that battle that two of my ancestors gave shelter to the Duke of Monmouth, escaping for his life. They were arrested, tried by Judge Jeffreys at the 'Bloody Assizes' in Taunton, and hung for it. My mother, despite her pacifism, awe-struck with horror at what happened to her relatives long ago passed on to me such a hatred of Jeffreys and the grim cloud of fear he left hanging in the air in Somerset, that I still use it as an example of how irrational prejudices linger from generation to generation.

When teaching about the Culture of Peace, I use this as an example of an irrational prejudice, which I should have been able to overcome long ago. If a three hundred year hatred lingers on even in a Quaker family, what hope is there for the human race?

Interestingly, one of my tutors, Professor M.V.C. Jeffreys at the Birmingham University's Education Department lectured to the MA Education Course I attended (1945-52). It was reputed that he was a direct descendant of the infamous Judge. However I thought it prudent to say nothing about this to him, despite the adage I used as guidance on many occasions, 'when in doubt, act!'

Maybe history should be excluded from the school curriculum unless it can resemble something like the South African Commission, which attempts to put right past wrongs, instead of hoping that sleeping dogs can be left to lie? One of the texts I used when dealing with prejudices was *1066 And All That: A Memorable History of England*[4] in the belief that hatred cannot withstand humour, even if the humour is black. 'Third Zulu War, Zulus exterminated, peace with the Zulus.'

Margaret Clark Gillett, my mother, ensured that her family kept in training for being different and assumed we would be unconventional. As a student at Newnham College Cambridge she had worn a dress for hockey, which showed her ankles and was known as Margaret's frills. About this time she went on a cycling and camping holiday in the Welsh border counties with her sister which at the time would also have seemed unconventional. After Cambridge she learned to weave and accompanied Emily Hobhouse and a Rowntree cousin to South Africa to teach weaving to the Boer women. Their homes and farms had been burned to check the guerrilla movement and they were enclosed in barbed wire camps with their children. Hitler called them the first concentration camps. A wool-weaving industry was established to earn some money as well as providing an occupation, which lasted fifty years. The British army did not like Emily Hobhouse's intervention, indeed it pointed to their incompetence, but in those days war was not 'total' and she could not be prevented from following her convictions.

Out of this sprang the close friendship of my parents with Jan Smuts. He had written in his diary, which he kept in his saddlebag during the war that another John Bright was needed to make a lasting peace, not expecting that he would ever meet one of his granddaughters, my mother.

As was the custom of the time she took on no paid work, but she set us children an example by her love for books. I recall being set to work rubbing oil on her many leather-bound volumes, but she was in no way a mere collector of old books, though in literature it was the most famous authors rather than the latest whom she preferred. She was an expert in poetry being able to quote appropriately for any occasion, thus enhancing both experience and understanding. She often read to me at bedtime, one of her favourite poems being Southey's critical account of the battle of Blenheim.

> But what they fought each other for
> I could not well make out
> But everybody said 'quoth he
> That 'twas a famous victory.'[5]

Although my mother worked with the Boers, she strongly supported better race relations. For example, my parents knew Davidson Jabavu, an African Quaker whom Nelson Mandela greatly appreciated as a teacher, and they took responsibility for his daughter Nontando when she came to school in England.

My parents had also befriended an Indian couple the Kumaramangalams, who later became well known in India as politicians and who were studying at the university in the early years of the twentieth century. In the following years they had three boys and a girl who were much the same ages as my own brothers and sister. Often they came to spend parts of their holidays with us, sometimes at Porthcothan Cove in north Cornwall, sometimes at 102 Banbury Rd. They appreciated this so much that, Paramasiva the eldest of the Kumaramangalams before joining the forces during the war, where he was to fight the Italians in northern Africa, delighted my father by naming him as 'next of kin.' My father gave his Lombard street address in the hope of better treatment for him if taken prisoner. Their mother introduced my mother to Gandhi, at the time of the Round Table Conference and as it was one of Gandhi's silent days, they sat and communed together as in a Quaker Meeting.

As children we all felt so close to each other that we all developed a healthy form of colour blindness and could understand the five-year old who invited a friend to tea and when her mother asked her what colour she was, replied 'I don't know, I'll look tomorrow.' The boys went to Eton and my father recommended Badminton School for Parvathi, one of a group of internationally minded schools. Being friends with Nehru, Nehru sent his daughter, Mrs Gandhi the future Prime Minister of India, also to Badminton school.

For a period after the war Paramasiva had served as Commander in Chief of the Indian Army, it was said of him that the only orders he gave were on the polo field. Meeting after many years break we talked about our holidays together in Cornwall as children and about our parents and then we moved on to major matters. He was strongly in favour of the UNA and of the Retired Generals and Admirals Association. We then moved on to the Gulf War: 'one of my favourite books on strategy' he said 'is Sun Tzu's *The Art of War*,[6] written in 500 BCE.' He went to fetch the slim volume, now worn and heavily marked for suitable quotations for speeches and he read out the following passage: 'the practical art of war, the aim is to take the enemies' country whole and intact, to shatter and destroy it is not so profitable ... supreme excellence consists in breaking the enemies resistance without fighting.' It was the very day the papers reported bombing of the air-raid shelter in Baghdad. There was no need to comment on the barbarity of modern warfare, so we discussed the role of the UN and the position of Saddam Hussein.

He soon came to the subject in which we have both been involved, namely education. For India, like many other countries, this means examinations. He had become the Chairman of a Board in Delhi as well as at home and had become so disturbed by the influence of examinations that he had written a paper on extra-curricular activities and won the Prime Minister's, Mrs Gandhi's

9

support for it, only to have it blocked by the Ministry of Education's officials.

Seeing my interest he fetched a quotation from Einstein's address at Albany, New York, October 15th 1936.[7] 'Knowledge is dead, the school, however, serves the living ... on the contrary the aim must be the training of independently acting and thinking individuals, who, however, see in the service of the community their highest life problem... the English school system comes nearest to the realization of this ideal.' The 'grand old man of world peace' as the encyclopaedia styles Einstein, taught in Germany, USA, and Switzerland but not in England.

By chance Paramasiva's successor as Commander in Chief joined our lunch party each day when we were in Mumbai (Bombay) as he was the brother of our hostess. Sam Manakshaw is a kindly man who said he pressed Mrs Gandhi six times to give preference to Paramasiva, especially because Paramasiva came from Tamil Nadu which is a big province in the south, and the army tends to be too biased towards the North. We were very amused to find that restaurants in the south used to be either Civil or Military according to whether they were vegetarian or not. The gentler vegetarians live in the south, the fierce meat eaters in the north, an observation, which draws attention to the heavy meat eating in Belfast.

Sam was upset at having to confront the pushing for promotion in the army on behalf of relatives, a practice, which could defeat an army more easily than an enemy can do! His anecdotes put him at the centre of any discussion. Whether Sam knew that a nuclear bomb was soon going to be exploded in India, I cannot tell. I doubt that Paramasiva, who has now died, would have supported such a rash policy.

Looking back now it seems odd that though I was closer to my father I appear to have followed my mother's ideas. They were both supporters of the League of Nations Union, the body that campaigned for stronger support of the League, and there was an influential branch office in Oxford on account of the University. Though my father ministered more often in Meeting and read to us from the Bible each morning, his banking work led to a more conventional view of public affairs. He was the owner of one of the last four private banks in Britain, the Gillett's Bank in Oxford, and also later he became a director of Barclays Bank and Vice-Chairman of Barclays Dominion, Colonial, and Overseas, after selling his own bank. Despite this conventionality he was a strong proponent of ethical banking and seen by his colleagues as somewhat eccentric. By that time father was a trustee of his uncle's Joseph Rowntree Charitable Trust so he liked to hold forth on what he called the right use of money to his wealthier clients from the Duke of Marlborough onwards. It was this kind of ethical banking he wished me to maintain. Before he sold out to Barclays he had a very positive response to the wide spread unemployment among coal miners and invested in a project for converting coal into petrol. That proved to be a false hope; when I visited the plant with him, there was already evidence of a disaster. Another one of his clients went bankrupt and he wrote an unsolicited letter offering him a loan should he ever wish to borrow. He was greatly impressed when his client set out on his bicycle to win enough prize money to repay his creditors, even though he was not obliged to do so. That was William Morris, Lord Nuffield, the founder of Morris Motors.

My father's newspaper was *The Times*, whilst my mother took the *Manchester Guardian*. The long-term influence of one's daily paper is more powerful than is generally recognised. The views of one's chosen newspaper become absorbed by an invisible process akin to osmosis. They both had very strong principles, my father's were indicated by his banking and by serving as a Liberal Councillor on the Oxford City council, they were also indicated by his choice of bedside books such as Thomas à Kempis, *The Imitation of Christ*, and Marcus Aurelius, O*n a Sense of Duty*. From such books, which often inspired his frequent Sunday ministry in the Quaker Meeting, one would never guess what a jovial person he was. As his college friend E. M. Forster wrote in his obituary, he seemed to have a private joke shared only with the Creator of the Universe.

He was eagerly awaited when he returned from the bank. The whole house and household seemed to be lifted by his jokes, his gentle teasing and the games he played with us four children. This lightness of touch is something to be remembered when negotiators are in demand and can deal with grim disputes or for training that is designed to help them. How it can be expressed without appearing to treat the consequences of fear and hatred too lightly is the question.

My father's family included his uncle Joseph Rowntree whose remarkable work for peace through his charitable trust will be described later. My father was a trustee from the beginning because he was needed for his financial advice. J.R., as he is still called posthumously, was the founder of the well-known firm Rowntree and Co, which has now been taken over by Nestlé. He first went to work at the Rowntree Grocers Shop in Pavement in York as an apprentice, his fellow apprentices were George Cadbury, Ruth's grandfather and the founder of Cadbury's of Bournville, and my Gillett grandfather who died young of appendicitis while my father was still at school. There is unfortunately no record of the conversations of the two famous visionaries but to judge by their two model villages, they must have influenced each other. J.R. at the age of eleven had already been taken by his father to Ireland at the time of the potato famine to find out what Friends might do about it. Nowadays children experience the horrors of television news, but it is seldom put into the context of what might be done about it. The public, the journalists, and the owners of newspapers and television may all be blamed for omitting an essential part of the news in that way.

Other members of the Gillett family, as of the Clark family, included inventors, creative people who played with their thoughts, which is an inventiveness that now needs redirecting to social problems. The most famous of these inventions was a machine driven by clockwork for producing Latin Verse. It was restored to use in the fifties to take part in a 'Britain Can Make It Exhibition' as part of the collection of inventions, which can never have any use. It was demonstrated on radio. Unfortunately small boys no longer have to write Latin Verse for their homework, as we did! The playfulness of mind it indicates is one of the needs of the peace movement after a century of failure. Latin Verse machines may be dismissed with a smile, but the same distant relative invented a new way of waterproofing cloth and sold the idea for five pounds to a man called Mackintosh, who went on to manufacture the famous raincoat.

Over the course of two centuries there have been a variety of beliefs about the prevention of war, which have been shown to be false or inadequate. 'If all men had the vote,' it was argued, then they would demand a policy against being sent to war in distant lands. Later, this theory having proved unduly optimistic, hopes were attached to votes for women who were assumed to be more caring on behalf of their children and other victims of war than their husbands were. The Marxists genuinely believed that the profits made by arms firms were the main force for war, which would tend to overcome the rational arguments of the peacemakers. Certainly throughout the twentieth century in the USA and in Europe such firms were involved in corrupting politicians, and disturbing peace and disarmament conferences. However socialist governments turning against each other showed that the public ownership of arms factories was an inadequate aim for the peace movement. Similarly the campaigns for disarmament have gained wide approval though there is plenty of evidence that disarmament is not enough. In Africa it is obvious that machetes have been used to kill when other arms are lacking. Such theories about the causes and prevention of war must be discarded and replaced by more thorough peace research.

How far forms of government, such as constitutions, affect the tendency to go to war is not agreed. Recently a theory has been discussed that there is evidence that democracies do not fight each other as much as autocracies. This theory is confused both by a lack of definition of Democracy, and that, as war threatens, democracies tend to reduce their democratic ways.

Michael Howard, Regius Professor of History at Oxford, who deserves to be heard on this elusive but important subject, concludes that cultures contain a degree of 'bellicity,' which determines their likelihood of causing war. This term is not, as far as I know, found in the dictionary, and was coined by Howard. It denotes something different from militarism, which suggests above all soldiering, and is also different from bellicosity, which means a readiness to pick a quarrel, but is best described as a cultural trait directly opposed to a culture of peace. It may well come into use now that the decade 2000-2010 has been named The Decade of the Culture of Peace. Culture is acquired usually over several generations and this may cause dismay, on the other hand it is better to face the truth if a lack of it leads to a nuclear war. Whether the negative concepts of bellicity or the more positive implications of a Culture of Peace are adopted, their implications may be much the same and are an invitation to probe more deeply into the causes of war.[8] If there is such a quality, it may be developed by long-term influences such as exposure to a special climate or diet, and may only be countered in the very long-term.

None of these simple proposals for abolishing war are likely to be adequate. A more persuasive approach though daunting in its implications is shown in Appendix 1. For any peace worker or peace organisation this appendix will encourage a search to establish a list of priorities, though it may be thought to be incomplete in itself.

In addition there are those who believe that nothing short of 'a change of heart' can bring peace. Father's first cousin, but to us Uncle Henry, a medical doctor, author and Mayor of Oxford propounded this view with conviction in response to his daughter and my brothers and sister who joined the Communist Party when no governments went to the help of the democratic government of Spain under attack from Franco. Henry Gillett believed that no system of government or economic system could thrive without public-spirited and caring citizens. Such people can be developed by the patient work of religious sects, schools, colleges, and perhaps psychiatrists. As far as he himself was concerned, he saw his work in the Society of Friends in this light.

My brother Jan, the eldest in the family, had the self-assurance of a man who obtained a double first at Kings College Cambridge. His discussions, sadly, usually became argumentative so that I cannot recall him ever accepting that an opponent was right. Due to very wide reading he was well informed on an extensive range of subjects. In doing this he taught me to brief myself well and to look carefully at ways of improving methods of discussion so that they could become more educative. Tona, my second brother was also older than I was and had warm qualities, which made him a good leader. It is a pity that I found difficulty in copying him and I concluded that such qualities, though highly desirable for peace-workers, are more often innate and are seldom acquired. Helen was younger and I realise that older brothers are little influenced by younger sisters.

14

My siblings' membership of the Communist Party became a barrier between us. Jan seemed to me to have become a fanatic, Tona went to prison for refusing to apologise for his part in the 'Mass Trespass' on Kinder Scout, and Helen organised a student sit-in as a protest against hip-baths (individual little bath tubs with no taps) at Newnham College Cambridge.

In general their devotion to their causes set a high standard for me to emulate. They may have known little about the virtues of democratic citizenship - concession, co-operation, and consensus - but they showed public spirit and selflessness in putting their ideals before their own interests. The slogan of the French Revolution, 'Liberty, Equality, Fraternity,' has inspired regimes to make liberty or equality their principal aim but no regime has done the same for fraternity. Such a regime would be more likely to lead to peace. It would have to apply the ideas in *Small is Beautiful*[9] by reducing the size of large countries, firms, schools, and perhaps families in order to enhance personal relationships as they are described in *Freedom in the Modern World*. [10] No doubt this would accord with the 'change of heart' prescription for one of the conditions of peace. At that time a change of heart was taken to mean becoming active in a Christian sect, accepting God's guidance developing friendly relationships with all and sundry but particularly with all those having a special need for charitable friendship.

CHAPTER 2

Finding My Feet in the World

IN EDUCATIONAL CIRCLES the influence of the informal education in the home is often underrated. In my case, school education was introduced by the little school following the Parents National Education Union syllabus in Aunt Sarah's house at Street. This prepared me for the more intimidating school in Oxford. It was five small fields away by footpath from Millfield, where I at the age of five, was living while my father and mother were in South Africa. The first day began inauspiciously for a future education-alist. In the first field I encountered a bunch of frisky cattle, which certainly had no udders. The way they scampered in front of me seemed to imply that I was taking an unreasonable risk, and so I retraced my steps and went back to report. I felt that I had not described their threats sufficiently vividly when I was told to go back and ignore them. On the second attempt I got by with the greatest difficulty. Despite my shyness, school was easy by comparison!

As it happened the Dragon School at Oxford was barely ten minutes away on foot. Being a younger brother it must have been much easier for me, than for Jan and Tona. A majority of people felt that starting school was an ordeal, which could have been eased for them, and Jan in particular had paved the way for me.

The School did three things exceptionally well. The daily lessons in Latin and Greek made it easy to excel in those subjects, even so I was taken aback when asked to write Latin verse for home-work. The Roman Imperialists would have wondered had they heard us using their language nearly fifteen hundred years after they

16

had left. It not only occupied us in class but formed part of our playground lingo because at one time schoolboys had been compelled to speak Latin all day. It had after all been the international language for Western Europe. At present, views are divided on whether agreement on an international language, such as English or simplified English, is desirable or whether it is more important to preserve a variety of living cultures for which, a variety of languages is essential. At the Dragons we began Latin at the age of seven, French a year later and added Greek at ten. This left us assuming that a precise translation was possible rather than welcoming the many occasions when, owing to differences in culture, an explanation ought to accompany the translation. This still bedevils the interpreters in such institutions as the United Nations where interpreters are not permitted to make corrections even when they know misunderstandings are occurring.

The school also laid stress on rugby football as a means of toughening the otherwise cosseted sons of well-to-do homes. At that time the majority of them were boarders so that we dayboys felt somewhat on the touchlines of school activities. Girls were accepted only if they had brothers in school, one once gained a place in the first XV Rugby team. One school cancelled its fixture with us on the grounds that 'our boys don't tackle girls.' The school and its ethos were surprisingly unconventional and congenial at the time I attended (1922-28); the jingoism due to the recent war was to be expected. Some teachers seemed freshly home from the trenches, and liked to be coaxed into recounting their experiences. One had lost most of one cheek, but the one who suffered from shell-shock terrified me for a whole year and I promised myself that I would take it easy under the kindlier teacher during the following year. The school supposed that I was home-sick for my parents absent in South Africa. An annual Navy League Lecture added to adulation of the armed forces, there was an opportunity to practice with rifles in preparation for joining the Officer's Training Corps in the next school after the age of fourteen. I enjoyed trying to get bull's eyes but, when new cardboard targets were put up with an unmistakable drawing of a German helmet in the centre, I gave up without explaining either to the school or at home.

The third activity to which the school attached importance was swimming and diving. At that time few schools had access to swimming baths so full use was made of the river Cherwell which passed by on the far side of the playing fields. The diving boards provided an opportunity for daring. Trying to keep up with Tona I had put myself down for the under eleven's diving competition despite the fact that I had never dived from the high board in the willow tree some ten feet above water level. Instead of practising, I calculated that in front of a crowd of onlookers I would not dare not to dive. The day came, the crowd assembled and I somehow contrived to get to the water and came second in the competition. The confidence I gained that day lasted me a long time and later coloured my approach to 'A form of education in which everyone is good at something.' For the sake of their self-confidence, or self-esteem.

Despite my successes at school, I only learned twenty-five years later that I was thought to have even more promise than Jan. I was well aware that the ways of the school were not our ways, the teachers never penetrated my thinking, I was like a stranger in a strange land. Had I not at the age of five, with my cousin Jenepher aged four been sent out into the streets to collect for saving German children from the famine, which I could barely imagine? A tall indignant lady reproached us: 'What, German children?' She asked with a severe emphasis on the word 'German.' I was dismayed. Before I could say anything Jenepher replied for us 'Yes, but they are children.' I felt reassured when the lady stamped away. Some time after this I walked in a League of Nations Union procession under a banner saying PAX, a word, the meaning for which, I was proud to know already from our childhood games? It meant of course peace.

It was puzzling for me when elections came in 1924 and the whole school seemed to be supporting the former pupil of the school who was standing for the Conservative party. Was it because he was an old boy that there seemed to be only two other boys wearing yellow ribbons for Labour and not many red ribbons for Liberal? I wore yellow to school at first but eventually courage failed me and I told my mother, I am ashamed to say, that I did not want to wear it again, although I knew it was her colour. My father was a Liberal despite his elder brother Uncle George being elected as a Labour

M.P. Later on Uncle George was appointed Commissioner for the Special Areas, to do what he could about unemployment. The answer was 'Not much.' By this time I was old enough to wonder whether unemployment caused wars, following the principle that 'The devil finds mischief for idle hands to do.' I am still wondering. By now it is apparent that there is a dire flaw in the economic system causing labour-saving machinery to result in excessive unemployment, despite the obvious needs for more work to be done. That flaw could well be a contributing factor to the instability which sometimes leads to war.

The year I left the Dragons, when I was thirteen, I screwed up courage to enter the speech competition in the belief that the ability to make speeches was essential for would-be reformers. My passion at the time was building crystal and valve radio sets so I wrote an account and learnt it by heart. As may be imagined I did badly because what was expected was an effective debating paper not a handbook of how to do it, but I had at least broken the ice. On the other hand I lived in great fear of the initiation ceremony at the boarding school, at which I would have to sing or drink soap and water.

As a result of going to South Africa the second time, I arrived at Leighton Park in the middle of February 1928 and then missed most of 1932 due to a serious mastoid operation followed by the third visit to South Africa. Having had diphtheria when I turned four and coming on to suspected ulcers in my forties I have always had time for reflection, a re-shaping of my values and a form of meditation to use a current term. I shall never forget the end of the period of deafness after the mastoid operation when all the world seemed new because I could hear sounds again. It may well have accentuated my interest in Quakerism that my brothers and sister were casting away. It was about this time that I was taken to visit Mrs. Mallory, the mother of the climber lost on Everest.[11] I was aware of the deep suffering in her gaze, and wanted to speak but could not find the words. Sometimes silence is better than words, but I was not sure that mine was better, because my silence was based on shyness. Later on I was to hear of my mother's great aunts who lived in Bristol by the Downs. They were thought to have died of broken hearts when the peace ended in 1914. Hearts do not seem to break nowadays, though as I walked past their houses on the way to the University in the morning, I seemed to know how they felt. I wish these great aunts could have known that much later after their deaths, at a meeting in a crowded church nearby, when asked whether I could imagine Jesus pressing the button for an atomic explosion, I replied that it would have been unlikely that anyone would have asked Jesus such a question, and this was loudly cheered. It was impossible to tell how far my bad health caused my subsequent academic failures, after studying classics for a first year in the VI form, I was persuaded by my friend Michael Foot to change over to History. From then on I never felt I mastered my academic work and ended up with a Third Class degree, in Politics, Philosophy and Economics, which might well have excluded me from teaching.

The atmosphere at Leighton Park in Reading was a delightful change from the Dragons, instead of living in fear of the teachers, I found them to be people I admired or even hero-worshipped. It is a Quaker school which was set up to provide at least one public boarding school without an Officers Training Corps, which could offer courses leading to Universities. Although the Council for Education in World Citizenship was not created in time to influence much of the teaching, when a Scout Troop was formed the Scout officials had to give way and allow the flag of the League of Nations to be flown alongside the Union Jack. A branch of the League of Nations Union was formed and as we stood together to agree a time and place of a meeting, the History teacher said ' And you, Gillett, will be the secretary.' Michael Foot must by that time have moved on to Oxford University. By this time I had already decided at the age of sixteen to prepare myself for working in peace organizations by teaching myself touch typing and improving my French, with Lansbury as leader of the Labour Party, a political career was a possibility for me. It was easy for my mother to arrange coaching in French when there was time during holidays and I had gained a distinction in French and oral French at GCSE, despite the English accent which still amuses my children.

French teaching has become much better since those days, though my accent was not as bad as Mr. Edward Heath's, the Conservative Prime Minister 1970-74, one of my fellow students at Balliol College. It leaves a lot to be desired and the French do not appreciate people who maul their beautiful language. I had two valuable periods in France, once with my sister Helen in an 'Ecole de Vacance' and the other while waiting to go to South Africa in 1932. Nowadays more emphasis is laid on speaking the language and this is eased by the use of audiotapes, which were not available to me. Aunt Hilda used Linguaphone records for her international work but they were less convenient to use. There still seems to be much to do to help overcome shyness and gain languages orally while staying in a country.

Learning French and later German was an act of faith. I had no idea at the time that it was going to be extremely useful in widely different circumstances. This raises the important question of when it is desirable to explain to children the reasons for each part of the curriculum. At present the teachers themselves are not very sure, even though until recently each school used to be responsible for its own syllabus. For example one of my acquaintances was a great believer in Esperanto as a way open for every school to make a contribution to international understanding so she introduced it into the whole of her Secondary Modern School. Her success was striking and the children were glad to have a language which their parents couldn't understand, and this led eventually to a deputation of parents applying for Esperanto lessons for themselves.

At Leighton Park the new headmaster Edgar Castle had enthusiasm and very persuasive theories of education. They centred round the concept of 'the whole man,' which implied a new balance between the classroom, the gymnasium, and the games fields, the Quaker Meeting each Sunday in Reading and in the school's hall and the elaborate provision for hobbies each evening. It was this last activity of hobbies, which appeared to make the school unique, and the winner of the prize for the best exhibit gained as much prestige as the cricket or rugby captain. It was becoming common for radio sets to be made, fishermen might make 'flies' for catching fish, photography was in great demand, the list seemed endless. My brother Tona won the prize one year by designing and making an armchair, Jan had collections of plants and went on to become a professional tropical botanist. It came as a surprise that everyone was good at something in contrast with the academic classroom.

Everyone had an 'identity' a term now used in peace conferences to indicate that minority groups often have a sense of group identity which they may fight to maintain as fiercely as ordinary nationalists. One of my own contributions to the Hobby Exhibition was a tent, which I had made with considerable difficulty, not being accustomed to using a sewing machine, an indication of an inner urge to travel and thus become acquainted with other places and other ways of life. I chose a lightweight material of a sky blue colour and spent many happy hours stitching and thinking of the places where I might use it. I woke one morning and looking up, wondered why the sky seemed to have indistinct lines in it, when suddenly I realised I was lying in the tent. Years later, on a very separate occasion I restrained my anger when two of the boys, romping in my sky-blue tent, tore it beyond repair. When and how should anger be restrained? To me it was like the loss of a peasant's land. My dream had been broken; so I was angry, but Quaker-fashion I tried hard to swallow it and to this day, I believe, they do not know how upset I was.

There are many ways in which the years at school have influenced my work in education, which followed. The Hobbies Exhibition at the school appeared to be firmly linked with the hour each evening when we were expected to be occupying ourselves with hobbies. On such occasions instead of a whole class studying the same subject, individuals followed and developed their own interests and often grew in specialist skills and knowledge. In my time there were stories still circulating of a previous boy who had written a book on The Green Roads of England, while still at the school. Another boy captured a very rare malaria-carrying Anopheles mosquito in the school grounds, and a third boy recorded the eruption of the volcano on the island of Krakatoa, off the coast of Java with a seismograph. Such a tradition of enterprising activities had a profound effect throughout the school and encouraged us to raise our sights. Creativeness of this kind is not appreciated in all schools and yet it is well said that you can always judge a person by what he does with his spare time. It is when he has leisure that he becomes truly himself. Leisure activities, to counter the overuse of television, were, and remain, of very great importance to schools, parents, and children. During the exhibition we learned who the people were who might help us with our hobbies, as I received help with my photography. I won a prize for my first photo that appeared in the school magazine. Others were also interested in the lightweight tent that I had made. Often the hobby pointed the way to a life-long career, a boy became a chef this way, my brother Jan became a botanist, an amateur meteorologist became a professional, one boy who kept hens, set up a poultry food business based on the new knowledge of the value of vitamins, and so with many others. In any case hobbies help anyone who has time on his hands to avoid getting up to mischief.

I turned this experience of my schooling at Leighton Park to good account when teaching at Turves Green for my own class. The exhibition of hobbies on this occasion was spread over several weeks so that everyone had a chance to answer questions about how their work was done. In brief the idea of an exhibition could be adapted to a whole school, to a class, to one or more Parent-Teacher Associations, or to holidays. When teaching, the staff could build on the confidence derived from the skills exhibited, and it made an excellent background for parent's day; in this way parents are able to deal with the long school holidays, though they may have to pay for it. One mother put up with a lathe in her front room and was well rewarded; her son became an outstanding performer on the lathe, and was chosen to meet the Prince of Wales. In Birmingham not only were many schools willing to hold exhibitions, but the most imaginative objects, with a lesson or suggestion for other children implied by them, were gathered in a department store, so that all parents and many teachers were able to visit, sometimes bringing children with them. With these exhibitions I felt we were touching the main joint field of interest of both teachers and parents. Teachers wish to develop such interests to be so strong that they spill over into leisure time: one commented to me 'I had no idea Tom kept bees; I'll base some of the arithmetic on bees and honey in future'. It seemed as though the film Kes of the boy who had difficulties at school until his teacher learned that he kept a pet Kestrel, had come alive. I was happy that teachers and parents cooperated so well and that my early experiment at Turves Green had taken root.

Again, later it proved possible to publish 'Holiday Books' containing suggestions for occupations at home, but this was less successful than the school or class exhibitions. Some of the head teachers said that their pupils did not do anything when they were not at school with the exception of watching television programmes. Several were honest enough to admit that they had made a mistake. There was much support for the schools exhibitions from parents who took pride in what their children could do and were glad to play their part by providing facilities. One commented 'I have never thought I'd see a canoe being built in our front room!'

Teachers also saw the great advantage of knowing their children better. The son of a poverty-stricken smallholder had a great day when he was able to show the class round the smallholding. When they came to the pigs, which were his special care, he was very proud to be able to answer questions about feeding the piglets. It was not so good when, at the school exhibition, one of the pigs escaped from their pen, rushed past the beehive, nearly turning it over. The BBC reporter looked aghast as though no one would believe her if she told the story.

Strode School, at Street was of special interest because it had successfully applied to a charitable trust and appointed a teacher Peter Preston to spend half his time 'improving the quality and quantity of the leisure activities of the pupils in and around their homes.' It was assumed that he would work through his colleagues, and partly with parents to ensure that the facilities were provided, as well as with the children themselves. In two cases this led to the building of sheds, one for bicycle repairs, and one for building radio sets. The exhibition was obviously supported by the children who made friends in a new way, learned from others ideas about developing their own interests and discovered to whom to turn to for help when in difficulties. That occasion at Strode School was made famous by two boys: One of them found instructions for making telescopes and asked for some help from the Metalwork Department, and then they set to work. It was a Secondary Modern School, but of such high standard that when they found constellations and wanted to take photographs of them they took themselves off to the public library for some books to help them. They noticed that one of the authors lived thirty miles away from the school. He turned out to be willing to see them and so they went off on their bicycles and had a very good time with him and his apparatus. The exhibit of their photographs and equipment was so impressive that it was given pride of place at the entrance to the exhibition. One nine year old boy, who did not have an expensive Meccano set to make windmills, cranes and tractors, hammered out empty tin cans and used nails to make the holes for his home made set.

After the introduction of splendid work such as this it was unfortunate, to put it mildly, that it was not continued. We have ourselves to blame if our time is filled in coping with juvenile violence and delinquency rather than providing time for creative alternatives. A culture of peace is best created among the young and the opportunity was missed to create it by methods and exhibitions such as these, at the end of the war.

It was not that Leighton Park was out of touch with the state system of education. On the contrary, Edgar Castle not only helped found the council for Education in World Citizenship but also went on to be the Professor of Education at Hull University. However, he may have been unaware of the potential of the Hobbies Exhibition. A good subject specialist should judge his own teaching of his subjects by how far it penetrates leisure interests. In schools people matter and people are made up of bundles of interests that need to be cultivated more than they are at present.

The virtue of leisure activities is that everyone can do something different, and be good at it. The evils of a highly academic competitive system can be avoided. Some examples from a variety of schools came to my notice. This was more than lateral thinking it was lateral living and my friends and I were ready for anything. Hugh Doncaster, who shared a room with me was of like mind and also shared my interest in birds. We were allowed to ride our bicycles into the countryside at weekends and we talked as we went. One of his recurrent thoughts was about a personal God. 'Why' he asked 'do Christians create such difficulties for us by expecting us to believe in such improbable, if not ridiculous doctrines?' I wanted to move on to other subjects but he wanted, it seemed to me, to keep worrying about the one question as though he was planning to convert everyone to his point of view. Later on in life he became a lecturer on Quakerism at Woodbrooke College in Selly Oak, Birmingham. I was more interested in finding out the purpose in life, 'what are we here to do?' I kept asking. Some six years later I got an answer which was satisfying if not satisfactory, a girl from the London School of Economics talking in a home in Vienna quoted Goethe: 'Der Zweck des lebens ist das leben selbst.' I stopped listening after that, I had at last got my answer 'The aim of life is life itself.' She spoke with such delightful gusto, wie ein wasserfall (like a waterfall) as one of the Austrians commented after she left, while I was busy digesting, what may seem a platitude from such a wise man as Goethe, it meant that I no longer needed to keep asking my question, now I could replace it with 'How do the good people, whom I admire, spend their lives?' It is, after all, their most important expenditure, but no one looks at it that way so far as I could learn from what was spoken in the Quaker Meetings. I never met her again to tell her how much Goethe's saying had meant to me; by encouraging me to say 'Yes' when in doubt, to making the most of life with gusto.

When Hugh and I, sometimes with a third boy, could not cycle we might visit the nesting holes of the Greater-spotted Woodpecker and watch the goings and comings, or, during an autumn evening listen to the calls of invisible waders migrating overhead. As if that was not enough for the two would-be naturalists' worship and wonder, there was often a Red-backed Shrike on the fence by the playing fields and a nightingale in the lane nearby. The nightingale sang so loudly that some boys complained they could not get to sleep. There is always more than one way of looking at a thing. Its song is certainly not a lullaby, but anyway, what does a nightingale think of the average boy? 'Oh would that god the gift would give us, to see ourselves as others see us,' comes readily to the lips of any would-be peacemaker.

In terms of international understanding this dictum is of the greatest importance, when teaching I made use of the journalist's unintentional joke: 'Fog in the Channel: Continent Isolated' as well as the intended joke of a Dutch writer 'Britain is an island off the Dutch coast' to convince my students that we all suffer from prejudices which may exacerbate animosity. A school can mitigate prejudices, and dispel xenophobia by encouraging good foreign travel but also by including on its staff at least one teacher from abroad and some pupils with roots in other countries. However, it is best if this happens in a context of mutual appreciation of other cultural values. Variety is a blessing to be nurtured, uniformity makes for a dull life, and variety depends on freedom. There is a famous poster showing a barbed wire stretched across a patch of sand. On one side are two human footprints and on the other side three human footprints. The caption runs 'I like you. You're different.' Such abstract ideas may not make converts – nobody seems to know what does – but they certainly confirm and strengthen those who are already convinced.

We were spellbound when Mr. Maw came to speak to us at our Sunday evening Meeting at school, dressed in his Indian clothes. He had used them, he told us, when as a Quaker missionary he had joined other pilgrims to go to the source of the Ganges. After the injustices of British rule in India, this was an act of reconciliation, of apologising maybe, or an act of solidarity with another religion. He knew how Britain looks when seen through Indian eyes. It was especially interesting for me because a number of the friends of my parents worked in the Indian Civil Service and came to stay with us when on home leave and appeared to be very able people, sensitive to the feelings of the people they were serving and committed to their work. With the help of my father, one of them arranged for E.M. Forster to go to India. This led to the well-known book and film Passage to India. My father's activities included acting as Treasurer of Somerville College and Governor of Leighton Park.

Michael Foot had been on good terms with my brother Tona and had learned to tease us for not following more closely in John Bright's footsteps by supporting the Liberal Party. It was against tariffs and most of them believed, along with the 'Manchester School,' that the contacts made in commerce would promote international peace both because there was a financial interest in maintaining trade and because international understanding would be enhanced by business friendships. Already in mid-Victorian times Liberal industrialists sent their sons to learn French or German in the factories of their counterparts abroad. As for Michael, he used to like chanting such lines as: 'The land, the land, the land on which we stand God gave the land to the people.' Alternatively he would point to some article of clothing and again chant its supposed previous owners 'George Fox, William Penn, John Bright, Jan Gillett, Nicco Gillett.' Later in life he was to suffer from teasing by his

Michael Foot became a close friend at school. At that time, he was a Liberal and I was Labour.

fellow journalists about his simple inexpensive dress intended to show that he preferred to spend money on books. I have prided myself on getting married in a recycled Oxfam suit for the same reason. He came from a very political family: in the 1945 election his father, two brothers, and he himself were candidates. He was the only one not standing for the Liberal Party and the only one to be successful. I always wondered what this surprise result did for family relationships! Moreover, they loved books even more than we did. I remember reading books he lent me with his father's markings in them, sometimes just an ordinary line to indicate interest but also a hand and cuff complete to mean very interesting. I was shocked at first at such treatment of a book, but have accepted the value of such markings since, though instead of the pointing fingers I put a list of topics and their page numbers at the back. It was Tona, I think, who invited him to take a holiday with us at Porthcothan in Cornwall, but when Tona finished at Leighton Park, I saw much more of Michael. He played wing-forward in the rugby team and I was scrumhalf, we shared responsibility for the club for younger boys from Reading, where Leighton Park is situated and helped run their summer camps. We acted together in Barrie's play 'The Admirable Crichton' as the two domestic servants from the country house. We with our employers shipwrecked on a desert island had to take over the running of the makeshift company, the others being too incompetent. This attack on Britain's class system was much appreciated by the audience and, I like to think, may have helped Michael move or prepare to move from his strong Liberalism to his strong socialism, a change which John Cripps did much to help at Oxford. Michael was never at a loss for words in political discussions, what he believed he believed passionately and I used to listen with admiration.

We never doubted at the time that Parliament was the place to bring about progress. It was assumed in the history we studied, and in the families from which we came. The question was: what else does one do? For Michael it was journalism, which provided him with the information and skills for politics. If we are ever to have peace, he might have asked, how can this be achieved without first persuading the House of Commons? At that time I agreed with him, and before leaving Balliol, after hard work during vacations in the Clarion Campaigns for the Labour Party in rural areas, I was invited to stand for Parliament in a strongly Conservative constituency, but I refused. At that time I did believe that arms firms helped create wars by over-selling their products and that nationalising them would be a good step towards peace, but at that time it was too difficult for a pacifist of any sort to enter politics. Nowadays it looks differently, almost as though parliament has become an agency for helping campaigners, as the post office has always been an agency for helping those who write letters. Large companies and the media have as much or more power than politicians. When the Oxford Research Group identified eighty people as the most influential persons concerning nuclear weapons, only two were politicians.

A further inspiration was Bernard de Bunsen who came back to Leighton Park School to speak about the virtues of the new Village Colleges in Cambridgeshire, as an administrator in a local education office. He had become an education official in Wiltshire and he described the work of Henry Morris in glowing terms. The Colleges were to become the social centres of the areas they served by providing school education during the daytime and adult education in the evening. He indicated some of the advantages of strengthening communities and community caring by providing communal activities, which would provide scope for the flowering of friendship, while reducing social barriers. He hoped that the level of conversations and discussion would rival those in residential colleges such as Oxford and Cambridge. For this kind of education, he said at the opening of Bottisham College, the countryside will be our textbook where young and old can contribute from their own local experience and build upon it. He spoke as a former member of the school and his message went right home. The school could be developed in such a way as to make it the educator not just of individuals but of the whole area served by the school until it could be said that it was an education just to live there, a life-long education for some. As I listened to him I did not guess that years later, on the opposite side of the world, I would be introduced as coming from England – the land of Village Colleges. In this connection I was once asked 'Who has ever heard of a revolution which started in a Garden Suburb?' Peasants, who often have a mystical relationship to the soil, may be forced into going to war; unlike town-dwellers, they seldom go willingly.

Leighton Park was frankly experimental and taught by example. It responds to the idea that democratic principles should apply, at least to some extent, and therefore set up a School Council. Previously my brother Jan had got into trouble for collecting up all the mats beside the beds in his dormitory and throwing them out of the window. The miscreant owned up at breakfast time and made a speech in self-defence about 'harbingers of dust' but did as he was told and put them back in their places. Corporal punishment was not used at the school as it had been at the Dragons, we were treated with respect and did not live in fear, and perhaps for this reason bullying was almost unknown.

Respect for people is one of the characteristics of a good school and of the Culture of Peace and likewise respect for the truth. It is considered likely by many people that Michael Foot lost his position as Leader of the Labour Party because he said what he believed to be true about nuclear weapons. Well-informed people believe that Lord Mountbatten, a brave member of the Royal Family died for the same reason when the American CIA persuaded the IRA to kill him. Since his death his remarks such as 'Nuclear devastation is not science fiction, it is a matter of fact,' have been amply justified.

I recall with shame an occasion when a teacher accused me of diving into the swimming bath after the whistle had sounded for getting out. I answered with a direct lie. Journalists, advertisers, and politicians have much more reason to depart from the truth. Those who maintain a high standard of truth deserve admiration, more admiration than is usually accorded to them. Telling the truth, specifically when it hurts to do so, is another contribution towards peace. When war breaks out truth is the first casualty and quickly a web of propaganda around the enemy is spun, whether his name is Hitler, Saddam Hussein, Milosevic, or Osama Bin Laden.

Sometimes as I read political history both in the sixth form and at University, I longed to follow in the footsteps of John Bright and learn the political way of life, including the difficulties in the House of Commons. I had acquitted myself well in the Clarion Campaign for Labour in the rural areas, but I was not sure that I could make any difference. It seemed to require more power to exert any influence over party or Parliament than I could muster, despite the example set by George Lansbury as Leader of the Labour Party and later by Clement Attlee. The question whether change can more easily be brought about best by sudden revolution or by gradual reform has always intrigued me, as it was a bone of contention between my two elder brothers and myself. I keep an open mind at the present time regarding the better way to challenge the monopoly of power by the large firms. Their short-term policy of maximising profits is a threat to the whole world by exhausting resources and blocking a more just division of wealth. They ride roughshod over parliamentary democracies.

At Leighton Park it was too early in the century for this problem to have been recognised. We were engaged in discussions about the merits of free trade and tariffs and about the methods of reducing unemployment. Such discussions were supported mainly by those from Quaker families and those sympathising with Quaker values rather than by those who had difficulty in getting in elsewhere, either because they were from abroad or because they had difficulty in passing examinations. The age-range was fourteen to eighteen and we numbered a hundred. This low figure was due to the economic slump. Having such a small number of pupils enabled the staff to know all the pupils personally and some of them made good use of it. There was one member of staff for every ten boys, a ratio, which is about right if the intention is to train democrats and not be driven into producing fascists. I made this my main theme when speaking at a National Youth Parliament in 1939. Three of the staff won my admiration early on.

It was a crisp September morning, a new teacher of gymnastics had come to replace the Sergeant Major, and we were gathering on the gravel outside for "breathers", when suddenly I felt a heavy punch on the shoulder. I swung round to see who was spoiling for a fray and saw a short strongly built man, the new teacher who had introduced himself in this unorthodox way. Our friendship never looked back, my anger melted and I felt intrigued by such treatment. He had been an Olympic gymnast and then trained in Denmark in Danish gymnastics before starting to teach at

Bootham, the Quaker boarding school for boys in York. We responded eagerly to his teaching and some of us were soon doing handsprings, headsprings, and backward flip-flaps on the grass or in the gymnasium. The purpose, I learned later, was to substitute gymnastics for military training in the ordinary boarding schools as part of the education of the whole person. It was a pacifist move in the reform of the curriculum, clearly in accord with the wishes of Quaker parents.

Thomas Hopkins, or Hoppy as he was known, was an admirable advocate of the subjects he taught and could demonstrate his prowess by kicking up to handstands in the most unlikely places, such as on top of a gate, or in the middle of a dining table laid with crockery. On one small point we differed. After a rugby match in which as usual I was playing scrum half, I was blocked, contrary to the rules, by an opposing wing-forward swinging sideways from his pack. The referee did not notice and Hoppy urged me on another occasion to charge him in the ribs with my head so as to wind him. Hoppy demonstrated what he meant and left me gasping for breath. At the time I felt doubts about playing that way. Thinking it over now, I feel sure that in children playing field-games and in playing other games respect for law including international law can gradually be established. A greater respect for law is essential for campaigners against war and pollution; the same interest in law and order locally has to be extended to practices, which are inevitably international, and this can be best taught during childhood. The sports coaches who encourage youngsters to defy the rules are guilty of a serious offence. If there is any difference between international law and local law, then international law has become more vital.

Another brilliant teacher was Billy Brown. He always had new ways of looking at old things. The geography he liked best was not the geography of books, but the geography of adventure, of landscapes, of peoples and their customs. He arranged a journey for two of us on the Berkshire downs, a weekend camp and a climbing holiday in the Austrian Tyrol, in which he joined himself. I regretted very much indeed that in describing to my father how we lost our way to the Alpine Hut where we had booked for the night I conveyed the idea that excessive risks were being taken.

Reasonable risks have to be taken if pacifists are to believe in themselves and not be regarded as cowards. Unfortunately the people left at home suffer, and suffer more sometimes than the people travelling in dangerous places.

Billy Brown had a great scar across his cheek from the war but he seldom indicated his views about the war, with the exception of the flag incident before setting up the Scout Troop. I thought at the time that he must share more opinions of mine. He did not accept the schools ethos; so much as create it by contributing his delight in new ideas, along with adventure. It was left to de Bono to coin the term 'lateral thinking' but the habit of mind preceded him. When invited to speak to the Sunday evening Meeting he began 'I was an unhappy baby.' Teachers in those days were expected to hide pacifist views for fear of being accused of abusing their positions but the issue now is how best to avoid and abolish war. There were many gaps in my education when we as a family travelled to stay in South Africa, and it might be supposed that these big gaps in my schooling would put me at a disadvantage. However, Dr Douglas of *Home and School*,[12] reporting his researches to a very large meeting of teachers, indicated the supreme importance of parental encouragement and 'We found to our great surprise that children who were away not frequently but for substantial periods of time not only caught up, on average, but went ahead of where they would have expected to be if they had remained at school.' My comment to the meeting was 'In the Parent-Teacher movement we would not be surprised because parents would be likely to show their concern for school work in such circumstances and encourage their children to read while convalescing by talking with them about their books.'

CHAPTER 3

The General Among the Quakers

TOWARDS THE END of his life my father Arthur Gillett remarked to me: 'The great thing in our lives has been our friendship with Jannie.' It lasted half a century from the time of the Boer War until the death of Smuts in 1950. Winston Churchill wrote to his widow describing him as 'a warrior-statesman and philosopher, who was probably more fitted to guide struggling and blundering humanity through its sufferings and perils towards a better day, than anyone who lived in any country during his epoch.' King George VI added 'The force of his intellect has enriched the wisdom of the whole human race.'

Unfortunately when I wrote a page about Smuts for a textbook for schools dealing with the United Nations, which was produced for the United Nations Association and adopted by the UN for translation into many languages, it was submitted to the African National Congress for their approval and then rejected at their request. This was unjust to him. He spoke against the colour bar (apartheid) at Stellenbosch University and when he came home that evening he retold the story of an African Chief, which he had told the students. 'The chief inflicted a crushing defeat on some Boer troops but then went to plead for peace. Would you pass a colour bar against a wise man like that?' he asked the audience. It is easy to dismiss the reputation of leaders of a past era, by applying contemporary values and end up with no one to admire. Smuts was the one leading politician to receive an African in his home. When he entered a football stadium for a rugby match against the New Zealanders, the crowd of 'coloured people' cheered Smuts

35

Jan Smuts, Close family friend during my childhood, who was seminal in the creation of League of Nations and United Nations.

not the Prime Minister, the crowd then went on to cheer the New Zealanders not the South African team! Smuts was often kept out of power by being called a 'native lover.' It is the fate of many politicians to be too radical for some and too conservative for others, but I never heard him complain. In a sense he had no reason to be dissatisfied by his achievements. After military defeats in the Boer War he was able to help General Botha win the independence of South Africa by negotiation.

Within fifteen years he was invited to join the Imperial War Cabinet in the middle of the First World War. In the Versailles Treaty he failed to remove the desire for revenge expressed by Clemenceau, which encouraged the Germans to foment the Second World War. His life, as he might have said, was full of shadows but the sunshine made them all, the motto inscribed on one of the steamers that took us to South Africa. He must have been informed of the making of nuclear bombs, because he was drawn into consultation with Churchill from time to time. In his letters to my parents after the bombs were dropped at Hiroshima and Nagasaki, he wrote 'There can never be a war again.' The context provided no explanation of the way he arrived at this conclusion. Did he mean governments fearing a nuclear war would allow the United Nations to insist on settling their disputes in courts of law, or did he mean that war would end the day it began on account of the massive devastation? He was so optimistic in general that, I would guess he meant the first. His biographer Professor Hancock went so far as to call the first volume of his work *The Sanguine Years*[13]. But there would be justification for using the same title for the second half of his life.

In a period of pessimism when politicians appear to be corrupt, journalists cynical, and businessmen slaves of profit, it is those who bring positive news who are capable of giving a lead by inviting their audiences to look to the future eagerly. In speaking to a meeting of fifteen hundred people and three thousand more in overflow rooms he spoke in this way: 'Let the greatest war in history be the prelude to the greatest peace. To make such will be the greatest glory of our age and its noblest bequest to the generations to come.' These were not empty words. In the First World War he had written *The League of Nations: A Practical Suggestion*[14], at a corner of our big dining room table. This booklet, which was used by President Wilson in setting up the League, became the essential precursor of the United Nations, and Smuts lived long enough to give the opening address to the San Francisco Conference for establishing the United Nations, nearly thirty years later.

When writing a book entitled *Men Against War*, I chose Smuts for one of the eight biographies, not because I knew more about him than the other candidates for inclusion, but because it seemed important to show that some military people have done much for peace, other than 'fighting' for it! Not because there was a shortage among those who looked to political institutions such as the League of Nations and the United Nations and to the development of international law, but because Smuts combined these achievements with others. He opposed all those provisions of the Treaty of Versailles, which led to the Second World War. He insisted that the terms of peace were a form of revenge by crippling Germany. 'We cannot destroy Germany without destroying Europe ... we cannot save Europe without the cooperation of Germany.' He wrote. Speaking to the British delegation he said 'If the Germans are prepared to swallow the treaty ... it will make the operation of the League of Nations impossible: the fires will be kept burning and the pot be kept boiling until it again boils over.'

It was about this time that John Maynard Keynes wrote his important book *The Economic Consequences of the Peace*[15], with some help from a suggestion from my mother. Smuts exclaimed on one occasion 'I want no overwhelming victory.' This, when applied to the Boer War, meant making peace before being forced to do so, thus preventing a desire for revenge fomenting the desire for a victory later. When applied to the First World War it meant preventing Clemenceau, on behalf of the French government, demanding reparations for far beyond what could be paid, if it had been successful it would have either prevented Hitler's rise to power or at least removed the sting from his speeches. A Carthaginian peace, as Smuts termed it, referring to Cato's regularly repeated four-word speech 'Carthage must be destroyed,' is both foolish and wrong, Smuts argued.

Despite writing frequently to those mainly concerned he had to give way to Prime Minister Botha's need for signing on behalf of South Africa, despite all the letters to his wife, my aunts and parents suggesting that he would protest by refusing to sign, as described by Hancock.[16] 'It is a terrible document, not a peace treaty but a war treaty, and I am troubled in my conscience.' He wrote to his wife. If any people were entitled to keep writing on this subject by virtue of experience it was certain that Smuts was one of them. He had identified one of the causes of war and shown how it could be overcome. He knew it was not easy from the difficulty the British and Boer South Africans found in overcoming the hatreds engendered by the Boer War. Smuts spent much of his public life seeking reconciliation between Boers and British in South Africa. Reconciliation is often a thankless task and he suffered for it politically by having to serve under nationalistic Prime Ministers belonging to the Nationalist Party when a coalition was formed.

Few had suffered more in the Boer War or distinguished themselves more, nevertheless people grumbled. They never forgave Smuts for changing sides as they saw it, and never associated themselves with the thought that: 'You can have the Boers as opponents or you can have us as friends.' The offer made to the British Liberal Prime Minister Cambell-Bannerman, before home rule for South Africa was wisely granted.

Fortunately Smuts was much more than a wise military statesman. He was famed as a philosopher after completing his two-volume work on *Holism and Evolution*.[17] It recorded his reflections on nature, the universe, and existence, and would therefore be beyond me to think that I understood it well. On the other hand it is easy to start pondering some of the issues it raised. If, for example, a cell is based on a cooperative principle leading towards its own replication, at what point in the history of the Earth did this begin? The scientists did not take kindly to the implications that they had anything to learn from philosophers. Being inclined to eclectic conclusions, I would be prepared to argue in favour of periods of analytical thinking being followed by periods devoted to holism. The extreme specialists from the present are more apt to favour this view. I have always regretted my refusal to travel to South Africa to spend my last long vacation talking philosophy and walking with Oom Jannie, as we always called him, on the farm round

Doornkloof. I was shocked by my parent's extravagance, but there was also a young lady at that time, who influenced my decision.

Another feature of the Smuts' book was the proposal for a new field of study which would be called 'personology,' a suggestion which the psychologists and psychiatrists did not take to kindly, but which has a strong appeal to teachers.

Mediators and diplomats attempt to make friends with unlikely people, sometimes they sound as insincere as salesmen because they have an axe to grind. They might benefit from some help from personology, particularly if it were to be reinforced by believing in there being good in everyone, as Quakers try to do. Teachers of difficult or emotionally disturbed children are taught to find out how their pupils were treated at home, how their personalities were formed, so as to have more sympathy for them.

Despite the criticisms of Holism as presented by Smuts it was a very great achievement, considering the time he had available for writing and that his library at Doornkloof was his main resource. Professor Hancock calculated that Smuts had written the 140,000 words in 29 weeks, nearly 700 words a day, while serving as leader of the Opposition. My mother was a great help to him by acting as his reader. Astonishingly large parcels of books arrived from Blackwell's bookshop from time to time. She read them or skimmed through them with understanding, separating those she thought he would wish to read, and posting them to Doornkloof, from those, which she considered of less interest, which were returned to the bookshop. Her degree which, combined philosophy and political economy, was exactly what she needed for this welcome task, to help Jannie's work as a politician, peacemaker, and philosopher.

The weekly exchange of letters often dealt with the books my mother had read, and the family read aloud Oom Jannie's replies when we were older, for discussion. In addition to philosophy, which sometimes took the form of communing with Nature, often when riding one of his horses, he had farms to supervise, and he was a keen botanist, especially in regard to South African grasses in which he was one of half-a-dozen experts. He might be regarded as both a Renaissance Man and as an example of Plato's philosopher-kings who were to be trained not just to rule but also to rule with wisdom.

This was the man who came to London in 1917 at the age of forty-seven from fighting first in German South West Africa and afterwards in German East Africa. He was to attend an Imperial conference of representatives of the Dominions but was soon offered various posts by Lloyd George, the Prime Minister who followed Asquith. He ended up becoming a member of the War Cabinet, though the British Constitution did not provide for any such appointments. The question arose whether he would accept a constituency to regularise his position, but that offer he refused. Already towns and universities seemed to be queuing up to honour him. He brought words of encouragement and hope at a time when the German submarines were threatening the sparse food rations in Britain. As a boy of three I remember the lack of sugar and the black treacle with my porridge, and Oom Jannie bringing boxes of sweets for us, something which became unobtainable in Oxford.

He came to us at weekends for the most part. Like one of John Macmurray's 'real people,' we felt his presence as soon as he entered the house. My first memory at the age of two was of his car. Cars were a great rarity in those days. In the road near our house the Hansom cabs with their horses stood instead of taxis, and when we went to the station we hired a Victoria Coach. Once or twice he travelled in his car, a green, open Vauxhall that he had used in Africa. Driving along one day he took both hands off the wheel and exclaimed 'See what a good car it is? It drives by itself.' He seemed to adjust to us whatever age we were, how he did it I cannot understand. He had a large family of six children at Doornkloof by the time the First World War began and no doubt they helped him.

He could tell stories to quieten us before bedtime, but earlier in the evening there might be riotous games such as when he looked for a walking stick to chase us round the house or garden. There can be few biographers who have been chased by their subjects with a big stick! At the age of three, during one of these chases, I slipped on a mat and cut my knee on a sharp piece of furniture. My mother would not help me until I stopped crying. I think she was afraid of upsetting Oom Jannie and anyway believed in the stiff upper lip response to pain, the scar remained for fifty years. I felt she did not understand what had happened. I had already formed a view that soldiers must be very brave people and especially Oom Jannie.

41

It was in 1906, that Smuts attended the Quaker Meeting at Street in Somerset, dressed in a General's uniform with my mother and her parents, he explained: 'I had nothing else to wear.' It caused some doubts among Friends but it inspired him and certainly helped me to make friends with military people at various points in my life, despite my pacifist views. My mother and his biographer, Piet Beukes, believed that in that Meeting for Worship a turning point in his life was reached. Some kind of vision came to him of a world fit for making friends rather than enemies.

One characteristic puzzled us greatly. Like Napoleon and a number of other outstanding people, his hours of sleep were few, but when he slept he slept very soundly. His active mind did not prevent him going to sleep and when he woke after his short night he read avidly. He read so many books about philosophy and politics that he must have been wide awake at this time. Fortunately for us we were encouraged to go and visit him early in the morning and he sometimes welcomed us with a remark about 'The old Hippo is rolling over to make room.' Then conversations about the plans for the day might follow or he could sometimes tell another story. Perhaps because he spoke High Dutch and Afrikaans in addition to English, he was fond of playing with words. Here are a couple of examples:

> There was an old man called Britz
> Who sits on his stoep and spits
> He sits and he spits
> And spits and sits
> He's a funny old man is Britz.

> Little Rex the labourer
> Little wrecks (or recks) the labourer
> When his day's work is done.

Laughter would break out at the mere mention of the word rex, in whatever context it was placed. Smuts sometimes complained that his own work was never done, but he never said 'I've got a lot of things to do today,' which has become the password at Oakcroft, where I currently live. He always appeared to have organised his work well. How such a busy person had time to write so many letters it is hard to say. It was customary last century to regard

42

letters as a form of literature, written not as a message for the day, as perennials rather than annuals, as gardeners might say. Written between friends they might range through all the realms of human thought, rather than dealing with the trivialities of day-to-day existence.

Such a person as Smuts endeared himself to my brothers and me, I know less about my sister Helen's reactions to him, as she is the youngest in the family. Smuts provided, not at part, but at all stages of our growing up, an educational experience, such as few schools can claim to do. The core of education takes place when the teacher passes on to the pupil a zest for his own enlightened interests; the personal contact is usually essential to the flowering of a personality slowly taking shape. He gave us memorable presents as though he knew what we wanted, a pocket knife at four or five, when we visited him in the Savoy Hotel, a silver spoon with a cock on the handle presented to him at the signing of the Treaty of Versailles. He never commented on the cock but I think he must have known it was an offensive French emblem representing the chauvinism of the time. A further gift was a book on Arabia, on which he commented: 'this is the country of the future to be watched'. Finally, on getting married to Ruth, Smuts gave us a set of floor rugs from the little industry set up by mother when she was working with Emily Hobhouse in the camps during the Boer war. How far these gifts were suggestions of my mother it was hard to tell.

We knew him both in Oxford in what must have seemed to him very urban surroundings but from time to time he would take a few days off and stay on or near the Berkshire Downs. On one of these occasions he went to see a Mrs. Smart, the owner of a large house near the Thames. Being war time and he, dressed in his general's uniform, she was taken aback when he said 'I'm wanting your house.' He soon added 'No not this house. All I want to borrow is your empty game-keepers cottage in Ham Wood.' The deal was soon settled. He was always fond of pulling legs, regardless of the consternation caused.

It was while staying there with Oom Jannie and my parents in Ham Wood that they were walking through the village of Aldworth, the nearest village to that cottage. It was Armistice Day in

November 1918. An elderly Vicar came out into the lane and greeted them: 'Should the church bells be rung?' He asked. Oom Jannie replied without a pause 'If you think it's a time for rejoicing.' The old man looked baffled. Oom Jannie was already aware that making a just and lasting peace was going to be a greater difficulty than winning the war.

The advantage of the gamekeepers cottage was that it was close to the open unfenced Downs. There the grass grew so tall and yellow that it reminded him of the tall, yellow grass of the High Veld round Doornkloof, where he sometimes rode a horse, sometimes walked to examine the flowers more closely. He found his own name for a small wood of Scots Pines; 'Sacred Grove' he called it and the name stuck. It was about the time when he wrote "The League of Nations – A Practical Suggestion".

My father was over-stretched by keeping the family bank going, with a minimum of help during the war, and his break-down led to him welcoming any opportunity for enjoying fresh air and exercise. After the Bank was sold he was able to combine some work for Barclays Bank in South Africa with prolonged holidays, following his newly found hobby of ornithology and this was repeated many times. Each time they took two of us four children with them. My first time at the age of eight and nine was with Helen. The second time I was thirteen and fourteen and was with Jan, the botanist, and again with him when I had been seriously ill.

Travel is likely to help children in their lateral thinking, a skill that is essential for peacemakers. The acceptance of war, which is such a cruel, devastating, despicable form of human behaviour, over a long period of time, points to the need for drastic new responses. The enlightened despots of the eighteenth century contrived a partial civilisation of the armed forces, when total war was unheard of, but since then war has grown worse, weapons are worse, and those who make and use them have become more callous. Now is the time for some fresh thinking. It is time to 'Disarm or perish,' in the words of the inscription in the original building for the League of Nations in Geneva.

The first journey to South Africa was on the 'Saxon Castle' of the Union Castle Line and among the passengers one caught a

44

whiff of the Empire. At that time the Cape to Cairo road, the length of Africa, passed over 'British' territory all the way. There may have been a hint of decay, but not noticeable to an eight year old. When the ship anchored at Madeira, small boys of my size came in boats to climb up to the deck to dive for silver coins thrown by passengers. Their bravery in diving the great height marking the pressure of poverty which I was soon to meet face to face. Writing nearly eighty years later I can recall some of the feelings I had at the time, unfortunately the diaries I kept to maintain academic skills dealt with bare facts not feelings so I let them go. They were as dull to read, as they were arduous to write. I suppose I needed some coaching about what would be of lasting interest.

I had little preparation for the spectacles of flying fish, spouting whales or those sinister fins of sharks, looking like submarines. The sense of wonder was stretched to the limit. Having seventeen days together the passengers exchanged travel tales in plenty and some were told to me. I was never quite sure what to believe. It is not only in war that truth is the first casualty. I recall some questionable stories of fishing for sharks with the help of petrol cans as floats. They sounded very convincing, on the other hand fishermen and storytellers do not have a good reputation. Yet those flying fish really did fly, I saw them with my own eyes. It was later that I had good reason to disbelieve my own eyes.

We passed Robben Island where later Nelson Mandela spent many of his twenty-seven years of imprisonment, and where he planned his remarkable contribution to peaceful government, and we landed at Cape Town. The Boer War between the Boers defending their two republics fought, it seemed vainly against the might of the British superpower of those years. It was still fresh in people's minds. Bitter memories linger for centuries if nothing is done to counteract them, from time to time I caught glimpses from fragments of conversation. To begin with my mind was taken up with Groote Schuur (Big Barn) where Oom Jannie lived while Parliament was in session as it is the Prime Minister's residence. The Dutch grandfather clocks with their rolling ships and other clockwork marvels, the huge sea chests and outside the peacocks overwhelmed me. Is it any wonder that powerful politicians, housed in this way, become corrupted by power?

45

It had been the home of Cecil Rhodes, who had grandiose ideas about the Empire; he is believed to have started the Boer War for the sake of the newly discovered gold in Johannesburg. This is an example of a war for scarce resources, not essential resources such as water or oil but luxuries, though gold for many countries with currencies fixed on the gold standard might be regarded as essential.

When not staying with Oom Jannie at Cape Town or Doornkloof his farm outside Irene, we visited mother's many hospitable friends elsewhere. When staying with the widow of President Steyn of the Orange Free State I recall my confusion when I overheard my father in discussion with her son-in-law a Minister of the Dutch Reformed Church. The Minister admitted to preaching sermons against making peace with the British, and against reconciliation and I overheard my father say angrily 'I don't know how you can preach such hatred in the name of a religion of love?' I was mystified, 'How could such words be used when we were visitors in the home of his parents-in-law?' I asked myself.

Even the opposition of black and coloured Africans did not compel cooperation between the Boers and the British. The power of hatred is very great and very few people know how to deal with their own prejudices let alone the hatred in others. Some months later on Dingaans Day December 16th we accompanied Oom Jannie to a large outdoor meeting of Boers who came to hear his speech marking a Boer victory over the forces of an African Chief. He spoke about reconciliation and paused to bring the four of us up onto the long ox-cart traditionally used as a speakers platform. He wanted to illustrate that there are many different views among the British so he spoke about Emily Hobhouse and my mother's work in the camps, let bygones be bygones was the theme of his speech. It is easier for a democratic leader to act as a demagogue maintaining his influence by stirring up hatred like Hitler and Ian Paisley than to offer the less attractive, but wiser path to reconciliation and peace. If only Boers and British could learn the skills of peace making, he thought, they would become capable of respecting the Africans and of cooperating more justly with them. Tolerance and friendship thrive on cooperation and a willingness to put the past behind.

At Groote Schuur we made many excursions and on one day I came across a snake in a garden some twenty miles from Capetown. I had heard such stories of snakes moving as fast as a galloping horse that I had became convinced, as I lay in bed at night, that the snake might be finding its way and would climb into my bed and bite me, so I burst into tears. Some days later I could be brave, despite the lapse, by running on the sharp gravel at the back of the house in my bare feet. The soles grew hot as I ran.

One thing about the garden puzzled me very much. Red-shirted convicts under armed guards came to pick up the acorns under the oak trees for pig food. Who were these people? What had they done? Would the guards really shoot them if they tried to run away? It was something I had never heard of, something sad and perhaps evil, so I did not ask the adults and no one spoke about them to me. Similarly on the road back from our bathing place at Muizenberg on Friday evenings we saw a number of drunkards and drove carefully past them. It was said that Friday was payday and some were paid partly in wine, so they got drunk on their way home. I wanted to know more, they were the first drunkards I had ever seen.

Money was carefully managed in my banking family; even at the age of eight I earned my pocket money by keeping accounts. What did these people do when they got home? How did they explain? There was little talk about such things, little opportunity to digest experiences. My sister was too young at that time and my parents had little gift for talking to children of that age. I have since attributed this to my grandmother's mother having died when my grandmother was only two years old so that the passing on of good mothering practices down the generations was broken in this way. I hasten to add that my parent's intentions were always for the best, they were always kind, and for older children able to make good contacts and provide a stimulating informal education. We regarded the cold baths before breakfast as a challenge rather than an imposition!

On the rail journey north to Irene, beyond Johannesburg, I was baffled by surprises. As the train slowly climbed up the long gradient to the plateau of the Karoo, I was looking down the slope into the grass far below, suddenly I saw little animals about two inches long moving among the grass. I exclaimed with delight at the thought of such toy-sized animals being real. It was very disappointing to be told that my eyes had taken no account of the dryness of the atmosphere near the Karoo desert, and that I was looking at ordinary cattle. It was more difficult to accept this optical illusion than it was later when the train approached a vast lake and I was looking for a railway bridge ahead, only to be told that the lake was a mirage. Yes, I had heard of mirages but had not expected them to look so real!

We spent some time on that long journey talking about surprising weather conditions. A storm wrenched a corrugated iron roof from a house and sent it spinning up into the air. Many stories were told of strange winds and unlikely accidents. At Christmas time there was a hailstorm of hailstones nearly as big as tennis balls. I did not know how worried the adults were about the cattle. Could they live in such a bombardment, they wondered. Fortunately they were half a mile away in perfect safety because the storm missed them completely. However, my parents went out for a walk and saw a 'fireball' four feet high moving across the Veld. On another occasion the loudest noise I had ever heard startled me in my outside room, it sounded like a clap of thunder on my doorstep. I opened the door and a dog pushed its way past me. It was terrified. A few days later I discovered that lightning had struck a metal pole a few yards away but it was not earthed, so it bored its way in a zigzag through the dry soil, like a mole half underground, and finished up at the trunk of a pine tree. It was so close that I was lucky that my room had not been struck and burned.

Looking back on such frightening events, it appears that they provide good practice in coping with emergencies and hardships. I began to feel quite wrongly that I could cope with anything. When we set out with Oom Jannie on horseback he looked as though he had been bred in the saddle and he needed that confidence. He seemed to relish the crises that punctuated his life and liked to tell the story of the African pastor who leading his congregation in prayer, said 'Times are very bad, Oh Lord, so bad you must come to us yourself this time and not just send your son.'

As I think about these three periods of four months in South Africa I realise what an inspiration it was to be with Oom Jannie.

Sharing his wisdom, his sense of fun and his readiness to talk about all the things that matter in life; people more than success, spiritual values more than shopping, good conversation more than food, and nature which is at its best in South Africa at dawn and dusk.

When Oom Jannie shared his wisdom it was not so much the slow wisdom of a sage as the quick reply that Gandhi also favoured. He knew when the law required him to send Gandhi to prison that he was up against a great man each of them quick to out-manoeuvre an opponent. Gandhi when in prison made him a pair of sandals. The thought behind the gift was much appreciated but the sandals were passed on to my mother. Oom Jannie living in a different countryside even slept in his boots when camping. When we asked him why he did not do the same as everyone else, he replied, 'Once in the war (meaning the Boer War) we were surprised by the British at night. I didn't have time to put on my boots and had to run barefoot through prickly pear country. Never again.'

The Afrikaners often called Smuts 'Slim Jan' which means much the same as crafty. When the Welsh miners threatened to go on strike during World War I, he was the cabinet minister chosen to go to Cardiff to speak to them. 'I come from a little country far away,' he told them 'but I've heard of the fame of your singing. Before we come to business may I hear you sing?' Their response was so enthusiastic the sound filled the large hall and afterwards they proved willing to do as they were requested and keep their grievances until the war was finished.

So far as we were concerned the best times of all were when cars were loaded with camping equipment and we went off to distant places in search of plants and birds. One day, high in the eastern part of the Zoutpansberg Mountains, he commented 'You know Nicco, we may be walking where no white man has walked before.' He had a great sense of the adventure and magic of Africa and used it to throw light on the equally adventurous advances of the human race, exemplified by his work on the League of Nations. He looked back not to be immersed in history but so as to look forward the better. Camping at his Bushveld farm Rooikop he walked off one day to visit an old lady of whom he had heard. He came back full of wonder, it seemed likely that she was right that she really remembered being left for dead when the Zulus had

49

advanced across the country, killing as they went. If so she must have been about a hundred and twenty years old. His son Jannie was my age and took up archaeology. On two occasions we came across stones convenient for sitting where some person had been making stone tools or weapons. Some of the chips even fitted together with a discarded spearhead; the Stone Age came to life. Recently I read how some prospectors for uranium in northeast India had been chased away by indignant tribesmen using bows and arrows. They might be still living in the Stone Age but they were aware of the dangers of mining uranium in their hunting area.

It was in the evening when the campfire was alight and its warmth welcome in the cool evening air that the best stories were told. At Fuggers Paradise where a lion visited our camp, one story was told of a piccaninny who had wandered too far beyond shouting distance from the village and was caught by a large python. I had a photograph of a python containing a fifty-three pound pig in my diary so I guessed what would happen. The boy was old enough to know what to do, he pretended to be quite dead, so limp that the python did not bother to squeeze him anymore, but began to prepare its meal by spewing its lubricating saliva from side to side and from head to foot. Then just as the snake had finished it turned to move round and start swallowing. Quick as a flash the clever boy rolled over from front to back.

The snake appeared to be puzzled by the lack of lubrication and went through the whole process again from side to side and head to toe. The boy lay perfectly still until the snake had finished and had turned away. Quick as a flash the boy turned over again and presented to the snake a gritty mixture of sand and gravel stuck in the lubrication. When the hungry snake tried to begin its meal it found itself in such difficulties that it went away unsatisfied and the lucky boy got up and ran for all he was worth. You could not tell from Oom Jannie's face whether the story was true or not, so we did not dare to laugh. The lion roared.

In South Africa real life is so extraordinary there is no need to make up stories. At Dudley Zoo the visitors found the feeding of pythons so terrifying that they had to be fed in private. The visitors may have had too much imagination and yet imagination such as is promoted by make believe is in short supply. How does this come to be?

The other kinds of stories that he liked to invent were about the disappearance of the Transvaal Republic's gold hoard during the Boer War. A common theme among these was the tendency of the robbers to quarrel among themselves, often leaving only one robber alive. My father was entirely in accord with this theme and enjoyed reading *Sister Gold*, by Laurence Housman in the *Little Plays of St. Francis*.

Often Oom Jannie was unable to be free for camping expeditions, so we would then visit other friends. On one occasion we stayed with a man who had been blowing up railway bridges during the Boer War and the next night with a man who had been rebuilding them. They should have been paired off in some way perhaps! The stupidity of war needs to be exposed and there is not much to say for it except that it keeps people busy. Only now is it recognised fully in high circles that finding work for ex-combatants is an essential part of peace building as Marrack Goulding of the UN pointed out recently in a lecture. How can the IRA in Northern Ireland find another way of living after thirty-five years?

We also went six thousand feet down a goldmine, that is one thousand feet below sea level. I was appalled by the coarse language used by the Afrikaner foremen of the team of Africans. It lingers with me to this day and I wonder whether Nelson Mandela has made a difference.

When I was fourteen I met Mandela's favourite teacher at Fort Hare, Davidson Jabavu, a Quaker. Later Smuts invited him to coffee, arranged by my mother, a brave move for a politician at that time. In Mandela's autobiography there is an important and informative account of a non-violent campaign supported by a minimum of force to right the wrongs of apartheid. It is a warning to military dictators of all kinds that there is a limit to their power even though it may depend on an astonishing freedom from bitterness and a willingness to forget. Due to the development and diversification of ever worsening weapons of oppression even so-called realists can consider the merits of well-organised civilian defence. Modern armies look more and more like wallowing dinosaurs, embarrassed by their own clumsy weight and with bad prospects for the future. Kosovo was a case in point.

We travelled through the Transvaal, the Orange Free State, and Cape Province mainly by car, stopping here and there to suit my father and me for birding, or for mother and Jan for plant collecting. Mother and Jan were so successful that they have a number of plants and even bushes named after them. In Africa, bird species are more numerous than in England but in any case having one's name used in this way can be a mixed honour. Who was Jardine, who had a variety of Babbler, named after him? I thought I would prefer to avoid it, no doubt in the spirit of sour grapes.

The behaviour of the birds was far more interesting to me than the rather tiresome identification of species, though I set myself the task of learning the Latin names and finding out their meaning. For example there is a shrike belonging to the large family of Butcherbirds once common in England that hang up their insect prey on thorns or barbed wire until they were ready to eat them.

Another extraordinary example of cooperation is the teamwork between human beings and the family of birds called the Honey guides. They make their call to draw attention and then lead people through bushes and trees to the place they have discovered containing a bee's nest. They wait close by while the bees are smoked out and expect a reward in the form of a piece of comb containing grubs or honey. There are a number of species of honey guides, some work with animals, as well as people, and some actually vary the call note when they get close to the bees nest.

Rooks in England have difficulty in controlling anti-social members of their rookery which steal nesting materials from their neighbours, just like bees robbing from neighbouring hives, with no Security Council to call them to account, so I was fascinated with the thought of studying the customs of Social Weavers. They build small haystacks in thorn trees to keep out the snakes and other predators. Unfortunately we were not staying near enough to one of these marvels of cooperation for me to form any idea of how it was achieved. Like flats in a tower block each pair had its own hole in the big nest. Not having much of a common language, they might be compared to the United Nations building in New York, and yet they cooperated successfully.

Lastly the Trek Duikers, which belong to the same family as cormorants, worked very well together. We watched them fishing at Saldanha Bay in their hundreds. Instead of working individually each formed a part of a military front advancing on an invisible shoal of fish beneath them. Significantly the two wings of their diving mob were well in advance to prevent the shoal of fishes escaping to one side. It was a great sight and was repeated the following day. A rugby team could hardly do better.

In 1939 at the outbreak of war Smuts wrote to his friend Tom Lamont,[18] 'Shall we never learn the lesson? There is no solution through war. This war, whatever the ultimate issue, will be followed by another peace which may be no peace, for after a devastating conflict there is no mood for a real and wise peace, as you and I found at Paris in 1919. Meanwhile civilisation is falling back and the light of the Spirit is being dimmed . . . And so the caravan (of humanity) passes on into the night.'

As Joan Baez said, 'They tell me non-violence does not work. The only thing, which works even worse is violence.' No wonder Smuts never attempted to convert me to his view that the war must be fought regardless of his sympathies with the pacifist position. He understood all too well that, when leading a group of four British representatives to the treaty-making at Versailles in order to reduce the vindictive demands of the French, he had failed completely to persuade them that a sound lasting peace has to be built on justice. In 1919 the French became the victims of their own war propaganda and thus 'let slip the dogs of [another] war.[19]

It seemed very strange to me to leave my very different world at Whalley Farm in World War II to visit Smuts in his hotel in London. I arrived in his hotel during a shower of rain with David aged two or three under my cape. When I dropped him down in the middle of the foyer, he gazed in amazement and the attendant, without a word from me, informed us of Mrs. Gillett's room number. It seemed as though all of my mother's visitors looked so eccentric that they could be recognised at a glance, without further investigation! At lunch Oom Jannie said to David, 'Will you marry me and live with me always?' How he loved to tease young and old.

Accepting the wartime principle that 'careless talk costs lives' I left Smuts to tell me whatever he thought fit to say. He had to return home soon because this time the war was a matter of dispute. The extreme Afrikaners who had lost the vote about entry of South Africa into the war by such a small margin that Smuts, as the Prime Minister was needed at home. He had, in fact, come mainly for consultations with Churchill, and to inspire parliament and people with his own optimism. It was a pleasure to hear his voice on the BBC. By the following day I easily slipped back into ordinary life, though stirred by what I had heard. The Search for Peace demands action among the Establishment. I doubted whether there was anything that I could do. I was too shy and too Quakerly perhaps to feel at ease among those who wield power. No doubt my father and mother felt the same, but if they did, they contrived to hide it. My father being neither a teetotaller nor a pacifist had little to conceal. His bonhomie brought him many friends. My father did not use the new word 'Establishment', but both my parents liked talking with people with interesting jobs or experiences while recognising that if democracy was to be effective, the media, and the people in the street must be involved.

CHAPTER 4

Balliol College and the Oddities of Oxford

QUAKERS HAVE ALWAYS been a small minority, separated at one time by their speech and dress. Nowadays they are regarded with some suspicion as likely to be teetotallers, and pacifists, a race apart. It was not surprising that I felt some misgivings about starting to study at a college, which had a reputation for academic success among students from Eton and other well-known schools. On the other hand it also had a reputation for an interest in politics, mainly of a variety of socialism and under the famous Dr Jowett had built up an ethos of public service. Despite my shyness and doubts about my intellectual capacity, I began to enjoy the atmosphere and set out to make friends.

One of the first things we had to do was write a paper and read it to the Master; A.D. Lindsay was an important figure in the university and it now astonishes me that he had time for such a purpose. He was known to me for his work in adult education helping the unemployed miners of South Wales, and his wife came to the Quaker Meeting in High St. Unfortunately I chose a topic about the danger of cars to pedestrians, which I knew was a subject dear to him. Thinking he would be amused with a challenge to his views I wrote on the theme that it would be better to spend time attempting to deal with war casualties than car accidents. To my surprise he winced and showed his disapproval.

The exhilarating air of intellectual enquiry, of the search for a meaning in life and for wisdom was a great delight but it did not help my studies. I was living in college for the first two years, though only a mile from home, in order to make the most of its social life. My father and mother made it very clear that this was as important as anything. I suspect that my father had in mind that I would be able to make good friends who would work with me later on in business. This was the reason for choosing Oxford for me despite my parents and brothers having been at Cambridge. My father only once intervened in my student life by inviting me to the theatre to see a skit on youth. As it happened he had confused two plays and what we saw was a skit on bank directors. We laughed loud and long. From time to time I went home to borrow the car on Sundays to take fellow students who wished to go to outlying Quaker Meetings. At the time I was more at ease when communing with nature than listening to the ministry, but I was not good at knowing how to do either the one or the other. I was a slow learner.

In some ways Oxford was of little help in this respect. Life in North Oxford was succinctly described as eternal Sunday afternoon and lacked the challenges we felt we needed. Life in the University was strident as well as exhilarating, making it necessary to pick and choose. I did not want to drink with the son of an arms manufacturer who came back to college on his hands and knees, nor with those habitual drunks, making use of their new-found freedom who came back pretending to be cars by stopping at the traffic lights. Another went out for a drink with his father and returned with a garage sign saying 'IN', which he fixed up at the top of his stairs. The more troublesome ones invaded my room with some kind of battering ram and poured scorn on the soft drinks they found there. On my return they would not leave but needed a push. It seemed as though my reputation as the best scrum half in the college may have helped, I wondered how some of the frail members of the college would have fared. Freedom should have its limits at some point. J.S. Mill wrote that if you wish to produce men of genius, you must first cultivate the ground in which genius can flourish. One might add that if you want peace, you must first cultivate the culture of peace in which peace can flourish. Much later on our five-year-old daughter, Candia, provided the ideas and almost all the words for a poem, which was published by the BBC; it is worth quoting here, as it is a good comment on the experience of students who had been kept in a straightjacket at boarding school and then passed on to university. They tended to abuse their free-dom.

On Liberty. (I like you. You're Different)

If I only read my book, if I eat but half my tea,
If I leave my clothes about, mummy soon gets cross
    with me.
'Leave your book a minute, make a tidy plate
Why can't you be like the others?' That's what I
    horribly hate.

If she wants us all the same,
She shouldn't give me all the blame,
But have another baby now,
And make it twins, then she'd see how.

To complete this list of those who saw Oxford differently and enjoyed tolerance of eccentricity, the student at the House, as Christchurch is known, may be added. To evade the rule against student's cars being kept in Oxford itself, he kept his car at the required distance away and had a chauffeur to bring it to him. He is unlikely to have met the student who was discovered by researchers to have no growth in his fingernails at all. On further investigation he was found to be living on one meal each day, the compulsory dinner each evening. The researchers were looking for a convenient measure of malnutrition.

Tolerance of differences was no more common in the univer-sity than outside it, or so it seemed to me. We resented the song, which Trinity College students sang over the wall separating them from us. 'Balliol bring forth your white man,' they chanted, refer-ring to the Balliol policy of including Indians and others. Colleges differed as much as individuals and Trinity had the custom of recruiting solely from well-known 'public schools.' When the rugby teams of the two colleges had a draw in the semi-finals, excitement ran high.

One of my first friends in the first term was an Indian. Chandra Mal was being trained for the Indian Civil Service. It was he who introduced me to Professor John Macmurray's book *Freedom in the*

Modern World,[20] in which he describes what he means by 'real friends' and 'real people.' It echoed what my father had said to me before starting at college, but made it more precise and persuasive. Much is said about friendship, how it halves troubles and doubles happiness and how you can always judge a person by the friends he keeps, but Macmurray takes his readers further than this by implying that real people make friends more easily and more deeply. Real people are those who are on good terms with themselves, who know themselves and like what they know, without, of course, being selfish or egocentric. Yet, at the end of reading the book it is clear that it is necessary to forget oneself so as to be able to overcome self-consciousness.

Chandra or Chandi as we often called him, had been helping Gandhi as a secretary before he came to college. He was a devotee of the great man. Often conversation turned to one of his many facets, so once he began talking about what an Englishman could wear, comparable with Gandhi's loincloth, to show that he took the side of the poor. Laughingly we decided that the brown corduroy trousers and red spotted handkerchief of the farm labourer were the nearest we could get. Now in my retirement this is what I use on the days when I go out to work in the market garden. It serves as a reminder that the poor are always with us, though not so much on the farms as among the unemployed, and in the Third World.

Unknown to most of the others, we had among us the son of a farm labourer. Somehow, despite the large number of his brothers and sisters, he had made his way to writing books including one on agriculture with Seebohm Rowntree, the authority on poverty at that time. I lived in awe of anyone who could write a book. Books were treated as something very special in our home and I reacted accordingly. Authors such as E.M. Forster and Malcolm Darling came to stay from time to time at '102' and added to this feeling of awe.

Then there were the Rhodes Scholars. Two from every one of the United States came to Oxford each year and Balliol seemed to have more than its fair share of these older gifted people, many of them trying to get their theses published. I was sorry when one of them earned great notoriety in the war in Vietnam later on. At the time he was developing his theory of a take-off stage in the course of a country's development. I would have liked to have known Phillip Kaiser better. He became among other things the President of the Encyclopaedia Britannica. I met him years later when he was presiding over a meeting for teachers.

Amiya Chakravarty had already served as a professor of Calcutta University and had come to Oxford to write a doctoral thesis on Hardy's *The Dynasts*. He had been with Tagore at Shantiniketan (The abode of peace) where his followers developed their culture of peace with the help of Tagore the wise poet. Amiya was more than a good friend to me. The Italians were invading Ethiopia at the time and he taught me the depths to which compassion can reach in speaking about the suffering caused. On another occasion he invited me to meet his friend Paul Robeson, who had just returned from West Africa. He had been studying the similarities between the music he found there and the jazz introduced into the USA by the descendants of African slaves. He stood up and sang and sang. It seemed to me that the whole college and not just the room resounded with that great voice. He sang for peace and tenderness, but I do not know how many people see it this way. Robeson was unfortunately later dismissed as a communist by the establishment.

Afterwards Amiya moved to the USA and I did not keep up with him, but I read that once he had been honoured as the educationalist of the year. When I listen to such people or hear Paul Robeson or Joan Baez singing I feel that any hardened diplomat or businessman could be persuaded to change sides. I often found myself singing on my bicycle. Sometimes the songs were those of the wander-vogel who, despairing of civilisation, took to the roads and footpaths, to seek the good life in the open air. Sometimes they included love songs, which struck home.

Another student whom I worked with closely was Dr Ranyard West, or Roy, as he was known, a psychoanalyst. He believed that his speciality was an important contribution to make, to the understanding of dictators and their power as demagogues and to determine the emotions imposed by war propaganda. He was an enthusiastic supporter of the application of psychiatry to world order. In the longer term, he wrote a number of books such as *Conscience and Society*.[21]

For the short term we formed a Child Psychology Study Group in the college and linked ourselves to Margaret Lowenfeld's Institute of Child Psychology, London. Her methods of understanding children were novel; we could watch the new ways children revealed themselves as they played with carefully designed toys and learned to relax after demanding exercise. The children were tested by being observed as they used these toys that represented the 'world' as they saw it; the results were extraordinary and I believe that, if the war had not intervened, Nursery Schools would have been promoted more widely and sooner. To us it seemed to imply that a new sort of education should be given to children, especially those of Nursery school age. I truly believe that creative and constructive play is an antidote to fear and hatred.

The happiest student I can recall is Billy Hughes, his nickname derived from the name of a prominent trade union leader. He even laughed in his sleep when on a vacation reading party with me. I never learned the secret of his contentment or the significance of his laughter. He could not recall the dream of which the laughter seemed to be part, but it occurred more than once. Dreams and their significance were an important part of conversation when the interest in Freud and Jung's work was at its height. Afterwards he became Ellen Wilkinson's Parliamentary Private Secretary in the Attlee Government and visited me anonymously in the depths of my despair at Saltley Teacher Training College. Then he became Principal of Ruskin College. His happiness was infectious and the College was fortunate in having him.

In the first months in my acquaintance with him, I had such an extraordinary dream that I wrote it down in the morning. About three years previously I had been travelling through Tunis and Algeria with a French businessman, who was buying produce for his Paris shop. The day before we arrived in the town of Constantine there had been a riot among the Arabs there on account of a rumour that a Jew had desecrated an Arab Mosque. The Arabs broke into many Jewish shops, killed the owners, and hung their brightly coloured rolls of cloth on the bridges, which crossed the deep gorge half surrounding the town, and on lamp posts. The French authorities restored order with the help of their colonial troops from Senegal, who were posted at street corners at the time of our arrival.

The dream began in the middle of Broad Street Oxford, showing the place in the road where Hugh Latimer the martyr, was burned at the stake in Queen Mary's reign. In a state of great anxiety I was walking towards the house of the Master of Balliol College with an urgent message. Miraculously there was no wall between the pavement and the drawing room of A. D. Lindsay, the Master and his wife. They were holding some kind of party in honour of General Smuts, who was accompanied by my parents. Mrs Lindsay, knowing Oom Jannie's fondness for babies and there being none in her family at that time, had borrowed one from an Oxford orphanage. In fact Oom Jannie used this as an escape from the small talk of social occasions.

The three of them agreed to come but not with the sense of urgency I possessed. As we looked into the street, we saw from windows upstairs in Exeter College furniture and books being hurled down and thrown onto a huge bonfire. There seemed to be Arabs everywhere running and shouting, with no one else in sight. It looked as though we had left our departure too long. To my surprise no one took much notice of us until we reached the crossroads beyond Blackwells famous bookshop. There an Arab in his white robes stopped us wanting to know who we were and where we were going. At that moment I felt a table-fork in my hand, which stuck out backwards so to say. With a big swipe I struck it into his chest and he folded up and collapsed.

We hurried on down Holywell Street and turned left into Mansfield Road to enter Balliol's former rugby ground. As we did so, Arabs entered the usual way from Jowett Walk and hurried to intervene. Suddenly there appeared a fence and very high gate in front of us, my heart sank and I assumed we would be captured. However, just then an aristocratic couple riding very high horses appeared from nowhere, the gates swung open for them and we were close on their heels. The gates swung together and we were safe for the time being.

Then we made our way by a devious route on the far side of the river Cherwell the sequence of the dream broke, Oom Jannie disappeared and my parents and I were at 102 Banbury Road expecting some kind of attack. I was still in great fear and I took on the job of checking that all the windows and doors were closed

61

and locked. I covered upstairs as well as downstairs but was still very afraid of what might be going to happen throughout the town and thought I had been meticulous when suddenly, as I was standing at the far end of the hall, I heard the front door open, it had rollers fitted so that it was obvious when it was used, I was horrified that I had forgotten to lock it and amazed when a little dark face of an Arab boy, who might have been six or seven years old, peeped round the edge of the door. When he saw me, using both hands, he flicked the contents of a frying pan towards me but it was badly aimed and it hit the edge of the inner doorway. He quickly slammed the door and ran. In horror I went to pick the object up. It was a large piece of fried human flesh so I opened the door and threw it away as far as I could.

The dream might have ended there and still provided enough for my friends to try to analyse, but the most extraordinary part was yet to come. Moving back across the hall I remembered that in my haste I had forgotten the front half of the drawing room which looked onto the Banbury Road.

When I opened the door I was astonished and my feelings ran amok. My father who was not a pacifist, indeed had volunteered, but unsuccessfully, in the First World War, had opened all the four windows as wide as could be. Then he had sat down in an armchair, seeming to be quite relaxed, reading his friend Laurence Housman's *The Little Plays of St Francis*. They are plays, which I knew well which teach such strange lessons; as the best place for stolen gold is underground, where it can rest unremembered, the wise insights of illiterate people, non-violence and the value of retiring from positions of power. As an otherwise conventional banker he savoured such teachings and relished them.

My reaction was strong and immediate. I was more than aghast at my father doing what I should have been doing, if only I had not abandoned my principles when my first trial came. With a very strong feeling of nausea I woke up, it took some time for the nausea to disappear, and the dream stayed with me as a reminder of the importance of my pacifist principles. I had let my fears betray my convictions in my dream life, and this was something I was determined to avoid in waking life.

With this dream to strengthen a belief in the importance of the unconscious mind it is no wonder that I turned to psychoanalysis to deal with one of the main roots of war. Contrary to Billy Hughes' Marxist claim that Capitalism is the main cause of wars, and also the more vague belief that it is a religious change of heart that is crucial; on closer examination human motives, represented by psychoanalysis, offers a chance to produce a culture of peace in place of a culture of aggression, militarism and hatred, perhaps by some process of group hypnosis.

At this time there was little going on to dispel the fears of war. There was a group promoting Federal Union, there was the much discussed motion in the Oxford Union where the debate concluded with a majority voting that 'This House will not fight for King and Country' leaving open the possibility that some might fight for other causes. After the failure of the League of Nations to ensure collective security in what is now Ethiopia, came a similar failure in Spain. The Spanish Civil War was the result of a democratically elected government that was eventually overthrown by a military dictator, General Franco. As a response, a number of Oxford people I knew, went to fight there in the International Brigade and several never came home. One young woman had been my teacher when I started Latin, the daughter of the Professor of Moral Philosophy, another was the son of a member of our Quaker Meeting. Life seemed to be a deplorable muddle and my reaction was to offer such help as I could give to the local League of Nations Union.

It also gave the Soviets the chance to show that they would support a democratic government according to the principles of the League of Nations collective security, while British and French governments remained neutral because they feared the socialist sympathies of Spain. No doubt the two governments were formed by short-sighted politicians who preferred to look at questionable 'national interests' rather than a long-term plan for establishing effective law courts in order to have an alternative to war. Sixty years later the lesson has not been learned that crises can be avoided by early preventive action, but not very easily if war propaganda is allowed to flourish until the time for making peace has passed. Most languages have a version of a stitch in time saves nine, and they are surely appropriate when applied to pollution and its avoidance.

Prophets are seldom popular figures and their words fall too often on deaf ears.

The debates in Parliament and the Oxford Union lacked gravity and sincerity even in the days before the war started. I spoke once in the Union but found the debates promoted insincerity. What was said was often clever or humorous as when debating the merits of the Union's officers having to wear white bow ties and coats with tails, Lyall Wilks stated 'God made the conservatives and gave them tails, but the socialists he left to come to their own conclusions.' With this command of language, in the course of time he became a judge.

Though not wanting to speak in the Union I did want to learn how best to speak in public. There was an office of the League of Nations Union in Oxford and they seemed glad to accept my offer of help, so I often went out to some of the villages in Oxfordshire to speak to one of the Women's Institutes.

One of my acquaintances was Moss, a Canadian student; he was a gentle serious young man who enjoyed walking in the countryside. In North Oxford there was a private housing estate for middle class people and when a Council Housing Estate was built behind them a barrier wall was built on their private road to prevent the working class tenants of the council houses taking a short cut to the city. This expression of contempt for another social class upset him deeply and, supported by another student, he took tools and knocked off the top foot of bricks in an attempt to remove this high barrier wall. At this point the police intervened and he was arrested, after this his sadness deepened. He went walking another day and his body was found on a half-burnt haystack. He left no explanation. Tragedies like this added to the gloom created by Hitler's Germany and the betrayal of the League of Nations to make this a very sad period, similar to what we now see at the beginning of the twenty-first century.

'When I am Hungry'

When I am hungry, may I find some people to feed,
When I am thirsty, may I offer water for their thirst,
When I am sad, someone to lift from sorrow,

When burdens weigh on me, lay on my shoulders the
    burden of my fellows
When I stand in need of tenderness, may I find someone
    who yearns for love,
May loving kindness be my bread, and gentleness my
    strength
May a culture of peace be my resting place.
Adapted from the French 'Prieres de Foi'

One of the difficulties of peace is that the word suggests that it is
something passive that undermines the willingness to face the challenges of a harsh, competitive, and aggressive society, rather than
something active. In this respect I was glad to be able to play rugby
to reassure myself. The first season I captained Balliol's second XV
and the following year was chosen as scrum-half for the first XV. I
was ashamed to hear that previously University College, our main
rivals had suffered so many injuries when playing against Balliol
that half their team could not play in their next match. Vengeance
was expected. Our best player was put out of action very early in
the game and I had the questionable honour of having my leg and
knee twisted by the captain of the Oxford team. The result of the
match was decided by a free-kick the captain took as a drop-kick
on the five yards line, and more than twenty-five yards from the
scoring line where the goal posts stand, in other words as far as
could possibly be attempted. The ball soared into the air and struck
the cross bar so that, by some miracle, it struck the bar again coming
down. It fell the wrong side for us and we lost the cup.

People argue about football matches. Do they enhance or subli-
mate aggressiveness. My personal guess on this matter is that it
depends on how it is played and how the coaching is given.
Unfortunately for me when rules are broken and the game gets
rough the scrum-half is apt to suffer most and I was injured both
at Oxford and later at Carnegie College in Leeds where my partner was the exceptional international player Bill Davis. I had only
to get the ball into his hands and then he often scored tries without being touched.

When not playing rugby I obtained my exercise by walking the
footpaths of Oxfordshire, sometimes by following the towing paths
of the river or canal, often on the hills and often in the footsteps of

Mathew Arnold and his Scholar Gypsy. In this poem by Arnold, an Oxford student left his companions and his books and wandered through the countryside 'waiting for the spark from heaven to fall' and learning from the gypsies. The appeal of learning from more practical people and attaching less importance to academic studies has often haunted students at Oxford, even in the new century. It was more than exercise I received. Like the scholar gypsy I often felt stabs of loneliness, and found myself also 'Waiting for the spark from heaven to fall.'

Often, I envied the gypsies their way of life. I had visited a gypsy caravan near Bagley Wood once where a gypsy's wife unfolded her treasured tablecloth. An heirloom that had been passed down to her through the generations, but she explained that she could no longer read what was embroidered on it in the ancient Gypsy script, but suggested that it was some parable for life.

One evening at Puckham I was leaning over a gate and enjoying the view when a stranger approached. Later on he admitted that, when I responded to his greeting, he concluded that I must be the Scholar Gipsy from the poem. I was pleased to have my own search associated in some way with that of the Scholar gipsy.

At times I had friends with whom I could share walks and thoughts, both boys and girls, one said to me 'living is like painting a beautiful picture, and we should use all the richest colours we can find.' He stopped as we walked, as if to emphasise his point, but I failed him on that occasion, by not giving him enough encouragement, and years later I failed him again, due to my shyness when we met by accident on one of the Aldermaston Marches against nuclear weapons.

What is it that constitutes a colour? How can richness be measured? What sort of picture should it be? I was troubled about the purpose of life, without a purpose there seemed to be no hope. Without hope we might follow Moss.

At this time I needed all my strength to survive what was for me a very sad love affair. My feelings were strong but got no response. I talked about serious matters such as work-camps, unemployment, and wars, she was interested in music and climbing. To my astonishment she turned up likewise at one of the Aldermaston Marches.

Studying at Oxford in those pre-war years was, to a large extent, a matter of choice. When asked whether I was reading for a first class degree, I answered with an emphatic 'No.' I was clearly informed that one would be no advantage if I entered Barclays Bank, whereas I was offered an extra year by my father if there was any chance of me playing for the Oxford University Team. To this I pointed out that the Oxford scrum-half was staying on an extra year in order to play for England.

My first impressions of the teaching at Oxford startled me. It was a dark October evening when I knocked on the door of my tutor. Philosophy, Politics, and Economics were such diverse subjects that I had many tutors, each one lasting for a short period, but on this occasion I was visiting my personal academic tutor, who would be helping me choose which lectures I should attend. Humphrey Sumner was an extremely able academic who afterwards won the most envied post in the University, the Wardenship of All Souls, the college with no students. It specialises in research. Being accustomed to the quirks of Quakers I was all the more appreciative of what I saw when I opened the door, the only light in the long room was a table light at the far end and bent over a table was a handsome head of long hair and the silhouette of a very large goose quill at work.

I have seldom told this anecdote for fear of Oxford being mocked for its quaint outmoded ways. I have found feathers a very difficult implement to use for writing. A first tutorial is too imposing an occasion for a discussion on the origin of pens, so we talked at random. Although he was an historian specialising in Russian History I never found conversations with him easy. He was kind enough to say after my degree was announced, that I had spent my time very well. I doubt if he knew that I had been attending lectures on psychoanalysis, and on unemployment by Professor Meade and G.D.H. Cole on life in cooperative communities.

'All works of love are works for peace' was a saying in accord with one lecture about the value to society of groups of people who follow their consciences. Sometimes the lectures on ethics called into question the doctrines related to economic man who was supposed to benefit everyone by following his own self-interest; however, nothing satisfactory was erected in its place. Human motivation might be part of a psychology course but it could have received better treatment in moral philosophy.

These were outside my course but life seemed short: ominously in 1934 I had been offered free training as a pilot, and, though pressed hard by an influential tutor of the college, I rejected the offer. I was more attracted by the chance to do something useful immediately. Finding the political and economic causes of war, solving the problem of unemployment, living in a community, and promoting international understanding seemed more worthwhile, so it was to these lectures I went in so far as I could find them.

This proved more difficult than might be expected. In political theory much was said and written about the relationship between the individual citizen and the state, and the various views about the nature of the state, including, for example, federal states. However, it did appear as though a topic did not deserve attention unless Plato, Rousseau, or Hobbes had written sage words on the subject. Unemployment was taken as a purely economic phenomenon; the political impact on countries such as Germany was not mentioned, presumably because it was so new that its significance had barely been detected. A future Professor of Philosophy suggested that I was taking Moral Philosophy much too seriously and that it should be ranked as a pastime such as chess. If philosophers ignored their vested interests and reached final conclusions they might have to join the unemployed, he confessed

Researchers into cancer are said to suffer from this same inhibition. For the most part I failed to cope with the course I had chosen and ended up with a third class degree. It was little comfort that a fourth class existed and I was bitterly disappointed. The news came at a bad time, a very bad time, capping the failure in my main friendship. Working for peace is hard enough to arrange without a bad start. I could not expect to find a job writing as a peace correspondent, nor find ways of slipping in messages related to peace as an ordinary journalist.

CHAPTER 5

Active Work Camps in a World of Unemployment

BEFORE LEAVING MY student years the work camps, which I joined or led each vacation, must be described. The work-camps movement looks back to its roots in the thoughts of Jean-Jacques Rousseau who wrote about the equality of all people and the educational value of practical and craftwork. Leo Tolstoy took these ideas further and glorified the work of peasants. 'Every day…I either dig the ground, or saw and chop wood, or work with scythe or sickle or some other tool…as to ploughing …it is pure enjoyment!' Bread-labour he called it, and he inspired his family to help a neighbouring widow in haymaking. Some communities inspired by him were formed to follow his 'New Life'. In 1909, speaking at a peace congress he said: 'War is murder by another name.'

John Ruskin, especially in his book *Unto This Last,*[22] developed these ideas by stressing in lectures the dignity of manual labour and also leading groups of students to build a raised track across the water meadows to the village of Hinksey from Oxford, the same village Mathew Arnold mentioned in his poem *The Scholar Gypsy.* This information became much more vivid when I learned that the father of a friend had taken part in the building of the raised track.

I used to regard it as an act of historical piety to walk on that same footpath to Hinksey. Gandhi valued Ruskin's contribution to the concept of International Student Service for Peace, which originated just after the First World War. Pierre Ceresole and an Englishman started this kind of 'camp'; Pierre was from French-speaking Switzerland, and he hoped to make this service an

69

alternative to conscription into the army. The first 'camp' was in France, near the Belgium border, and its practical outcome was to restore buildings in a village, which had been destroyed during the fighting. There is usually a shortage of labour immediately after a war; so volunteer work was welcomed, but later it became a little more difficult to find suitable projects without appearing to take work away from the unemployed.

The first International Voluntary Service for Peace camp in Britain was held in Brynmawr in 1931, a town with 86% of its workers left idle by the closure of the coalmines. A coal tip was being turned into a park intended for children in particular. It was before the days of bulldozers, and there was a need for plenty of strong men to work with shovels and wheelbarrows. My eldest brother Jan took part and came home with a poisoned blister, which needed a fresh poultice every hour. As I was the only person at home, being too young to go myself, I had a difficult task. He came home with tales of working with people from all over Europe, many of whom spoke little English. They had sung songs of an evening and all the world seemed young and hopeful.

Some years later when I was busy work-camping, Jan, faced with the ever-growing problem of unemployment, which no one knew how to remedy, joined the Communist Party. He hoped that unemployment could be brought to an end by economic planning and he felt that Capitalism could not manage to remedy it. It is often said that Hitler's rise to power was due to such economic problems in Germany, and it also explains the growth in the desire for revenge after the First World War. Certainly the lack of work for more and more people, and the lower level of unemployment pay, caused people to become more desperate, which disposes governments to enlarge the armed forces. At times we had visions, rather than expectations, that volunteers would undertake the unpaid work which is never the less badly needed on a mass scale, such as caring for handicapped people, children, and the elderly, and work for charities. Tennyson wrote, 'How dull it is … to rust unburnished, not to shine in use!' We were idealists who were committed to our own high hopes, so we responded warmly to such thoughts both for the sake of ourselves and for the unemployed. Maybe we thought that, in the long run, planning was part of any cure for unemployment, for recycling human resources.

On the top of these hopes we wanted to be regarded not as 'townies' but as people who knew one end of a spade from the other; not as soft-headed academics but as practical people able to take the rough with the smooth; not as callow youth but as people with a range of experiences; not as the privileged elite ignorant of human suffering but as friends who cared about people. These were high hopes and we were often disappointed. Mixing with other people of many different backgrounds was in itself a first step towards wisdom.

My first camp took place in the summer of 1934, a year after Hitler's seizure of power. Hugh Doncaster, a school friend, and I stayed with Pitt and Yves Kruger. Two other German refugees helped re-establish a previously abandoned farm in the Pyrenees, above Prades and Perpignan. Pitt, who was in charge, decided to make the farm self-sufficient in food as much as possible, with goats, hens, vegetables and some fruit. Meat was restricted to once a week. Bread, tomatoes, and cheese were our staple diet and some vegetables cooked for the evening meal. I recall bathing the baby in the yard in front of the house. In the village of Mosset a kilo-metre below, the long list of names on the War memorial provided the explanation for many farms being abandoned. Their terraces were beginning to crumble away, their fruit trees unpruned. The place reminded me of Alphonse Daudet's 'Lettres de Mon Moulin' in which the rabbits and the owl eventually became the sole inhab-itants, except for visiting cows which slept *à la belle étoile*, a phrase which has delighted me ever since by conveying the enchantment of a starry night.

How far doing work for refugees promotes peace I have never been sure. Is one dealing with symptoms or causes? It goes against one's heart to ignore these needs and confine oneself to preven-tion, and this has puzzled us in many different situations. It is likely that it depends on how the caring for the refugees is done. The existence of refugees is generally caused by neglecting peace educa-tion in their country of origin. This should be made clear to all the people involved: firstly, to the members of their government who need to take more national pride in their own tolerance, hospi-tality, and friendliness, qualities which, incidentally, favour the tourist 'industry'. Secondly, to teachers and parents who need to demonstrate an appreciation of people of different kinds on the principle of 'I like you, you're different'.

71

My Aunt Esther had taken boys from Yugoslavia into her home after the First World War. Aunt Hilda had also been active in helping refugees, as was Ruth's family.

Refugees are not a separate issue from war. War usually causes people to try to escape either from the fighting or from the consequences of extreme nationalism associated with war propaganda, as was the case with Pitt Kruger. Unlucky man, he was betrayed to the Nazis when they invaded the south of France by the priest in Mosset. He was sent to the Russian front where he was taken prisoner by the Russians and almost died of hunger in what was then Leningrad. He finally made his way home in 1948, long after the war had ended. The story of his dealings with his gaolers in Leningrad is such a perfect example of non-violence that it is unfortunate that it was omitted from the book on *La Coûme*.[23] The book explains the extraordinary atmosphere of friendship for all, established at *La Coûme* by Pitt and his wife Yves.

Our work at *La Coûme des Abeilles* (The valley of bees) consisted of harvesting potatoes and tomatoes in preparation for winter, chopping firewood, and occasionally herding the goats. It was on a later visit that I was trusted with a scythe, only to cut my thumb when sharpening the blade and developing such serious blood poisoning that I barely reached Switzerland for the next part of our holiday. A mule carried me up to Saas Fé, for there was no road at that time and I was unable to walk.

The next year my Aunt and cousin, who owned the farm, invited me to find other students to follow on. One of these was my friend Denis Healey from Balliol who described his visits to *Coûme* in his autobiography.[24] The *Coûme* developed into a home for Spanish children, refugees from the civil war, and later into a well-known experimental school for those children whose parents doubted the value of the over-organised French education system. This was a system, which undervalued spontaneity, intuition, and creativity, and over-rated uniformity and convention. It was a perfect example of Bernard Shaw's comment that too often 'schools are like prisons, only worse'. Pitt was an admirable head master, especially for such a school as *L'école des buissons* (the school among the bushes), which contrasted sharply with schools following national curricula.

The next so-called work camp (we were never under canvas) was in Oldham in Lancashire. The work consisted of digging up the turf on the top of Oldham Edge to make allotments for unemployed people. It was hard work and we developed good appetites so it was a good way to learn how it felt to be unemployed and have barely enough to eat. We were billeted in pairs in the homes of the unemployed people who were not necessarily the same people as those who were digging with us. When my friend and I laid out two pounds for the two of us on the table, for our week's board and lodging, our host commented: 'It's a long time since we've seen as much money as that in this home'. The dole at that time amounted to about thirty-two shillings.

One cause of conflict in many countries is the growing gap between rich and poor. It could be a part of education to live for a week on the diet of the poor, as a prosperous Quaker grocer once did, so as to generate enough sympathy to ensure that action is taken to reduce the gap. John Hoyland, Jack to his friends, who organised these work camps, was a magnificent speaker. His deep voice stirred the consciences of the privileged children in the many so-called public schools where he spoke, in a way no one else could do. He had been a missionary in India and his first wife and part of his family had died there. His suffering served to deepen the passion with which he spoke: 'Come and see how these people live and live like them for a bit. You can learn by talking over your spade better than any other way'. This was the gist of his message in his book *Digging with the Unemployed,* one of Jack's many books. The title sounded ironical at first, but it became apparent that the morale of the unemployed workers often needed to be raised before they would grow their own vegetables; they were surprised and pleased to have our help. Such a method can often be used effectively when violence comes to an end in an international or intra-national conflict.

In Oldham I slept in a front room, which overlooked a cobbled street. We were woken in the early morning by the sound of the wooden clogs on the cobbles as people went to work in one of the few cotton mills still working. The women wore cotton shawls over their heads. They seemed to be summing up a whole period in the history of Lancashire, but the period was fast coming to an end. Up on Oldham Edge one morning I counted one hundred and thirty-two tall factory chimneys. I mentioned the figure to a local; 'Yes', came the reply, 'we've never been able to count them before because the air was too smoky, but now they are closing them down, the air is clearer'. Then the speaker added with a trace of bitterness in his voice, 'the managers have gone to Egypt; the machinery has gone to Egypt. It's just us who are left behind'. I have often wondered whether to rejoice that the poor, often children, of the Third World have benefited from this move, which threw people into unemployment in the 'North', for the children now work in such bad conditions. No international trade union has been able to give work to those who need it most while safeguarding reasonable conditions of work. A fair bargain is rarely struck between the rich and the hungry, because the hungry have no bargaining power. The rich tend to be corrupted by the power of wealth and the poor tend to be corrupted by the powerlessness of poverty. The result is called structural violence, a hornet's nest for the would-be peacemaker. For such stings there was no obvious antidote, as we learned from our studies at college.

Crabbs Cross, south of Birmingham, was a dull landscape for the following work camp. It lacked the glamour of a disappearing industry and yet had its quota of unemployed in need of the opportunity to add fresh vegetables to their diet. Considering the plight of the unemployed it is surprising that there was not more shoplifting and burglary occupying the time of the police. In Crabbs Cross the reverse was true and it sounds as though it had at least one characteristic of *Utopia*. The local 'bobby' had a country footpath as part of his beat, where rabbits abounded. His tailcoat moved in a mysterious way because he kept a ferret in his tail pocket for catching them. Happy is the country, which has such policemen!

After Crabbs Cross came a proper international work camp held at Marienthal which lies well to the south of Vienna. As in Lancashire, cotton mills had been closed down, leaving men out of work. By some freak of management the cotton goods they had previously produced passed seven times between England and Marienthal for the different processes in the course of production. No wonder they could not compete with cotton goods from elsewhere. These people were in need of vegetable plots.

The men of Marienthal were more familiar with vegetable growing, than the cotton spinners of Oldham, due to cotton factories being relatively new in Austria, by comparison. In a more industrialised country such as England, people lose touch with their ancestors' skills in gardening, and fight shy of showing their ignorance. Then they need some assurance of help, or at least advice, to be available to them around the gardening year, which is much more than a work camp can offer. To this camp, the campers came from several different countries but mainly from England. We were suspected by the Austrian officials of being Nazi sympathisers on account of the Anglo-German naval treaty and because the Nazis had their work camps too. We were housed in huts, which had belonged to a socialist youth organisation called *Kinderfreunde* (Children's friends). Our first task was to clear up the litter, which had been left behind when, for political reasons, the place had been closed. Among the rubbish I found a number of songbooks for children, which we put to use. The songs were about peace, friendship, and travel, and some had a political slant so I worried that they might be confiscated during my weeks in Hitler's Germany, where I was to stay later. The songs were so striking that there is one, which haunts me still:

Auf spielman stimme deine fiedel	Come fiddler give voice to your fiddle
Jetzt geht's zum thor hinaus	Now it's time to leave
Zum abschied noch ein lustig liedel	One more merry song at parting
Ade du gastlich haus.	Goodbye you hospitable house
Wir wandern in die weite	We are wandering afar
Wohl in die weite wunderschone welt	In the wide and wonderful world
Ade zum frischen streite	Goodbye as we take our eager steps,
Ade du gastlich haus.	Goodbye you hospitable house.

These simple words caught the feeling of the time, of 'World, world I am coming', of good company and adventure. I often wondered whether it sounded equally good to the German speakers. It may have expressed their wish for the freedom of the open road and their dislike for regimentation. Songs can play a special part in education for peace. They speak to the heart directly, achieving on behalf of peace, especially for international friendship, what nothing else can do. Joan Baez, like Paul Robeson, stirred people for peace with her songs, as the Marseillaise moved Napoleon's armies. Napoleon may have claimed that armies march upon their stomachs, but men do not live by bread alone; nor does the devil have all the best tunes.

Later in the same summer of 1935 I moved on to Berlin, ostensibly to improve my German but, as it turned out, to help Corder Catchpool at the Quaker Centre. His work as a representative of the Society of Friends was in disarray; the police had searched his office. A departing Friend had her address book confiscated at the frontier and an informer attended Meetings for Worship claiming to be a genuine 'attender'. Corder arranged with me to turn up at the centre without asking questions, but I had to be prepared to spend the night away. He had promised an English Friend would come as a protection if needed. Foreigners were given much help and consideration until Germany was fully re-armed; in addition, Friends were appreciated for their work of feeding the hungry at the end of the First World War, and so I felt doubly protected. It turned out that people who had exploded bombs previously had threatened a Jewish holiday home again. I spent an evening talking among people some of whom had surprisingly been allowed to leave concentration camps. It was hard to express enough sympathy for the people who had been left behind in the camps.

That night I was invited to teach English songs to a group of young girls before they all went off to bed; the lucky ones had already planned to leave Germany. There was a loud explosion and we waited to see whether the building would be burned but nothing further happened. On another occasion I was sent to Breslau to warn a Catholic priest that the address book carried his name and that he should burn papers of interest to Nazi officials. He had been working for a better understanding between Poles and Germans, which was highly undesirable in Nazi eyes.

It is not easy to recapture at this time the feelings I had towards the Nazis. During the war German prisoners had made beautiful toys for me and I had acquired an admiration for the way of life of the rucksack-wearing outdoor Germans who appeared to be a very large portion of the population. On the other hand I had watched Hitler's face, distorted with hatred, as he spoke to a large meeting of the Hitler Youth in Innsbruck. On that occasion he looked so ridiculous that I thought the Germans far too sensible to follow him, but he was a more skilful demagogue than I realised. He could persuade his audiences in a single speech that Germany was both an inoffensive country surrounded by enemies who might threaten Germany by working together, and also a sleeping giant able to take on the whole world.

I have recently found it much easier to understand some of the world's megalomaniacs since reading the USA author Alice Miller's book *For Your Own Good*[25] with its brief accounts of Hitler and Mussolini in which she describes the effects of a brutalising childhood. The theme that cruelty to children produces bullies like Hitler and Mussolini is vitally important for peace workers. It explains how wars begin, and teachers can help peace education, if classes are small, and examinations do not press too hard so as to leave little time for dealing with problem children. The book is a study of greed for power among school children. They build up their gangs in order to threaten other children with violence to compensate for the violence, which they had experienced at home, to such an extent that these children become excluded from school on a regular basis. Additionally, she has explored the theme of educating younger children about peace, as a route to peace. Those who do something to heal such emotionally disturbed children are making a significant contribution to peace.

Experiences such as mine in Berlin provided me with contributions to make to the discussions, which emerge spontaneously during work camps. In Germany these discussions were far more restrained for fear of spies. While working in a camp back in Wales, my account of the denial of some newspapers of the existence of concentration camps in Germany produced the comment, from an unemployed coal miner in the Rhondda valley: 'The trouble with the papers is that they get everything upside-bloody-down'. He was working in a co-operative project of the Unemployed Miners Club in Tylorstown, which was based on permission from the mine owners to obtain free coal for themselves by driving a coal level into the side of the mountain. They had been given the wrong advice for their first attempt and needed a boost for their morale before trying again. The cheerful way that they addressed us as 'Boy-o' made it apparent that they enjoyed our gesture. We were in the early stages of excavating the tunnel or level so the coal was not reached until after we had left.

The unemployed miners of South Wales were the aristocrats among the unemployed. In the Rhondda there was an adult education class in classical Greek, provided by WEA, among many other classes. They spoke with authority about political affairs, and yet the social gap between employers and employees was greater than elsewhere. My Uncle George was commissioner for the Special Areas, districts where unemployment was at its highest, and he found difficulty in getting a hearing for the plight of the poor, when he returned home to the city of London. Unemployment at that time in London was 'out of sight and out of mind'. No wonder the class war, as many Marxists called it, was at its height. One indignant man entered the law court to witness a trial, and as he did so the heavy hand of the policeman in attendance came down on his hat, crushed it up, and passed it back to him. He felt offended for being treated that way. I suspect that policeman knew nothing about ferrets; like the policeman in Crabbs Cross. Higher up the valley the milkman of the co-operative called his horse Stalin and was able to carry on his propaganda by addressing the horse with a loud voice and a careful choice of words. I was disappointed that my host for the camp in Wales, had no interest in politics, but instead owned a tent and frequently took his wife camping. I had made the mistake of thinking that the miners would have worked out ways of curing unemployment without the complications of the Soviet system, and that they would be keen to hear the views of others about them. It is sad to report that it was the Second World War, which solved their problem, by providing them with military jobs. How is it that today at the start of the new century unemployment is not solved by creating jobs through training to deal with pollution and the needs of the environment?

At another work camp in South Wales our hostess remarked, 'my grandmother used to speak "fancy" just like you', and I realised more clearly how rifts in society are noted and sometimes resented. The miners had been so proud of their craft that they looked up to no one and valued only the fellowship of the miners. We heard of miners working eleven-inch seams by lying on their sides, of rescues from danger and privations, and of strikes. They had every reason to be proud people on good terms with themselves.

The Bruderhof Camp provided an entirely different experience from that in South-Wales, although it also involved helping refugees from Germany and pacifist refugees from militarism, they were all people interested in communal living. It raised entirely different issues. When the life of monasteries was at its full height during the latter part of the Middle Ages, it was taken for granted that communal life was either the ideal way of living or at least a desirable way of living. At this period the Hutterian communities demonstrated that this sharing of private property could provide a sound basis for developing qualities of life, which are hard to achieve in any other way. Through skilled craftsmanship in wood, clay, building and gardening, closed mixed-sex communities often led the way in creating societies where it was a privilege to exist. Material needs were met collectively, thus allowing the main attention to be directed to the life of the spirit, including human friendship, loyalty, and responsibility.

The members of the Bruderhof believed that by living close together, as one does in such circumstances, they put into practice their belief in non-violence and mediation for disputes, and that this does much more for world peace than avoiding such experiences by living in modern tiny families or alone. Last century Edward Westcott wrote: 'A reasonable amount of fleas is good for a dog. It keeps him from broodin' over bein' a dog', which should suffice to encourage lonely people to calculate the substantial financial advantages of sharing.

The Bruderhof at the time we visited was near Fulda in Germany. The members came mainly from Germany but also from Britain and other countries, sufficiently varied to present opportunities for peace making among different religions, languages, eating habits, ages and ways of bringing up children. Already the Nazi Party had led to the young men of the Bruderhof being sent to safety in Liechtenstein and also a new branch established in the Cotswolds in England.

Later, when conscription was expected in Britain, they all moved to Paraguay and they came back after the war. I stayed a short time with them in Germany, but a longer time in the Cotswolds at Ashton Keynes. They were delightful people. They lived on a diet of beans, like the Diggers of the seventeenth century[26], they were earnest, and yet we enjoyed dancing country-dances, and singing, sometimes simultaneously and with great gusto. It was hard to believe that life would not become monotonous, but otherwise it was very attractive. In 1981 I encountered a man who had been one of the Bruderhof children. He had a French conscientious objector as father, an English mother, and he learned Spanish and Portuguese in South America. He retired from being a United Nations interpreter, like many others, owing to the stress of the work, and he was serving as a freelance interpreter, sitting between a British Cabinet Minister and the Prime Minister of Spain to negotiate Spain's entry into the Common Market. 'What do you do, when someone obviously misunderstands?' I asked. 'You can't do anything.' He replied. 'You just have to go on interpreting what they say without any suggestion that they are misunderstanding each other.'

Looking back twenty years later I wish that I had persisted and had asked him whether he had thought of warning a friend in political circles if an important misunderstanding had occurred. The principle of early warning against the outbreak of violence is widely accepted, and misunderstandings often lead to violence.

A number of friends from Oxford joined in these visits to the Bruderhof but no one, so far as I know, joined permanently in their attractive way of life; however, I hope we gave them some encouragement even though our practical work made little difference to them. Much later Ruth and I were able to compare them with the *communauté de L'Arche* in the South of France from where leaders were sent to practice non-violent resistance in support of the poor and the oppressed. This mingling of service to the world at large with the maintenance of community life appealed to me more. Law by itself is never enough for civilised living; there has to be created a strong public opinion in support of it in order to make it effective. With the development of international law under the auspices of the United Nations pacifists should recognise that they have a special duty to strengthen it. It is very necessary for isolated pacifists to have a strongly supportive base to which they can return for refreshment and also renewed inspiration. This role is sometimes performed by a quasi-religious order, sometimes by a university department or a family circle, but too often this support is missing and the people feel strangers in their own homes.

During the past century and now in the twenty-first century, material wealth has excluded these other human achievements from what has come to be regarded as desirable values. One might attempt to measure the success of monasteries, families, and individuals by the wealth at their command, but the comparisons would be obviously ridiculous. The 'good life' cannot be found and lived so easily. No one believes that millionaires are the happiest people. So where can we go from here? An Irishman, directing my wife Ruth, pointed with his finger and said, 'This here is the nigh road, but for safety and sanity I'd be taking this (other) one'.[27]

Animals can be a help to those in search of a better, peaceful way of living. For a sheep, it may be that the good life is to be found somewhere near the centre of the flock. Other sheep around it provide a cosy reassurance and it only feels deeply anxious when it is pushed by those behind into leadership or if it is cut off in some way from the flock.

Cats have different values. They appear to be most content when they are alone. Bees are particularly interesting creatures because they live together in communities and have highly elaborate social structures and yet, like humans, they go to war.

One spring I left the doorway of one hive open too wide. Members of a neighbouring hive discovered that raiding the honey supplies nearby was more rewarding than searching far and wide for flowers. This information was spread by the bee dance to the other members of the stronger hive and the robbers rapidly increased in numbers. Meanwhile the sentries of the weaker hive called, I assume, for support. When a bee stings it dies and the number prepared to sting in self-defence is extraordinary; soon the close-cropped lawn in front of the weaker hive was covered with the corpses of bees, many of them in pairs, still clinging together in death after fatal duels. After a great deal of study much is known about the behaviour of bees, but I doubt whether anyone knows how the killing comes to an end. Who gives the message to cease fighting? How are they selected? A humanist might add, 'Let's find the gene and transfer it to the human race!'

The figures for family members in Britain have changed substantially in the course of the past century so that most households now contain only one or two people and provide an inadequate preparation for living in communities of twenty or more. Already in 1953 I had found that a third of the students in the college where I was educating them to be teachers were only-children, and lacking in some ways experience desirable for teachers. It is reasonable to suppose that an only-child lacks the skills involved in sharing and co-operating, and that they expect to be in the limelight and receive much attention from adults. Smaller families may be needed, but adjustments in social lives are also needed and one of these may well be the development of social skills in groups of families such as the Bruderhof. Another may be the growing custom of creating aunts, uncles, grandparents, and above all cousins by adoption. In Quaker meetings, in theory all adults share responsibilities for the children; in practise this is not achieved. In the Bruderhof the sense of responsibility was more nearly reached and it was fascinating to watch the consequences. The children looked remarkably happy.

The next work camp I attended was in Salford in Manchester at a club used by unemployed people and their children. My main job was mending toys, many of which were already broken when they were donated. We also needed to keep children occupied and do the decorating.

CHAPTER 6

'Just Look[ing]' for Fifty Years

THE WORK CAMP I had attended at Salford in Manchester was an important occasion for me because I had only met Ruth briefly at her home, Barns Close, at New Year. We found we had so many interests in common, ranging from German songs to child psychology, that I picked up courage to write and enclosed the letter in a thin pamphlet of the Margaret Lowenfeld's Institute about child psychology. Then an extraordinary event took place. It was my first letter to her and I got no reply. I assumed that she wanted no further contact and that she must have other people in whom she was more interested. What had actually happened was that the pamphlet had remained unopened. To my astonishment a letter came two months later explaining that she had only just read mine when it slipped from the pamphlet as she was putting it in the waste paper basket. I was glad that I had written on sufficiently slippery paper! It was a chance, which changed my life.

To add to my astonishment she invited me to join her family on a skiing holiday. This presented me with a dilemma. The dilemma was that, after making one mistake by making a friendship with someone with interests different from mine, such as putting skiing before work camps, I was firmly convinced that I should avoid repeating it. Would I accept, or would I be true to my own values and refuse? I was well aware that you live according to the company that you keep. I also pondered on the thought that the history of religions shows how much easier it is to give lip service to high standards than it is to live up to them. I had no one from whom I could seek advice, though I was in great need of it. Even

My wife, Ruth (on left) always encouraged me in the psychological approaches to peace. This led me to act as rapporteur for the UNESCO sponsored committee on stress in primary schools. Ruth passed away after our golden wedding in 1988.

my favourite motto was no use to me; it states simply 'When in doubt, say Yes.' In this case it was not quite clear whether that would mean accepting the invitation or sticking to my principles. Had I not written a warning to my sister when she joined the privileged on sunny ski slopes? The following poem was my caution:

To a Sister Taking a Skiing Holiday

Mountain pleasures few may know,
Some ride o'er the winter snow,
But, however great their art,
They can but grieve the mountain heart.

Others smoke a cigarette,
Forgetting mountain etiquette.
Rain baptizes. Bear in mind
To leave the city's joys behind.

With rocks and cliffs the heights are fraught,
For mountain wisdom's dearly bought,
Bought with many a sigh and so,
Mountain pleasures few may know.

It was indeed a very difficult decision, although Ruth was also a member of Jack Hoyland's work-camp committee. However, when she attended I had been absent, and vice versa, so we simply missed each other. After tossing the question about for as long as was reasonable, it took some determination to write and say that I had made plans to join a work-camp in Salford would she too like to join? To my great delight she agreed.

At one point the lady organiser at Salford, Hilda was looking at Ruth who had a circle of little children around her, who were completely absorbed by what they were doing under her direction. We could not hear what was being said because we were outside the building, gazing down its longest corridor to a room beyond. Hilda commented 'Just look' and I just looked for fifty years even though at times I upset her, by taking my work too seriously.

On April 20th 1938 Ruth and I were married in the peace and quiet of Jordans Quaker Meeting House, which Ruth had attended as a child with her two brothers and two sisters, and where William Penn lies buried. We became acquainted by sharing not only the Salford work-camp, but also a Clarion Campaign on behalf of the Labour Party in the constituency near Windsor and right up to our marriage she worked there for a hostel for Spanish children, refugees from the Spanish Civil War.

By this time she had played a big part in my life by persuading me that I should give up thinking of banking as a career, despite the very good offer to follow my father by serving as a local director in Oxford. She also persuaded me that despite my bad degree I could become a teacher by taking up gymnastics as a main subject. At that time there was a great shortage of gym teachers, especially of those qualified to teach the new-fashioned Danish Gymnastics. Consequently I was accepted for a one-year course at Carnegie College in Leeds.

On top of this I was attracted by the idea of forming a Labour or Socialist Youth Service, by John Parker MP who commented when I consulted him 'We've already got enough people to deal with banking.' The Youth Movements in both Nazi Germany and in the Soviet Union were a warning that the ideals of young people are a powerful force and need to be tactfully harnessed by governments, particularly if society is adapting to new developments, such as the decline of the influence of the family.

Ruth and I spent our first summer doing some practical teaching, she in the primary school, and I in the secondary school, of Bottisham Village College. It was a remarkable new idea to envisage schools' purpose as being the education not of individuals but of communities. It is an idea, which might be compared with the Bruderhof, which educates its own children who live in the previously mentioned ready-made communities.

George Cadbury, Ruth's grandfather, was the founder of The Bournville factory and The Bournville Village. The factory was run by some of his sons. George Cadbury had strong political views and so at the time of the Boer War, which in reality was being fought over gold and diamond mines, he bought the Daily News, to bring this to the attention of the public, because none of the other papers

86

put the Boers' case positively. As a consequence a series of local newspapers mainly bought by Joseph Rowntree, but including George Cadbury's Daily News became known as the 'Cocoa Press.' The war propaganda had been left unanswered: 'We don't want to fight, but by jingo if we do, we've got the men, we've got the ships, we've got the money too.'

The phrase 'by jingo' dates from 1878 but achieved common currency in the Boer War. The Daily News under the editorship of the novelist Charles Dickens had exposed the sad and seamy side of British life at home and now was to attempt to paint a more truthful picture of the Empire, but truth is elusive in times of war. My parents met at Cambridge University over opposition to the Boer War. Ruth's father, who had read agriculture at Cambridge followed by a short period farming, was asked by George Cadbury to take over responsibility for the *Daily News*. It later became the *News Chronicle*, but by then Henry Cadbury's eyes were failing and he had to find other work to do.

Henry and his wife Lucy became wardens of Woodbrooke College in Selly Oak, Birmingham, we lived close by, first in Witherford Way and later sharing the large house 'Westholme' with them, which used to stand a short distance away on the other side. Henry and Lucy were able to act as hosts to Mahatma Gandhi during his visit there in 1931 at the time of the Round Table Conference and his bedroom remains in demand. A young student visitor begged to be given this room. When asked how he had slept, he replied, 'not very well. I couldn't decide how Gandhi would have slept, so I spent half the night in the bed and half the night on the floor.' The poet Tagore also visited, and Kenyatta studied there, these visitors all helped to create an atmosphere of non-violence and peace at Woodbrooke.

Ruth's father Henry was such a humble host during his time as Warden of the College that on one occasion a young newcomer from the Far East mistakenly offered him a tip for carrying his luggage! Ruth took after him in this respect and wished to disassociate herself from her famous family. I often teased her for telling me on the first day we met, that she would really like to change her name. I don't think she had realised the implications of such a suggestion!

Two years later when I was looking for a teaching post and I wanted her agreement in advance, she said 'I don't want to be in Birmingham, anywhere else will do.' I replied 'But the School Inspector who examined my work recommended Birmingham very strongly.' 'All right' she answered, 'As long as we're not in Bournville.' In fact we ended up in a house in Bournville so that I could bicycle to work in a new school nearby. Bournville is best understood by standing on the Village Green, where we used to gather for Christmas carols. Surrounding the Green, revealing the hopes of the founder, were the primary school, Ruskin School of Art, the Continuation school for young factory workers who were released from work for one day each week, the Quaker Meeting House and a short line of shops.

For some reason, despite the remarkable eloquence of Ruth's step-grandmother, who remained very active in her old age, the hopes of the founder were not understood by many as a means to a better way of life among people both friendly and public-spirited. The Director of the Bournville Village Trust remarked one day that our starting of a vigorous Parent-Teacher Association was the best thing, which had happened in a decade. It brought even those often tied to their houses by children to meet and learn from each other. Ruth and I never knew what great-grandmother thought when she made an unexpected visit after the war and found us parents away at a meeting and the two great-grandsons not only out of bed, but out of the house, bicycling up and down the street dressed in pyjamas. She lived on to the age of ninety-six and died of catching a cold when sea bathing.

Ruth's mother was Lucy Bellows, daughter of John Bellows, the printer of Gloucester. I was glad to be able to speak about her with enthusiasm at the Memorial Meeting at Bournville. She was herself a person of great enthusiasms, which ranged from polar exploration to individuals such as Jomo Kenyatta, the first president of Kenya. As she had known him well when he was studying at Woodbrooke College, she went to see him in Kenya where he was in prison, after being found guilty of leading the 'terrorist' organisation Mau-mau. He claimed he was not guilty and she believed in his honesty and wisdom. He survived to become one of the highly successful and admirable leaders of newly liberated African states.

Lucy Cadbury played a fine part as grandmother of our family of six. From 1951 until the time of her death we shared the large house 'Westholme,' formerly belonging to uncle Edward, which we divided into two but with a well-used connecting door upstairs. It was a big adjustment for the children to move from a very small house to a very large one. One of our sons was described as the boy who lives in the park. On the other hand he was embarrassed by the old age of our 1938 Austin and asked, on the rare occasions he was driven to school, to be put down round the corner where he could avoid being seen to have any connection with it. Bournville School being in the state system, non-Quaker children attended it, though it was partly built at George Cadbury's expense. He wanted the classrooms to be so small that it would be impossible to have large classes and travelled to Whitehall to obtain permission. He may have missed out some of the factors affecting desirable class sizes and classroom sizes, but it was a brave effort to apply educational principles.

However the demand was so great, after school building had been suspended during the war, that at least one of our children was in a class of over fifty, and another son of ours commented when out walking with me 'That boy over there is in our class.' When asked why he did not wave to him, added: 'No. I don't know him, he's on the other side of the class.' None of the rest of the eighty descendants of George Cadbury had attended the school, partly because their name would have made relationships difficult, partly because smaller classes were available in private schools.

As social distinctions can turn into a form of unjust apartheid and lead to violence in the longer run I was lecturing both before and after the war on the harm done by larger classes and large schools in keeping the private schools in business. In this connection I wrote an article and leaflet headed 'Law-breakers in School,' giving the statistics for over-size classes; because there were legal restrictions on the size of classes, the children appeared to be 'aiding and abetting.'

The size of the gap between well-to-do and working class homes, I should admit, can be shown by describing the household in which I grew up. Ruth's family name added to the oddities of our well-to-do Quaker homes. Our Quaker ways would astonish those of later generations they might well be described as not easy to reconcile with Quaker beliefs. In those days it was considered desirable to employ servants as much as possible for those who could afford the wages, especially if the workhouse was the alternative. Moreover a banker had to live, not extravagantly but not as though he was hard-pressed, for fear of losing the confidence of his customers. If that happened the house would have had to be sold and we would have been 'out on the pavement.' Although, my father could print and sign his own bank notes they would not have been accepted when his customers lost their confidence. His bank was one of the last four private banks to be bought up by the large banks and the risks he ran led to a breakdown in his health.

During my childhood we had two or three servants living in and a gardener who came by day. With the exception of the gardener they all came to the reading of the bible or similar book before breakfast. In the evening my mother came to us one by one to 'say blessings' on family and friends and from time to time she would read a story or more likely a poem and this has left a lasting impression on me. I have often felt that life should be led with a poetic rather than a matter-of-fact quality. This would mean that feelings could be both a better guide and a better experience than pure academic reasoning; that a better balance between the two sides of the brain should be sought. The Quaker silence before meals was both a reminder to be thankful for our good fortune and blessings and a time to remember that many children were hungry.

It was difficult at that time to reassure Ruth that we were making the right choice in sending the children to Bournville School, but Dame Elizabeth Cadbury was delighted as chair of the governing body. I hold firmly to my belief that unless socialist principles are allowed to reduce social inequality, the gap between the rich and the poor, the social oppression among the deprived will drive some of them to violence. Fraternity or solidarity can reasonably be the goal for all. Justice is a vague term, which changes in import from generation to generation and place to place, if society has to wait for all to feel satisfied with the social system it might wait for ever. It is necessary to question the wisdom of those who claim that they are fighting violently for peace with justice. In the USA discipline in some areas is so lax that children may be allowed to take guns to school for self protection and armed men police the schools. The statistic in the USA that a school child dies every two hours from gunshot wounds indicates the size of the problem caused by the gun-lobby, which maintains the law allowing everyone to carry guns for self defence, and by the excessive size of schools, which are very difficult to control.

I remember once deciding with Ruth that, as the headlines of the *News Chronicle* were worrying our older children some ten years after the war, we would change to the Guardian. We were sharing our home with the children's grandparents at the time. I did not realise how much it would sadden the old man. He felt that his life's work had failed. He was characteristically gentle about it. The Cocoa Press, as the collection of Cadbury and Rowntree newspapers were called, failed in the end to raise the level of journalism, but for fifty years they had been at least partially successful.

Headlines are chosen to draw the reader into reading further, a paper's headlines affect its readership, and the editor has the important task each day of checking the effectiveness of the selection and wording of headlines. The variety of front-page headlines each day is a fascinating introduction to the subjectivity of truth and can be easily studied at any newsagent's. I was always interested in what Henry had to say about the day's papers. I had assumed that the day's news somehow dictated the headlines, though left-wing and right-wing papers might put different gloss on them. There is, however, much more to it than that. At Leighton Park School, Michael Foot repeated the old ditty, which refers to two Press Lords:

> He who would drink at the well of Truth
> And quaff its waters clear,
> First he must dam the Beaver-brook
> And drain the Rother-mere.

It was difficult to accept Michael's decision, to work for Beaverbrook later in life, as a journalist, even though he claimed that he was given freedom to write what he wanted.

My father-in-law Henry Cadbury and I had always enjoyed our conversations very much. At the end of the war our shared interest in farming led to his offer of a partnership, and believing that I could give as much time to it as I chose, I accepted the offer. A

91

farm was purchased on hills in Worcestershire facing towards the east and it had a huge cherry orchard part way down the slope in front of the house. Unfortunately, he had a severe heart attack and had to change his plans; otherwise my life would have been quite different.

Ruth herself was much of his way of thinking. She favoured country rather than town, corresponding with his interest in farming. She always looked to mountains for holidays in Wales the Lake District or Scotland as a refreshment of the spirit. This provided a life-long interest for our children and has established quite a strong family tradition. Our daughter Jean has insisted on living near the Lakes most of her life and loves these desolate and open spaces, which appear empty but in reality very enriching. In the same way, a Quaker meeting can have this appearance. David and Bevis who each have two boys have passed on their love of challenging expeditions and wild landscapes. Jonny, my youngest son, took a postgraduate degree in Landscape management.

In social work they all, Henry and Lucy Cadbury included, shared a social-democratic opinion that the world can be made a better place, and that it is right to devote one's life to the attempt. They, both young and old, have had little idea what a strength they have to me when the going was rough.

Ruth's family also passed on to her a sense of the value of help for refugees. Her grandfather John Bellows, with crucial help from Tolstoy, had succeeded in gaining permission from the Czar, for the pacifist Doukhabors to be allowed to leave the country and thus avoid conscription. It was a long story ably summarised by Ruth's sister, Kate Charity, in her biography of John Bellows[28]. Ruth's parents had housed Jewish refugees from Nazi Germany and Ruth began early in life before our marriage by working in a Spanish children's home for children from the Spanish Civil War. I still remember one of them, the young Alberto, son of a Basque miner whose big round black eyes led us into giving the top storey of our wedding cake to share round the many children. 'Is it all for me?' he asked.

German refugees followed, Ruth and her friend shared a hat for visiting the appropriate official in Whitehall after finding work for each one as well as a financial guarantor. It was a hard job unrewarded by personal contact, but she was persistent. Later in life she corresponded with a prisoner in Chile; one day a mysterious message arrived that she should fetch a parcel, and on one of her visits to York, a complete stranger handed the brown paper parcel to her. 'It comes from my friend in prison' he said 'I went back to Chile to visit him. It is something he made in prison.' It was a beautiful crucifix with carved, painted and embossed emblems, which appear to carry a coded message saying 'My home weeps for me. My head may be struck from my body, but my soul goes marching on.' How that was achieved and brought to England remained a mystery.

In the course of bringing up our six children Ruth became adept in helping parents to cope with their own problems. Ruth and I had a common interest in the care of emotionally disturbed children and enjoyed being governors at New Barns School, she as a Psychiatric Social Worker and I as an educational psychologist. She visited homes and talked with parents, who were often part of the trouble. She would come back with wonderful reports of conversations such as Michael's mother, who remarked: 'Michael's such a liar; why, you wouldn't be believing the Lords Prayer if you heard it coming from between his lips.' She also often worked with refugee children and due to her reading was in sympathy with these hopes of psychiatry, so she was delighted when her closest school friend married Ranyard West.

In my first book *Parents Only*[29] I tried to capture some of her spontaneous skills in managing the family or household. She did not always say 'Now it's time for bed.' After there had been strong complaints at going to bed during the previous week she asked: 'who is going to turn the tap on tonight?' which soon created a competition among the children as to who was going to go upstairs first! On another occasion, when Ruth wanted to help the children in dealing with their individual fear, she would endeavour to help them look at it from a different angle such as when a four year old called downstairs in fear, 'I know there isn't really, but I can't help thinking there's a fox under my bed,' she replied at once, 'Is there really, ask it to tea.'

Changing the agenda like this such as discussing the best ways of abolishing nuclear weapons, instead of the value of nuclear weapons, should become almost a recognised way of advancing business. As circumstances change this is a very necessary device, but it depends on some very creative thinking by someone well versed in the subject or in lateral thinking, to use de Bono's term. It was a great help to me to be in situations both at home and at work where there was scope and some encouragement for this creative way of looking at the world.

The children were indeed an influence to be compared with that of our ancestors in helping focus on the main peace issues, though the ancestors, some of them looking down augustly from their picture frames, seemed to set impossibly high standards for emulation and a certain cold remoteness, as though they had nothing to say to small children. The children and their friends were the opposite and prompted a much lighter view of life, full of laughter, fun, and games. Once, in a game of hide and seek, they had heard me go upstairs and were almost indignant at finding me sitting in the living room after complaining that they could not find me. They had never thought that I might jump out of an upstairs bedroom window. No wonder they accepted our having no television set. To most of them, especially those who remember the war, it was obvious that peace was an important matter, as when one five year old remarked: 'We have friends in many other countries, don't we? It would make a muddle of a war wouldn't it?'

At a later age a game of football broke up almost in tears with accusations of breaking the rules. The very next day as one of the boys passed by he remarked 'we're going to play football again. This time we're going to see if we can play without quarrelling with the referee.' The value of childhood games, which depend on rule keeping, has not yet been investigated. It is necessary to plan to develop an automatic tendency to keep rules and therefore laws, if international law is to be properly respected. Unfortunately some people regard laws as a challenge to their ingenuity to find ways to evade them. I am convinced that, if a public relations approach is ineffectual, it is necessary to do much more about keeping the rules during games in Nursery Schools and Classes, while making the reason explicit.

The National Curriculum does not interfere so much in Nursery Schools so it is possible to provide Social Education, which includes Peace or Negotiation Education. As clearly stated this takes the form of coaching through knowledge of what part a teacher should play. It is certainly not leaving the children to knock off rough corners by themselves.

It is a long delay for a social change, waiting for the children to grow up, but it is likely to be more successful than persuading adults to change their deeply rooted habits. I am making a strong plea for the new Peace Education Centre in the bombed church of St Luke in Liverpool, to have a section for research and education among Nursery School children.

I once tried to interest the Red Cross in Nursery School education and found them quite willing to listen that the failure to respect the Red Cross and its workers is best dealt with during training teachers for this age group. Just laws deserve support from sports coaches too. Jeering at referees should be seriously discouraged. My own research into the testing of social attitudes, which I did for my degree in Education, suggested that the respect for regulations, rules and laws is developed early in life, mainly in the homes and only confirmed at secondary school age.

Even when they were quite young the children made comments and asked questions, which we found very thought provoking. When asked 'Do doctors go to hospitals to help the nurses?' I replied after a pause for thought 'Yes, you could say that.' One son was very troubled by death and dying and frequently asked questions about old people. It was wartime and we wondered what conversations he had overheard. Fortunately he linked the idea of death with old age. Thinking he was too young for a discussion about war, I tried variations of 'When people get old they get very tired and need to rest. It must be very nice for them to be tucked up under the daisies.' I was glad that the news had not reached him that a ferret at our neighbour's house had climbed into a pram and killed the baby.

It is interesting to speculate whether his excessive interest in death was connected in some way with the air raid during his birth. His mother as it happens was born in London during a Zeppelin raid. One night, when he may have been five or six he called out 'I want to be near you.' 'You are very near to us.' I reassured him being in a large room for three beds at my parent's new house. 'No,' he replied, ' but I want to be as near you as you are.' To avoid anxiety, shyness and fear one has to strike a sound balance between expressing confidence and taking reasonable risks on the one hand, and warnings about dealing with fire, electricity and traffic, and similar dangers on the other.

Another son commented that when he grew up he would gather all the bombs and drop them to the bottom of the sea. When asked about his plan for housing the homeless in armchairs, regarding wet days he said 'Oh, but they'd all have umbrellas.' His concerns stretched further at the age of five, and he suggested finding the lonely mummies and taking them to the lonely daddies. There seems to be a need for parents and teachers to deal with serious social problems at the level of childhood and no occasion to worry so long as hope is not undermined by ridicule or contemptuous dismissal. In other words, children should be given enough respect like other people and their questions on life taken seriously. At all costs ridicule should be avoided.

Unfortunately television programmes give little help to parents; they tend to enhance the effects of playing with toys. Producers sometimes excuse themselves by saying that we live in a violent society and that their job is to show it as it is. Over a space of forty years those responsible for programmes for children for the BBC have told me that their brief includes encouraging children to spend less time watching television by providing suggestions for other things to do. If children's worries about violence have to be acted out in one way or another it is at least better for them to be active. I am indebted to Miss Rosa Wake, a former colleague at the Dudley Teachers College for her reply to students who kept asking what to do when boys insist on changing drama lessons into gun battles. 'You may have some shooting' she would say 'but then you must have burials, mourners, and maybe prayers for the dead. For the wounded you will need doctors, nurses and ambulances. Shooting is no game. It is deadly serious. We cannot have corpses lying about our school, can we? Do you know how to put a bandage on a leg or make a splint?' Acting out in this way has proved very effective and is accepted by most teachers.

Parents and teachers need to encourage cooperative games now that most argue that our society has grown excessively and aggressively competitive. Some children come to hold the absurd conclusion that a game must have a winner and a loser. There are now a number of books of cooperative games, when we did not have them to suit the beach, the garden or indoors, we invented them. I wish we could have made a film of some of them; it would have helped Children's Television Programmes to implement the BBC brief. Of course, uncertainty still encompasses the acting out of these aggressive scenarios, and it becomes questionable at to whether or not it would be better to encourage the children to act negotiations rather than playing at war, showing them alternatives and prevention rather than always simply fighting. When two of the children rode home in a bicycle sidecar one day from their nursery school, armed with toy guns given to them by a mischievous member of staff, they shot at every pedestrian along the way. 'They needed to do that to get it out of their system and balance their Quaker upbringing' claimed the teacher the next day, with tongue in cheek. There is no agreement about this among educational psychologists whether, or how acting out one's aggressions is a satisfactory process that leads towards peace or not?

As the children grew older their ideas about peace became less childlike. The elder ones persuaded the whole family of eight to take part in the Easter Marches between Aldermaston and Trafalgar Square. One year the boys and their friends made a black coffin, marked 'Bury the Bomb,' and carried it all the way. Another time one of the girls aged fourteen walked the whole way, refusing each of the three days all offers of a lift.

We marched up Whitehall in our thousands, the place where government and the armed forces nestle together and the horse guards do their quaint propaganda. The statues often honour the wrong man. We felt a fresh dawn had broken, as though we had come to negotiate a peaceful take over from the militarists. If there was no need for an army in Costa Rica in Latin America, perhaps people could be persuaded that there was no need here on an island. When Michael Foot was Secretary of State at the Department for Employment, I went again to see him. It was at the height of the Aldermaston marches when by sheer numbers we felt as though we, not the government, felt ourselves to be the voice of Britain. Despite their success, which was obvious to the tens of thousands who took part, the daily and Sunday newspapers gave us little space. Michael took a prominent part often heading the huge procession and I knew he would give me a hearing. "To avoid being neglected," I said "we must do something more sensational." On several occasions I had lain awake at night trying to screw up courage to have my hands fixed with nails on a crucifix. I was to wear a mask so as to remain anonymous and there would be some words of explanation such as: 'Father forgive them; for they know not what they do.' However, before I explained these details, Michael's voice rang out "Crucifix! We cannot do that. The religious people would howl." I did not press the matter further, but I would guess that the religious people may have been better than he thought. A clergyman blessed the first atom bomb but now most of them associate nuclear weapons with genocide and wish the governments would accept the Advisory Opinion of the World Court. The campaign for Nuclear Disarmament has made steady progress. At that time I had no vision of how the forces could find a new role in dealing with the defence of the environment. That was to come later when I made a joke of the armed forces failing to achieve what they claimed to be able to do.

For the army this was to defend every inch of British soil, but they did nothing when the soil of the uplands in the war was ploughed and cultivated each time allowing vital humus to be blown into the North Sea. The navy claimed to guard every mile of the coastline but allowed the sea to become so filthy with radioactive waste and sewage that bathing will soon be dangerous. Similarly the Royal Air Force given the task of defending British airspace has added to the pollution of the air instead of preventing it. Lord Judd was so pleased with this that he sought permission to borrow it, and meanwhile I tried to catch the theme in verse.

Recruits for Real Defence

The army claims to fight for every inch of British soil,
But they don't shoot down the farmers: who, let centuries of toil
Be blown to sea from uplands, which their fathers never
    ploughed,
But kept the thin turf sacred and their heads by greed unbowed.

98

When soldiers will not do their work, they'll hear the
    grumblers say,
They may be brave and all that, but they haven't earned
    their pay.
The tax-man need not come our way, until the job is done,
Poor children will have more to eat at the setting of the sun.

The sailors in the navy, likewise, made an idle boast.
That they would be the guardians for each mile of British coast,
But they turned their eyes - well blinded - to the foe they failed
    to spot,
From nuclear power pollution to the sewage left to rot.

The RAF may be better? Our whole island they can scan,
So they know more of the problems, which beset the fate of man.
Their task is much more simple and they look a likely crew,
The airspace overhead is theirs to see what they can do.

They fly high and low and often, they fly by day and night,
They must think the roar of warplanes is a reassuring sight.
Someone needs to tell them we can drown in CO_2,
It's just one of the gases which their planes are adding to.

If you want to be secure and safe from such defence,
It's no use to stay and grumble, while sitting on the fence.
Be bold and seek a bunker in an island still unmanned,
Unless you think that's just the place for nuclear bombs to land.

Come then join peace builders' own defence against defence,
To wear transparent royal robes makes very little sense.
We'd like to fan your hopes and your many skills and flair
There's a future for your world, for you we'd also care.

                                              A.N.G, Jan 99

    The armed forces need to be subjected to the challenge of the
expansion of the ethical movement, a movement that merits an
historian of its own. Already it has secured a strong position in

investment and soldiers are provided with some knowledge of the laws governing the conduct of warfare. It should certainly be applied to the bringing up of children. I remember with great regrets a period which stretched out to two years when I was working in Cheltenham while our home was in Birmingham and returning on Fridays to be pummelled by a tiny daughter for being away too long. At this time it was very difficult to find both a home and schools to suit us all. Sometimes I wonder whether the absences and preoccupations of parents during wartime sow the seeds for the next war.

In our case it was certainly not a lack of attention from adults, which affected our children. From the point of view of education for international understanding they were highly privileged. One scene I shall never forget. Before he could talk one of the boys paired with a visiting politician from the Ukraine who had no English. They went on walks together, one speaking Ukrainian and the other Double Dutch, with maximum expressiveness to compensate for the lack of meaning. The two eldest met German prisoners, some of whom made toys for them.

Mainly however they got to know the young women who were glad to come to learn English when the war was finished and to help Ruth coping with what nowadays would seem a large family, six in all. They made a sound basis for our children's education for international understanding and they also provided an encourage-ment to the children to learn second and third languages. One of our sons even had a reputation for having cow's language as his sixth. I have been glad of the arrangements, which my mother made for me, to have additional French and German lessons during the holidays and I now wish more of the grandchildren had the same.

They absorbed from them almost without knowing it that we can have friends in other countries, and that we can have close friends in other countries although languages and customs may be different. There was competent Trudy who came as a Nazi but left otherwise, the children still visit her family when they go to Germany, she had been in charge of a hospital ward at the age of sixteen. Later she came back with her husband-to-be for a holiday with us in the Lake District. Then there was Violette from Paris, in the course of time we also got to know her family.

Pepi came as a small boy from our friends in Vienna. He looked lean and hungry and he came to escape the harsh post-war conditions in that city. The value of speaking another language was evident to our children, Ruth and I slipped readily if not easily into French and German and the children have become far better than we were. Some of Pepi's remarks are still quoted 'Du siest aus wie einem Bauer in ein Wirthaus' (You look like a farmer in a pub.) he said to one of the boys. Then, on another day, he hung a notice on the fire-guard or high fender 'Diese Tiere muss nicht erfuttert sein.' (This animal must not be fed) Then he tried to keep the cat in the cage he had made for it. We also had Oba Awolowo from Nigeria for Christmas. He enjoyed our family custom of roasting sausages outdoors and laughed when his sausage fell off his stick, as only Africans can laugh; the whole of him shook and laughed. Later on he was runner up in the presidential elections in Nigeria. He was an extraordinary man whom the children loved immensely.

These contacts for the children were not specially arranged by us, rather they could be said to have happened without our being fully aware of the likely results. It was a very culturally cultivating time in their lives and as a consequence they find it easier than most people to undertake international work owing to the culture of peace, in which they were brought up. This culture of peace was something that was taken for granted in previous generations of our two families. This may be described as treating everyone with respect, expecting that friendship can be developed despite differences, and that people from afar are often more interesting to us than conventional English people.

This was a very enriching time for us all as a family and we were often reminded of that hilarious family, the Gilbreths, described in *Cheaper by the Dozen*.[30] The Gilbreths had a family double the size of ours, and if they wanted to have a day out, an event as simple as getting into the car, was no small feat for them. Guided by their father, a time and motion expert, the entire Gilbreth family somehow all managed to find their seats in the family car, despite there being no less than fourteen of them including the parents. The whole operation took place in strict order and with the utmost precision despite the fact that there was much sitting on laps for them all to fit in. However, these events necessitated the calling of the roll when going on expeditions and other curbs on the more curious members of the Gilbreth team. Individual attention had to become subservient to cooperation. Our family, though we had no television, derived very enjoyable fun from the games we played, many of which involved our international guests and friends. The games were often spontaneously invented and I do not mean invented by me!

CHAPTER 7

The War Years: A History Lesson for All

PEASANT ENGLAND WAS still in existence in remote parts of Britain when war broke out in 1939. It is worth asking in what circumstances peasant life tends to preserve peace. Mahatma Gandhi had a vision of an ideal life for villagers in India that would preserve peace and make war an anachronism. He assumed that the care of one's own land, crops, and livestock would overcome the 'bellicity' of industrial countries. Nowadays the question might be asked, 'Is this process of overcoming bellicity, the influence of fresher food and exercise?' Beyond the food and exercise there is a deep feeling of satisfaction at being even partly self-sufficient. I well remember towards the end of harvest time when a field of oats and barley was being cut and the rabbits were gathered in the middle, catching one with my hands and proudly bearing it home as a welcome variation in our otherwise vegetarian diet. We were hungry but not starving at the time and those farm labourers, who were able to do so, liked to supplement their rations one way or another. A farm labourer by the name of Archie is a good example of how difficult things were for people in peasant England at this time. He was so short in stature that he would stand near enough to the auctioneer to bid for piglets and did so by secretly stepping on the auctioneer's toes. Archie had the sympathy of others because he had such a large family to feed in a time when there was so little food.

Small farmers and labourers tended to overlap. In the thirties before the war a Canon of the cathedral at St. David's walked into our holiday camp with a story to tell. He had been walking along

103

the coast that morning and stopped for a chat with a man trimming a hedge. He asked him who owned the fields where he was working and was intrigued by his reply that he could not properly say. 'It's like this,' he replied, 'it used to belong to a farmer but when bad times came he didn't have enough to pay me, he said that he was sorry, but that is how it is.' 'How would it be,' the labourer replied, 'if you paid me what you could and if I took the rest in land?' 'That's alright with me,' answered the farmer. Bad times continued and one day the labourer said, 'Look, I own more than half the farm now, but there's no need to worry, I'll take you on to work for me on the same terms. The farm has changed hands several times, and who the farm belongs to now, I can't properly say.' On that farm, conflict and unemployment were soundly defeated. Maybe the moral of the story is that if there is trust between people many problems can be solved. It is easier to trust people who are well-known for their honesty, than it is to trust strangers across national and cultural frontiers. Otherwise, peacemaking would not be as difficult as it is. Every time someone honours a promise and rejects corruption, trust increases like some kind of social capital. Parents and teachers who practice what they preach produce and encourage the development of this social capital.

As the war approached, feeling that I would be dismissed from school on the grounds of being a conscientious objector, I wrote to the husband of one of my cousins who ran a farm, to find out if I would be welcome to come and work there. It was a five hundred acre farm with pigs, poultry, and mixed crops and so there would be a variety of work to learn. It was called Whalley Farm, and the farmer wrote saying that he would be delighted for me to come, as a consequence we became great friends. At Whalley Farm I met people and worked with some of them drawn from families who had small farms of their own or worked as farm labourers and both might be held to be coming from peasant stock, though some might have claimed to be yeomen farmers. They retained attitudes and practices, which belonged to earlier times. The ploughman of Whalley farm was partly Gypsy and lived in what was known locally as Bug Hut, several fields away from the nearest dwelling, with no electricity and only a single tap. One local peasant from the village was a builder and was known as 'Mr. Nigh Enough,' because he didn't work with all due precision, as a consequence he was never given work at the farm because his work wasn't nigh enough! The peasant's humour attached itself to people in this way; they laughed at the results of my trying my hand at sheep shearing because a sheep shorn by me could be spotted a mile away! They were more impressed with my horse-hoeing the potatoes, which was a skill I seemed adept at despite no previous experience. The rows of potatoes amounted to a hundred and fifteen miles of hard walking, in the field where a Roman tessellated floor has since been found. I wish I had known that it was there at that time; the days would have been even more enjoyable. I also recall that at Whalley Farm I had never had the same work for two weeks in a row, except one winter when carting manure to the fields, and even then I was regarded as particularly lucky to be able to draw on the heat of the manure heap to keep my feet warm.

The peasant's life was full of ritual for example; May 10th was the right day for the cows to go out to the fields, though the new grass-seed mixtures led to earlier grazing. There was a good date for tailing the lambs and for shearing the sheep. The farmer James Rowe was a very gifted farm manager who made the most of his work-people, and I suspect that he sometimes gave way to their opinions. The ritual found a place in the thoughts and language of these people. The last sheaf of corn to be unloaded in a day might be greeted with 'That's the one we've been looking for' and a man would be described as 'Old so and so is alright, but see you don't get his braces twisted.' Jack the foreman of Whalley farm, kept the workshop and was much respected for his many skills. His two brothers won prizes for ploughing and shooting and Jack himself when mending a fence in the least visited field on the farm remarked to me, 'A botched job won't do. You never know who might come by.' When a forester was teaching four of us how to bind up some hazel for pea-sticks, Jack learned the knack much more quickly than the rest of us. 'Nigh enough,' was not good enough for him.

The use of dialect was fascinating, often I could not understand what was being said: 'Make some yelms out of that straw' seemed to Jack an obvious request, but I had to ask for an explanation. 'Get all the straw lying the same way, he added. 'Coign' meaning corner was easier to guess, and I picked up 'teg' from its context, as meaning a yearling sheep. I would have liked to have learned to speak with a thick Gloucestershire accent, but my ear is not good enough. Sometimes I felt as though I was nearest to the secrets of the peasants when I savoured their proverbs. I began making a collection of books of proverbs from different cultures such as China and Russia, in the hope of finding in them some pointers for peacemakers, and peacekeepers. Proverbs being a ritual of thinking, and being a powerful influence on behaviour, should be known and used by mediators to show that there is a basis in their own culture for reaching an end to violence, hatred and discord in general.

Here are some thoughts about proverbs:

A proverb is to speech what salt is to food.

A proverb is the wisdom of many but the wit of one (who spots how to apply it).

Patch grief with proverbs (which satisfy by the pleasure of matching them).

An argument may be clinched by a proverb.

And here are some proverbs to savour and relish:

A drink is shorter than a story. (e.g. for patching a dispute).

Time is a good story-teller (A story is improved each time it's told. Beware!)

The trotting horse can't hear the story-teller. (Settle down first.)

To ask well is to know much. (i.e., good questioners are better than know-it-alls)

We look at others with our front eyes (i.e. clearly) but we see ourselves with eyes at the back (with bias).

A lie may seem to be wise, but truth is wisdom itself.

Not to know is bad, not to wish to know is worse.

Experience is the looking-glass of the intellect.

Knowledge is a wild thing and must be hunted before it can be tamed (i.e. made your own).

Doubt is the key to knowledge.

The best fighting is against oneself (i.e. to counter one's own prejudices and anger).

No one gets ahead of the cock.

Advise no one to marry or go to war. (They will complain about
   your advice).
Every new thing has its special delight.
One who is accustomed to kicks, will never listen to reason.
An ass cannot be made into a horse by beating.
Who travels alone tells lies.
An ant in a cup (i.e. can't get out).
Go a mile to see a sick man, go two miles to make peace between
   two people, and go three miles to visit a friend.
Farming, writing letters, worship and the tightening of your
   horse's girth, you should do for yourself.

In present times of rapid change, proverbs favour old age and
experience too much and yet sometimes the application of a proverb
exemplifies lateral thinking as vividly as others justify the status
quo.

The people in and around Whalley farm caught the full flavour
of the story of the family of the farm further up the valley. They
lived with an earth floor in their tiny farmhouse and took a day off
each year to do their shopping; on the allotted day the powerful
horse was harnessed into the small wagon. The wagon was laden
with sacks of corn for grinding, eggs, cheese and bacon might be
added to bring in some money for new clothes, boots, salt, sugar,
tea and something for a treat, leaving the balance for deals with
neighbours and hawkers who came to the door. No one was quite
sure when this came to an end, may be it was in the years before
the outbreak of the First World War.

Long before that it was said the whole valley had been a sheep-
run worked by Cistercian monks, good at producing high quality
wool. When I stood in a sacking bale to press down the fleeces as
tight as possible, suspended for packing from the rafters of the aged
stone barn, the hazy mist of history closed round me. I trampled
each fleece into place, to make ready for stitching the big bales,
which contained about thirty fleeces in all, knowing that I was, at
least temporarily, transformed into 'something rich and strange.'
It belonged more to past centuries or to nursery rhymes handed
down from one generation to another.

The war started slowly and broke the tiny world of Whalley apart more quickly when news of the Battle of Britain set tongues wagging. It seemed that even the farming community would now be effected by the devastation of war. 'Where is Scotland? asked a neighbouring housewife in her naivete. 'My husband has been sent there. Is it overseas?' The number of German planes shot down increased day by day, or so it was said at the time, now it is a well know fact that the figures were falsified to boost the morale of the country. The constant question in my mind was about facing up to German officials, as a pacifist should do. Should I organize resistance underground? I had heard that they were especially afraid of pacifists for being potential troublemakers. Was my German good enough to explain my pacifist position in defiance of their threats? If I were tortured how would I manage to conceal the identities of my friends? Such were my constant worries, but I was never put to the test.

It is very hard sixty years later, to remember how it felt to be ignorant of what was to come. It is one of the drawbacks of history and historians that they have difficulty in putting themselves in the shoes of those who were acting in the dark. It is often that those who are wise after the event call people stupid. About this time Hitler was boasting that the Germans were about to finish off the British like wringing a chicken's neck. Winston Churchill, in his radio speech, which followed, commented dramatically 'Some chicken, and some neck!' To some extent leaders become leaders because they are optimists and the wise took Churchill and his persistent optimism with a pinch of salt. On the other hand he had more information than the general public. Anyway the fortunes of the war varied, the Battle of Britain in the air was won, so that a German invasion fleet could get no effective air cover, but then came rumours of new weapons, which the Germans hoped to use to make London no longer habitable. From the German point of view they came near to driving the Soviet forces out of Moscow and the support of Japan seemed to be a promise of final victory. These ups and downs throughout the war might have exhausted the strength of many men but Churchill survived to lose an election at the end of the war and demonstrate how to accept the thumbscrews of democracy. I have often wondered whether he remembered that he had said in a wartime speech 'A great war minister is seldom a great peace minister.' He might have added unless he knows how to resign gracefully, avoiding a military coup, and later returns to power.

These topics were seldom mentioned on the farm either among the workers or in the farmhouse. This may have been because we wished to avoid clashes of view, or it may have been through the sheer hard work, which left no energy for other things beyond the work itself. We were certainly a motley crew. In addition to the eight regulars, there was a mixed bag of conscientious objectors. A skilled carpenter came from London and made a home for himself, his wife, and daughter by putting three shepherd huts on wheels together. His wife, a real Londoner, never settled; one day she surveyed the broad view of the Cotswold Hills to the south, where only a handful of farms were visible, no shops, just woods and fields. She remarked, 'The blitz is nothing to this.' Clearly living in the countryside for her was far more traumatic than living among the falling bombs of London. Her husband, to be sure, was a highly skilled worker, but he never seemed to realize that livestock have to be fed and watered, jobs in the country do not necessarily finish as they do in the city, on the tick of five. He was a trade unionist. Then there was a powerful woman from Vienna, an Olympic discus thrower. Her husband being in politics had arranged to be in India with a climbing expedition when the war began, having sent his wife to safety in Britain. A young Jewish boy George, a refugee from Germany, proved to be a textbook case of adolescence; it was he who distinguished himself when driving one of the chariots, low box-like vehicles, drawn by horses. He took charge of a spirited horse and offered three of us a lift from one of the upper fields down to the farmyard. As soon as we started down the lane after stopping at the gate, the horse increased its speed rapidly. So fast that when reined back by George the one rein broke and having no other means of braking George stepped off the open-ended char-iot, leaving the rest of us to fend for ourselves with a runaway horse galloping home. Two of us swung our legs over the edge of the box to land with a crash into a bed of nettles. There was soon no one left and the horse arrived at its tying-up place at the stone wall of the meal house, almost breaking a shaft as it stopped.

It is an odd quirk of humanity that such minor disasters serve as major topics of conversation for months. The events of the war took second place; no wonder the newspapers make much of disasters, especially those near at hand, to the exclusion of more positive reports. It is good that more positive material is being shown to exist by the quarterly English periodical *Positive News*. Sometimes there appears to be a conspiracy among journalists and news editors to spread gloom far and wide. The excuse given sometimes is that society is thus forced to face its problems; however facing problems is not enough. In addition, there must be hope and determination to ensure action. 'When hands are needed, letters and words are useless,' runs an appropriate proverb.

A more sensational event occurred in the local wood by the farm. The International 10/20 tractor with its spade lugs instead of rubber tyres was being worked as a back up to Jack copsing the hazel. It was in my hands, an inexperienced driver, who did not see the little hazel stump in front of the large stump just beyond. The small one caught the front wheel and forced the large rear wheel to mount the large stump, as the land was sloping down to the stream, this was too much and in slow motion the tractor began to fall on its right side. There was no time to jump clear, but the tractor continued rolling upside down with me leaning backwards, being pressed in the back by the spring seat, with my chest very firmly pressed into the ground. The steering wheel and column, being normally the highest part of the tractor, carried most of the weight. The tractor continued rolling and would have rolled onto its four wheels and continued travelling ahead with me still in its seat. Unfortunately the front axle broke so that it fell back on its left side. Jack hurried up to 'pick up a dead'un' as he said, and was astonished to find me not only alive but also unhurt. The farmer took it very well, considering that he had to find a spare part for one of only two tractors, but it remained a topic of conversation for months or years afterwards.

The influx of people new to farming due to the war had an impact on earlier ways of life. There were changes in the labour force of Whalley farm, which also included a Land-girl as the members of the Women's Land Army were called, and her brother an architect. Most of us were conscientious objectors and the farmer being a Quaker was very well disposed towards us, and skilled at keeping his mixed work force with all our eccentricities working happily together. In general it could be said that the war served a useful purpose in shaking up the population, bringing different sorts of people together and producing a tolerance, which is much needed today. The tolerance was even extended to conscientious objectors, though the cowman did say to me that if it was up to him, he would put me up against a wall and shoot me!

We never had an opportunity to explain our strange views. Difficult, potentially disruptive topics were carefully avoided. This does not necessarily lead to an appreciation of each other's values but it may be an initial step towards that. A country is seldom so united as when it is under attack. I have often wondered whether the nations can ever be united without elaborating the environmental problems, which threaten them, and the opportunities for dealing with them. How can global warming and extravagant consumption come to be seen as dragons or ogres that might overwhelm the human race? Lord William Beveridge, a founder of the Welfare State, created his giants, to sum up his official report on the social services of the future, but now a different team of ogres is needed to unite the country.

Our own personal family life was changing. Our son David had been born in 1940, Bevis in early 1942, and Ruth had to give up cooking for everyone at Whalley Farm to move to Puckham Farm, the two farms were worked together. We adjusted to a quieter and simpler way of life. By this time I had had a serious back injury trying to throw a one-hundred-weight sack of potatoes onto a wagon, which was moving away. Dickie, the horse, was not trained to stand still and wait if he could see any food ahead. The consequence for me was that I spent much of my time in the farm office keeping records. Otherwise I fell down with acute muscular spasms. Eventually I had to go to Oxford for treatment, while working in the Agricultural Economics Research Institute and later at Avoncroft College, Worcestershire on Young Farmers Clubs. Life at Puckham Farm was free of any modern conveniences; a hipbath in front of the kitchen range, one cold tap and yet Ruth managed the household for the two boys. She added to her responsibilities by making Puckham a self-catering Youth Hostel and began preparing to work for the Friends Relief Service, a dream that never came true.

It is very hard to say whether it was the people or the new machinery, which did most to break up the old ways of thinking and feeling. Agricultural machinery has replaced the old ways of working. To begin with we provided a service to local farmers by taking the threshing drum from farm to farm during the winter months. This was always a pleasant social occasion in the breaks for lunch, when local news was exchanged. The remark, which began 'The bomb dropped just as I was half way across my piece of bread and cheese ...' came from such lunchtime chat.

The operation could easily occupy half a dozen people; one feeding the machine helped by one pitching him the sheaves of corn from the corn-rick. Down below there might be three for the straw, the chaff, and the grain, with a sixth building the straw into a rick or binding it with a baler. Cheerful teamwork is a blessing for those who often have lonely tasks to do; the coming of the combine harvesters ended it all. They worked neatly and efficiently but I missed the threshing parties. The ploughing, which had once been done by oxen, one furrow at a time, was now done by a caterpillar tractor pulling a six-furrow plough. One machine which was new to me, and which I called the mechanical cow, was the muck-spreader, which carried manure from the manure heaps and spread it on the fields. Patient farm labourers working, often with horses and people for company, were replaced by hurried mechanics driving tractors, subjected to terrible noise and rushing to get their work done.

Does this make for peaceful people in a peaceful world? Are noisy industries competing for a place in a world market one of the causes of war? No one seems to know the answer to this question. Certainly excessive competition and concomitant hurry are taught early in life in schools and colleges, in what appears to be a self-motivating change of culture out of keeping with the culture of peace. It is time for a book to be written on the last of the British peasants.

From time to time I heard of friends and acquaintances in the war. My brother Jan was in Burma on the far side of the Japanese troops. His knowledge of tropical botany helped him and his Indian troops when food supplied by airdrops was scarce. One of my closest friends at school was killed in Italy but in general it was civilians who suffered most of the casualties during the war years, a fact which made it easier to reconcile pacifism with conscientious objection to military service. At times it became difficult to believe that Nazism could be opposed non-violently; at other times when Dresden was bombed and later atom bombs were used on Japan it seemed that it could not be opposed any other way. In opposing Nazism Britain had become almost as ruthlessly cruel as the Nazis themselves, without any justifiable excuse.

Looking back on these experiences much later I concluded that Tolstoy and others were right in identifying the corrupting influence brought to bear on anyone who holds a position of power as one of the major threats to peace. It is a difficult subject to study because no one can expect to find rulers who have the time to allow a researcher to cross-question them. Moreover autobiographies are bad sources of accurate information.

Shakespeare's inspired guess-work revealed in such plays as Julius Caesar, Hamlet and Macbeth gives more understanding of the process of corruption than it gives confidence that all the relevant factors at work are faithfully presented. The words in Macbeth (v.iii. 20) 'Canst thou not minister to a mind diseased?' point to the question whether the hunger for power may unbalance the normal personality? William Pitt's father, the Earl of Chatham, in 1770 in the House of Lords, anticipated Lord Elton's famous dictum by stating 'Unlimited power is apt to corrupt the minds of those who possess it.'

In Chatham's lifetime 1705-1778 there came to power in Europe the so-called Enlightened Despots. They might be cited as evidence that power does not necessarily corrupt, but certainly most individuals who achieve power believing that it will not corrupt them, are proved to be wrong; just as it is doubtful whether all the Enlightened Despots would withstand investigations of their so-called enlightenment.

Constitutional Monarchy is based on the assumption that power like muck and money is best when well spread. Democratic prime ministers have to share power with their parliaments, containing their own parties as well as the opposition; they have to keep in mind the opinions of electors, who are waiting to be given the

113

chance to express them at the forthcoming election. There are also the media, the laws and conventions of the constitution apart from the President and as a last resort the armed forces. It is little wonder that the pressures become so frustrating that the prime ministers by-pass and ignore some of them and then proceed to use illegal forms of influence.

The process by which a politician in a democracy arrives at the premiership by overcoming all the hurdles along the way, weeds out all those who have no hunger or even greed for power and the corruption feeds on itself. Those who achieve power are linked by having to deal with the governments of neighbouring countries, dealings which cannot easily be avoided. The electorates cannot reasonably be blamed for failing to recognise a dangerous lust for power.

A country needs a large number of citizens who are quick to expostulate when this occurs. They have to watch events closely enough to know when laws are being broken, despite the assurances reiterated by the officials of the public relations sections of the prime minister's offices. When democracies become involved in wars, the crises provide strong reasons for extending the powers of the Prime Ministers for the duration of the wars. They perceive more or less clearly that, along with arms firms, the armed forces and secret services, they themselves stand to gain by occasional wars. Margaret Thatcher, in the eyes of her opponents, extended her regime in this way, and learned to use wartime propaganda for her own purposes. Propaganda has become so much more skilful in the course of the twentieth century that it is apt to deceive even those who create it. 'In time of war, truth is the first casualty' is a warning which cannot be repeated too often.

The development of psychology is largely responsible for the lack of truth, though a stronger peace movement could equally turn it to beneficial uses. Already new and better methods of improving research are being devised. One ingenious US researcher, accepting that national power holders were too difficult to approach, decided to study the impact of wielding power among local politicians or more precisely local politicians willing to help him.

On the principle what you sow that you reap, this should be a strong encouragement to those who have to deal with unhappy

114

violent children, often excluded from school, who become the future bullies among adults. Schools and teachers should be valued, not just according to the exam results, but according to their work showing their affections for social misfits. It may be that identifying present day decision makers for extra attention can be supported by identifying the larger number of possible trouble-making power holders of the future and converting them to accept a culture of peace. So far as I know no one has examined this possibility. There are some significant experiments with violent prisoners. This would side step the discouraging work of trying to convert the whole, or the majority of the population.

Finally corruption by power has been accidentally depicted, and more vividly than is likely to be repeated by the secret tapes made at the White House of President Nixon talking with Secretary of State Kissinger his principal confidant. These tapes form the basis of a play and show the depths to which politicians can descend in their ruthless pursuit of power. When I attended a performance of this play in 1999 I was strongly reminded of the face of the Principal of Saltley when he dictated that letter to me.[31] It reflected the borders of insanity itself. Is it possible that wars are started by men who, at least for a time, have lost touch with sanity?

Either by a lucky chance or as a deliberate policy, teaching using activity methods developed and spread rapidly during the war and provided evidence of its therapeutic value. The children revealed their anxiety in their play and many of us not only believed in what was shown but also in the healing process, which accompanied these revelations. How far this depends on the words or coaching of the teacher it is difficult to say. Both the activities and the coaching of individuals become more difficult in larger classes. It seemed to me that activity methods, measured in terms of progress in reading, writing and arithmetic were judged unfairly on account of the period when they were introduced. The large classes and the children's fears prevented them from experiencing a happy childhood in which creativity and mental health could flourish.

Mental health is a thought-provoking term at a time when genocide is threatened by weapons and by the destruction of the environment. Maybe the human race as a whole is suffering from madness in a race towards self-destruction. The sane people who should be giving a lead, are disheartened. Most people have such a restricted vision they seem to be not crazy but simply stupid. It was once shown by a research worker that the number of people using the same front door to a block of flats was related to the number of violent attacks. Is it possible that the increase in violence per million people is related to the size of the total world population? In the USA it has been found that the larger the towns and cities, the larger the number of police are required per thousand of the population to maintain order.

Do the people involved in making war ever know how to count the cost? It is far greater than the cost of lives, of wounds and the cost of arms. War sets humanity back rather than allowing it to move peacefully and actively towards 'Going to Court Not to War,' which has become essential for human survival. Power must be not so much tamed as sublimated, so that the impetus can be put to good use. Everyone can help set an example in the years 2000 – 2010, the years set aside by the UN for developing the Culture of Peace, by making such an effort for peace.

CHAPTER 8

Training Teachers for Creativeness

AT THE END OF the war my father renewed his offer to find me
a place in Barclays Bank with responsibilities in Oxford and for
work overseas. I had a strong difference of opinion with my father
about my future career. 'Schoolmasters are men among boys' he
remarked one day, 'but boys among men.' I was never able to
convince him that I had made a wise choice. There is a quotation
inscribed in a stone above the entrance of a certain school in the
Lake District, and had my father known the quotation he may have
had more empathy for the choice I was making: 'An opportunity
of a lifetime must be taken during the lifetime of the opportunity.'

I had already been interviewed by the Chairman of Barclays
Bank on the work I might undertake in Africa, France, and Oxford.
'You can go and learn your banking in Timbuktu, if that is what
you want,' he said. I was very sorry to disappoint my father, who
had set his heart on my acceptance. However, whatever length I
had stayed there, it is doubtful whether I would have found a way
of lending to the poor. It was difficult enough in my own country.
But it was a good offer and now I wonder whether I made a mistake.
I think not though, because I always remember that doing a little
against war is better than doing a lot against poverty. John Parker
MP, and Chris Mayhew MP, encouraged me to join the politicians,
but that was, I thought, out of the question, in view of people's
dislike of conscientious objectors just after the war.

This dislike was soon to be put to the test. I was appointed to
teach physical education at the Birmingham Emergency Training
College for Teachers, by an admirable Principal. I bore him no ill

will when he wrote two weeks later to say that he had made a mistake in thinking that there was no regulation against this. No wonder that I made my own error in accepting by phone a comparable position at a Training College belonging to the Church of England situated near the gas-works and partly funded by a brewing firm. In mitigation of my error, it should be said, I was recommended by my tutor at Carnegie College in Leeds, who had been teaching in the college in Birmingham doing the work which I was to take on myself. Later on, maybe recognising his mistake, he was glad to be in a position to offer me one post at the University's Department of Physical Education and another at Bournville Works designing exercises to off-set the impact of working, at a variety of machines, work which had harmful effects in the long run. These offers I had to refuse, partly because I was still suffering from a bad back, and partly because my interests became centred in the teaching of Education.

The Principal of Saltley College was a very persuasive man indeed, especially when appointing staff and selecting students. For the first term or two I was living in the college, taking lunch in the hall with the students and staff and in the evening I was alone with the Principal for dinner. He talked with enthusiasm about the college and the students as well as about his own teaching. At first he sounded a good man and believed he could win my admiration. On one occasion, however, he failed to impress me at all. 'It is strange' he said, 'What a large number of students are attracted to those rails,' indicating the Birmingham to London main line just across the football pitch from the college buildings. It did not occur to him, it seemed, that the way he ran the discipline of the College, forcing students to report on other students, may have accounted for the plight of those desperate young men who had attempted suicide. Nor did he see that the former youths of eighteen to twenty and the ex-servicemen could not be treated alike. If a man has served in the forces all over the world it is unlikely that he will accept lights out in the dormitories at ten o' clock! To make matters worse he expected me to turn them off myself. Despite this the students seemed to go out of their way to welcome me. They invited me to play rugby football with them, but the Principal soon put a stop to that. Then we tried to form a debating society but he also stopped

The model house, which was a result of a partnership between UNESCO and the Thai government, was an educational project at rural schools that encouraged learning by doing in home economics.

Another Thai project was supported enthusiastically by Mr Suwan, the travelling ballad singer. It dealt with the parasite hookworm.

There were few books in rural Thailand in 1956. The "wall newspaper" was produced by children and others, and helped promote literacy.

These oversize teaching props were used to help students think creatively about the use of visual aids in lesson planning.

This mobile library, designed by an official from the UN, was another means for promoting literacy in rural Thailand.

Dealing with racial prejudice early in life. Ubon, Thailand 1957.

that. From other members of the staff I learned that his miserliness was so great that our salaries, for example, were four months overdue, and that the Vice-Principal had consulted with the doctor as to whether the poor man should be certified.

It seemed to me such a serious situation having the library permanently locked for fear of losing any books, having some students running a burglary racket, with the help of Sten guns and ammunition so that they went to prison and other similar failings, it was necessary to blow the whistle. To their shame no one else was prepared to help me. I appealed to the College's Inspectors through a friendly colleague of his who knew me, but he was about to retire and wished for no trouble.

Most of the forms of corruption were visible in the management of the College by the Principal. He relished too much the wielding of power, he disliked any actions which lessened his influence and that meant making disparaging remarks about anyone whom he considered too popular with the students. By using objectionable methods of extracting information he maintained his influence throughout the institution, which he made his own. To minimize outside influence he barred the staff from meeting the Governors. He used his monopoly of power to his own financial advantage. The Bishop described him as spiritually exhausted.

All the time I was lying awake at night wondering whether I was doing the right thing, until my wife became so worried about me that she moved to Birmingham to make it possible for me to go home and relinquish my residential duties. The Bishop was the next person to visit. I asked him to alert the Governors but would not give the details myself. He knew about the students in prison and may have asked the Governors to send someone. As previously mentioned I invited one of my MP friends, Billy Hughes to visit the college incognito and report to Ellen Wilkinson for whom he served as Parliamentary Private Secretary. Finally I wrote to another friend, Vice-Principal of another college, who took it upon herself to write to the clerk of the Council of Church Colleges. She cannot have been a skilled negotiator because she let the Principal know the source of her information.

A strange scene followed when the Principal, his eyes blazing with his mental disorder dictated the letter I was to send, to

125

qualify the previous information. I feel ashamed to admit it, but his eyes were so wild that I humoured him and sent it. How can truth and madness be assimilated?

After two years his successor came and dismissed me, but the Vice-Principal had it revoked the same day, so I stayed a third year before moving to another Church College, St Paul's at Cheltenham. In its social atmosphere or ethos St Paul's was as good as Saltley had been bad.

St Paul's was a good college in many ways, but the effect of the war on the schools near by which were used for teaching practice was even more obvious. No wonder a bright Infant School teacher remarked 'I'd like to live to see the day when the RAF had to organise jumble sales when they need a new fighter-plane, like we do for our equipment.' In Gloucestershire the schools were antiquated. One building was designed for the monitorial system of teaching and proudly carried an inscription in large letters outside 'Founded by the Duke of Wellington fresh from the laurels of Waterloo.' In another even older building the headmaster reached up to a pigeonhole to show me a dividend voucher dated 1782 of the Canal Company that had built the office for its own purposes. I found a student whom I had come to help, teaching in a very narrow stone building originally used for weighing canal barges and their cargo. The lively teacher aged fifty-seven told me that as a boy his headmaster had been very good to him and allowed him to learn his physical education by spying on the police through a keyhole while they performed their exercises. This was his training for teaching, which he carried on with exemplary enthusiasm.

The Director of Education for the County at the time insisted that the scarce funds would be confined to those required for following the Parents National Education Union (PNEU) courses. This resulted in my listening in one class to the story of how Horatius defended the bridge over the Tiber until he was ready to dive into the river. When I moved next door to a parallel class of the same age, Horatius was just hitting the water. This is the death of creativeness both for teacher and class, I thought to myself, as I left. This will not prepare them for living in a rapidly changing society, or for tackling the issues thrown up by pollution or the threat of another war. National Curriculum enthusiasts should beware.

A rebel headmaster, so far as the PNEU went, insisted that every boy should learn to grow his own vegetables and that wartime 'Digging for Victory' campaign should be made permanent in this way. He had no use for training college lecturers and was never seen by any of us except in his Wellington boots ready for gardening. He had more sympathy from me than he ever discovered, even though he would insist that the students called the manure 'by its proper name 'shit'.' He was punctilious about his impoliteness.

It was apparent that the government in the year leading up to the Second World War gave physical education a very high place in the curriculum and accordingly, after my year at Carnegie College in Leeds, I was able to get appointed to a post wherever I wished. At one point I was invited to become an inspector of schools (HMI) specialising in this subject. One HMI even joined the students in my class one day. But I was bent on other things and had joined a huge class of seventy studying for an M.A. in Education. The course was severe, and it took three years of Saturday lectures and four more for writing a thesis for me to pass as the seventh out of seventy students to complete it. I thought Birmingham University rather stingy in not granting a doctorate. I wondered whether I was being penalised for my Quaker views.

At Saltley and St Paul's I insisted on teaching Education in the hope that I might make a tangible contribution to the improvement of teacher education as it was coming to be called instead of 'training', a word which suggests that teachers rely on a bag of tricks rather than setting an example or model for the children to emulate unconsciously. With my new degree I could consider myself to be fully equipped for my new work so long as I continued learning.

My next appointment was made to teach Social studies and later on Education at Dudley Teachers College. The Principal had watched me 'facilitating' leaderless groups at a vacation course for teachers and as he believed that Social Studies should be learned by the students contributing their own experiences, he hoped I would be able to organise the students less by dominating them than by drawing them out. He was undoubtedly right in believing in democratic methods for learning about democracy, but was aware that most schools and teachers feel they can only cover the syllabi by authoritarian means.

The discussions on such matters at Dudley among the staff and to a lesser extent among the students reached a very high level indeed. It was an inspiration to take part in these discussions. I notice now that these discussions confirmed my greatest hopes as the Three Ps are now accepted as the basis for educational reform. The three Ps are as follows:

Power spreading for Peace education is essential in the core of Social Studies.

Parents' interest and encouragement are vital.

Play for the younger becoming creativeness for the older opens a new approach.

These three statements are not an attempt to define the whole of educational reform and much less a definition of education. Defining education as promoting personal growth does not prove very helpful in educating teachers, whereas a lively discussion follows the statement that educated people are those who can entertain themselves, can entertain their friends and even more importantly can entertain new ideas. The Handbook of Suggestions for Teachers has a longer definition, which ends with a significant phrase of people when educated being 'willing to lend a hand to anyone in need of it.' The three statements overlap at various points but it is proposed to take them here one by one.

The Home and School Council in England began in the thirties; the Council benefited parents when it fostered an enlightened interest in their children. It benefited teachers when it gave teachers a deeper understanding of their children and thereby helped the children. The Council worked most easily in Nursery Schools because the parents have to bring their children to school in the morning and fetch them home at night so they meet other parents and can easily approach the teacher when they need to do so. The schools and classes are small enough for everyone to know the others. I was so impressed by these schools that not long after completing my thesis I applied to become secretary of the Nursery School Association. Unfortunately I was turned down initially for being a man and when minds changed I had already obtained another post. I was hoping to get into the Public Relations side of education, which has been neglected for too long.

Although teachers and parents have the common interest of helping in the education of the children, misunderstandings easily occur. The mother of a secondary schoolgirl had never attended the Parents and Teachers Association (PTA) meetings but there was real trouble at home when her daughter came back after school and burst into floods of tears. She was overweight and the teacher had called her a scurvy elephant and 'she'd no business to be rude like that.' The mother became as indignant as her daughter and the very next morning, asked to see the headmistress. She was clearly very upset and needed time to recover over a cup of tea. She was then able to explain her indignation to the headmistress who asked the teacher to come. The teacher heard the story and looked very puzzled. 'No I never said anything like that.' The mother looked defiant but then the teacher added 'Just a moment; I did call her a disturbing element.' After that all was well the girl accepted polite criticism!

I like to think that PTAs provide a good opportunity for people to learn how to work together and sort out disputes, either in this kind of case or in others. In being slow to anger and quick to mediate, as the headmistress was, she set a good example to all who heard the story as well as to those directly involved. I was less successful on one occasion when called in to mediate between staff and parents, being shouted down when attempting to explain the one side to the other. Feelings were running so high that I got no chance to speak.

There is a somewhat similar failure occurring frequently in China. Owing to the successful policy of insisting on parents having smaller families to limit the growth in population there are many one-child families, but this has had results which were both foreseen and unforeseen. These 'little emperors' have the attention of both parents and up to four grandparents anxious to meet their every request. They come to expect grown-ups to wait on them hand and foot, and they learn little about sharing or taking turns. In consequence they may appear to be selfish and spoilt. When they begin school they tend to complain about their teachers who do not have the chance to give them undivided attention and the children's dissatisfaction spreads to their parents. On a visit to Beijing I was informed that relationships between parents and teachers have never been so bad as they are now.

129

FROM PARENTS TO PARENTS

TAKE STEPS
TO HELP YOUR CHILD

Her progress and happiness depend on harmony between home and school

ISSUED BY
BIRMINGHAM & DISTRICT
FEDERATION OF PARENT-
TEACHER ASSOCIATIONS
240, POUND ROAD, OLDBURY

DESIGNED BY
Mrs. MARY ALLEN

BEFORE SCHOOL

A calm sense of things planned.
Wake her in time so that

she has time to eat and start early for school

without having to rush. Give her time — give her love.

Her interests and needs must be the concern of parents and teachers.

If you can meet her — be on time and be pleased to see her.

Be interested in all she tells you about school.

Let her share in the activities of home, but don't set too high a standard.

AFTER SCHOOL

MOTHER HER — DON'T SMOTHER HER
MORE "DO'S" LESS "DON'TS"

Stress in the Primary School, this work was produced by one of my mature students at Dudley College.

130

The opportunity to demonstrate how to dispel this clash of expectations has not yet been taken. It can safely be stated that this part of education for peace is still in its infancy. In some schools, however, great progress has been made in reducing the number of competitive games and increasing the number of cooperative games. It is not only in the cabinet where personal ambition spoils the achievements of the team. Most boardrooms of firms suffer from the same difficulties due to this special form of corruption among the powerful. In this country Mildred Masheder is well known for her books of games to play at an age when the personality is rapidly forming. She has a vision of the world where people suffer less from competition and aggression.

The work of the PTA was greatly encouraged by the findings of Dr. Douglas, which he reported in his book *Home and School*.[32] In summary they suggest that the interest and encouragement by parents is more influential in determining success at school than the quality of the teaching. Rapid advances in education could be made if it were easy to show parents how best to help their children. Often the ambitious parents are anxious about academic success to the exclusion of everything else including creativity. This is unwise because it has been proven in American statistics in Maine, that schools which, provide artistic and creative lessons as part of their curriculum, achieve greater success in the other more 'academic' subjects including the sciences and mathematics.

I have sometimes warned such parents that the greater their success the further away their grandchildren are likely to live, high academic achievement being usually followed by jobs at a distance. One head teacher attracted a high proportion of parents to a meeting by giving as a title 'What I want my child to be.' The parents were expecting a talk on how to become a lawyer, a doctor, or a high-paid business executive; instead of this what they got was a talk about 'What sort of *person* do I want my child to be.' It was a salutary reminder that there are more important considerations than status and wealth.

Suggestions for Parents

One yes is worth two nos.
Play with your children, and see the world through their eyes.
You can judge a child by what he/she does with free time.

Mother love, like wealth and muck, does best when well
   spread.
Good mothers never hurry – a big change from office work!
No teamwork with no team, no leadership with no followers,
   no originality with no freedom, no grit without
   difficulties.

In the 1930's at the final meeting of the Home and School
Council, where it had been decided that due to lack of funding,
the work could not be continued, I decided that something could,
and must be done about cooperation between parents and teachers. So Ruth and I started the PTA at the Bournville School, an
easy job thanks to a welcoming headmaster. We had our own periodical 'Children first'. This magazine set a good example to the
children and parents and teachers, and through it they all learned
a great deal from each other about the children in their care.

Having established the PTA in Bournville School, which all our
children attended, the next step was to set up a Birmingham and
District Council and later in 1956 we formed the National
Confederation of Parents and Teachers Association (PTAs). It
should have provided a useful channel for the best of the new ideas
for education, which circulated after the war. Although my name
appeared in the letter headings as the founder of the organisation
I did not get much of a hearing, largely because of repeated absences
abroad with the United Nations Education Science and Culture
Organisation (UNESCO). Our current periodical *Home and School*
is published professionally. Previously the Birmingham periodical
'Children First' had developed a lively image, but we found we had
to write too much of it ourselves and had little time for increasing
the circulation. We had to choose between advertising it elsewhere
and a public relations firm. I chose the PR firm because I lacked
experience of how such work is done.

One of our PTA activities was when the BBC arranged a competition to find the most skilful pair of parents; they asked me to help
judge by viewing films made especially for the occasion, and inter-
viewing the competitors. They were charming people to meet, even
though a bit overawed. It is a great pity that it has not been repeated.

I had early on built up a reputation for writing articles for the
magazine. My articles tended to be outspoken, one of them was

*We founded the National Confederation of Parent Teacher Associations
(NCPTA) in 1956.*

133

'Law-breakers in school.' In this I called the children in classes over the maximum size, 'Law breakers.' Another suggested that there was more to be learned from France, Belgium and similar countries than people liked to hear. A third 'To Whom Do Children Belong?' accused advertisers of stealing our children to turn them into the slaves of the consumer society.

I had written a book-length manuscript previously on PR in education in the hope that if parents valued education more highly everyone would benefit. The book covered PTAs and Education Weeks to allow the schools to provide parents the chance to see the work of the schools and ask questions of the teachers; all the schools of my Education Authority did this. In Birmingham we fixed a day in March for all the schools to have individual open days and spent a year making preparations for it but a couple of days beforehand thirteen inches of snow fell and all the meetings had to be cancelled or postponed.

My next undertaking was writing a series of letters to parents to help them know what to do at each stage of a child's development. They included suggestions for toys, games to play indoors and outdoors, visits to make to places of interest, what to look for in a school and what books to read both for the parents themselves and their children. The publishers did not wish to take them on as intended because it would have meant too much work for them to send the letters out every six months or yearly. However I published my letters in book form under the title *Parents Only*. It has long been out of print.

It was followed by the 'Robinson Crusoe Holiday Books' I wrote with the help of a student, providing suggestions for activities and craft-work during holidays. I derived the idea of these books from France and adapted them for us here. These holiday books were designed by me to be provided by the schools at the end of each term. They contained suggestions and occupations for school holidays, ranging from games to play to books to read, and places to visit. Their aim was to provide the incentive of an exhibition of work at the beginning of the next term. These proved popular and led on to a comparable activity. It seems that my colleagues were astonished at my forthright writing. These become more important as the roads became more dangerous for children, and parents give less time to looking after them. It is more difficult for parents to take their children in to see their own work, where machines may be too dangerous. Compared with a peasant farm two hundred years ago, a factory workers council house is a frustrating place for children despite the television set.

It was not easy to bring parents and teachers together. Parents often had unhappy memories of school and teachers felt themselves to be on the defensive. Sometimes a line was drawn on the asphalt playground and a notice announced 'No parents are allowed beyond this point'. A number of head teachers confided in me that they were afraid that Communist agitators would break up meetings. We were thought by some to be agitators ourselves, and this mistake was only erased when we persuaded the Duke of Edinburgh to be our President. The Nursery Schools Association helped initiate the Birmingham and District Federation of PTAs. It was at one of these meetings that a mouse kept running out and sat contentedly in front of the crowd, washing its face. We didn't frighten a mouse but several head teachers shook in their shoes at the thought of parents getting together. Year by year patience and tact prevailed until nearly half the schools in the country belonged to the National Confederation and the voice of parents was welcomed in Whitehall. When a committee was invited to draw up a report on periods of psychological stress in primary schools with the help of a grant from UNESCO, I was surprised to be appointed as the reporter for the sessions. This was interesting considering my views at the time revealed by these excerpts from my writing:

Children are misfits in this fast age of machines.
As teachers are no longer a branch of the police force, they can become more like parents and vice-versa.
An Inspector of Schools can report on the effectiveness of schools by visiting the homes.
Teachers who walk to school teach more than teachers who ride.
To love a child is to love the future; to love the future is to love peace.

Following the parent's role in education and especially education for leisure, some comments on creativeness are relevant. Obviously creativeness thrives as a form of play in leisure time and

135

like play it is also valued as an aspect of school subjects. Creativeness is the flower in the tree of life and has little place in the many treadmill schools where the books and teachers are geared to passing examinations only. It can be fostered by a favourable ethos in the school set by teachers who are themselves creative, and it is normally associated with the fine arts that form the core of a civilisation. Only in the twentieth century has it been recognised that creativeness has anything to do with children. Cizek was an early practitioner in child art; examples of his pupils' work were used to raise funds for feeding the children in Vienna after the First World War as I well remember. Dr. Viola came to England to expound his theories regarding child art. Discussions arose about how much help a teacher should give. 'To touch a child's painting is forgery' said Viola. It is possible to teach the handling of a brush and the mixing of colours but when a child wishes to paint a picture he is on his own. He may wish to talk about what he is going to do, but the teacher at this point encourages rather than giving instructions.

Once child art became well established creativeness began to spread. A ten-year-old girl in a Wolverhampton school began her poem with 'My stallion black with its querulous mane...'. This was an amazing example of how a child could not only use a word that many other children may not have understood, but she had used it in a new context with such creativity. The headmaster in her school used to give the pupils a sense of 'a good word to use,' he not only taught them to understand their language more effectively with new words but encouraged them to use these words creatively. The poet Auden must have had the same effect on his pupils when he taught at the Downs School in Colwall. Each of Auden's pupils produced a passable poem for the collection that was later published. A writer on business management coined the phrase: 'He who quickens the sense of life in me is my leader' and aptly described the quality of a teacher of creativeness. Such thinking characterised the ethos of Dudley Training College when I started teaching there in 1950.

1945-48	Saltley College, Birmingham
1948-50	St. Paul's College, Cheltenham
1950-56	Dudley College
1954-55	UNESCO Philippines

1956-58   UNESCO Thailand
1963-65   UNESCO Iran

Creativeness does not belong exclusively to painting and poetry. It also finds scope in craftwork, which in younger children may mean using their imagination while making use of scrap materials. It is applied in music, in dance, in drama and especially in combinations of dance with drama. The cynics complain that children have too little experience to justify relying on their imagination, but it is precisely their freshness, which needs to be valued and preserved. Within every child there is a potential poet and often it is to poets we must turn to appreciate fully what this word 'creativeness' may mean. Shakespeare in *A Midsummer Night's Dream* wrote these lines:

> The poet's eye, in a fine frenzy rolling,
> Doth glance from heaven to earth, from earth to heaven;
> And, as imagination bodies forth
> The forms of things unknown, the poet's pen
> Turns them to shapes, and gives to airy nothing
> A local habitation and a name.

Shakespeare's words 'frenzy' and 'airy nothing,' describe experiences of successful teachers of creativeness. I recall one of my own student teachers bringing me an egg-shaped lump of clay, which a boy of ten years had made and lent to her. It looked, it must be admitted, rather a heavy 'airy nothing'! My student teacher went on to tell me the story of how the boy explained his little egg. She said, when the egg was opened there was a hollow centre with a tiny figure lying in it. 'What's that?' she whispered to him. He must have felt her to be a sympathetic friend as well as his teacher because bit by bit he explained 'That's me, lying alone in the dark.' 'Yes?' she commented. 'No I don't like it, not the dark. Dad and mum go out and leave me in the dark.' The student learnt that the parents apparently frequently left him alone in the house at night when they went out, despite his fear of the dark.

As often happens the full story remains to be guessed. Psychologists still disagree about the value of 'acting out' in ways such as this, so that fears can be managed or even mastered. It was a very important issue during the war and after, when the trauma produced by air raids was at its worst. As weapons have developed soldiers are no longer sent out to 'die for their country' as the phrase had it, but more and more to kill women and children and traumatise others. It is time for psychologists to agree among themselves and then make recommendations for responses by schools to the prevalence of fears of violence. The stresses imposed by the National Curriculum are likely to prove more of a hindrance than a help. It crowds out the play-way of learning by concentrating on basic literacy just at the period when there is a very large movement in the USA, based on elaborate research, to attain higher results in the 3 Rs by focusing attention on creativeness.

The six trends in teacher education, which I tried to support, are not distinct from each other but overlap. They began with the three Ps – Power-spreading, Parents, and Play – and go on to the three Cs, namely Creativeness, Community, and Citizenship.

Creative work is normally practised by individuals, on their own; you cannot write poems in a committee or paint pictures as a group. However this does not imply that there is no place for teamwork or group work. The reverse is true that there is or should be a very important place for social education within the wider field. If creativeness is the flower of the educational tree, community education may be regarded as the roots.

By encouraging the individualism associated with the Miller of Dee, the specialists in curriculum reform have unknowingly contributed to the social chaos, which appears to lie ahead. When the turn-round begins and awareness prevails the schools may prove to be the best means at hand for introducing the community service schools. Their aim will be to produce Good Samaritans rather than Nobel Prize-winners; social education will be given preference, even over intellectual education. Trees will develop their roots as well as their flowers, roots consisting of loyalties to families, to neighbours and friends in addition to the more usual loyalties to work place and nation. Each school will ultimately serve the community around it and seek to turn it into a place where it is an education just to live.

At Dudley College I was already speaking in these terms. The students were expected to consider, the community served by the schools that they had previously attended as pupils. They were to discuss the needs of the local community and draw up plans of action for the schools to meet these needs, with the added help of the local people. At this time I had no knowledge that this was already normal practice in the Philippines.

There were plenty of objections to Community Schools in England. It was said that teachers cannot be trained in such a variety of skills as would be required if schools were to become the agents of social change and especially as no one could foresee what changes might be demanded. Secondly it was argued that people had shown clearly that they valued their privacy much more than sharing in communal life.

Citizenship is increasingly discussed in education, the more so now that young people in many countries, even in Switzerland, are becoming less willing to use their votes. This may be because other activities such as watching television are more attractive or it may be that they feel that their votes count for little. Just as power tends to corrupt, so powerlessness tends to corrupt, and absolute powerlessness corrupts absolutely. Democracy is intended to spread political influence but Edward Heath, the former Tory Prime Minister, stated with emphasis 'the invention most needed today is how to produce democratic citizens'. He was appalled by the growing apathy. Educationists should be applying the principle of learning by doing in this matter. Talk about constitutions is too abstract, practising democratic procedures takes more time than ordinary schools believe they can afford.

It is perhaps for this reason that the two most impressive examples I have witnessed were in schools for disabled children where the pressure of time and curriculum are least. The first example was when I visited a school south of Shrewsbury at Condover for blind children who had a secondary handicap. Mr Myers the headmaster was conducting an assembly of the whole school that met weekly. A boy complained that someone had been disposing of waste paper by pushing it behind a radiator in the hall, although there was a waste-paper basket in each classroom. The headmaster asked the assembled children 'Who knows *how* he could have made his way to the proper place?' Someone suggested, 'Surely he might have asked for help in finding a basket?' And somebody else volunteered that 'there is a basket behind the door and everyone knows where that is.' In this way most of the business of the school was conducted by question and answer rather than by more usual discipline, and a public concern for the well being of the whole school was enhanced. Speaking up like that was a public-spirited act, and it was a feat on the part of Mr Myers to have created an atmosphere in which it happened. I suspect that children in such a school attract public-spirited teachers who pass on, often unknowingly, their attitudes to the children.

The second example was a school where John Cross was in charge. It was a school for children who were so disturbed emotionally that they had to have residential treatment. I took my own teacher-students to visit and sitting at the back of the weekly assembly we witnessed an extraordinary scene. It was like a trial where a confident twelve-year-old was conducting the business of the meeting and, I suppose, had been briefed for the occasion. I could hardly believe my ears when I heard him explain to a new member of staff that no one is above the school rules. The offence in question at this particular point was that this new member of staff had lost his patience and had been hitting a boy who was still up, and who was refusing to go back into bed at one o'clock in the morning. 'Yes, that is certainly against the rules,' said the chairman firmly, 'Chris is new here and doesn't know our rules.' Then turning somewhat fiercely to the boy, he added 'And so what were you doing at that time of night?' The boy looked ashamed and mumbled his excuses. There followed some consultations which I could not overhear and then silence was called for, to hear the verdict: Chris was told to take the boy out to supper in the nearby small town and the boy had to report to another adult, meaning not Chris, every four hours for a set period. In this way both of them were tactfully but firmly reproved. This is learning citizenship by living it and is likely to achieve more than hours of chalk and talk. The numbers in such situations have to be small and the pace of life different; the teachers have to be skilled even though the children would normally be easier to manage, than this story suggests.

If the young Hitler had been treated like that, history might have been different. My group of teachers gasped with astonishment, some said 'yes' and some 'no' to this daring demonstration of democracy for keeping law and order.

There needs to be in addition a greater recognition that it is difficult to inculcate a loyalty to something abstract and distant. When writing *The Swiss Constitution – Can it be Exported*[33] I worked out that no politician in Bern, the federal capital, lived more than two hours from home. This favours a much more democratic government than can be found in the USA. It also implies the importance of local government and the principle of subsidiarity, which assures local government a significant role. The teachers of Social Studies may build the piers of a bridge to national and international governance but they depend on the politicians reaching out to meet them from their side if the interest, loyalty, and public spirit that are vital to good citizenship are gradually to be formed.

CHAPTER 9

UNESCO Technical Assistance in the Philippines

THAT FIRST MORNING in the plane travelling east from Paris on my first UNSESCO assignment, I rubbed my eyes as I wondered how I came to be there. I had a UN Laissez-passer or international passport, international money in the form of UNESCO coupons valid for any country, to buy educational equipment, and I myself had become an international civil servant. I seemed to be witnessing the opening of a new era of worldwide cooperation. UNESCO itself, the united Nations Education, Science and Culture Organisation had sent me a letter out of the blue, like the proverbial letter on the breakfast table, to ask whether I would let my name go forward. Awkward as it was for us considering our six children, I regarded this as call-up papers, which a pacifist cannot refuse, especially after the easy life I had enjoyed during the war. Ruth never fully shared my view. 'Two wrongs don't make a right' she said, referring to the splitting of our family.

With both the Ministry of Education and the Ministry of Labour phoning to know whether there was anything they could do to secure my release, it was clear that something very unusual was happening. This was no ordinary job I was being offered, this was a mission. Would I join the UNESCO Mission to the Philippines? My parent's friend Professor Gilbert Murray, the internationalist, had been heavily involved in UNESCO's predecessor, the Committee for Intellectual Cooperation and he would have used a word of that kind which implied service and the selflessness of a real profession. From my work camp experience I knew that idealistic plans are not always appreciated by the people who have already been on the job. The Canadian official at UNESCO in Paris was in doubt about the nature of our work. It was a project worked out between the officials of the country and the UNESCO officials.

The Canadian was very glad to hear from me in one of my early letters in response to her question, that I fitted the situation so well that I might exclaim, 'I was born and bred in a briar bush,' a quotation from the Uncle Remus Stories, about Brer Fox. In the story Brer Rabbit was caught by Brer Fox, with a sticky tar baby and thrown into a briar bush as a punishment. I was thinking in particular of my remaining in UNESCO House in Bayambang where our work was centred, instead of returning on Fridays with the others to the fleshpots of Manila, the capital city, which lies a hundred miles to the south.

I belonged to a team of six:

Urban Fleege from the USA Chief of Mission and
    Primary Education
An Australian for agriculture
A Dane for Secondary Education
A New Zealander for Science
An Indian for Adult Education
Myself for Teacher Training

Looking back on the work fifty years later it is easy to perceive that we might have given more help to each other. We were all supposed to be strengthening the community education, which was adopted as the educational policy after the USA granted independence to the Philippines. I should have persuaded the Australian to provide more help over school gardening. Urban Fleege was committed even to the advanced forms of community education and felt quite at home with the many senior officials, who had studied in the USA, the country where community schools first took shape. The Indian was likewise fully committed and we sometimes organised courses for teachers together.

My brief, I gathered in Paris, was to devise a very practical system of teacher training, which would enable teachers to cope with the very practical work of community schools. This never happened, I never found any official who was interested in anything

143

I wrote or said in this respect. What I was able to do was to write articles in praise of the Filipino Community Schools and to give help over English teaching, in my spare time. This may sound like failure, certainly my experience in the English teachers colleges was never tapped and my proposals for child studies to be included, as part of teacher training, was never accepted. This is remarkable considering the country is English speaking throughout, especially among teachers, so there was no question of misunderstanding. There are fifty to eighty different languages, depending on who's doing the counting – a new language was discovered while I was there in the hills I could see from my window.

They said that they preferred English-English and would I make some tapes for them. That was a delicate question, with many Americans involved. The English specialist Fe Manza worked me hard. I shall never forget reading *Forsaken Merman* by Mathew Arnold, to a very large group of English teachers until so many were in tears that I had to stop. Nor shall I forget the group of younger teachers, on another occasion, sitting on the beach at sunset who appeared to enter into my own enjoyment of every poem I chose to read. A rumour had circulated that my home was near Stratford-upon-Avon, and that was enough to ensure that I was treated with great respect throughout the whole province of Pangasinan, thanks to the work of Fe Manza, in regard to Shakespeare.

In my week of briefing in Paris I had gathered that I should expect surprises. That seemed to be true of every aspect of life and not just education. A roadside notice proclaimed 'We have spare parts for your car, we've no spare parts for you. Drive carefully.' When the Filipino's say they are moving house, they mean exactly what they say. I met a man astride the ridge of his thatched roof urging on a team of neighbours carrying his bamboo house on long poles from one village to another.

Coming home at dusk one evening I found a crowd of some two hundred people, watching in wonder the flames among a spout of water where a new artesian well was about to be made. I came away with some of the gas in a bottle; it turned out to be ordinary marsh gas. To the crowd, burning 'water' was a miracle, which pleased the vendors of the nuts and fruit, who had lost no time in

144

setting up their stalls. I did not stay long because we were supposed to be in by 5.00 pm for our own safety. Up in Mountain Province next to Pangasinan (the people of the salt country), two Americans took a wrong turn and never came back. When Krishnamurti and I passed that way and we came to that turning he said, 'No we won't go that way. You can never be sure.' On the mountain slopes facing us I counted a sequence of ninety-six terraces holding up strips of precious soil, some of which seemed to be as high as they were wide.

The Philippines are made up of seven thousand islands, many of which have coral reefs. I spent some time there with a snorkel living in what seemed to be paradise itself. The Principal of the College to which I was loosely attached said that as a boy he had often gone to fetch guano from an island cave. The odd thing was that every bag of bird manure he filled had a bowlful of human teeth in it. A story must develop from there, but I never heard it.

The most important day of the year was festival day and as the floats went by, there was Princess Elizabeth of Britain, represented and her consort the UNESCO expert from England. What sort of teasing was that? How could that be made to further community education?

When asked how the Americans came to be so popular, in what had been their colony until independence in 1946, the reply came without hesitation: 'We found that American soldiers are different from other soldiers; they have candies in their pockets and their pockets seem to leak when small boys are near.' Is this an idea for peacekeepers? It's the best ammunition that I have ever heard mentioned.

In this startling environment it is little wonder that the schools were also startling in their innovations. The first lesson I happened to witness was a lesson in hospitality. It was the beginning of the autumn term and the children of what had previously been the youngest class were preparing to entertain the newcomers with songs and dance. 'Where will they sit?' asked the teacher, 'Where will our guests sit?' The reply soon came 'They can sit on our chairs, we'll sit on the floor.' The teacher looked pleased and accepted the suggestion and continued with other arrangements to ensure that the newcomers felt themselves to be welcome.

In Filipino schools the Home Economics building is not only very large and well equipped but it is used to entertain visitors to the neighbourhood. I found them so hospitable and they expressed their pleasure so strongly that I almost seemed to be doing them a favour. Later I found that teachers were hesitant to invite me because English people there had such strong colour prejudices that it was awkward to invite them. I, of course, was delighted to be amongst them, and when one evening I was attending a very late event in a remote village I was invited by a family to stay the night. I watched in wonder as the entire family gradually retired to bed on the same huge mat, which was unrolled a little further as each family member became ready for sleep. The children made no fuss at all and the matt filled almost the whole of their tiny hut. I felt that this was such a beautiful act of friendliness and hospitality, and carried out with such shyness, I found it very moving. A place was kept for me at the end of their bed mat.

My first proper school visit was a very memorable day. I was put on a large dugout canoe and taken down river, a long way down river, it having been explained to me that the only alternative was to walk and I had missed the cool temperatures of early morning. I introduced myself to the headmaster who was expecting me. 'Yes, I'd like to show you round' he said. Being used to such visits, I assumed he meant the classrooms. When he turned his back on the school buildings and made for the great gateway out of the school grounds, I was puzzled but hesitated to ask where we were going. I might well have guessed that we were going to see the work of the school in the surrounding community. First we stopped by a new rectangular fishpond, which had been made with some help from the oldest children. It was setting an example to all the neighbours of one way to provide their families with a supply of protein. Tilapia, the new wonder fish, which came originally from Mozambique, was being introduced into many countries through UN technical assistants. At first mistakes were made, the water was not sufficiently cooled by shade, for example, and the fish bred before they had reached a reasonable size. Sometimes the water was too shallow, but the fishponds had spread throughout the province.

Further on, pegs had been pushed into the ground by older school children to mark the edges of the new road. It was intended

146

to encourage farmers to take their surplus produce to market with the help of horse-drawn carts. I began to wonder whether we had been located in this particular province because it had an exceptional Director of Education but later I found that the enthusiasm for new work of community education was widespread. It may have formed a part of the response to winning independence. All schools and colleges were requested or invited to take part and the list of projects, which I saw in operation as I travelled in the course of my work was astonishing. I knew by this time that the Community Education of which I had dreamed of in England was widespread in the Philippines. This cross between a Cambridgeshire Village College and work-camp, this education in democratic citizenship on the principle of learning by doing, this formative interpretation of Ivan Illich's book *Deschooling Society*[34] is capable of ensuring that the urgent environmental problems can now be faced by the world. The schools in their new form could save the human race from disaster.

It is hard for me to exaggerate the effect the schools had on me. I ceased being a cautious academic and became an enthusiastic believer in this particular development in social education, which gives the school the prime place in dealing with social problems by planning a visionary utopian future. People speak of dreams coming true, but it was more than that, it constituted a response to the pessimism produced by the war, a reward of hope, an association of hope not just for my generation but for the generation of my children. One morning I awoke and planned that, with the help of the Rowntree Charitable Trust, some pilot community schools might be established in England. UNESCO, wishing in its early days to confirm its leadership in education, would promote community education wherever there was a response. As I reflected on them, I found that I could repeat the words of Keats:

> ...Then felt I like some watcher of the skies
> When a new planet swims into his ken;
> Or like stout Cortez, when with eagle eyes
> He stared at the Pacific – and all his men
> Looked at each other with a wild surmise –
> Silent, upon a peak in Darien.

My feeling of surprise increased on closer acquaintance with the Philippines, instead of fading away as might be expected. The Community Schools undoubtedly deserve more attention than they have received. It is difficult to describe them without a warning that the example of only one school can be misleading, because the essential principle is that each school's work should be based on a compromise between the 'felt needs' and the so-called 'real needs' of its community. The real needs being those for which wise outsiders might be able to establish and win the approval of the local inhabitants, either using books or by their visits. In whatever was undertaken this distinction produced profitable discussions. I took my training to become a wise outsider very seriously both by writing and by reading as my diary letters show. Many of the projects were well woven into the learning of ordinary school skills such as the three R's. Reading and writing about matters of interest and importance to the children have often been shown to improve results in their literacy skills. See Appendix 2 for a letter home at that time.

Before reaching an account of the work of Philippine Community Schools, it is desirable to write something about the surveys made in each of the villages before the projects were chosen. Sometimes the teachers took on the task, especially if the children were younger or in the early days when the idea was new. They had to be very careful not to impose their own ideas and thus risk losing the willing support of parents or children. They had to learn the difficulties of drawing democratic initiatives from people who had been accustomed to powerlessness and obedience to heavy-handed officials. The surveys were indeed the first step in community education. Sometimes the teachers contrived to obtain parental involvement through questions taken to the homes by the children, sometimes in those days, owing to the absence of television and the scarcity of radio sets, it was very easy to call meetings at the school and many schools had parent-teacher associations.

The respect in which teachers were held was an advantage in that their wishes tended to be accepted but a drawback in that it hampered the expression by parents of counteracting views. On the other hand the recent acquisition of political independence created an atmosphere in which changes were expected, and sometimes very ambitious programmes of work were agreed risking disappointment later. One of the rules developed was to plan for at least one early or short-term project suited to providing the essential experience of success. Later it might become possible to undertake something requiring more patience, more time, more skilled work and more funds. Occasionally surveying by the schools was used to provide the local or even national government with the statistics needed to measure the success of a campaign. Rough measures of literacy were provided in this way. Along with many other countries in the 'South', they considered they were very poor. One day when I was on my way to a school the driver of a caratella commented, 'We are a very *poor* country,' meaning that the people, had little or no money, but when I disagreed with him saying 'I think your country is very rich.' He looked puzzled, so I added 'Rich in sunshine, and smiles and children. In England we are very poor, in this respect.' And anyone having visited England or lived there for any length of time will know how dull a climate we have and how dour the general populace in the streets seems. He brightened and looked happy at this comparison. The quality of life is hard to measure. For the most part life is neither good nor bad, but thinking makes it so.

A country such as the Philippines should be urged to reject the materialism and over-consumption of the West and pride itself on setting an example of how to live better on less, a lesson which the West will need more and more as sources of energy become exhausted and expensive. The UN might be planning already how to provide this technical assistance in reverse. Such evidence could be supported by the fate of those who win large prizes in the national lottery who often lose more in real friendship than they gain in financial security. Unfortunately this is seldom reported to the controllers of the media who stand to profit by over-consumption and the advertising which inevitably accompanies it.

One of the difficulties is that surveys of material welfare are more easily made than surveys of smiles and friendship, though I have attempted both! But that sign in the Philippine island of Leyte showing the projects planned for the future is worth repeating:

A cemented church.   Reformation, a strengthening of religious and perhaps spiritual life.

An artesian well.	Providing cleaner water.
Basketry.	Industrial arts may form a main money earner.
Poultry and Duckery	(The Filipinos are good at adding to the English language).
Learning farming skills.	
A barrio string band.	For recreation.

The spread of projects accords very closely with the usual, not to say official section of Philippine Community Education which are listed as:

Health
Food production
Industrial arts
Recreation and culture
Moral and spiritual

Moral education often meant campaigning for the prompt payment of taxes, which is usually a hard task, though a source of funds for carrying out other projects. Industrial arts leading to a money income for the members of the community was likewise hard to teach. It was significant that during my visit the Technical Colleges throughout the country were making a survey in their areas, of unused raw materials, of under-used or teachable skills, which could be matched with potential markets at home or abroad.

As an example of their work I bought myself a tie embroidered in colour, which is so striking that I have seldom worn it for fear of attracting too much attention! The country has highly skilled needlewomen, as their national costume indicates, sufficient to attract consumers among tourists, but the quality of the spinning and weaving of the cotton cloth was not in keeping with the embroidery of that tie.

In one particular village a visiting official spotted a number of palm trees of a species noted for the hardwearing quality of its leaves. He easily persuaded the villagers that they could weave hats if only they knew how to do it. Eventually a teacher was found who agreed to go to Manila to take a course. On his return he taught some of the older children what he had learned and they in turn taught their parents. When I visited, school had just finished and it seemed as though everyone was weaving palm leaves into hats, young and old, men and women, all had shared in turning the village into a kind of disorganised hat-making factory. I kept one of those hats for a long time; in fact until it wore out, feeling it had something to do with the Mad Hatter's tea party in *Alice in Wonderland.*

Soon regular lorry loads of hats were leaving the village for sale in Manila, and temporarily their financial problems were solved and they had funds for their projects. Whether they had the fore-sight to plant more of the palm trees I never heard. In every soci-ety it is difficult to persuade people to look into the future and care for their children in a practical way. When I think of the few pesos these people were earning for their hard, and by now, skilled work, I cannot bring myself to spend money going there just to satisfy my curiosity by revisiting some of these places and people. The popu-lation has doubled and nearly trebled in the past fifty years if offi-cial estimates are accurate, so there is no shortage of customers, but the villagers may have been replaced by factory workers, despite the drawbacks of commercial industrialisation.

In another area the schools demonstrated their flexibility in adapting to new situations. Many projects are long term but when a plague of giant snails got out of hand instead of turning to a firm for pesticide, the requirement was attached to school attendance that every child must turn up at school with a Giant Snail, dead or alive. Failing that, they were sent home to find one. The snails could not withstand so many enemies. This treatment could not be applied to a plague of rats in Cotobatu, part of Mindanao where many of those who had accepted land were forced to become rat refugees. Among the scientists with their many proposals for look-ing for predators no one was successful at the time of my visit, no Pied Piper was discovered. How much it was discussed in Community Schools I never heard, but it was certainly worthy of their attention, as with any other social problem, from atom bombs to lack of smiles.

The spread of ideas was remarkable. An Agricultural school, which I visited, had applied the principle of combining theory with practice by providing enough plots of land for the students to grow their own food. They spent half of each day on their plots and did

151

not regard it as a device of the tight-fisted Mr. Squeers, a character from Charles Dickens, but a sensible arrangement, which imposed no hardship on their parents.

The imagination, which is required for finding good projects to undertake, spilled over into the methods used to carry them out to a conclusion. In the province of Laguna, which is near the capital Manila, on the island of Luzon there was an enterprising superintendent. He found that many teachers hesitated to take their classes out to study the environment, so he standardised a system in which the school caretaker regularly took the blackboard and fixed it among the group of houses to be used on that particular day for a particular purpose. On the day I was watching, the subject was sanitary-toilets. After listening to the teacher explaining the need for sanitary toilets to reduce disease and increase cleanliness, the pupils were presented with a list of good points to notice when inspecting the toilets. Then the class was divided into small groups and allotted certain houses to visit to ask their questions. When pupils returned to their class, they helped to compile the statistics on the board, of the number of houses reaching a satisfactory standard, in each of the 'good points.' It is easy to see what social pressure was brought to bear, but the local inhabitants did not seem to resent the inspection, or else they absented themselves. For the most part the adults came to join the lesson and then went home to receive their young inspectors. In the Philippines it was not unusual for an adult to join classes to improve their arithmetic or English for the sake of the work they wished to do. Their presence in the classrooms set a good example to the children and raised the prestige of the subjects and the teachers.

The question of setting a good example arose in a separate context. I had been attending and speaking at a Saturday course for teachers and laypersons. At one stage, a small discussion group working under the shade of a particular tree, sent a teacher across the grass to talk to me. He told me that one report described the difficulty caused by a lawyer, the most highly educated person in the community, who had refused to cooperate with the community by fencing his property against straying animals. At this point in the discussion, an illiterate rice farmer intervened and said: 'You've got everything the wrong way round. He should be one of your leaders, not an unwilling follower. You should be planning to make him one of your officers.' So this is what they did. It is clear that this humble farmer had found an answer to Chaucer's well-known question: 'If golde rusteth, what shall iren do?'

In concluding these impressions of the remarkable Philippine Community Schools it is natural to ask what they do that is relevant to a search for peace in England. The signs of the times are more difficult to read and digest than might be expected. The combination of factors beginning with the breakdown of family is widely accepted but seldom considered in its import for children. First of all they grow up and often copy their parents failures and already the schools feel the impact of having a third of their pupils suffering from broken homes.

To this the English schools have not responded by building smaller schools to enhance the possibility of warm teacher-pupil relationships and pupil-pupil relationships. In former times there were aunts and uncles to make good the defects of the nuclear family. In Geneva the frequent and transitory comings and goings of the United Nations Officials bring extra stress upon its workers, making living extra difficult. The UN's home magazine carried an extremely persuasive article on the theme that if one does not have three friends so close that they can be phoned for help at 3.00 am in the morning, one is at risk of mental breakdown.

In selecting teachers the education authorities again make mistakes by unintentionally favouring individual candidates who have come from one-child families. It is common for more than a third of the student teachers to come from such families. These are generally people who have missed the pleasures of a shared childhood in which they automatically acquire the skills of sharing the limelight and so they resemble the so-called Little Emperors of China. To make matters worse secondary teachers and possibly primary teachers are not local people who can share with their pupils the warm pride in the schools environment. Roots in an area are an asset which is not often fully appreciated though both people and places are capable of forming a part of healthy homesickness, a form of loyalty, the very ground and basis for friendship with others who have much in common. It is worth repeating Aristotle's wise words 'How shall I learn, unless it be from my friend?'

Without a development of loyalty and trust, selfishness will grow apace including crime, violence and other social problems and the first step for many schools especially Community Schools should be to foster a sense of community. It is made more difficult by the size of modern schools and towns. The USA is showing the way in dealing with it, by being the first to set up community schools.

Professor Johan Galtung has written a remarkable article suggesting that social chaos, caused by alienation and lack of guiding values (anomie), may prove to become a more serious problem than the threat of nuclear weapons. The Community School is the best response to this growing crisis, providing the chance of a well-designed social education. After one of my periods with UNESCO, I wrote a book with this message, but failed to get it published, now the crisis has deepened.

It was many years later that I fully recognised the importance of 'parish patriotism' of having roots in a place and community for which one can feel homesick.

The anarchism that follows anomie and alienation is a powerful threat to peace. The ultimate form of individualism is when every person is for himself and family ties are broken, loyalty to others is disregarded, chaos reigns as each one struggles alone for the necessities of life. Before extreme individualism is reached, questions should be asked: what kinds of social education will have been squeezed out of the curriculum? Already the prevalence of civil wars as opposed to international wars is widely recognised. The social confusion of former Yugoslavia is a warning of what the future may bring elsewhere.

An American missionary invited me to take charge of the United Nations Studies programme of an international student work camp. After some hesitation, I accepted it in place of local leave of absence in the hope that it would throw some light on the value of such experiences for members and leaders of the Community School movement. At the last moment an earthquake shook the northern coast of Mindanao, the largest of the islands in the south, where we were needed to help re-build schools. We transferred our plans despite the difficulties of working where security could not be guaranteed.

154

Mr Boutros Boutros-Ghali, the former Secretary-General of the UN wrote in the introduction to his 1992 *An Agenda for Peace*: 'Preventative diplomacy, peace-making and peace-keeping – to which I have added a closely related concept, post-conflict peace building.' He devoted two of his forty-eight pages to it (32 & 33) 'I have in mind, for example, projects that bring States together to develop agriculture, to improve transportation or utilise resources such as water or electricity that they need to share, or joint programmes through which barriers between nations are brought down by means of freer travel, cultural exchanges and mutually beneficial youth and educational projects.' This is the nearest he got to recommending international student work-camps which have helped an influential group of young people to shed their prejudices and hostility and open themselves to friendships which cross national frontiers, by sharing some practical work together at a very impressionable age.

I failed to persuade the Philippine Government of the value to them of the work-camp idea. It is a country with a record of non-violent resistance of which it can rightly be proud but the Catholics' bad relationship with the Muslims has lasted too long, which suggests that some outside help could be useful. It will soon be fifty years since my visit, and the trouble has continued ever since that time as well as before it. Violence is widespread and not confined to dealing with the other side. The Governor of the province told me that, when he was talking with a Datu as the Moslem chieftains are called, and another Datu opened the door, they pulled out revolvers and shot each other dead. The Governor seemed to be only just recovering from the shock.

The American missionary was determined to miss no opportunity. Somehow he arranged for a whole crowd of Moros from their side of the invisible frontier to come to put on an afternoon's entertainment. They arrived on a lorry with all drums beating, it was not very clear whether this was an ordinary announcement or a threat. The work-campers were fascinated. I asked to take a photo of a man in a purple robe with a babe on his arm and a sword in his belt. I didn't get permission until first one, then two, then three, of his wives were lined up beside him. When I enquired how it was that a man with three wives should be looking after the baby, I was

155

told 'The women, all of them have to work in the fields so the babies get attached to the father.' We were told that the Moros' entertainment was a gesture of peace and sympathy. A disaster brings neighbours together in a way nothing else can; one hopes that forthcoming environmental disasters may have this effect worldwide, but there is no evidence that Governments realise that more will have to be spent on the environment and less on conventional defence. The results of the earthquake were more obvious and directly visible, it seems that there may be a need for schools to prepare pupils for facing future problems. An example might be using vivid details such used when writing home about the earthquakes. See Appendix 3.

Although the conflict between Moros and Christians was one of my earliest connections with conflict management and I was almost too new to the skills to be able to learn much, I was aware that I was learning from the camp leader Paul Dotson. He was always optimistic about what could be achieved and friendly to those he encountered. In particular he involved people in entertaining each other and after slightly grim encounters turned to laughter, it was clear that progress was being made. The question arises: for whom was he paving the way? Was it other Americans, Presbyterians, work-campers or the new conflict managers? Even when little is achieved in the short run, it is possible to prepare the way for those who follow.

I felt this in my own case, during the year in the Philippines that I was a representative of UNESCO and through UNESCO of the UN and if I could be friendly and enthusiastic I was preparing the way. I was completely baffled in Iran when a student commented to my counterpart 'Now we have seen how Mr. Gillett works, we can understand how the British Empire held together for so long.' My loyalty to UNESCO and the UN had been overlooked.

From the little virtues such as punctuality to major ones such as friendliness and a wider concern for other people, the technical assistance official can set a good example and establish an appreciation of his organisation or institution for which he is working, even in countries where he or she does not speak the local language. As was the case provided by my unexpected journey to Mindanao, questions about conflict often arise and offer an opportunity to provide help with a major concern of UNESCO. UNESCO seeks peace in unusual ways, through science, education, and culture. Already much was being done in the Philippines about peace education in schools. United Nations Day on October 24th was widely celebrated. At one of the schools, where I was invited to speak on United Nations Day, the teacher had ordered a dress for the occasion, which had UN symbols embroidered all over it. The heavily illustrated history textbooks in use in the Philippines, however, had fighting or corpses in almost every picture and had little space for any useful information about the UN. I expect the contents in these books have since improved.

It was unfortunate that sovereign states were too jealous of UNESCO to allow it to operate its own radio stations, especially in trouble spots or areas such as the Balkans. They have been urgently needed to counter hatred and war propaganda. Some very interesting radio programmes were broadcast for Afghanistan, in the midst of its past troubles in the nineteen eighties. The funding came from a variety of sources including the BBC, and the programme was presented in the form of a soap opera, which continued to include some elementary teaching about health and agriculture but to a small extent, so as to keep the audience keen on the entertainment. A site chosen was in Pakistan for reasons of security. A survey confirmed that listeners were numerous and a reasonable number were taking the advice. It was planned to incorporate some peace education for this warlike, war torn country. The young nun who was to advocate bringing the violence to an end was barely introduced when the project was abandoned for no clear reason. It may have been due to the victory of Taliban.

Other attempts also have been unsuccessful such as the radio programme funded by George Soros from a steamer in the Adriatic to former Yugoslavia and the provision of radio equipment to Uganda, which was used for war propaganda instead of peace!

No doubt the programmers in Afghanistan intended to make use of the biography of Badshah Khan, *Non-violent Soldier of Islam: A Man to Match His Mountains.*[35] He was also known as the North West Frontier Gandhi. He exploded three myths: That non-violence depends on gentle people, also that non-violence does not work against ruthless oppression, and that it has no place in Islam.

157

He achieved this by converting the notorious, trigger happy men in the area of the Khyber Pass to become a non-violent army, having laid down their arms and being brave enough to die for the sake of freedom. It was calculated that some 100,000 took the pledge; the British officers with their Indian troops were baffled by such willing victims. Never before or since have so many soldiers fought without weapons. This was a new way to freedom and peace. The story should be made known to all those who were fighting in Afghanistan. It was when I was staying in Kabul, on my way home in 1958 that I inquired about their Independence Day celebrations. 'Independence from whom?' I asked. 'From the British of course.' He continued, 'The British garrison outside Kabul was killed off, all except the one man who was sent away with the news.' Badshah Khan had taught that all men are brothers, according to the Koran. 'How can a man kill his brother? It is better to die and go straight to heaven.' The Afghanis never accepted this part of their religious teaching any more than Christians have accepted their similar teaching. The radio can be used more widely in conflict situations, for spreading accurate and relevant news. The absence of such news is the crux of the difficulties in such a conflict, I concluded.

CHAPTER 10

UNESCO – Thailand 1956-1958

NO DOUBT IT WAS my experience in the Philippines, which led to great pressure to leave Dudley College and its inspiring students within a year of returning to them, to go off and work in Thailand. The Thai officials were very impressed by the Community Schools and wanted them, or something like them, introduced into their country. Thailand is one of the least westernised countries and the Philippines perhaps the most. Spain ruled the Philippines for the long period from 1565 until they became a colony of the USA in 1898. In contrast, Thailand had always remained an independent country. It always maintained a very distinctive culture of its own, heavily influenced by Buddhism, akin to those of its neighbours, Myanmar (Burma), Cambodia, Laos and Malaysia, but nevertheless distinctive.

Buddhism was in evidence not merely because according to their calendar the year 2500 was fast approaching and the temples had mostly been repainted for the great occasion, but mainly because of the saffron robes of the monks or Bhikkhus as they are known. It was customary for most men to spend a year as a Bhikkhu attached to a monastery, going out on their alms rounds with their begging bowls for others to feed them. The Bhikku's would go from door to door, each time simply standing at the doorway, not actually asking for anything, because that was not the way, but waiting for the people of the household to bring them just a little food. In this way they would collect small quantities of food from each willing household, rather than an entire meal from just one person. This, according to tradition, was forbidden. Even the King had followed this custom while living like a Bhikkhu until the roads became too blocked with the cars of those wishing to see this remarkable sight. He also set an example on Teachers Day, a day set aside for appreciating the work of teachers. The King did this by teaching a lesson himself, to learn to appreciate what skill is required in teaching.

Dissatisfaction with the government did not affect the King. He was greatly respected. The supposedly democratic constitution did not, however, prevent the abuse of power and changes were made by frequent military coups, unlike the Philippines. It might be the government backed by the police prevailing over the government by the army or vice versa. These changes were brought about with very little bloodshed. I once explained to a Thai student studying in Birmingham about the occasion when the Royal Air force dropped a bomb down the funnel of a naval vessel in the river during a coup. On board the vessel was the Prime Minister on a visit, who had to swim to shore after damage to the ship. The student commented: 'Yes, that was my father, but three weeks later he was playing golf with the new Prime Minister.'

During one such coup, Ruth and I had to send our two boys aged seventeen and fifteen on their own, through Bangkok, itself 300 miles away from us, to the airport. Difficulty was added to this situation by our not speaking the language. We were advised to do this because the four younger children at Ubon needed both of us more. Reports about what was happening were few and not of violence and cruelty but, for example, of the tank which knocked over a letterbox containing letters from the previous two months!

We had two unusual sources of information about local people. The first was a tall man from the United States Information Service who, we read later, was some kind of spy, employed to counter Soviet influence in South East Asia. He came frequently of an evening when the children were in bed. He did not accompany himself singing with the banjo as he did in youth groups but he made himself very acceptable by passing on information about current international affairs. I had the impression that he saw no future for the United Nations. He was always witty and never self-centred and we missed him when he no longer appeared.

160

The other visitor who had even more local information to give us was the chief of police. He had been seconded to the Lancashire police for a period and spoke excellent English. He told us the story of the Prime Minister who travelled to England to learn about the Mother of Parliaments and how democracy works! He was taken to Hyde Park to take a measure of the freedom of speech. This impressed him so much that on his return he had a Hyde Park established in every provincial capital. 'That was all very well' the chief of police continued, 'but he did not like what was said about himself and his government. So an additional ruling was made that a loudspeaker could only be used by those supporting the government. However can I enforce that, when I know they change their tune as soon as my jeep comes into view? As a matter of fact, this afternoon, I took a microphone from a member of the opposition and spoke to him through it, so that the crowd could hear "much as I love you. I don't really want you locked up with me, so give up using this mike." That's the best I could do.' He ended. It sounds like a very civilized way of policing; courteous, non-violent, and effective. I can only hope that international policing becomes equally effective as the years pass on, by living in a culture of peace.

Shortly after that, the chief of police went to the Philippines. He did not explain whether he was on leave or on business. It may have been a diplomatic exit, because while he was away the army staged a successful coup to take political power from the police. A short time before that happened, he had been to see me to offer me armed guards to protect us from riots against British people during the Suez Crisis. When I refused, he said 'Mr Gillett, you are a very brave man.' Later, as the situation worsened, despite my refusal, some guards arrived. It proved difficult to protect the household from the soldiers.

According to law, certain offences require capital punishment, but executioners are so hard to find that foreigners such as Chinese are requested to help. Gentleness is noticeable everywhere and this applies to man and beast. I never heard of corporal punishment in school or home, whereas I will never forget a huge picture of bastinado in an Iranian teashop in which a young man had been tied up with his legs in the air and was being beaten on the soles of his feet. When I asked my counterpart whether this still went on, he shrugged his shoulders and said: 'It was done to me when I went to school.' The way he said it made me avoid questioning him about the circumstances.

In Thailand it was too hot to hurry even when driving cars, the quietness of life was such that it showed in the way the pace of oxen set the pace for walkers, as they passed our house on their way to Ubon market. In a related way the deep influence of Buddhist culture and the meditative steps of the Bhikkhus (monks) and the smiles on their faces removed any possibility of mental stress. Smiling was one of the general rules of health included in the posters on the classroom walls. Even major disasters such as a bus accident were treated with laughter, and a high level of concern.

The schools with their uniforms, their punctuality, their authoritarian ethos and flag ceremonies did not seem to fit in well with the rest of life and I kept wondering whether Scouting for boys and Red Cross activities for girls on Thursdays were designed to mitigate the effects of other more usual school work. The former King had been in the habit of sending his sons to England to look out for good ideas for introduction in Thailand and Scouting had come in this way. The children gained experience of cooperation, teamwork, leadership, and public service, which fitted them for embarking on the new community education we were helping to introduce. It was significant that the schools that did not wish to participate were those where the pupils lived within reach of the secondary schools who had a possibility of becoming teachers and civil servants. I was reminded of the four year old in London who began attending a Nursery School but was found putting on his coat to go home. He complained, when the teacher asked what he was doing, 'All those toys and games won't get me through the Eleven Plus Exam.'

Further away from the provincial capital, the response from parents and teachers was enthusiastic. It is difficult, however, to maintain discipline in ordinary schools where competition does not provide the main motivating force. For helping our project a professor of sociology had been sent in advance to prepare a more thorough description of the local culture than we could provide for ourselves. I did not understand why he omitted the social or cultural changes and some account of how they had occurred, including

162

the names of individual innovators, so that we might know to whom we might turn to for help. Social change is an essential and major part of UN Technical Assistance programmes and it is vital to take into consideration the changes, which have already taken place, whether they failed to take hold or succeeded.

These were the circumstances into which the work at Ubon had to fit. The work was in two parts, a large institute, the Thailand UNESCO Fundamental Education Centre, known as TUFEC, in which a dozen UN officials trained community development officers who had been picked for senior posts. The nature of their course is indicated by the list of expatriates.

Donald Faris	from Canada for Food and Agriculture. Advised me on making compost in unfamiliar conditions.
David Smith	from Canada for Adult Education. On the arrangements for courses, seminars etc.
John Allen	from UK for English Teaching. See below.
Nurse Heafey	from Dublin and the World Health Organisation. On making a set of slides about the life cycle and treatment of hookworm.
Dicon Nance	from UK and the International Labour Office for Crafts. Designed a special basket wheelbarrow for making compost.
Jan Kinket	from Holland for visual aids. Especially photographs of the lesson about elephants.
Conrad Opper	from UK Chief of Mission for both TUFEC and TURTEP. Helped with his wise administration.

I believe that it was Dr Malcolm Adiseshiah who held a senior post at UNESCO, who conceived the ingenious idea of putting the Thailand UNESCO Rural Teacher Education Project (TURTEP) on the same campus as the Teachers' College. In that way we had access to the specialist expertise of the TUFEC staff. There were three of us at TURTEP's, one of them Mr Ertem, came from Turkey. During his work in Turkey the future rural teachers learned to make their own ploughs, and breed and train their own horses so as to establish themselves fully with the peasantry, as part of an agricultural reform movement. Mrs Jesse from the USA was the third person in our little group. She said she had learned all about developing countries by working in Kentucky. She concentrated

163

on education for girls, Mr Ertem on school gardens and I took the wider brief of community education towards which all of us contributed. We did not work well together but we each thrived individually. Thinking about it afterwards, I decided I should have asked Con Opper to call us together to coordinate our work more effectively. In very strange circumstances it is easy to miss spotting what needs to be done. We agreed that each of us should select three schools spread along the same road for thirty miles to simplify transport, both for the students and for ourselves.

My meeting with the Minister of Education soon after my arrival, augured well for the future. Despite the heat I borrowed a jacket from a friend for the occasion and I was glad to have done so, when I saw the size of his office and the brilliance of the Buddhist shrine in it. I had no wish to look disrespectful to this man who, I later learned, was both a general and a poet. He had begun writing poetry in English when studying at Christchurch College, Oxford. I would have liked to have asked him whether he had ever read 'The Scholar Gypsy' with its reference to 'The lines of festal light in Christchurch Hall.' The Minister quickly came to the crux of his briefing when he said: 'Go and see what the rural schools are doing. We know it's all wrong. Then find out what the real needs of the villages are, and start making a new curriculum from scratch.' He knew, and welcomed the fact that I knew what the Philippine schools were doing, but we were both too diplomatic to suggest learning from another country. Instead of that he went on to explain that European schools had been copied, although the conditions were quite different. I was elated by the invitation to look for the real needs. I knew full well that the so-called real needs might appear differently to the teachers and the parents from the list, that UNESCO or I might identify. This, however, was my mission. As an epigrammatical introduction to our pamphlet, 'Briefing of International Consultants.' We had written Jonathan Swift's provoking words:

> To guide his steps afford your kindest aid
> And gently pity whom ye can't persuade;
> Leave to avenging Heaven his stubborn will,
> For, O, remember he's your brother still.

Unfortunately a tacit assumption is being made that one is always right oneself, which is obviously untrue. In the end, all we are really left with is, at best, our own opinion, or even worse, our assumptions.

I would have valued any attempt by the Minister to explain how real needs can be discovered, but either he thought me too new to the country to benefit, or it would come better on some future occasion. So far as the Minister was concerned, it appeared over the two years as though we could not put a foot wrong. The work after one year was planned to be spread to all other rural teacher-training colleges before there were enough teachers trained to do it. We were embarrassed by the offer to increase funds because we thought that teachers should not have to suffer a cut in resources once they had left the college. The third indication of the satisfaction in the Ministry was that in the course of a few years the two bright young men who had served as my counterparts were appointed as head and deputy head of the Ministry of Education dealing with the Primary Schools.

UNESCO failed me by the end of my mission. Con Opper left, presumably without having reported on our work. Maybe we should have invited him to visit. Years later he begged me to join him in Iran where he 'Was having a hard time.' His successor, formerly an inspector for the London County Council, who said of his colleagues that they were the best group of educationalists in the country, went to UNESCO Paris for his briefing but must have missed seeing Dr Eagleton who had recently visited us and acclaimed our work. I can only assume this because when I showed him the village work he remarked curtly at the end of the day, 'You've no business to be doing this work. No one in Paris knows what you are doing.' He was so rude that I did not argue the point but left him to find out what a mistake he had made. He may have been influenced by members of TUFEC who saw us as rivals, or he may have believed in plain work on reading, writing and arithmetic not backed up by practical applications.

By this time I was due to hand in my resignation to rejoin my family. They had not thrived in the difficult climate. Ruth lost a third of her weight, and Candia found sleeping even more difficult than she did at home and Jonnie the youngest caught hookworm.

Nevertheless they spent a year learning how interesting novel ways of life can be. Jean the eldest daughter, aged ten at the time, still insists that it was the best year of her life. She quickly picked up enough of the language to talk with students and Bhikkhus who made frequent visits to our house and garden. One day she remarked to me with a smile 'You've no business to be here. These people are perfect. They're more Quaker than the Quakers are.' This was a remarkable opinion in itself but the story was enhanced at the Hague Peace Conference forty-five years later, when a Thai Buddhist sitting next to us laughed so loudly on hearing this story that I looked puzzled. 'That's what I say,' he said, 'Only in reverse. We had two Quaker visitors to my Buddhist community and I had to tell my people that the Quakers were more Buddhist than the Buddhists!' That made a very happy story and a good introduction to the year of the Culture of Peace, and a good way of fitting into other people's shoes.

We were much helped by the four children who occasionally came to the villages and played regularly with the children of the Teacher Training College staff at games like Oranges and Lemons, hop-scotch, Paper, Scissors, Stones, or climbing up an obliging ox either over the tail or over the horns. They learned songs and dances. After ten months Jean helped me by coming as my interpreter to the villages on a day when my counterpart was absent. My second counterpart for my last few months was Mr Saiyut Champatong, who was just back from studying in England. It was a pleasure to work with him.

Counterparts are a vital part of UNESCO technical assistance, indeed of all technical assistance. They are too easily overlooked. They are expected to learn enough from the expatriate to be able to carry the work forward when he or she leaves; or at least mark time until a successor arrives. They are therefore expected to do two jobs rather than a single one. Interpretation from one language into another is in itself difficult, and the mastery of the technical words of the two languages may be far from complete. In addition they have to learn the substance of what is being taught. Mr Panom Kawkamnerd, for example, my counterpart of whom I cannot speak too highly, had to know details about compost-making, water-seal slabs for latrines, hookworm, classroom teaching, the use of puppets, flannelgraphs and paraffin slide projectors as well as being

166

able to teach both students and school children. No one can be master of such a wide variety of skills, but they must have enough confidence in their own versatility and a willingness to 'have a go.'

Mr Panom adjusted to village work admirably. At the end of long hard days his sense of humour did not fail him. On one occasion travelling home at dark, he began speaking so seriously I was quite misled, 'You see that broken tree over there, it looks sad. I want to stand beside it and then, if you take a photo of me, I will send it to my mother and she will be sorry for me.' One month he had lost his salary cheque and at first would not accept any help from me. Finally pretending to be a bit angry I said: 'you are a friend of mine aren't you?' 'Yes' he replied suspiciously. 'Well, friends are people with whom joys shared are doubled and troubles shared are halved. Here's half.' He acquiesced with a smile. Nearly thirty years later, to my embarrassment, he told the story to a large lunch party of the English Speaking Union in London. Making friends with a counterpart is the best first step, sharing goals and experiences follow. They may feel overshadowed and everything must be done to build up their confidence, noticing their successes more than their mistakes. It is very tempting as the expatriate picks up the language to correct him in front of an audience, it is usually wrong to show off in such a way. I wish we had written in our UN pamphlet 'Build up your counterpart's confidence, not your own. Then your own will look after itself.' Unfortunately the counterpart/expatriate relationship varies widely from person to person, from skill to skill, and from country (culture) to country, so that it is difficult to give general advice.

Mr Panom had been instructed to get everything down on paper. This explains my efforts to get details of all our projects in some written form. This overcomes the difficulty in most countries that there is always a language gap and spoken instructions are only partly understood. By the time the expatriate has explained to the counterpart, the counterpart to the students – in our case – and the students to the schoolteachers, and their teachers to the children, and their parents, there is ample room for mistakes and misunderstandings to occur. Even though my English had to be translated into Thai with its unique alphabet, it was worth spending evenings drafting pages of instructions. They would have been better if there had been time to try them out first, to find out how clear they were, for example, by the time they reached teachers.

As I normally spent only one day each week in the villages and there was a limited amount of opportunity for teaching English, especially as I was requested to teach English conversation to a hundred students at a time, the production of this written material was possible but this happened more by accident than design. It is very difficult for UNESCO officials in Paris to envisage the circumstances on the ground and one has to become a kind of educational entrepreneur with a gift for spotting scope for initiatives and seizing them. For this a light teaching timetable is essential.

Often we worked in the dark only guessing whether villagers, students, or other UNESCO people benefited, despite the advice we received about the importance of evaluation. One lesson that we learned was that every project needs backing up with some appropriate message about its importance. Action needs to be backed up by a public relations section. If a new kind of cooking stove is introduced to save fuel and reduce smoke, it may well not be used unless a salesman's skills are applied. In Thailand, UNICEF offered fish meal for villages where lack of protein was widespread but the children refused to eat it, and TUFEC's expert in Home Economics was working on new recipes. The children, who normally brought sticky rice for lunch in little, woven baskets, at first refused to bring anything to eat at all, for fear of having to eat the fish powder with it.

The government asked us to do whatever we could to reduce hookworm. For this, toilets had to be both made and used. I did not think it sound policy to be involved in a campaign, which implied that people had dirty habits, but agreed, a little unwillingly, in view of being useful to the government. We taught the students how to make water-sealed concrete slabs. As the slabs came out of the moulds the onlookers used to cheer as if they were watching a goal scored at football. They had taken the job to their hearts, but there was still a long way to go. It was desirable that more people should understand the lifecycle of hookworms. Where no toilets are used the tiny eggs blow about in the dust until the ground is damp in the rainy season, then they hatch out and the lucky ones find some thin skin between the toes or fingers and so get into the bloodstream. Via the heart, lungs, and throat they reach the intestines and there they hook on and feed on the food as it passes. Finally they produce eggs at the rate of 15,000 a day. 'You'd do well' I would tell the villagers 'if your hens laid that number' and so the process begins again. A person can feed up to roughly eight hundred hookworms, but if they have many more they begin to look pale, feel lifeless and find they can't feed so many and also remain strong enough for work.

With help from Nurse Heafey I made colour slides of the process of the lifecycle of the hookworm. These slides were later to be used for showing in the community schools. Coming from Oxford I understood the feelings of the villagers about their boat-race day, to them the most important day in the year, when the huge dug out canoes with dragon figureheads race down the great river, a tributary of the Mehkong. The last slide in the series shows one of those races and the caption runs: 'If you get rid of hookworm from your village, your boat-crew will be so strong they will win the race.' This produced a roar of applause.

The slides may have been helpful in persuading the students to support the anti-hookworm campaign but not, I suspect, the villagers, nor would many of them learn from the written word in the village news. It was the students who exclaimed one day 'We must persuade Mr Suwan. People listen to Mr Suwan and they do what he says.' They talked to him with good results, and later I went to hear him one evening. He is a peripatetic ballad singer, available for weddings and other celebrations. At that time, neither radio nor television had reached the villages where we were working, so that homemade music and musicians were in great demand.

The song was translated for me and was something like this: 'The headman of a village near here had a very beautiful daughter, with large eyes, and arms and hands as supple as an elephant's trunk, but she suffered from stomach ache. After waiting for it to pass without success, her father said to her "Go and seek advice from Uncle Prasobchai who lives deep in the forest." So she filled a basket with presents of food he might not find in the forest and set off. She was expected to go alone even though there were tigers in the forest. She knew how to sing loud enough to keep the tigers out of the away. (That was how Mr Suwan himself had come to know so many songs.) When she arrived she bowed down to greet her uncle and said "Uncle, father has sent me because I have stomach ache. It is bad and I still don't know what to do." Her uncle had been living in the forest a long time and even knew the fruits and leaves that monkeys choose to eat. He gave her the names of certain plants and told her how to find them, and when she returned home she boiled them in a pan and drank the brew.'

'But the stomachache was not cured. She still held her arms across her stomach and groaned a little when the pain was bad. Next day her father said to her "Either you or your uncle has made a mistake. Today you must ask for help from the Buddhists at the temple." She went there quickly and explained her trouble to an old monk who was an expert regarding herbs. Early in the morning when the herbs are good, she went with a friend into the forest and did exactly what he had said. She put some first into the pot and some only needed dipping at the very end when the water was boiling. When she sipped the medicine it seemed to be having a strange effect on her and, her friend asked, "What is the matter, you look paler than before?" She became frightened, but when she had waited all day, the ache in her stomach was still there. She was walking along the village street that evening when who do you think she met? It was the new students from TURTEP at the Teachers College. They saw her arms folded across her stomach, her pale face and the look of pain in her eyes and guessing her troubles they said, "You must have hookworm. Go and ask the doctor for the medicine against hookworm, but you must take it exactly as he says." So the next day she took the bus to Ubon and saw the doctor, he told her when to take the medicine and how much to take, on condition her father built a toilet, and she went home and did as he said and soon the stomach ache was cured like a miracle. She was able to live happily ever after.

Mr Suwan's ballad sounded throughout the great crowd who had gathered to hear him and all went home that night, thinking they were wiser than they had been before. I was not happy about the implied criticism of the monastery because they were keen to help us in our work in the villages, they even built a hostel for the students to use.

170

Mr Suwan and his ballads were a great assistance in the education provided by the new community schools, because he sang in many villages and people liked him and his music. He could be of help by singing about any of our projects. In a similar way the village newspapers were flexible in that they also gave support to other projects. In particular they helped by providing acceptable reading material for all those school children and adults who had learned to read and were glad to display their new skill. They had a wide range of subjects, I found, whenever I asked my counterpart to translate. From the Suez Crisis to a child's story to an advertisement for a second-hand dug out canoe. What was never omitted was recent Community School work, introducing poultry, making compost heaps suited to the climate, meaning, near enough to water to provide for rotting in the dry season, and yet protected from excessive rain by a thatched roof in the rainy season. One student used a large bamboo to make a drainpipe for washing up water from the kitchen to go to the compost heap. In praising him in front of all the other students, the idea was spread.

Many students took initiatives like that. One of them showed me his notebook written, to my surprise in English. He was attached to a school where there had been difficulties. 'My plan,' he said, 'is to build a school dining hall and kitchen. The fathers will either bring a stout post or thatch a part of the roof.'

I looked dismayed, 'I happen to know that that school has only half as many children as last year, so there is plenty of room for them to eat in the old building.'

He replied politely, 'You do not understand. A school with no lunchroom does not believe in itself.'

'I'm not sure' I said 'anyway the bus turned over by the school and several people were killed. The people believe it is bad for their children, if the place is haunted by spirits.'

'No, I've thought of that!' he smiled 'The abbot, the chief priest has been and the place is alright now.'

He went away after hearing my doubts and wrote his notes for teaching. The notes ended with a memorable remark: 'If I do all my plan, I shall smile all day.' He did smile all day and the school gained a roomy dining hall and kitchen. I liked being proved wrong.

The school did begin to believe in itself. It is little wonder considering that the conditions were such that the student and some of his boys had to hire themselves for removing tree stumps from a side road to earn enough money to buy nails for the two wooden buildings.

I was proved wrong on another occasion. Working in an unfamiliar culture where rules are different, we had to be prepared for making errors of judgement. It happened like this. On my first visit to a group of students I was annoyed to find that they had failed even to begin a survey of the real needs of the village as they had been told to do. I said 'I'll come back next week, will that be all right?' When I came back the following week to the same blank faces and learned that nothing had been accomplished, I was not annoyed, I was angry. It is the height of bad manners to show anger in the Thai way of life and I hope I did not show it. Clutching at straws I said 'I'm bringing a cine-camera next week to make a film of what you decide to do. So you will have to have made a plan by then.'

The next week I found myself filming without having any clue about their plans for a village activity. The film starts with a carefully rehearsed line of children leaving their school building, by the gateway to pass down the main street. No one had made use of the cattle manure which was lying about but I was still hoping that the village was not so difficult to activate as the students implied. The procession turned across the road and through the gate in the bamboo fence and formed a perfect semicircle for the students to begin their lesson. I gradually gathered that the lesson was to be about a flowering, climbing plant, which was held up for all to see. Flowering climbers are very attractive but with every village suffering from kwashiorkor (protein deficiency), hookworm, malaria, periodic famines, and other similar threats, they seemed of less importance. I was fuming when I asked the students the aim of their lesson. I approached the question remembering that they had attended a good lecture on the vicious circle formed by Ignorance, Disease, Hunger and Despair, but they had also been taught to ask the villagers themselves. The villagers felt that the children should learn to look after old people who were so unfortunate as to have no children of their own. When I heard this my jaw must have just

172

dropped and I realised that it was I who was taught the lesson which I needed on account of my western eyes. How can we weigh a Good Samaritan in the same scales as a doctor providing pills against hookworm? It may well be that Good Samaritans are as rare in the West as good doctors are scarce in the rest of the world.

This, like the dining hall, may be regarded as successful initiatives by students, perhaps Mr Suwan should be put in the same category, other methods of giving a message were flannelgraphs for compost making and puppets for the same purpose. The Thai ways of campaigning were much more effective, we thought, and they took to puppets very readily. Slides need more justification. Someone discovered that an unlimited number of projectors were available free and it seemed a pity not to accept the offer. We had to run a training course in the use of slide projectors but I fear that no more sets of slides related to community education were likely to have been circulated.

Going back to the village Newspapers, they were both a project in their own right by providing an essential part of a literacy campaign and at the same time another way of boosting the support for all the other projects. It is true that only a minority of people were able to read and an even smaller minority of the population were able to write, but they would be influential people who could give the most help in carrying out projects and in winning support for them. I think they suffered from the over-helpful education officer. I was speaking to a very large meeting of head teachers about how to find enough writers and readers by making the writing and pictures as interesting as possible, for example parents like to read the work of their children. I wanted to make the activity voluntary on the part of the head teachers so as to avoid dull news bringing the project into disrepute, but the official made it compulsory and I could not get round a huge area to check what was happening. Journalism is not everyone's skill.

Finally the best project was planned in the absence of the three expatriates at a committee in Bangkok. We joked that we were not needed any more. It was decided by our counterparts that each year each school should select and present a model house with garden, compost heap and toilet where children could come and learn each week alongside the house owner. This gave the chance to make reading, writing, and arithmetic more closely related to practical things in which they had a strong personal interest. According to our counterparts when the children were tested at the end of the first year, their performance in the three R's was improved despite giving less time to formal classroom work. It also helped draw the attention of adults as well as children to the value of improvements in the villages; and very conveniently involved girls equally with boys.

When sleeping in one of the villages, I was woken one morning by a man who invited me to his house in order to suggest further improvements he might make. It was a beautiful house and so well equipped even with fruit trees in the garden, tools on the wall and playthings for the children that I could think of nothing to suggest. I do not know whether he was pleased or disappointed! It was easy to praise what he had done. In some villages there were long waiting lists for house owners who wished to accept the adoption offer and sometimes more than one house at a time had to be adopted. It was more difficult to be fair between rich and poor. In one place the house chosen already had an expensive corrugated iron roof, but we were very far from wishing this to be copied by people who lacked money and we doubted whether the extra protection in the rainy season compensated for the extra heat during the hot season. I wanted to know if a leaking roof was a common problem and whether it was possible or desirable to have either a thatch on top of the iron sheets or vice-versa. In any case, the 'houses were getting better.' The Ban praprung (the house that is getting better) as they were modestly called in Thai, were an enormous success. Villages became places where people were pleased or even proud to live in and thus were able to tempt the men back home from the slums of Bangkok to where they had gone to seek work. Bad harvests had split families in this way and sometimes caused old people and invalids to be left behind, without anyone to care for them. With help from other people I had written a short story about one such family in order to have a text for teaching English.

The opportunity to teach about the UN and UNESCO, as was noted for the Philippines, was reinforced in Thailand. Again United Nations Day was taken much more seriously than it is in Europe. It fell to me to speak to the huge meeting of TURTEP students. I pointed out the value of international law and the importance of strengthening support for it. With TUFEC close by it was easy to refer to the individuals sent by the Food and Agriculture Organisation, the World Health Organisation and the International Labour Office. Real people and real projects seem much more distant in England and I closed my speech with a ringing call to uphold the new institutions. I was not expecting nor prepared for the questions that followed. 'Why was the Peoples Republic of China refused admission?' 'How much longer would the seat at the UN be held by Taiwan and the real China denied its rightful place?' 'Don't the United Nations and the United States begin with the same word and isn't the UN really a United States institution for fighting communism?' I replied 'no on the contrary part of my salary was paid by the Soviet Union and the UN was genuinely international', but I was on difficult ground when I was asked how long it would be before China became a member. I never knew how prevalent the feelings against the United States were among the audience. Meanwhile the United States was trying to win the support of the students by paying for all the new buildings the college required. The USA, which is the home of public relations and advertising, seemed to be slipping. I wondered what the reason might be. It was not until many years later that the US air force took over the grass airport at Ubon to use it for bombing both Vietnam and Cambodia. My friends wrote to discourage us from returning to Ubon for fear it would break our hearts.

Working so as to give UNESCO a good name, thanks to our effective counterparts in Thailand, proved to be easy. I discovered how much the work in international teams revealed both opportunities and difficulties in working closely with people from different cultures. Sitting behind a very clear empty desk may mean that the person knows how to keep on top of the administration tasks allotted to his post, or it may mean that the person believes administration is a sinecure. Obligations to share living expenses with relatives vary a great deal from one culture to another. It would be difficult for the extended family of a UN official left behind in a third world country, to fully understand the enormous expense their relative would have to pay for rented accommodation in Paris. The thought that an international organisation such as UNESCO is an ideal, worthy to receive loyal service, may be rare but is extremely valuable.

A very different aspect of teamwork is that differences in dress and diet have to be appreciated, and not allowed to grate. It is not for nothing that the briefing of the UN officials includes a section on etiquette. This cropped up in a conversation with an English friend who happened to be holding the important post of chief administrator in Tehran for the whole of the UN technical assistance programmes in Iran at the time I was there. I never discovered whether he raised the matter because he felt I was living too simply. Partly because I was wishing to keep in touch with the Iranian officials with whom I worked, I chose fairly cheap lodgings in preference to a small hotel. At any rate my friend spoke at length about his own problem in being expected to live like the ambassador of a major state if he hoped to be taken seriously, by the Iranian government officials as the administrative head of the United Nations agencies living in Tehran. Where understanding of people's importance is always being assessed in the absence of a common language, it is very tempting to fall back on trappings of power, such as the size of the car or the number of servants to indicate how much of a hearing one must be given. This may lead to misunderstandings back home in a more egalitarian state. I may be a Gandhian by disposition but I learned to avoid judging my colleagues in this respect.

One of the troubles of living with the trappings of power, even though the power is very moderate, is that it quickly goes to the head even among those least likely to be corrupted. I noticed it in myself but I never noticed it in Conrad Opper, even though he had started his career in the colonial services in what was at the time Rhodesia. In Thailand he was greatly appreciated for his gentleness and was very content. In Tehran, where Conrad Opper was head of the UNESCO Mission, I fear that his gentleness was taken for feebleness and he was so unhappy that I fear he was 'walked over.' The day after I arrived there to join him, he was very happy to receive an invitation to move on to New York to serve as UNESCO's liaison officer at the head office of UNICEF, the UN's International Children's Emergency Fund.

CHAPTER 11

UNESCO – Iran 1963 to 1965

THE PHILIPPINES COULD be described as the most western-ised of the countries in South East Asia, and Thailand on the other hand, the least westernised, never having been colonised by a European country. Iran had completely different lessons to teach about development. The Shah was introducing reforms fast. Votes for women, no more veils, at least when attending any official func-tion, a 'White Revolution of Land Reform,' a new literacy campaign and so on. A student leader complained to me that 'He is stealing our programme from us.' The Shah, however, kept a plane in his garden, fearing it was possible that he might have to escape in a hurry, or so the rumour went. Working in such an unstable coun-try made it a new experience, as any long-term planning is not taken seriously. The coups of Thailand seemed very gentle compared with the mysterious threats in Iran. There is a well-known saying 'He knows not England who only England knows' and I would add that 'He knows not development who knows development in only one developing country.' Fortunately, I like surprises and Iran was full of them. Once on an Indian train, after my time in Iran, I was asked by a fellow traveller, one of two bank officials going to take a course:

'Would you mind if I asked you a personal question?'

'No, of course not.' I replied with some hesitation.

'Do you ever feel embarrassed, coming here, as you do, from the ex-imperialist country?'

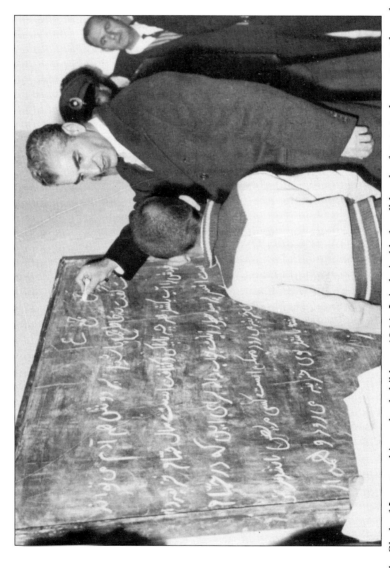

The Shah of Iran teaching school children, 1964. It is desirable for all heads of state to demonstrate the value of education. For example: in the UK, the prime minister might hold a class in good citizenship.

'Yes, of course I do.' I replied hastily. 'But not so much as you might think, because my family has been anti-imperialist for generations.'

It is a pity that he laughed without pursuing the matter or I would have told him about my father's claim that Barclays Dominion, Colonial and Overseas, was training the future Civil Services of independent Africa. Additionally, I might have mentioned John Bright's gibe that the British Empire was a gigantic system of out-door relief for the less capable members of the British aristocracy.

His question was, however, much more relevant to Iran than might be supposed. In that country on several occasions when looking for the Teacher Training College we made our way to the largest building in the provincial capital and found that it had at one time been the British Consulate.

'Whatever made them need such a huge building?' I asked.

'That was when the British ruled the country,' he replied.

'But Iran was never part of the Empire.'

'That may be, but anyone who put his foot wrong, tended to disappear.'

In this way I gradually learned some of the drawbacks of being English. It may affect British UN civil servants and would create difficulties for British mediators and such Non-Governmental Organisations as Oxfam. I realised that the same applies to Afghanistan. A.E. Housman's sad poems of soldiers dying overseas were, perhaps, sadder than he realised, sad for the soldiers certainly but also for their opponents. 'And there with the rest are the lads that will never be old.'[36]

That was the first surprise. Another surprise was the astonishing beauty of spring when the fruit trees blossom appears in all its glory with a background of snow-capped mountains. The comparable miniature paintings are true to life, even including the bright but narrow bands of flowers edging the tiny watercourses. I had been introduced to the glories of the famous Persian miniature painting as a boy, so when visiting a museum during my work in Tehran and finding a painter at work, I asked to see his brush. Yes, it did seem to be a single hair. How long was he taking to complete one picture? Yes, it was a whole year! It was to form the cover of a photograph album, a gift to be made by the Shah. A year may seem a long time but when I take into account the occasional lifetime sentence digging Qanats, the deep, wide, underground channels carrying water from the edge of the mountains out towards the desert, it seems short.

The beauty of Iran is summed up for many by the mosques, but for me it is best summed up by the carpets, gardens, and poems, which, in my mind all belong together. Carpets are used for all sorts of purposes such as decorating the exterior of houses at festivals. The landlords garden in each village seemed to be open to the public in his absence, so you could drive into the country, choose a garden, spread your Persian carpet and compose poetry, and the colours in each enhanced one another beautifully. Poetry is a main feature of Iranian culture. My counterpart said one day 'I want you to meet General so and so, a very great poet.' On another occasion I said to my landlord Mr Mirseyedi, 'I've been told that in this country people play poetry games.' Oh yes he replied and started playing against the driver, capping each line of poetry with a line which began with the same letter as the one at the end of the previous line supplied by the driver. After some time capping each other's lines, the driver won. Needless to say such people carry hundreds of lines in their heads, which they have learned by heart at some stage in their life.

Perhaps it is due to this passion for poetry that the quality of conversation was so very rich. I used to say that there is more good conversation per square mile in Tehran, than in the other towns where I had lived: London, Paris, Oxford, or Birmingham. Television may have had quite a lot to do with this lack of richness in conversation in western countries. In Iran this conversational atmosphere may be due in part to the presence of many servants in the homes, and you should bear in mind that even poor illiterate Iranians have dictated and published books of poems. I brought such a book home as a curiosity.

Good conversation may arise partly from the importance attached to hospitality. There is a story of an American visiting Iran, he was a lover of horses, he found a very special steed that he wanted to buy and he offered almost any sum of money for this horse. Unfortunately he could not persuade the owner to part with the much-loved animal. When he got home he was complaining about his failure, and his Iranian host said, 'Maybe I should not be telling you this but it is a custom to give a guest anything he wants before a meal begins.' So the crafty American arranged to get an invitation to the home where he had failed previously, and then brought the conversation around to the horse, wondering whether the host might have changed his mind. His tribal host held up his hands in horror explaining that there was no longer any question of this because, having no other meat to offer, he had sacrificed the horse. The horse was on the table before his eyes. It was explained that there had been nothing else to offer to him the honoured guest.

It seemed to me very important to learn about the aggressive nature of the Iranian way of life and promote discussion about its similarities and differences from the way of life in England. It seemed best to delay publishing it lest it upset anyone in Tehran. I later published the article under the title 'Why Iran Erupts' and based it on the theme that the climate and diet should be taken into account when looking at these differences and similarities in ways of living. See Appendix 4

Having set the scene in which my work was to be done, I cannot do better than describe the preparation during the first year, for my teaching during the second year. It included travelling to see how teachers were being trained, the variety of villages and village problems and learning the attitudes to education among villagers as well as the civil service. For some pages based on my diary see Appendix 5.

At that time I was busy completing a small volume to be published by Gollancz, *Men Against War*,[37] which was successful in reaching three editions. I had started writing it in 1958 and by immersing myself in one after another of these great men's lives, it was possible to take six or seven years to complete the task. How was it possible to choose among the large number of the potential heroes of peace? One of my cynical colleagues in Thailand proposed Napoleon for having fought the most wars and therefore obliged to make peace most often. The selection proved to be highly complicated. Eventually each person was chosen for their distinctive contribution to peace, and their interesting lives, their geographical spread, but also for their attractiveness to the expected readership.

No doubt someone else would produce a completely different list with the exception of Gandhi. No doubt I chose them because I had special information about all except Asoka. Gandhi was known to many of my friends, particularly Jan Smuts. John Bright was my great grandfather. Tolstoy was a close friend of Ruth's grandfather, from whom photographs and letters were handed down. William Penn was buried where we were married. Dag Hammarskjöld I met in 1937 when a member of a Fabian party producing a book in Sweden. Ceresole was the founder of the Work-camp Movement, but known to few.

This list looks much more political than it might be made today. It includes no educationalist, no psychologist, no peace researcher, no film director, and no poet. This may be because such people lead lives which seldom make a story. It's criteria look too much like those of the people who award the Carnegie Peace Prize. Here are the thoughts behind my choice.

Asoka the successful military commander who nevertheless was struck by the horrors of war and ended them.

Penn who set an example of treating a minority fairly.

Bright who promoted peace by the sheer power of his oratory.

Tolstoy whose novels ended the glory of war.

Gandhi whose non-violence made him most people's first choice.

Smuts having shaped the League of Nations lived to open the UN's first conference at San Francisco.

Hammarskjöld the inspired administrator of the UN.

Ceresole whose work-camps started the process of reconciliation, after the First World War.

As this writing finished I took on at Roger Wilson's request, the manuscript that he and Waclaw Micuta had begun, a pamphlet to help UN officials working in cultures other than their own. The first job to undertake was to seek the help of the Resident

Representative of the UN's Technical Assistance Board. This man's work, involved co-ordinating the services of all the UN's agencies from the large World Health Organisation (WHO), and Food and Agricultural Organisation (FAO), to the much smaller Drug Control Unit. The Resident Representative turned out to have attended the Dragon School and so may have been extra keen to help me to identify the UN officials based in Teheran, who might have useful anecdotes illustrating the mistakes easily made when working in unfamiliar cultures.

There was someone who told me the well-known story of the picture of a magnified mosquito. It looked large enough to terrify the bravest people. However, when pressed to take part in an anti-mosquito campaign the audience was unwilling to take part. Someone explained 'We don't have mosquitos that size.' I spoke with a colleague who had arranged to set drug smugglers free if they would take part in anti-drug films. It was difficult to get much support when even the Deputy Minister of Education complained that his father took opium every night and had lived to a ripe old age. In the end we decided to avoid local examples and placed at the beginning of the introduction this passage:

There is an oriental story of a monkey and a fish, which were caught in a great flood. The monkey sprang to safety in a tree. Looking down (as the water rose), he saw the fish swimming hard, head on to the current. At considerable risk, he moved out along a branch and swung down to scoop the fish out of the flood. Great was his disappointment when he found that the fish was not pleased to receive this technical assistance.

Aid needs to be appropriate to the needs of the recipient. Sometimes the wrong help is worse than no help at all. Whether we are dealing with technical assistance or conflict management, we often have difficulties in understanding the points of view of both sides and westerners need to know what Gandhi said when asked what he thought of western civilisation. 'It sounds like a good idea' he replied.

By the time Roger Wilson had contributed from his deep wisdom and Waclaw Micuta from his boundless enthusiasm, I had little to do other than editing, as Waclaw said he could never be sure of his English. My role proved to be to write a concluding section and choose some quotations as section headings. I think in this example of good cooperation we were all pleased at least with what the others had done. In particular Waclaw liked my headings such as Aristotle's, which I have already quoted, 'How shall I learn, unless it be from my friend?' and Mary P. Follett's 'Like electrical engineers, we must set friction to work for us,' a maxim or apothegm appreciated by peace-makers.

The thirty-page pamphlet was printed by the UNDP in New York under the title 'Briefing of International Consultants' in several languages and used for some years, and much of what it contains is relevant to others going on business to the tropics. I write 'business' recollecting that we used to confront ourselves with the story of two salesmen for two shoe manufacturers, who had studied the market opportunities in a West African country and had met in a hotel. One grumbled 'Most people do not wear shoes. I've wired home to say I'm coming home tomorrow.' That's odd replied his new friend 'I've wired home to say 'Most people here go barefoot, send all the shoes you can.' That is a thought provoking version of the stories about optimists and pessimists.

There is the old story about the two frogs which fell into a pail of creamy milk they found no way out, one of them gave up and drowned, the other kept on swimming round and round until it could leap to safety from a pat of butter. These stories are useful for anyone on a peace platform, because there are often some members of the audience who still believe that there will always be wars, which they attribute to human nature, despite the Seville Statement on Violence sponsored by UNESCO. It is of course true that there have always been wars, but the situation has changed as weapons have become more dangerous. There are still 400 farms in Britain banned from carrying livestock as a result of the Chernobyl explosion, though the explosion was very small compared with what nuclear bombs could produce.

During my first year in Iran I acquainted myself with the good and bad features of the system of teacher training. I sometimes wondered whether I was doing what was needed, and what was wanted by the officials of the Ministry of Education, who would be continuing my work after I left. I had failed to make such warm friendships as I had experienced in Thailand, and yet they responded so eagerly to my harsh comments on the teaching methods and my description of the value of extra-curricular activities that it was decided to put extra-curricular activities into the curriculum! I enjoyed the irony of the logic but wondered whether the leisure activities would become formal like other school subjects.

Turning over my papers this year (2001) it seems that I wrote countless reports and memos for officials, sometimes at their request and sometimes on my own initiative. The language problem for this was considerable, because the second language for older men was often French, and yet I was never asked to get one of my colleagues to translate. On top of that it is difficult to work thoroughly when a regime is not secure and it is probable that one is going to be replaced. I think it was at this time that the UN's Technical Assistance Programme was threatened with a major cut in resources, putting our posts at risk, and we were flattered when the receiving states got together and decided they would finance technical assistance themselves. Morale rose markedly! The relationship between local and expatriate officials needs to be managed very carefully because it often appeared that we were paid much more than our counterparts for doing the same work. The penalty of leaving a family behind is often overlooked, as is the difficulty of working in different circumstances. I remember the acute homesickness I experienced at Karaj. I tried treating it with such lines as:

> Oh tarnish late on Wenlock Edge,
> Gold that I never see;
> Lie long, high snowdrifts in the hedge
> That will not shower on me.
>
> A.E. Housman *A Shropshire Lad*

But the medicine was counterproductive as was Gerard Manley Hopkins' *Inversnaid;* the favourite poem of Ruth, containing those words, later to be used at her memorial service:

> What would the world be once bereft
> Of wet and of wildness?

I decided to learn the whole poem by heart when I spent half the week at Karaj.

The new work at Karaj arose through the success of men like Mr Azmoun which was described in an article in the Times Educational Supplement in March 1965. The Ministry and Mr de Clerk, chief of UNESCO Mission, made plans for training the best of the first group of the Literacy Corps, or the Army of Knowledge as they were known. They needed extra skills to help their successors. It is clear from the description of Mr Azmoun's work, who was one of this first group, that they had many skills to acquire. First they had to teach the ordinary reading, writing and arithmetic, made easier by the enormous eagerness of the children to learn and the strong backing up by the parents. They had to add to these the knack of relating these to the village work they undertook by reading and writing about agricultural work and animal husbandry which were often rather new fields for the young men who had grown up in towns and who had tended to despise peasant life. Then they had gradually to acquaint themselves with the needs of the village so that the schools could become the centres of sustainable village development. For this it was necessary for me to learn something about land ownership in Iran. The landlords varied more than might be expected, there were some very wealthy, like the one who admitted that his estate was about as large as Switzerland, some younger and irresponsible like the father of one of my friends who lost a village one evening by gambling at cards. According to the villagers most of the villages were the sole property of relatively poor men who pressed them harshly for their rents. A few might be described as reforming landlords, inclined to follow the example of the Shah, by selling them cheaply to the families who worked them. My counterpart and I visited a few of them to explain what was going on at their schools and solicit their interest and help in the improvements in the village.

One village reminded me of Glastonbury and Street, where for a long time no agreement could be reached about the site for the new school building. I made a prophet's speech about UNESCO's interest in encouraging cooperation and the many considerations to keep in mind when locating a school. In an extreme case they might benefit from employing an outsider to decide for them after hearing the two sides of the case. Schools should welcome opportunities to demonstrate conflict management. I had rather a stony reception that day, but blamed myself for lack of experience. It is hard to lighten the atmosphere when working through an interpreter and trying to raise a laugh.

In each village a survey was made with a view to finding out the improvements most desired. For the most part both students and villagers could not imagine their villages being different from how they had always been. One student came to me and spoke with indignation, 'There have been no changes here' he began, 'the trees are the same, the endless mud is always the same, the houses made of mud bricks are always the same. I have nothing to write.' He added fiercely. Knowing that he was speaking for many others whose English was less fluent, and realising that I had not explained their assignment sufficiently well, I replied 'Where is the headman's house? Let's go and ask him.' Soon we were sitting on the ground in the headman's house listening to his replies to the questions I asked through an interpreter. I started gently:

Are the clothes and shoes you are wearing different from what your father or grandfather wore?

Do you eat any food that they did not have?

Who do you think might have been the first person in the village to eat that?

(The innovators are the potential allies of the educators who are necessarily concerned with social change.)

What changes in transport have there been in your time?

How long has the school been going?

Conversation sprang up about the number of people who could read, about what had been learned by going on pilgrimages to Mecca and to places nearer home such as Qom. After this session, the student came to me again and his eyes were alight: 'I see what you mean now' he exclaimed with delight. 'I am going to write a book about my village.' Another student said that he liked what he called learning by asking questions. 'It is a good way. Although it is difficult, I will bring up my sons that way.' Memorising text-books is very common in developing countries and the system of examination tends to perpetuate it and produce the well known problems of very conservative administration, of uncreative teachers and the marginalizing of poets and artists.

187

Sometimes the work took unexpected forms. Waclaw Micuta sent me a solar cooker to test. It was shaped like an umbrella upside down. In place of a handle there was a container to hold the cooking pot on which the circular strips of wood covered in foil were focussed. It cost almost nothing to run but it was rejected partly because it produced no light in the evening, and also because paraffin was extremely cheap due to the fact that Iran was an oil producing country. Hay-box cooking was unknown at this time in Iran. I hope it will be remembered when the oil supply begins to dwindle. I was very impressed by the extraordinary amount of heat produced from this solar cooker, and wrote to my friend Denis Healey, when he was Chancellor of the British Exchequer, to ask that all 'council' houses with south facing roofs should be fitted with solar panels. All I got in reply was a civil servant's answer. Democratic politicians have difficulty in looking ahead so as to avoid crises occurring without warning.

Measuring the amount of water coming into villages seemed so important in preventing water disputes that I sought the help of a Dutchman working for the UN. When I thanked him he answered: 'My work is my play, my play is my work.' Lucky man, I thought, one could wish for this for everyone. Measuring the water was also an enviable task. It involved working out the volume of water between two points and then floating objects down the stream to find out how fast the volume of water was passing. A neat little formula was provided.

My help was sought by a UN architect for the design of schools in Iran; I told him about the mistake of a British architect who had been designing school buildings in New Zealand. When the day came for an official opening someone asked 'Why does it face the south?' The architect was about to reply 'To catch the warmth of the sun,' when he realised that he had not allowed for the change of hemisphere. I went on to explain how in the Philippines and Thailand schools were designed to keep the direct sunlight out, either with windowpanes of oyster shells or by building long schools from east to west, with windows facing north or south.

My own calculation is that about two new words are used in any good lesson, not counting areas where the home language is different from the schools. Also the pronunciation of new words

This class demonstrates the potential of alternative energy, with a $4 solar cooker.

has to be heard distinctly so that the children can learn their meaning effectively and use them themselves. This makes it vitally important that the acoustics of the building, including the interference of noise from one class by another, are made clear to architects when they are working on such projects. This can be avoided by thicker partitioning walls, by acoustic tiles, or by situating classrooms appropriately to avoid traffic for example. Acoustics is for architects a relatively new study. Not long ago I went to see a new building in England where a special room was equipped for music. But it's acoustics were so bad that it had to be converted into a library. This process of careful planning and the rethinking of the basic rules, that an architect must go through, especially when working in new cultures and new climates, is exactly what peace makers need to adopt as they search for solutions to the ever increasing number of different circumstances they find themselves up against. Acoustics have, I believe, a relevance to cultures of peace, but it is merely guess work that noise creates stress, which in turn creates aggression. Who ever heard of a violent garden-city or garden-suburb?

In the final month of my stay in Iran a large international conference on literacy was held in Teheran, and so I was invited to write about the village work of these future school supervisors, which they performed on a one-day weekly plan during their Karaj course. The resulting thirty-three-page brochure or report was published by the Organisation for Teacher Training and Research and was given to those who attended the conference. If I were writing it again, I would make much clearer the ways in which the reading and writing of the children could be related to the village work; thus explaining the value of reading and writing. At this time seventy percent of the population in Iran could neither read nor write. Most of them wished to remove the stigma but had little idea how it could help them in dealing with shopkeepers and other traders. The report is called 'Village Work At Karaj – A Report of the Work of two-hundred Future Supervisors of the Education Corps in Twenty Villages. February – August 1965.'

In addition to village development this pamphlet stressed the importance of children, their friendships, their needs and their families in planning their education but it was too late in my two years to do any follow-up. One very interesting UNESCO conference had been held in the previous year in which I had a minor part. Believing on the basis of past experience that literacy itself is of little value unless there is a good supply of books, it was decided to hold a meeting for all those involved. Besides authors of children's books, illustrators, publishers, librarians, book-sellers, and teachers, in fact everyone except parents and children met to describe their roles and explain what they needed to perform their functions better. Having set up an exhibition of children's nonfiction books at the request of the Ministry of Education in London, I was fascinated. I would support a campaign to bring books to children, in a country, such as Iran, before they become used to television filling their spare time. It could avoid the dull sameness of knowledge and opinions, which the mass media and the national curriculum combine to produce.

Most of the expatriates working for UNESCO were highly specialised teachers working in a new technical college and the rest of us had little to do with them. Our smaller group included a scientist dealing with earthquakes, he was willing to listen to my proposal to send the bill for a major earthquake to Moscow. This had occurred just before my arrival, killing, or so it was claimed, twelve thousand people. I hazarded a guess that it was caused by the lowering of the Caspian Sea by several feet caused by otherwise excellent Soviet irrigation schemes. The Iranian houses are built with clay roofs, which are added to yearly, so that they become very heavy, and lethal when they fall down without warning.

Statistics such as the deaths from the earthquake are usually not believed by the local people, so no one was surprised when the literacy figures showed the number of new readers to be more than the total population of the country. To meet this need a specialist in statistics was appointed by UNESCO. I do not think he remained long. The trust in officials adhering to the truth is a very valuable part of social capital, and not to be lightly allowed to disappear.

If I were to be asked what it was like to work in Iran at the time, I would have to admit that it did not have the same warm quality of the work in Thailand, but there I was extremely lucky. The Iranians did not trust each other, they had no reason to trust expatriates any more. From time to time I annoyed them by refusing to order equipment with UNICEF funds until teachers colleges had permanent buildings. There were stories of equipment being piled high outdoors at the end of the academic year for anyone to plunder. Eventually the Chief of Mission took the matter into his own hands and gave way to the requests.

On the whole UNESCO was doing a good job in very difficult circumstances, and I was sorry when it was not given credit for my minor successes. If Mr Conrad Opper, who was sent to be the UNESCO-UNICEF liaison officer in New York when I arrived, had remained in his post, my work would have been much better. As it was, Mike Easterly of the US Peace Corps appointed himself as my right hand man, and made life very much easier for me. He was well trained in community or village development and in a short time had learned to speak the language. He was able to report what the students were saying about their course, comment on my projects usefully and on occasions interpret for me. The Peace Corps attracted a very gifted set of people. It was a great pity that it fell into disfavour, mainly, I suppose, because the CIA infiltrated it.

It is odd that the Peace Corps and the Literacy Corps or Army of Knowledge have similar names. Each name hints that armies are becoming redundant and are searching for new roles, but one is made up of military people extending their functions to serve their country in new ways, the other is made up of civilians moving in the opposite direction by accepting a degree of military discipline for the sake of international service and peace. The Peace Corps might have fared better if its aims had been more like those of Pierre Ceresole's work-camps and had included international friendship. After leaving UNESCO's employment in 1965 I maintained whatever contacts I could with the large office in Paris where we were welcomed before and after our service abroad.

Community Schools as described by me are revolutionary rather than reformist institutions. They identify social issues in need of attention and then consider how schools can help. It is hard to understand how peace can be established or the environment preserved without the help of schools. Since that time I have always worked this ethos into teacher training courses in order to make society flexible enough to face the dangers ahead. After Thailand

192

I gave my time to a countrywide tour of Britain arranged for me by the Council for Education in World Citizenship (CEWC). I sometimes provided questions for group discussion and one of these being 'What corresponds to hookworm in this country?' the answer presented by a pupil to one large meeting was 'What corresponds to hookworm in this country is apathy, but apathy is even worse because there is no medicine for it.'

UNESCO honoured me by inviting me to give a lecture there on Education for International Understanding. I felt that I was being asked to teach my grandmother to suck eggs, but was glad of the contact. We all start with certain assumptions, the question arises: How can children acquire wide rather than narrow points of view so that they are fit for international friendship. An Iranian schoolboy came to me bursting with indignation because his pen friend in London had written to him asking him whether there were telephones or television in Teheran. 'How do I reply to such a stupid question?' he asked. 'Ask him how many drive in banks, and drive in cinemas there are in London.' I replied.

A letter reached me from the editor of the UNESCO Courier, to enquire whether I was prepared to write on peasant life. I side-stepped that one by writing on proverbs as being the window into the peasant mind such as 'When God made time he made plenty of it.' Once I spent a long railway journey translating a booklet of farmer's proverbs into proverbs dealing with education. It proved to be a very thought-provoking exercise but it did not suit the Courier.

For a periodical on teaching methods published by UNESCO, however, I wrote a number of articles, one of them was on how to deal with making use of classroom walls, and another, on the journey to school, as a teaching aid. In many countries the shortage of books and teaching equipment is so very great that the teacher's voice is the main resource and even little variations count for much. There are so few pilot schools to point the way that dull classrooms are taken for granted or even valued as being free from distraction. In England, classroom windows only reached down to above head height for this very reason until the twentieth century, but then they usually had textbooks.

The principal sequel to my years with UNESCO was an invitation to attend its conference on 'Peace in the Minds of Men,' held in Côte d'Ivoire, at the invitation of the late President Houphouet-Boigny. This conference had all the trappings of grandeur to draw attention to its importance, making as it did a change of emphasis in UNESCO in regard to psychology and, culture in the sense of way of life as opposed to the Fine Arts. He had decided to move the capital from the busy port of Abidjan to the village where he was born. To make a beginning he had built the famous Roman Catholic Cathedral modelled on St. Paul's but twice the size, a large Technical College and the largest Peace Research and Conference Institute I have ever seen, where we met. These grandiose surroundings seemed to be in keeping with the task we had been given which appeared to be to link psychology with peace. For a country with a population size comparable with Portugal to have such an institute is indeed good news. This was peace by trumpet by a man who knew that way of thinking, but I could wish there were more rulers who provided for peace in this way. I fear he may have died before endowing the Institute so that it could bear its share of the work in peace research. I hope it is endowed as handsomely as it is built. By now, going to war is so dangerous that funds spent on non-violent defence should be as great as funds spent on conventional defence.

At the conference itself its importance was marked by the presence of two past Secretary-Generals in addition to the current Secretary General of UNESCO. Our attention was redirected from disarmament and conflict studies to the nature of violence and the culture of peace. The lead seemed to be taken by an American psychologist who persuaded us to sponsor the Seville Statement on Violence, which asserted that violence is not part of human nature but an acquired characteristic, and that human nature is sufficiently flexible to make peace a possibility. This was thoroughly debated and accepted, thanks to the leadership of David Adams, whom, incidentally I did not meet again until the Hague Conference more than ten years later in 2000. He then went on to set the stage for the Decade of the Culture of Peace 2000-2010, and now heads the Division for UNESCO, which deals with that particular decade.

I have mixed feelings about this. I would like to substitute the word 'Culture' with 'Way of Life,' because it has already been confused with the fine arts, music, dance, and drama; nor has there been any attempt to identify a culture of peace in any human group such as the Arapesh tribe, described by Margaret Mead, or such as Quakers. The Quakers are so mixed up with the values of an ordinary militarist society that they are not such clear examples as they used to be in the Victorian era. John Bright was the most widely know Quaker at the time and he coined the powerful phrase: 'Force is not a remedy,' but he conceded to his fellow MP's that force might be a necessary condition for applying a remedy when riots get out of hand.

My own interventions in the proceedings were to propose a new volume of *Men Against War* composed of biographies of suitable people whose names might be put forward by Ministers of Education. I wanted UNESCO to prick consciences of its member governments by asking them to send in suitable names from their own country or region. Despite writing several letters to a UNESCO official whose name I was given, nothing came of it. Abstract ideas such as the culture of peace are best taught to children with the help of biographies and they are needed to balance the influence of war heroes. It seemed to me that to have such an outcome from a big conference would balance the fears that the conference had no visible success.

Secondly I explained the need for a book for student teachers about child psychology. At present this subject is omitted from most developing countries' curricula and teachers often work as though individual differences among children are of no account. I miss Dr W.D. Wall, my tutor at Birmingham University for my M.Ed course. He eventually worked for UNESCO and set up an Institute for Child Study in Bangkok for South East Asia. I was encouraged to follow up these suggestions with a plan of action but the Finnish lady at UNESCO fell ill and I became busy with other projects.

There may be insufficient time; the nuclear bombs may fall too soon for establishing peace by protecting children from bullying parents and schoolfellows. It may be, that considering the nuclear risks that are run by the whole of humanity and the rest of the animal kingdom, the Campaign for Nuclear Disarmament and similar organisations provide the best hope for children.

It is hard to tell where to put one's energies but at the time I was convinced that there were two options ahead. One was in peace education for children and the other was total nuclear disarmament. Because, despite the fact we cannot change nuclear technology, now we already have it, if we continue to harbour nuclear weapons there will always be the risk of nuclear war. Out of these two options, peace research needs to be expanded, and nuclear technology needs to be brought to an end.

UNESCO, I thought was entrusted to coordinate and encourage peace research but the governments which controlled its policy always seemed to stop short of committing themselves to any effective action, as they did in the same way for peace education. Most of the substantial work was left to private individuals and Non-Governmental Organisations (NGO's). Enough was done, however, to raise the suspicions of right-wing politicians in the USA and in Britain sufficiently for them to succeed in then persuading their governments to resign from UNESCO. Carefully designed dinner parties were held first in the USA and then in London to gather editors of right-wing newspapers and radio programmes at which pressure was brought to bear. Though the wording of articles was ridiculously repetitious, the move was successful. For many years the absence of the two powers of Britain and the USA was maintained. They made it difficult for people like myself to keep our connections with the various departments in UNESCO.

For Governments it is wise to remember that war is like a lottery: when they lose, they and their peoples lose hope and self confidence; when they win they soon become corrupted by power and lose their friends. It is only the cement of international friendship, which can prevent the ultimate holocaust. In John Bright's time, he spoke about friendship as an aim of foreign policy. He also talked of the importance of personal friendships between politicians, but this seemed unlikely in his day, on account of the difficulties of travel. Now travel has become much easier and the League of Nations, followed by the United Nations have provided the magnificent premises in New York and Geneva, where formal meetings can easily be arranged and casual meetings occur spontaneously.

Even the language barrier has become much reduced with the common use of English as the international language of business.

This is one reason for my regretting Britain's long withdrawal from membership of UNESCO. The Non-Governmental Organisations, churches, universities, and learned societies failed to compensate for its benign influence. Few British people realise the full extent of the insularity of Britain. Quite apart from the belief of the extremists that 'British is best,' there are the British tourists who assume that even a package holiday automatically widens their understanding and justifies their laying down the law.

UNESCO, like some of the other UN agencies, has as its major function the gathering of information from all over the world, which is then digested and circulated in various forms of report. In this way scientists including social scientists, educationalists and those who deal with culture, many of them concerned with development or peace, obtain the raw material on which to base their work. I was glad to be able to take a small part in some of this work after I left Iran.

CHAPTER 12

Bristol University

THE RETURN FROM Iran in 1965 was very strange. Miss Browne, the Principal of Coventry Teachers College and Professor Roger Wilson of Bristol University, had traded me in my absence to undertake work for which I was particularly well suited. The government paid me to go to an interview designed to help more people to work abroad.

So Ruth with her usual valiance had bought an old house for us in Bristol in the former village of Westbury-on-Trym. It had been re-shaped in 1834 out of half of the Westbury Poor House. It had plenty of room for our large family but was frequently in need of attention. It had a fine view from the crest of a hill, of Blaise Woods and was a convenient hour's walk across the downs to the University.

I felt at the time that it must surely be easier to have fresh thoughts in a unique house than it is in a standard modern house and soon began writing my *Utopia: Bristol in 2020*.[38] I told my students that as their future pupils might be in mid-career fifty years later, their education should be adapted accordingly to include future studies. At last I was writing a book, I thought, with a popular appeal, which was sure to be published, but my friend, an author's agent, assured me that optimistic utopias were out of fashion and he could not deal with it. Now, more than thirty years later the manuscript still makes good reading, and I wonder now whether it is time to try again.

My new work at the University was to develop a curriculum for those children whose age group would soon be remaining for an

198

additional year at school, when the school leaving age would be raised to sixteen. Often they had developed a sense of failure at school and would be needing to experience some new activities, and new methods of teaching. The sense of failure would already have made them some of the most difficult youngsters to teach. To achieve this it had been agreed by the Institute of Education to set up a course for those teachers who had already made a success of teaching the disaffected early leavers, the most difficult section of the school population to manage. It was to be a full-time course for one term. Unfortunately they proved to be the hardest to replace even for a short term, due to the unwillingness of their pupils to accept anyone else. The schools with head-teachers of wide sympathies who understood that this might be an expensive loss in the short run, but a wise investment for those willing to look ahead, were far too few.

Critical head-teachers may have thought that John Lang and I may have been unskilled at this novel task, which included helping the students to learn from each other. By good fortune I had always relished paradoxes and paradoxical situations. Whether the two of us were sufficiently hesitant in putting forward our own ideas and sufficiently encouraging when our students put forward their own suggestions, I am not sure, but the final document which I produced from our discussions, is clearly coloured by my prejudices. It was intended that it should cover a part of the curriculum according to the circumstances in each school, especially in the interest of teachers for whom it would be a new experience.

The headings overlap, community education overlaps with citizenship, just as education for leisure may overlap with work experience. Each of them is based on the assumption that the pupils appreciate getting away from their desks and making contact with adults outside the school, and also on the principle that much is best learned by doing. There is no great significance in the order in which they are written. The forms of practical work may well determine in what order they are taken, may be one or two or even four at a time. Most of us thought that the new type of work points towards smaller classes and to linking it with deskwork and group work. It is my firm belief that the less able academically, require small classes comparable with the smaller classes for A-level, so

199

that they gain the benefits in social education, which may be derived from group work such as co-operation and leadership.

It is very interesting to note that the present government is spending heavily to find out the best way of reducing the number of children excluded from school. Funds are usually better spent on prevention rather than cure as the teachers employed in the work are already explaining. A stitch in time, before habits are formed, may well save nine, when a life of crime is already started. This is the main reason for justifying smaller classes and it has strong connections with peace work, as the biographies of Hitler and Mussolini show. I made a ringing appeal for smaller classes when, as a young teacher in 1938 I spoke in the National Youth Parliament of that year. Speaking from the lessons learned in five or six schools where I had been pupil or teacher, I claimed: 'If you wish to produce Nazis or Fascists, make the school classes so large that a severe discipline has to be enforced to maintain order. But if you wish to create democrats, capable of thinking for themselves, keep classes small.'

George Cadbury, despite the many original ideas incorporated in the 'Village' he founded, never considered the possibilities of community schools. He did however, accept the idea of community, and may well have discussed this with Joseph Rowntree when they were apprenticed together in the grocery shop in Pavement, York. What they said about town planning is not recorded. My grandfather George Gillett was the third apprentice at the time, but he died relatively young so there was no chance to voice such questions with him. One may reasonably guess that in building their villages in York and Birmingham they were influenced by people such as Robert Owen, and the Malcolmsons

Patriarchal philanthropy regarding building homes and schools was taken for granted during the nineteenth century. It was assumed that capitalism could, in the long run, solve the problems it created, that competition among the captains of industry might lead onto competition in social reform and that there was no need for the State to intervene. In the event, the corrupting power of wealth has prevailed as has been well expressed in both proverbs and poetry: It is a great pity that more wealthy people did not learn from George

Cadbury, and his brother Richard and others, how best to use their wealth.

> Art thou poor, yet hast thou golden slumbers:
> Oh sweet content!
> Art thou rich, yet ist thy mind perplexed?
> Oh punishment!
> Dost thou laugh to see how fools are vexed
> To add to golden numbers, golden numbers?
> O sweet content, O sweet, O sweet content!
> Thomas Dekker 1570-1632

Some kind of community living such as may be found in Bournville or York was provided for people before the coming of the motorcar. Cars have offered them the opportunity to express their preference for privacy, however risky their choice may be. In search of privacy they have moved to suburbs, if they can afford to do so, and many fail, in both their work community, and their home community to become active community members. Like cars that provide privacy during travel to work, supermarkets provide the privacy of the anonymous crowd while shopping. In addition television provides privacy during entertainment.

Selfishness enhanced by the dwindling size of families leads to a variety of social problems ranging from loneliness, mental ill-health, to crimes, alcoholism, drugs, and suicide. Neither does absolute privacy, that unnamed form of insanity, lead to the good life, and to some extent most people need some social roughage much as we need fibre in our diet.

Too many people take too much of these changes for granted. It happens slowly enough for it to be overlooked and the ultimate outcome is not clearly pictured. Sudden floods, earthquakes, and even starvation are more easily understood than social chaos or global warming. It is the task of schools to teach the lessons which cannot be learned by any other means, such as parents or television.

The fact is that as early as 1980 the number of households of two or a single person outnumbered all the rest for the first time in history. This might be welcomed as an indication of a high standard of life, or it might be regarded as a failure in social education.

Have English people become so selfish that they are unfit to share a house? Absolute privacy may lead to non-participation, non-living for those who have never discovered the joys of communal living and the friendship that ensues.

In this situation social education including community education could be used as a counterweight. The sooner such measures are introduced the more effective they will be. At present community education is so little understood, even their potential value in solving social problems, that few take them seriously. At Bristol University I found a good base for promoting these new ideas. The distinguished headmaster Cyril Poster, of the comprehensive school at Lawrence Weston was two miles away from the University. He was not only a person to whom the BBC would call on when they needed a spokesman for the Community School Movement, but he also found time to edit two books.[39] Some people argue airily that all that has to be done is to base schoolwork on the local culture, the local set of values and visions. Would this imply that even more children in the USA should carry firearms to check bullying and if so does this apply to nursery classes? Should girls in Iran be kept at home rather than go to school? In each case the answer would be 'Obviously not,' despite the local cultures.

There is an interesting difference between the USA and Britain in regard to defence against armed robbers. In the USA it appears to be reasonable for householders to keep a revolver at hand, in Britain it still feels quite normal to live without such dangerous protection, though in many ways the USA customs are spreading. I have to admit that I have to think hard when the question of arranged marriage is discussed. It seems at first as though respect for other people would lead clearly to a right to choose a partner, but, after a consideration of the proportions of marriages that break up, it may appear to be a valid point that parents being older have seen more of life and may perceive more clearly the factors which make for a good partner, than young people overwhelmed with falling in love.

Cyril Poster began with Community Education in industrialised countries and moved on a little later to the Third World. My experience was the other way around, beginning with the Philippine Community Schools and continuing in Britain. In John Rennie's remarkable introductory chapter to the first of Cyril Poster's books he writes: 'The first (Sc. Matter of faith) might be that the seeds of the solutions to a community's problems are contained within that community.' This means that we do not have to wait for others to solve our problems, though we may have to learn how to choose the right outside experts to guide us.

For me it was an inspiration to be put into posts where I might be regarded as a suitable outside expert, sensitive to the hope and needs of the people I had come to serve. In the Philippines I may have been too young and inexperienced to do much more than learn on the job. In Thailand all seemed to go extremely well and in each case my approval was greatly appreciated. This may point to the need to pay more attention to public relations so as to create an acceptance and a demand among teachers, politicians, and others for the changes we demonstrated. Nowadays with the spread of the radio, and the television it would be much easier. Children practicing any kind of community education are easy to catch on film.

As explained earlier in the previous chapter, Iran was a very different assignment, being a country torn by political conflict in a way, which associated the United Nations with the Shah. His regime was to come to an end with a coup after we had left. There was plenty of work to do for the Army of Knowledge but it had as much to do with the literacy campaign as with active village development. My enthusiasm led to my undertaking lecture tours, which were intended to benefit UNESCO in addition to community education. On my way home from the Philippines the New Education Fellowship arranged a tour for me in Australia. It is a country where radical ideas flourish and one of my hosts had just published *Nature's Second Sun*[40] about the effect of parental affection on children with behaviour difficulties at school. It was in Australia that I began adapting ideas about community education to Western, so-called Developed Countries. Western countries likewise are not free of severe problems. When I talk to my eldest daughter Jean about the evidence she speaks of them with fervour, and repeats the list made earlier of loneliness, mental ill-health, crimes, alcoholism, drugs and suicide and adds unhappiness, broken homes, depression, stress, apathy, lack of friends, and lack of roots.

Not only are millionaires, it seems, not happier than the poor, but the people of wealthy countries do not appear to be more contented than the inhabitants of poor countries. Especially when the latter benefit from both kinds of sunshine that is the warmth of the sun and warmth of parental affection.

After the two years in Thailand I returned via India, to Afghanistan, and the USSR. In Moscow I spoke in the Ministry of Education to a group of twenty-five. After being introduced I asked who would interpret for me. 'There is no need. We all understand English.' This astonished me, but I did what I was told. Much later I got a letter from one of the audience, asking whether we could write to each other about education in Britain and the USSR. She asked whether I could send, for example, the timetable of a typical grammar school and a typical Secondary Modern School. I doubt whether she believed my reply, because they varied so much, that it would have made her work much more difficult. In regard to the Secondary Modern, I sent her the story of a headmaster who had recently moved from another county: 'What is your policy for Secondary Modern Schools?' he asked 'To be different from all the other Secondary Modern Schools in the county,' replied the official. In other words, the head teacher must think for himself about the needs of the area as well as his own belief, based on his experience. The official would have made this reply because he considered that we teach well when we teach what we think is important. In the USSR teachers were not considered good enough to be left to decide what they should teach nor how they should teach it. The national curriculum, however, was frequently revised by requesting experimental schools to use and revise new books, so that the curriculum could be changed.

Russians are very human people, Vera soon knew and remembered details about our family. The correspondence lasted into the nineteen nineties, though in all those years we have never met. A colleague of hers brought us a book from the Moscow public library to read . It is always difficult to know how freely one can write to a totalitarian country without getting one's correspondent into trouble and having no more letters delivered. Once I asked the censor in Russia to let me know about just how freely I could write, but perhaps I should have enclosed a present for him, because I got no reply. On the other hand it is always desirable to have pen friendships modifying a Cold War to remind people that war propaganda is never true.

After reaching home I found I had made a big mistake. I had given up my post at Dudley Teachers College, thinking that this was what the Principal wanted. Indeed I could see that I would be tempted to respond again to UNESCO's pressing requests. I was pulled strongly by my family, both Ruth and the children and I was pulled in the other direction that pacifists ought to recognise their call-up papers in peacetime. Ruth's line on this was clear and strong. 'You shouldn't have had a large family if you want to work abroad. The trouble is, you like it.' So I thought that I was making it easy for the Principal to appoint my successor, it turned out that he thought that I should have returned to the college.

These were the circumstances, which provided the opportunity to travel to schools in England, Scotland, and Wales; it was a lecture tour arranged by the Council for Education in World Citizenship. I learned the opportunities and difficulties of teaching world citizenship, as the national curriculum now requires. I hope some of the audiences learned to respect the work of the UN in technical assistance, of UNESCO's work in school and also some sympathy for those coping with Third World issues. An angry teacher in Wolverhampton asked whether I really could persuade myself that Britain had anything to learn from the Third World. I replied that the principle of using schools to help us to face new problems was certainly something that we could learn from the Philippines, but I could answer much more convincingly today. We have got to learn how we can live better on less, as the earth's resources become exhausted. The most devoted internationalists I met were at a school north of Swansea, and a very wise sixth-former in Glasgow.

At this time I was thinking hard about how to persuade teachers in England to establish schools different but similar to those, which had been created in Thailand. In both countries there was opposition to them from ambitious parents who wished their children to be prepared for professional work obtained by success in exams. In Thailand, village schools, which were remote from Secondary Schools were the most willing to participate. In Britain Eric Midwinter, backed by the Gulbenkian Trust was doing well

205

in a part of Liverpool where ambitious parents were few. In other places the larger Comprehensive Schools had classes of older children with no academic success to justify concentrating on academic subjects, who were free to explore practical activities such as those involved in community education. For them it is essential to have small classes for group or even individual work to succeed. Once at the beginning of the war, I had been given a class of mixed ages and abilities and I had used the methods of the Dalton Plan, whereby each pupil proposes a plan of work for the week, containing full references to pages of their textbook, which they were intending to cover. I had noticed what a stimulating experience it is for children to take such a responsibility but also that it sets a limit to the number of children I could supervise.

It became clear to me and I hope to my colleague Mr Lang and many of the middle-aged teachers on our course that one option for the curriculum of the hitherto early leavers should be community education. I used to lie awake at night wondering how to introduce this new idea into British schools. I had the possibility of winning the support of the Rowntree Charitable Trust. If I made the case out, they could have offered a salary for one extra teacher for a pilot school for as many of the Local Education Authority areas as they were willing to help. In a sense every Community School is like the Trust, each had to weigh up social needs and throw their weight where it is likely to be most effective, taking into consideration the nature of the need and the obvious difficulties in that this Trust is confined to finance, and the school, to unskilled labour of its children.

The recent additions to the National Curriculum make this similarity between the aims of grant-making trusts and schools much clearer. It will be examined in a subsequent chapter; here it suffices to draw attention to the desirability of both acquainting themselves with the development of campaigning as a new profession, which deals with the changing of attitudes.

It happened accidentally that, when creating a social attitude test for my thesis for an M.Ed in educational psychology (1952), I found in trying out the tests, the figures suggested that children's social attitudes are derived from their parents and homes much more than from their schools. It appeared to make little difference whether the school specialised in group-work or whether the children heard little homilies on right and wrong each morning. Group work carefully coached is widely expected to influence social behaviour on the grounds that it accords with the principle of learning by doing. I must admit to being biased in its favour and this makes it all the more remarkable, the tendency among researchers being to find what they hope for, and what they expect to find. I wish someone would follow up my work but unfortunately Professor Schonell, who initiated it, went back home to Queensland. He hoped I would find that there was a marked difference between one school and another according to the method they used, however, this did not prove to be the case.

The sort of questions a campaigner should ask might be: What are the target audiences? Teachers? Politicians? Journalists? Or more specific groups such as lawyers, or more general such as parents? Will a general appeal do for a periodical or is it worth rewriting leaflets, books, and articles for smaller groups? Are we clear that we have chosen the right message? Have we won the active support of people whose opinions will be respected by members of the target audiences? In addition to support, what information, such as statistics, will impress? Can we find a better name for our organisation?

I recall a very long wait before the name 'Saferworld' was found by that very successful think-tank. Many good slogans are related to names; so it is as well to consider the two together. Commercial advertisers have made us familiar with the value of brand names, but the point has not been taken by many charitable organisations. Public relations consultants are too expensive for all but the largest charities, but whether such charities as Oxfam and the National Trust have grown large because they employ experts, or they are large and so they can afford to employ experts, it is hard to say. They certainly have much to teach smaller bodies.

There are many lessons to be learned by the many small peace and environmental organisations. They are dealing with a future that appears to be more remote than conventional medical charities, so they are less attractive to donors, to judge by their applications for funding they could well begin by looking at the books on campaigning and fund raising so that, when they write their letters of application to grant-making trusts, they avoid major mistakes.

Campaigning needs to include some evaluation of apparent successes and failures, and can usefully be added to the often unattractive agendas of meetings of the executive committee. I have become a great believer in building on previous success, whether I am fund-raising or leading from the chair. It is not possible to be an effective democrat unless there is informed discussion to guide the activists who are prepared to give time to bring about changes in which they believe. Unless activists start young as in Community Schools, they are likely to become the apathetic non-voters, the political enemies of democracy.

Education for Leisure

The second part of the curriculum, which was developed with the help of the teachers on the University Course, was based on the desirability of preparing young people for making good use of their spare time. Spare time arises in various circumstances. It may take the form of unemployment. At that time among the school leavers it was exceptionally high and increasing so there was ample justification both for education for leisure and for vocational education to make them more attractive to employers.

There used to exist a belief that frustration leads inevitably to aggression, and that militarism flourishes on very strict discipline: this is worth bearing in mind. The exact ways in which it comes about have been questioned, because it depends on what is thought to be reasonable behaviour at the time. The human race is very adaptable but there are limits. It was our experience that even a large family gets restless when kept in by rain all day. Restless but never bored, boredom is a disease all on its own, the consequence of poor education and parenting.

Imagination or creativeness is a very important though elusive quality. A person who continues doing something repetitively is said to lack imagination; perhaps the clearest way to describe it is to quote a poet and a scientist writing on the same subject, for example the dictionary states that a lark is a member of genus

Promoting valuable leisure activities, in anticipation of a local economic downturn, at Strode School in Street. This pigsty was at the home of a local smallholder.

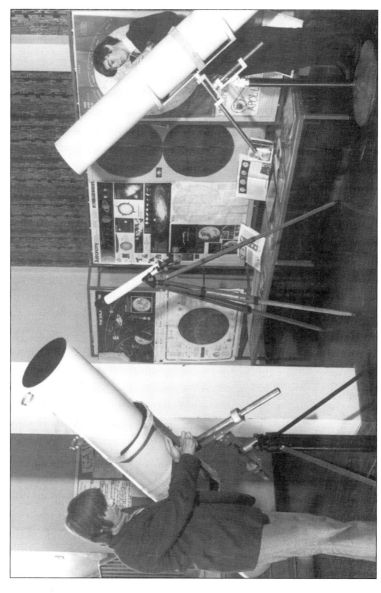

Two of the most enterprising boys made telescopes with the help of Strode School. They took the initiative, and enlisted a local astronomical photographer to assist them.

Alaudidae. Whereas the poet P.B. Shelley concluded his famous poem 'To a Skylark' with:

> Teach me half the gladness
> That thy brain must know,
> Such harmonious madness
> From my lips would flow,
> The world should listen then, as I am
>   listening now.

Some people, when they are losing their capacity for inspiration, become so desperate that they take heroin or similar drugs in the hope of recapturing it. The time may come when harmless drugs are available, but there are certainly none today and I would not take the risk. I wrote in my own unpublished *Utopia* that in the future when school children came to a creative class in school such as art or craft or poetry or other creative writing they would be issued with the appropriate pills. I did not continue to find out how much creativeness a school could contain. Some art-school students aim at being so creative and unconventional that they cannot fit in with institutions at all. It seems best at present to rely on special times of day or night to enjoy the unquestionable pleasures of being creative, playing with words, with sounds, with colours, and with ideas. Just as there are special times of day, there are special times of life when play comes to the fore, in childhood, and in Spring for example. The play of animals is mainly when they are young, I remember how the orphaned lion cub at Doornkloof, which had lost its mother and sister used me in their place as a playmate. Huizinga, when he wrote his, at that time, definitive work *Homo Ludens*,[41] on human play, had not the opportunity to benefit from the recent work of the ethologists.

Play is often full of imagination and creativeness. It is sometimes possible for artists and other creative people to learn to see the world with the fresh eyes of children, by watching them and listening to what they have to say. As I write, the BBC has held a discussion as to whether it would be possible for machines with artificial intelligence to be developed into machines with artificial imagination and even consciousness. It reminded me of a game I used to play by choosing two words from two pages of the dictionary and trying to fit them into a single sentence to see what new ideas emerged. To savour the randomness of combinations of words is surely becoming possible as a game. Imagination without words, and imagination with words may be two different things, or so it seemed to me, but it is important to encourage children to develop within the area of their creative strength.

In regard to peace, children have such simplistic views that one might suppose their views were of no use to anyone. Often adults make ideas far too complex. I would like to see a child's question or statement inscribed near the entry of peace research institutes. It is children who suffer most during wars nowadays and they put our efforts to shame. They are the people with the prospect of a long future ahead of them.

When leisure activities are well chosen they provide a psychological treatment well recognised by occupational therapists, who provide not just an occupation for people undergoing a long period of convalescence, but the opportunity to make something of which they may be proud. Just as a peasant farmer may become so attached to his patch of land, which is more than home to him, has also become an extension of himself, part of his personality. In this way the things a person makes may give that person a sense of achievement and self-confidence, which everyone needs, to live in harmony with the world.

It might well be asked whether this feeling of harmony with the world around us should become part of a peace movement, whether the cruel people who start wars were in need of occupational therapy when they were young, or whether their capacity for imagining or creating was never exercised?

Looking through my collection of proverbs I see that some warn against the dangers of failing to control anger and there may be rulers who get angry and lose patience with their opponents. Anger in rulers has become more dangerous as weapons and wars have grown worse.

Proverbs on Anger:
Anger is a short bout of madness, hatred is a long bout
    of madness.
He who rides a tiger can never dismount. (China)
The eye of hatred can bore through stone. (Masai)

The anger of brothers is the anger of the devil. (Italy)

The angry and the weak are their own enemies. (Russia)

He has wisdom at will, who can with angry heart be still.
(Old English)

Let not the sun go down upon your wrath. (The Bible)

Hatred never ceases through hatred, hatred only ceases
through love. (The Buddha)

Work Experience

The third heading of the curriculum we designed was related to unemployment and leisure in that it included work experience to help sixteen-year-olds to learn about starting work in different kinds of factory or office. In this way they could adapt more easily if they were lucky enough to get a job on leaving school in the following year. It is obviously much easier to plan and carry out a work experience scheme, if you yourself have been through the experiences. Before planning for the members of the course I tried to recollect what experiences I had been through. There was Whalley Farm, other farms during work-camp years, the Young Farmers Club office at Avoncroft College, a spell in the Oxford University Agricultural Economics Record Institute, a garage, and a bank. Yet if anyone had asked me what I had learned about starting work, they might have received a blank sheet. This made it even more imperative that we included this as part of the curriculum. Because even I had never noticed the role of the Trade Unions, the safety rules and the importance of cleanliness, especially when working in food shops and food factories, so what hope would school leavers have if we didn't teach them?

One of the headmasters who took our course was very shocked when the workers in the food factory did not bother to wash their hands after leaving the toilets. He wanted to know what he should do about it. That was not easy to answer. Another of our student teachers, with a very fashionable appearance fixed up some of her coloured schoolgirls to work in a food shop where there had been no coloured people working previously. 'On principle' she said 'I have not told the manager.' I replied 'Couldn't you drop a remark to explain who is coming. We don't want them rudely turned away.' As a consequence of what she said there have been coloured girls working there ever since. In fact we broke the ice of a difficult situation.

It appears that preliminary work-experience increased the number of young people in work but it is impossible to say how many. It is likely to make them more polite, manageable, and punctual through seeing and hearing of the manager's problems, and so become more employable. But unemployment is a worldwide problem, and demands a global answer. Cheap labour in the 'South' or Third World inevitably attracts factories to move, it may be better, if we think globally, to have jobs move to where there is no pay for the unemployed as there is in the 'North.' A way needs to be found for spreading wealth across the world, while reducing unemployment and increasing the number of jobs in teaching, nursing, and cleaning, which do not require substantial extra resources. If no way is found to do this the invisible movement of population from the 'South' to the 'North' will keep growing amid increasing violence. It is as inevitable as the rising of the sea level.

Citizenship

The fourth part of the new curriculum dealt with democratic citizenship. Here again, for the non-academically inclined children we had in mind, the principle of learning by doing was vital. The following quote comes from an article I wrote for the internet, it explains one way of making the mysterious, largely unwritten British Constitution, come alive:

> It would be useful if schools, or failing them classes, formed model states to carry out some of their business. At least an outing could be arranged. In the case of an outing, the Foreign Secretary would give the reason for making contacts with the institution to be visited, the Chancellor of the Exchequer would raise the funds and supervise payments and roles may easily be envisaged for the Ministry of Food and Agriculture, the Environment and so on.
>
> The Cabinet would meet and ministers would have to attain the approval of both the elected House of Commons and the House of Lords, the latter being appointed by the head teacher

214

or the teacher. An opposition could easily be formed and a major issue might divide the pupils into parties.

Mr Heath once commented that, of all the needs for inventions, the greatest was for ways of producing democratic citizens.

Work such as this on the Constitution is for older children and ideally they will have begun with something more tangible and immediate. Community Schools with their surveys to identify needs or issues, followed by action to make some improvements, are within the capability of younger children in their primary schools. The teaching will be about people and places known to them. For example a series of lessons about 'People who help us' could be designed to discuss the bravery of firemen, the attention to detail of postmen, the competence of dustmen and so forth. Is there anything we can do to help them, such as writing clearly for the postmen, and sorting rubbish for the dustmen.

Gradually the children will gain pride in their own area. It does not cost much to win a reputation for kindness and hospitality to strangers. When the children gain confidence and are referring to plans for the future, they will talk about 'We' rather than 'they' and walk tall with pride as they go down the street. They will be keeping up with the traditions of the great democrats from Pericles in Athens, some of the French revolutionaries, Tom Paine, Abraham Lincoln in the USA and John Bright, Winston Churchill and Clement Attlee in this country. It is odd that there is no widely accepted list of great democrats; their biographies are needed by the teachers of citizenship, because abstract ideas are most fully understood when attached to people. It is easier to explain what democrats do, than it is to say what democracy is.

Voting has been thought of as the central or core criterion of democracy, but authoritarian rulers seek to justify their rule by holding elections and many elections fail to make the voters believe that they really share political power. In Britain improving the political system seems likely to have some topical interest for years to come, but the alternative ways of voting are too complex for teaching in schools.

Of more importance is to explain the role of public discussion of the pros and cons of major issues. Political meetings nowadays are attended by so few people that they seem to be dying out. The papers have not yet replaced them and so it has fallen to television and radio to provide independent information regarding the policies of political party programmes. It is likely in the future the internet will supplement this by providing high-level discussions. 'No democracy without discussion.' Is the new slogan which I coined to apply to states which, recognising the level of technical knowledge required to gain a valid opinion, respond by imposing secrecy regarding such issues as genetically modified organisms and nuclear waste. The quality of discussions varies greatly and it is a task for schools to raise standards by:

Maintaining the aim of finding out the truth rather than being right.

Recognising what people and what points provide convincing evidence.

Encouraging suspicion of vested interests and the operations of public relations firms.

Valuing the formulation of key questions.

Appreciating the role of an independent facilitator of discussions.

CHAPTER 13

Bristol University Continued

Discussions.

(Participants in discussions are often in the position of
    judges.)
That judge is wise who understands a matter soon and
    judges later. (China)
A fox was asked for his witness. 'My own tail,' he replied.
Judges should have two ears. Both alike.
Yes, and No, divide people. (Germany)
The roots of quarrels are three – downright assertions,
    sarcasm, and abuse. (Tibet)
If you tell me I forget, if you show me I may remember,
    if you involve me I will understand. (China)
Mountains do not meet, but people do.
Use soft words and hard arguments.
To tear is easy to sew is difficult. (Discussion can easily
    be torn to pieces.) (China)

PARLIAMENTARY DEBATES demean democracy by the child-ish virulence between one party and another. This makes the teacher hesitate about staging a mock parliament, though the method when applied to the United Nations has been working well in the Model United Nations General Assemblies (MUNGA), which have now been held all over the country, usually by groups of Secondary Schools. These help in the understanding of the UN and its related institutions and of a non-violent way to establish peace. Conversely, though seldom put into practice, it could be applied to Local Government. I recall doing this once by writing a discussion about the building of their own school for a class in Birmingham. A session of the Education Committee was dramatised.

Knowledge of institutions, however, does not necessarily lead to a greater interest. Public spirit, I suspect, is an attitude, which is formed very easily in life by parental interest but many children have no guide to follow or they may suffer through the absence of their parents at meetings! A Lord Mayor of Chester invited representatives of societies in the city to a reception, and I attended as Chair of the branch of the United Nations Association. Living sixteen miles outside Chester and being a newcomer, I did not make contacts of much use to the UNA, among the hundred and twenty guests. But when the Lord Mayor began to speak, the value of the meeting grew in my view. He began by talking about the social needs of Chester, the need to overcome the stress from the speed at which we all live. As he warmed to his subject and coming to the climax of his speech he said, 'Your work on the various voluntary organisations and societies of Chester makes a huge difference to all those who live here. Indeed, it is you who make living in Chester worthwhile.' It was this sentence that kept ringing in my ears. Citizens are people, who care for their neighbours. Pericles might have made a comparable statement like that to his fellow Athenians, where a very pale version of democracy first took root in what we now call Europe, and Athens was a major part of the glory that was Greece.

The public spirit involved in citizenship is the spirit found among volunteers for the good of a large part of society who do a service without pay. Some firemen, some lifeboat men come into this category but teachers working overtime without pay come into this group, which assuredly deserves more honour than it gets. Alexander Pope's famous adage may be adapted:

> For forms of Government let fools contest
> Tis public spirit makes the best.

If public spirit is the oil, which eases the workings of society, how can it be taught? It must surely be caught by contagion from parents or teachers. As there is no test for parenting, teachers should more frequently be selected for possessing public spirit and opportunities for practising it can be provided by schools.

Whether education for citizenship is part of peace education or vice versa, is not worth discussing, but peer mediation to reduce bullying should clearly be included in the curriculum, though at that time we were not sure. We hoped that some treatment based on Elise Boulding's methods would be added; however the members of the course were not as enthusiastic about looking into the future and forming Utopias as I expected. It seemed unrealistic to turn back to the course on education for international understanding, which I had devised for students at the Coventry College of Education in the early sixties. Everyone should assume that they themselves and not just their opponents have prejudices, which they need to shed. Advertisers are professional creators of prejudices and their methods can profitably be studied by teachers who may be tempted to use their methods, instead of just exposing them as lies formed by vested interest.

For the university course I wrote a large number of papers, sometimes to hand out as summaries of the introduction to discussions. Being wise after the event, I should have added a short list of questions to ask in addition to references to books. Roger Wilson's phrase 'That's a good question to ask,' reminds me of the value of teaching so as to enhance curiosity.

Other papers were intended for publication and were carefully prepared as in the case of the one for the conference of the International Peace Research Association, which was held in Malta. I ought in this case to have found a sympathetic colleague with whom I could discuss it. Although I was on very good terms with John Lang, and full of admiration for him as a teacher, I wished to avoid his caution and try to write in a lighter style. My bad start in university work at Balliol left me with little confidence in myself as far as writing went. However, when I applied for Principalships of Teachers Colleges and I was short-listed four times, I began to wonder whether the Ministry of Education had a ruling against pacifists holding such important posts, but did not like making it public.

It is hardly necessary to add that leisure activities and Community Schools were other titles for the PTA Magazine. More surprisingly is the one of spring 1962, which began 'One evening soon, children in this country will go to sleep British and wake up

European.' It is followed later by 'We used to learn from the Scandinavians, who for many years have practised the exchange of textbooks between countries so as to rid them of stupid distortions.' Early on it proved possible to interest some of our British PTA Committee members in forming an international body to spread such ideas from one country to another.

I curtailed my PTA activities after I moved to Bristol in order to make time for other things. There was one exception: an invitation from a very friendly headmaster of Hartcliffe Comprehensive School, the largest school in the Southwest. Teachers on strike on account of cuts in education and the parents were angry. They were so angry, in fact, that they would not give me a hearing. It was a new experience for me except for the occasion in Yugoslavia when European students, fresh from the barricades in Paris in 1968 refused my chairmanship in order to establish an anarchic or leaderless meeting. Unfortunately I was never again invited to chair the student sessions, organised by the American Friends Service Council. These were intended to introduce older students from all over the world to major world issues. I recall two significant incidents. At the first, which was held in Munster, I felt that it would be possible to invite an Indian to state the Pakistani case regarding Kashmir and a Pakistani to give the Indian case. The audience listened spellbound, knowing the risks the two were taking, if their people back home came to hear what they had said. At the finish the applause was the greatest of the whole fortnight's seminar.

The second occasion was in Holland we were housed in a castle with a double moat round it, the inner one very close to the building. I had been provided with a rubber duck, which quacked loudly when it was squeezed, to use if anyone spoke too much. The young people of the seminar all knew its purpose. One day we had a distinguished and interesting visiting speaker who had spoken for quite some time when we were interrupted by a loud quack from the moat. The laughter, which followed, was so loud that I thought it best to explain to the speaker what had happened, so that he could share the fun. I was wondering afterwards whether he was shortening what he had to say!

Those seminars were good examples of one of the things, which need to be done. They gathered together in a friendly atmosphere the young potential leaders to brush away some of the misunder-standings, the prejudices and the hatred left by war propaganda and the memories of brutality left over from wartime. Many of us were on the edge of tears when a Jewish teacher from France described what an enormous relief it was when she was able to meet ordinary Germans for the first time. It was very difficult for her to explain this, but it helped many of us to hear it. I should have made more of it, perhaps persuading more people to share their strong feelings. I fear I am always slow to react in such highly charged situations. It was not that she was angry, it was rather that the sound of the German voices filled her with such fear and she was filled with sadness at the thought of the length of time it would take for reconciliation to be complete. Our seminars pointed the way, but the way was a long one. Is there a peace organisation that is genuinely searching for better ways of making that journey? Can psychiatrists help? It could be that Archbishop Tutu with the Truth Commission in South Africa has part of the answer.

By accident this is being written while the BBC is broadcast-ing the life of Albie Sachs, describing the ups and downs of his life on the BBC. Brave men like Sachs, and Joel Joffe, both lawyers who defended Nelson Mandela, are the people who should appear in a history of democracy. Their interpretation of the meaning of citi-zenship is a vital part and would be readily appreciated in schools.

It brought back to mind the travail of South Africa from the Great Trek of the Boers, to wind its way across what became Onze Rust. As a family we had stayed there, and mother had been in the Boer camps during the Boer War, which was caused partly by the discovery of gold and diamonds. Later as we grew up with Oom Jannie constantly in our minds we began to appreciate his vision-ary efforts towards reconciliation between Dutch Afrikaners and British as a prelude to reconciliation with 'coloured' and black South Africans, so that all could share their beautiful country on an equal footing. My parents who had become guardians for Nontando Jabavu could afford to be more radical, and practised the reconciliation they preached. A page I have written about Oom Jannie for a sixth form text on the United Nations has recently been rejected by the African National Congress, despite his opening address when the UN was created. It should surely be a rule of thumb for peace builders that there is more to be said for opponents than is usually admitted.

David Brockington, of the University of Western England, wrote a book on children who refused to attend school. It has grown into negotiations in which he arranged for all children to have their non-academic skills recognised by future employers as well as by higher education institutions. This development is going from strength to strength so that already nearly half the secondary schools take part with 120,000 students each year having their achievements or skills recognised, while following the National Curriculum. The Award Scheme Accreditation Network (ASDA) of David Brockington has done a great service by helping everyone to be good at something. Too many schools have only recognised academic or sporting achievements and failed to understand the effect on those who fitted neither category.

Discouragement in school is one of the factors undermining mental health. I felt very privileged to be appointed rapporteur to a UNESCO funded British Government Commission to deal with stress in Primary Schools. I wish I had been in possession of a text such as *Emotional Intelligence*[42] by David Goleman. This would have been an invaluable book for other members of the Commission to read had it been available at the time. They included educational psychologists, head teachers and officials, and they were mainly thinking in terms of examination stress, the difficulty of starting and changing schools and threats from bullies rather than other kinds of social education. The more delicate question to control impulsive emotions seemed to have been neglected. I cannot be sure, as I left to work for UNESCO abroad.

Goleman's book would encourage us to focus on outbreaks of anger and recommends that we should teach children to study the situation, and the options available, the consequences of different actions and the solutions, before reacting. It would also improve social relations in general in less impulsive cultures. Our Commission was aware of the adage 'Quiet teachers, quiet class.' But this theme was presented more thoroughly in the book *The Art of Teaching Peacefully*[43] by Michelle MacGrath. The popularity of the book should be doubled during the decade of the Culture of Peace. Although many teachers use a stentorian voice to quell noise, a more effective method is to deal with it by setting a good example oneself. I used to tease Ruth for reducing our ceilings to tatters by talking in violent terms about Mrs Thatcher. As it happens while she was at Somerville, Mrs Thatcher was tutored by a scientist so distinguished that she became Chancellor of Bristol University. Until then no women except members of the Royal Family had been so greatly honoured, and later Dorothy Hodgkin's portrait appeared on postage stamps. Her first act on resigning from Bristol University was to ask me to 'look after' two members of the staff who resigned on conscientious grounds. They did this when their agricultural research grant ran out and the work was turned over to the Ministry of Defence to fund. They feared that their information could be used in biological warfare.

In an urban civilisation the custom has grown up of teaching children to face violence with violence, they should be learning to understand the dangers of anger and attempting to view the situation from the other's point of view. It is time for Christians to learn from Buddhists, that one disgraces oneself by becoming angry and losing the impressive serenity for which Buddhists are well known.

A soft answer turneth away wrath.

Anger comes on horseback, but goes away on foot.

The offender never pardons.

At one period I used to go off to sleep at night while thinking of the wonderful serenity of the Buddhists whom I had met in Thailand. All in all I became convinced that it was as helpful to deal with the peace of the heart as with the peace of the mind. Quaker Meetings and the feelings and thoughts that arise there, are as essential to the peace movement as a whole, as the work in parliament or filmmaking. It was not as difficult a change, as those who resign from the armed forces have to make. I was daunted at one point when one of my nearest and dearest commented: 'When I am angry I feel I am being honest. You sit on your feelings too much.' Nevertheless I still believe that to promote co-operative democracy in the family, among friends and in ever widening circles is right. Even the simulated anger of parliamentary debates is a bad way, a non-co-operative way of making laws.

Anger and violence had little to do with the University Course. Corporal punishment had already been abolished and anger was out of favour, unless it was followed by an opportunity to do better, and a pat on the back of some kind, for the individual or class which had been offending. It is to be regretted that international 'pats on the back' are difficult to arrange! Many of my other activities did contribute to the course in some way.

I believe I was respected as a Quaker, though some of the teachers must have thought me eccentric when my non-payment of taxes led to my furniture being confiscated. Without my prompting them the BBC rang to televise the occasion but by this time a Quaker was already in prison and the government did not want any more 'bad' publicity and so we did not know when the furniture would be taken. A legal advisor to the government had already informed me, that if the case went to the Courts the government would be likely to lose its case, because in the non-payment of my taxes, I had specified nuclear defence, which was considered questionable long before the World Court gave its famous Advisory Opinion.

The conversation with the lady from the Inland Revenue who came to collect my furniture, supported by a silent bailiff, was extraordinary. By the time she had heard me on the tax refusals of early and recent Quakers, Ruth joined in and asked what becomes of a society when the conscientious are driven to emigrate and those who remain are the corruptible. 'You are sending the wrong people to prison and news will spread,' the lady already knew of the interest of the BBC to televise it. 'It is a tragedy' Ruth continued. Our visitor's eyes filled with tears of vexation at not being able to persuade us to pay our taxes instead of having our furniture removed.

They took, not the silver, but the chairs and larger furniture, calculating they could stop selling when the appropriate sum was reached. One piece was so large that I had to help with it, showing my sympathy for the work they were expected to do. At the sale, some of the family bought the handsome chairs and gave them back to us. It was after the event that I canvassed the family to find out whether they would join us in Ireland as refugees from a nuclear weapons state. They were interested but not keen so the idea was dropped. There was only one other opportunity to refuse to pay taxes and to make a stand and that was for such a small amount that I heard no more about it.

The family seemed lukewarm about going to Ireland compared with their interest each year in the Aldermaston Marches. They all came and marched valiantly, year after year, being rewarded by the singing and meeting many friends. We never saw enough of the Atomic Research Station at Aldermaston, to make those who worked there aware that many people took the view that what they were doing was evil. Years later there was a large explosion and Sir Richard Body, a Conservative MP told me that his barn near the boundary fence was demolished and a crack had appeared in his house. He asked for compensation from the Ministry of Defence and received the reply, 'We cannot pay compensation for damage done by an explosion which officially never took place.' The entire Nuclear Industry has become such a running sore in society, compounding lies with corruption that it has become not merely a financial disaster but undermines the quality of life by destroying the trust on which society depends. How can a government with such a disregard for the truth expect the sheep farmers of Snowdonia, not to sell their sheep after the fall-out from Chernobyl?

Esther Rantzen became a heroine for exposing the misrepresentations of the commercial advertisers, a brave champion of political truth is now needed to expose the lies of the spin-doctors in the political sphere otherwise the body politic will suffer the same fate as another Ruth:

> There was a young lady called Ruth
> Who had a great passion for truth
> She said "I will die,
> Before I will lie"
> She died in the prime of her youth.

The Quakers in former centuries were people of Ruth's calibre and there are tales of them adhering to truth in remarkable circumstances. Indeed this was how prices came to be fixed cutting out tiresome bargaining. Quakers in the corn trade announced their prices and that was that.

It is difficult to imagine truthful diplomats. They have even been defined as officials who are sent abroad, to lie for their country. They are still at the stage of bargaining for corn. They need to become frank, worthy of confidence, and able to admit the mistakes of their own government. Now would be a good time for such an experiment to be made. National interests and international interests are much less different from each other than they are made out to be. It is in the interest of all peoples to have an effective UN for example.

Considerations such as these were the only interruptions to normal university work. I received some stimulating invitations to travel briefly, to the Lebanon, Malta, the Island of St Helena, and later to Côte D'Ivoire. In the Lebanon the future of the large Quaker School at Brummana had to be decided. The war had been going on too long and had got out of hand, the older boys had been getting the younger boys out of bed very early to drill them for fighting, not a Quaker form of peace education! Originally the school had been started by a Quaker eccentric married to an Ethiopian Princess. It performed a very useful function by providing a route for the daughters of wealthy Arabs to university education. It had become coeducational. I listened to a lesson on the international situation in Arabic and intervened to talk about the UN and its function of ultimately bringing wars to an end. A bright looking girl put her hand up to say 'But we like fighting.' The school is very near Beirut with its buildings crumbling from gunfire, indeed the firing was from both sides as we came from the airport and the driver shaking with fear. Afterwards it was said to me by way of explanation: 'You see you have your United Nations, we have the Arab League.' I knew the secretary of the Arab League because he was a fellow student and attended the Oxford Quaker Meeting, because he had attended the Brummana School previously. I was very disappointed not to meet him again. I would have liked to discuss with him the Arab attitudes to the UN. The chance was missed in Dag Hammarskjöld's time of promoting the UN to take on the government of Jerusalem and Arabs and Jews have paid heavily for their mistaken opposition to it.

The flight to Malta was to read a paper at a conference of the Education Commission of the International Peace Research

Association. I was full of admiration for the number and high quality of the Americans and the Scandinavians. My reflection on those attending the conference were that academics know much more about what they would like to teach, than about the children and their learning. It is attitudes towards foreigners that matter, even more than knowledge of the UN and such attitudes are acquired at Nursery School age, partly from parents.

At Bristol University we had Professor Tajfel, a French-speaking Polish Jew, he was so concerned about group dynamics that he had set up and led a team in a very important experiment. They formed two groups of five-year-old children carefully balanced so that there was no apparent cause for discrimination. All of them were just starting school and it was arranged that the teachers taught in similar ways as far as possible. The findings were disheartening to say the least. On a variety of measures each group thought their own group was better. The implications of their findings are that people tend automatically to think of 'in-groups' and 'out-groups,' of 'we' and 'they' even when there is little reason for doing so. In every case the children formed the belief that their own group was better. I have to confess that I felt profoundly discouraged when I heard the result and began to consider how I would design lessons to avoid this result, how to promote cooperation, tolerance, friendship and hospitality, according to Mildred Masheder's methods as shown in her books. This may extend to the strange loyalties of football fans and chauvinists. As a very young teen-ager, my brother taught me a joke:

> We are the chosen few.
> All others may be damned.
> There's room enough in hell for you,
> We can't have heaven crammed.

This is an effective form of counter-propaganda, making the chauvinists ludicrous. Some people are so idealistic in thinking that everyone should be so rational even in their enthusiasms that there is no place for slogans, songs, mottos, rhymes, and jokes. In my view it is essential to understand that rational motivation is not enough to solve human problems. People have 'hearts' as well as brains. Perhaps I am biased after spending several months in Nazi Germany, because of the rationalised hatred I witnessed as I watched Hitler while he spoke, but what was more confusing was later hearing apparently quite reasonable people justifying Nazi policies while I was hitch-hiking. Living in Berlin, I came to believe that good will and reason were not enough to provide an effective opposition to conversion.

In addition to Malta a former student from my early days at St Paul's College in Cheltenham, whom I had not seen for twenty years, looked me up to invite me to go to the Island of St Helena to teach about Community Education, during the long vacation in the summer. The Governor of St Helena has some responsibility for other islands in the South Atlantic, stretching over a distance equal to the distance from London to Newfoundland. St Helena is the largest and has a population of four thousand people; it had four secondary schools with women teachers except for gardening, woodwork, and some sport. There was plenty of work for girls on leaving school, but very little for boys. The girls worked hard to win places as secretaries in the administration, in teaching and in shops. The boys failed to get work and often caused trouble in school. The situation was an intriguing challenge to any community-school teacher. The island was in fact a potential Utopia, in many ways it resembled Robinson Crusoe's island and was not inhabited until the arrival of the Dutch in the seventeenth century. Everything being in miniature seemed to be manageable at first glance; on looking more closely most attempted changes came to nothing owing to people's attitudes to change.

A businessman from Cape Town may have been planning an escape from the dangers of South Africa, in any case he established himself very thoroughly by buying a very large house and a shop. Fruit trees were planted, pigs and hens for his 'bacon and eggs' and so on. He seemed intent on 'developing' the Island's economy. I noticed some of the anomalies: In the government guest house where we stayed we were served fish-fingers imported I presume from the North Sea, but not the fruit growing in the yard outside, which I was told 'nobody eats.' The catching of fish for the island was organised by my nephew Simon who arrived before my second visit ten years later to serve as treasurer or Chancellor of the Exchequer for Mrs Thatcher's Socialist colony. The government was conducted in ways as close as possible to Westminster's with the elected representatives calling each other 'the Honourable Member for' and the name of the constituency followed. Across the wall behind the speaker's head was written a sonorous quotation from Edmund Burke, famous in constitutional history. It was in front of the legislature that I presented my report on plans for secondary education. I noted that the four little secondary schools demanding improved facilities, especially for science, each had on the average a hundred pupils. This figure was declining year by year, and the plan was proposed to build a new central school by the only playing field in St Helena, which happened to be centrally placed. I noticed that the grammar school was placed in a Prickly Pear desert by the coast, hot for studying, whereas high up in the centre there was a different climate, cool and with a rainfall suitable for gardening. Rather than this project be turned down on the grounds of expense I pointed out that the long school holiday in the summer originated in the Middle Ages. This was a time when all the older children were needed to help with the harvest, but in contemporary times it was kept as a tradition. Neither of these factors applied to St Helena. With the help of some lateral thinking it would have been possible to build a smaller cheaper school with the children coming in alternate days or weeks, or month according to convenience.

The assembly legislators may have been impressed by the flexibility of the reasoning but the main attack came from one who accused me of breaking up community life, saying a secondary school is essential for a community to thrive. Given the size of St Helena and its population I was not prepared for this, nor was I prepared to discuss the impact of birth control, but I have seldom been caught on the wrong side of the argument that 'Small is Beautiful.' I was able to say that I had walked the distance involved, and by English standards they were short, and hoped that taking to donkeys again would be welcomed by the children. After that as I went about my business, whether on foot or by car, the children large and small, used to shout 'donkey rides.' Having held meetings for parents and teachers in every school I was confident of democratic support but what would Whitehall say, when I got back to London. The official responsible for St Helena at the Foreign Office, who had been absent at my briefing complained strongly

229

that I had failed to look at the other ways of improving secondary education and did not believe my modest costings, based on advice from the Department of Public Works. For five years nothing was done and then, without informing me, a much greater building was erected costing very much more.

A new light was also thrown on international affairs. In the shop in the High Street where the Fairy Terns nest in the trees, there are English-Russian dictionaries on sale. From time to time the crews of Soviet submarines are allowed to come ashore. I did not meet any but the local inhabitants liked having them, finding them cheerful, kindly visitors, who spent their savings more freely. St Helena is a steep volcanic island with few places to land. Almost all ships lie at anchor off Jamestown, but the Soviets were very well informed and knew that in some circumstances the weather allowed a landing on the almost uninhabited side of the island where there is a small beach. They had landed there and taken some bananas, which they found growing nearby. Needless to say that was resented, as was the over-fishing on the African coast by large 'factory' ships. One may imagine the headlines in the papers in Britain such as 'Soviets steal from British Colony.'

There are, or were at that time only three routes for getting from St Helena; by steamer to Bristol, Cape Town, or to Ascension Island. At each visit I was pressed for time, but on my second visit I had difficulty in getting back so I took the steamer to Ascension where many people from St Helena, 'Saints' as they were called, go to do unskilled work. There I stayed with a Resident Representative of the British Government, who was answerable to the Governor of St Helena. From there I was the sole passenger to Johannesburg in a USA military plane. It was 1979 and the Cold War was far from finished and this forms the context for the following anecdotes.

The Commander of the Soviet submarine, weary of the cramped quarters either for himself or his crew signalled to the Resident Representative of Ascension Island, for permission to land. No doubt he knew about the landings on St Helena, but the Representative signalled back that it did not rest with him, he would have to obtain permission. He did not say from whom he had to get leave. Four companies Cable & Wireless, the BBC, NASA, and one other occupy the island. The Americans fire missiles across the Atlantic to the sea near Ascension and are sensitive about secrecy, even though the Soviets might well be afraid of precision or lack of it. Permission was refused. The Soviet Commander signalled back 'Pity. Humpty Dumpty sat on the wall,' leaving others to finish the sentence. I suppose that people, who hold the fate of humanity in their hands, have to make light of it for fear of becoming over-whelmed by their responsibility. I could well wish for more humour like that to lighten Cold Wars. If it had been possible I would have sent books of the 'Don Camillo' series to that captain. The World Court Project has ensured that British Commanders are aware of the fact that they undertake to commit an illegal act as they accept their post. It is now clear that the world becomes upside down when it is the government and their representatives who become the breakers of law.

When travel is difficult it is highly desirable to keep one's mind fresh, out of a rut and capable of lateral thinking by correspondence. Now I have a correspondent whom I met in Beijing but exchanging ideas is in its early stages and I am not sure that I can be of any use to him.

CHAPTER 14

Grant Making Trusts: A Look on the Inside

ONE SATURDAY EVENING in April 1951 I arrived at a large house in the Chiltern Hills, with a view down a valley. It had been Disraeli's home a century previously but had become a set of flats. In one of them lived Seebohm Rowntree, one of the sons of Joseph Rowntree. I had been invited to stay the night because the house was inaccessible and Seebohn liked to meet proposed new members of the trust of his father's, now famous, Charitable Trust. I was teased afterwards on the grounds that the other trustees were so anxious to persuade my father to resign on the grounds that his memory was failing, that they accepted his suggestion that I should take his place. I might be accused of sheer nepotism, Joseph Rowntree having been my great uncle. In those times so many of the trusts were family trusts that it did not occur to me to hesitate and question the principle.

Many of the trusts were Quaker in origin. Quakers had taken a principled stand against paying tithes to the Anglican Church and many emigrated to the United States and many moved to towns and played a prominent part in the Industrial Revolution as industrialists and bankers. When they became rich, they ceased being Quaker or they followed the accepted Quaker principle that, after meeting essential needs, all funds should be given to good causes. It is difficult not to smile at the consequent wrestling with consciences to which this may lead. Quakers do at least make an attempt to follow that guidance by living lightly.

By the time of my first Trust Meeting we already had five children and my quarterly absences would not have been possible but for the help Ruth had from the young women from the continent. They were mainly German, who wished to improve their spoken English. With several of them we have kept in touch ever since.

Before the first Trust meeting in 1951 I was sent the Trust's permanent documents containing advice for the Trustees. These showed Joseph Rowntree's wisdom so clearly that paragraphs were read out at our meetings before the business was begun. It may have appeared a little like ancestor-worship but the risk was well worth taking. I read in them phrases such as 'New occasions teach new duties, time makes ancient good uncouth' which both my father and mother repeated to me about their own trust. In other words they wished policies within the trust to change with the times, and not become stagnant and 'uncouth.' At some point in discussing a grant, a trustee remarked 'The advice should not be allowed to justify Sunday newspaper philanthropy,' meaning that fashionable giving should not sweep us and make us forget our well-considered strategies. Personally I was seldom quite sure whether I was following the vagaries of fashion or benefiting from recent research. On the major issue of what the Joseph Rowntree Memorandum called 'The need to search out the underlying causes of weakness or of evil in the community, rather than of remedying their more superficial manifestations, as a need could well remain throughout the duration of the Trusts.' I felt at the time entirely in sympathy. Even though it might mean hardening the heart against Oxfam's appeal for hungry children as compared with Oxfam's 'Cut Conflict' campaign, against the fighting which makes them hungry.

Dealing with the 'rooting' and causes of problems has only been questioned recently, for being too negative and for urging people to fight against wars as compared with building cultures of peace. The difficulty about that is that it is easier to raise public opinion against war, than it is to raise public opinion for peace. The new quarterly *Positive News* will have to face that question.

One of the more surprising suggestions in the Memorandum is that money should be given away within a person's lifetime for preference. Joseph Rowntree excused himself by writing that his wealth had come to him in old age. He had not had the time to make it and to spend it! As the capital value of the Trust's holding has grown and grown, it has become incredibly difficult to give away and Trustees have repeatedly decided to prolong the life of the Trust. Steven Burkeman, until recently the Secretary of the Trust wrote a paper on the motives for philanthropy. Even though the sense of power is diluted by the number of trustees, he concluded, the motives are always mixed and we all suffer wrongly by delusions of grandeur, wrongly because it is usually the grantees, the recipients of the grants who deserve the thanks and the honour for their work. We trustees should always remind ourselves that money achieves little by itself and can easily be wasted unless there are competent people able to determine what needs to be done; and then persuade others to help them.

I enjoyed being a member of the team, if Parliament is the best club in London; the best club for me was the Joseph Rowntree Charitable Trust (JRCT). Watching my favourite good causes being helped by financial support amply rewarded me. To me they were like racehorses only better. There were at times, of course, disappointments when what had seemed a good cause failed to win approval for reasons I had failed to spot. There were also occasions when a larger grant was approved than one dared to hope.

The four fields in which the Joseph Rowntree Charitable Trust operated were: peace, not through politics so much as through research, on account of the Charity Laws; secondly, Quakerism, and religion generally, and thirdly, social reform, and finally, education. Joseph Rowntree was hoping that all the four would benefit from the publicity provided by his newspaper when bought by the Social Service Trust. This scheme was being supported by George Cadbury's purchase of the *Daily News,* a national newspaper managed by Henry Cadbury, my father-in-law. He converted it into the *News Chronicle,* a paper of liberal leanings, which survived the Second World War before being squeezed out by less scrupulous proprietors.

If this aspect of the Trusts proved more difficult than Joseph Rowntree expected, it has been compensated by the good work of the Charitable Trust. In many ways it has become a model for other trusts to seek to emulate, and visitors continually come to seek advice about our procedures. Let me hasten to add that I had very little part in bringing this about. I was one of the learners and believe that I turned what I learnt to good account when establishing our two small family trusts. One of them was set up by my parents, rather late in life and the other by Ruth and myself when we realised that our children and their children had as much as they needed, to live useful and enjoyable lives. I often ask myself whether I should have taken my great uncle's advice on this point as in general he was usually right, and his judgement wise, and given away the capital. However my parents had taught me to be secretive about financial matters and it went against the grain. The Rowntree Trustees changed their policy about secrecy some time in the sixties or seventies. They concluded that transparency was desirable in a somewhat democratic organisation such as the Trust, which benefits from the non-payment of taxes by charities, and implies the importance of making clear how the money is spent. Its reports are now much more colourful and detailed. I shrank from this publicity and was glad that none of my friends seemed to know any more about the matter than they had previously.

One of the results of making more information more available and the increased number of charities and of grant making trusts is the rapid increase in the publication of books and articles about them. The Directory of Social Change, under the guidance of its founder Nicholas Albery, has published a large number of books including such practical details as 'How to write Letters of Application.' Likewise, Susan Forrester's *Peace and International Relations: A Funding Guide for Independent Groups* provides an example of specialist directories, which contain information about each grant-making trust.

An example of the steadily increasing number of articles is Alison Benjamin's, in the Guardian of December 13th 2000 'Crowded out by Competition' in which she reports that there are 5,000 new charities every year seeking funding. One result of this is that more money is spent on fundraising. The evidence for this is that the amounts spent on the real work have fallen by 13% of the total income in the five years to 1997. She does not think that this should point to mergers to obtain the benefits of larger-scale operations, but to more discrimination on the part of the donor trusts. For example the number of trusts now dealing with cancer has grown to six hundred and twenty. Such a number is absurd and implies that private initiatives get out of hand and also that new ideas are needed.

On the subject of new ideas, Roger Wilson, a former chairman of the JRCT once repeated the quote: 'Who ever heard of a good new idea coming from a man in a suit?' Ironically he was not only wearing a suit at the time, but Roger and I were discussing a plan for handing over a tenth of the Rowntree Charitable Trust income to a group of young people under thirty-five to spend as they saw fit. Our fellow trustees rejected the idea.

I believe it would have shown that it was a good innovation to develop. Too many trustees of the grant-making trusts are elderly men of an unadventurous, and conservative outlook, as more than one commentator has indicated. It is good for an older trust to counter that tendency by appointing more young people and include women.

Secondly trustees need to keep an eye on the warnings of futurologists that the future tends to encourage pessimism of more than one kind. The dangers of a nuclear exchange and of global warming are now obvious, but there are also the growing gaps between rich and poor countries and the sign of some kind of social breakdown, which are seldom discussed, but which have many implications for grant-makers. For example poor countries often have excess sunshine and they need to be put into a position not only to use solar power, but to export it, maybe in the form of electricity. The tactics of philanthropy are better than the strategy, since strategic insights come from the combination of young and old trustees who are open to new ideas, but not for the sake of novelty.

The Rowntree Charitable Trust has promoted a number of practices, which may be of interest to other trusts. It supported the Friends Provident Stewardship Fund, the first such ethical fund in the country, by funding the publication of 'Social Audit' and the accompanying research into the practices of companies. It demonstrated the value of a flexible trust deed, it offered help to its grantees over the disseminations of their findings, encouraged groups of related grantees to cooperate over the publication of books and conferences and gave help in interpreting the confusing Charity

Laws. Roger Wilson arranged that we met a couple of grantees on the Friday evenings, before our own Saturday meetings for business, to hear them reflect on the issues arising in the course of their work. This proved to be a great privilege for us to hear and raise questions about important fields of the Trust's work, and we benefited also from the personal contacts. Whether Roger Wilson thought of those meetings as part of the in-service training of trustees, I never knew, but he must have been thinking also of the in-service training of teachers, because it was a matter being discussed at the time.

To some extent we also learned from each other. I regretted that Michael Rowntree of the *Oxford Times* and the *Oxford Mail* seldom spoke of his experience there. Like several others he was a mine of information about Quakers both from school days and from the Friends Ambulance Unit or Friends Relief Service. William Fraser could speak of the Quaker College at Woodbrooke in Selly Oak, Birmingham of which he had been warden. There was no lack of good advice regarding Quaker enterprises. There were then and later a sprinkling of Social Workers and teachers, mainly at University level, two of whom were women. The original trustees were all men drawn from the Rowntree family. It did not astonish anyone in 1904 even in Quaker circles. There was an assumption that women were not interested in money matters, I suppose.

Since the Rowntree firm was bought by the Swiss firm Nestlé the Rowntree Charitable Trust has a great list of securities yielding some four million pounds annually and has become one of the largest trusts. Passing along a photographic exhibition of its work, I overheard one lady say to another 'What a lot of good work they do!' The reply was curt and quick, 'If I had all that money, I'd do a lot of good work.' Her tone was envious rather than appreciative and I have been wondering whether the great living donor philanthropists, such as Ted Turner, who gave one billion dollars to the United Nations, and George Soros who gave an enormous amount of charitable grants to Eastern European countries to allow them to become democratic; and Bill Gates who has given twenty-two billion dollars for general charitable purposes, may produce envy rather than an encouragement to others to give what they can, and derive some satisfaction that they are doing what is right.

Professor Roger Wilson speaking with me, at a meeting of the Joseph Rowntree Trust, of which he was chairperson.

238

This sum that Ted Turner has given is nearly equal to half the usual annual budget of the UN. The size of this gift is only matched by the wisdom with which it is being spent. The USA is being helped to pay its debts, the opposition to birth control by the Catholic Church is being evaded, the tobacco firms are to be defeated in moving their markets to the Third World and to children.

Two things need to be done as a result of this extraordinary generosity. Most billionaires are so deeply accustomed to accumulating wealth that they cannot stop adding golden numbers to golden numbers. The first is to ensure that he is thanked by people he would like to have thanking him. The second is to persuade others to follow his example and to invite some statements from him might help. Already Ted Turner appears to have tempted the Bill Gates Foundation to support him, with a twenty-five million dollar grant. Such people are able to stand up against the global firms, which break the rules. There is hope yet.

There are some things that a large trust can do on account of its size and it is appropriate for it, with its larger paid staff to look thoroughly into larger projects, knowing that smaller trusts often follow its lead, especially when they have little first hand knowledge of the people and the planned work. In our much smaller, and yet by English standards, the medium sized Polden-Puckham Foundation, formed from two family trusts of which I was the only common member, we avoided the family name for reasons of privacy and borrowed the names of the hills related to each part of the family. I notice that this is a rare practice, even among Friends. This was initiated by the younger members of the family who quite rightly shun publicity. 'Money is the thief of the soul' is for them a congenial proverb but nevertheless it is hard to persuade them to take Joseph Rowntree's advice and spend the capital. The only comparable body known to me, which did spend its capital, was the Society of Friends and it seemed to cause much trouble among the employees and others when the spending of capital came to an end.

There is a large preponderance of proverbs suggesting that it is best to avoid too much wealth as well as too little.

If thou art poor do not make a rich man thy friend. Chad.
Surety in poverty is better than fear in riches. Old English.
All doors are opened by a golden key. Estonia
Wealth comes and goes like the shadow of the palm tree. Bihar.
Fortune goes but pride remains. Iran.
Where there is more than enough, more than enough is
      wasted. Bantu.

Before the Polden and Puckham Trusts were joined together, when each was a very small trust, I had to manage the two separately. My fellow trustees were my brother Jan for one half and my wife Ruth for the other. Jan lived in Nairobi, in charge of the Herbarium and letters took a long time to reach him. Ruth was busy with our six children and the large old house in Selly Oak. In addition she was suspicious of money and the dangers it brings and was very glad to leave it to me. I was very far from participating in the organisations we supported as Joseph Rowntree hoped would happen with his trustees and for the most part gave small amounts to organisations or people with whom I was well acquainted. It does not surprise me that it was at that time I made a mistake.

Believing a woman journalist's stories about the many journalists with whom she had worked, we set up an institute to enlarge the knowledge of peace issues for journalists, who dominate the media and were beginning to overshadow parliament. It soon became clear that she had kept moving from one paper to another for psychological reasons and her outbursts against Quakers, teachers, and peace activists were so preposterous that the initiative was firmly brought to an end. Her language was so extreme that I ought not to have believed that she could make a success of what she undertook to do, but it is easy to be wise after the event. When Polly Toynbee wrote about Evelyn Waugh she expressed contempt for the cynicism of those journalists who prefer 'do-badders' to 'do gooders.' Journalists need to be saved from journalism and no one knows how that can be done, unless maybe by such people as the Buddhist writer Thich Nat Hanh, who might heal them with an eloquent smile.

Fortunately there have been plenty of success stories to compensate for this mistake, though success is often harder to identify. Anyone applying to have a grant continued is naturally keen to demonstrate that a further grant would be building on success. This is what appeals to donors.

The mysterious world of grant-making which I needed to understand both for the sake of the Joseph Rowntree Charitable Trust where I had been a student for the two little trusts which I had for a time to manage alone, left me still fairly ignorant. People involved in trusts tended to be secretive for fear of being swamped with applications. Factual information derived from the grant-making trusts themselves, omitted vital suggestions about the various ways of making grants and the even more varied purposes for which grants are given. Here are some examples:

Ways of Making Grants

One off: For example to meet some exceptional expenditure like office furniture.

A small exploratory grant so as to provide time to get better acquainted.

A continuing grant e.g. to provide security for an additional employee.

A tapering grant to ensure that fund-raising is continued and other supporters are discovered.

A matching or conditional grant to reassure the donor that others have a favourable impression.

A prompt grant. The donors on average meet between two and three times a year and fund-raisers, especially those helping new organisations, are likely to be in a hurry to get started.

Objectives of Grants

To cover core costs especially when others prefer to back projects.

To help 'prime the pump' by paying for fundraising.

To ensure the hunt for better ways of working is maintained by promoting travel.

To encourage new ideas by means of prizes for school children, students or the general public.

To encourage authors.

To ensure that the dissemination of good findings is fostered
   by Videos etc.
In setting up a new organisation, to ensure that e.g.
   Mark Lattimer's *On Campaigning*[44] is read.
Study-grants and sabbaticals for improving qualifications
   so as to avoid growing stale.
To act on the principle that campaigning has become a
   profession depending on many skills: e.g. by
   correspondence and seminars on strategy.

This sounds like a very cut and dried bureaucratic existence for
the trustees and administrators of the future, but this is very far
from the truth. Being agents of social change they have to deal with
the future and like teachers they have to keep a variety of Utopias
in mind. This is about as remote as a satellite from the conventional grant-making trust repeating its grants from year to year,
which may well have been inappropriate to the situation even when
they were first awarded. Susan Forrester, the author of
Environmental Grants published by the Directory of Social Change,
writes about the failure of trusts to fund energy conservation, and
alternative energy sources, appropriate technology, pollution
control, and population control despite opportunities and despite
the larger sums going into the conservation of the architectural
heritage and wildlife. Whether the BBC's efforts to remedy this
failure will be effective, remain to be seen. I received a polite but
useful reply from the National Trust when I wrote pointing out that
'Enterprise Neptune,' their campaign to protect the coast is nulli-
fied by the pollution of the Welsh coast, and part of the English
coast, by discharges from Sellafield.[45]

The major difficulty regarding charitable trusts is the scarcity
of good trustees. The Rowntree Charitable Trust after losing several
of its members who felt overcome by trying to keep their job, their
families and the trust all satisfied simultaneously, went so far as to
advertise for trustees, but that was among members of the Society
of Friends (Quakers). They look for someone with good committee skills; someone who knows when to speak up and when to listen,
someone who is informed about one or more of the fields in which
the Trust works, and is keen to learn about the others and knows

something about money and the difference it can make in good hands.

It is doubtful whether for the Rowntree Charitable Trust, it is necessary to stress the importance of new ideas because this is taken for granted. Other trusts may be glad to develop a routine. Considering how much time and unpaid work is expected of trustees they cannot really be blamed. On one occasion a JRCT trustee sought approval for travelling from London in a first-class coach so that he could read his pages of the agenda free from disturbance. This seemed un-Quakerly to the trust at the time, but that was before the resignations.

Neil Wates, the chairman of the building firm, came to York to seek advice about forming his trust and asked how we found trustees. An explanation was given of the Quaker method of laying a concern on their members. It makes a difference if the invitation comes not as 'Would you like etc.' but 'We think you should seriously consider etc.' He was a delightful man; I remember the pleasure with which he showed me how his cows were milked on his farm; the power for the machine coming from the biogas from the cow's manure. He asked our secretary on his visit to York how it was possible to fund projects in Northern Ireland while knowing what was going on over there. The reply began 'To begin with we have a trustee in Belfast' referring to my period there during the nineteen seventies. In general it is good for Quakers to work on conflict situations where they are already known for their welfare service. They are already known for their help before conflict management begins and they know to whom they can turn for help. This explains the name of the former Quaker Committee of Friends House in London, Quaker Peace, and Service. There must have been some very good reason for changing to the new name 'Quaker Peace and Social Witness.' In this connection it is worth noting that the UN benefits, to some extent, by the same association; where its social work has given it a good name it is easier for its Peacekeepers to serve when conflicts are finishing.

In establishing a new trust it is very attractive to the donor to make it a family trust. In that way the founders may meet their children on a regular basis, possibly extending invitations to friends or other relatives and making it an enjoyable social occasion.

243

Sometimes such meetings are strengthened by the attendance of a lawyer or an accountant and take on a more formal procedure. I have heard complaints that when no one outside the family attends no one can insist on one person speaking at a time! As the year's pass and new generations take on the task, they tend to drift apart. A very tempting solution then is to allot a fraction of the income to each trustee to donate. In the only case of this, which is familiar to me, it has not worked well. People like to point out that committees do not write poems and that inspiration comes to individuals, but good grants are different from poems.

The Network Foundation provides the opposite of a single person working independently. I attended its first meeting in England and we heard how wealthy young people who wished to give money to good causes decided to join together to discuss their grants. The proposal was made by an American who explained how it was done in the USA, how they became known as the Doughnuts because they were 'nuts' to give away their 'dough.' At an earlier meeting they were asked to carry a label to say 'how much they were worth.' Reading my face from across the crowded room, he added 'No Nick, we're not proposing to do that here. We know England has a different culture.' I did not attend another meeting, not because I disapproved, but so as to leave the field clear for those of my family who wished to take part by drawing on funds from the trust. It indicated another way of finding trustees namely by bonding together with others to help each other make grants.

Thinking about it later I began to wonder that there is no way for young persons or people retiring early to train as trustees before offering their services as volunteers. A practical study-course might be established consisting of visits to funded work in a variety of fields, visits to charitable trusts to hear and question their administration, mixed with some reading about the charity laws and the major recipients of charitable funding. No doubt the failure to fill important gaps in funding would create a good discussion. Very recently, having been told that our little Polden-Puckham Trust is nevertheless the second largest donor to peace organisations, I was appalled to think that, though the danger of nuclear weapons has never been greater either from suicidal terrorists, or from accidents, nothing is being done to reduce the risks. I was accordingly very happy to be invited, along with my son Bevis, to attend a meeting to form a new trust to deal with additional peace applications. The new capital was to be drawn from new sources such as highly paid musicians, and note might be taken of Ted Turners' suggestion that the very rich might be invited to join in supporting the UN.

Before leaving the issue of finding more trustees and improving their skills, it is necessary to point out that the future may lie with directors who make the hard decisions which are then rubber-stamped, or passed on the nod by trustees, whose main work is to choose effective directors. Issues such as this may be taken up by the new Centre for Civil Society at the London School of Economics as described in the LSE Magazine,[46] where one of the foci will be charities and their management. It is already a substantial Centre with 16 staff, and numerous post-graduate students. In a few years time charities will no longer need to work in the dark.

Another issue, which is bound to turn up, is ethical investment by the grant-making charities. Ethical investment has only spread recently. In Britain trustees were assured with confidence that the law required them to maximise the trusts' income without taking ethics into account. This requirement was due to the danger of the trustees corruptly supporting firms in which they had a personal interest. Now the reverse is the case, and Reed Abelson attacks Bill and Melinda Gates for funding cancer charities while investing in Philip Morris the tobacco firm.[47] He must have been joking for even if blocks of shares averaged a million dollars in value, there would still be 22,000 blocks to manage in their $22 Billion Foundation, and an oversight would be pardonable, one would suppose.

The view that 'If you have a large endowment, the power derived from investing to create change is probably greater than the power of your grant-making'[48] may be correct. If Chief Executives are sympathetic or interested in public relations, if the charity has skilled negotiators, and the climate of opinion is more supportive than in Britain, it is likely. In 1997 the Council on Foundations (USA) found 15% of its members had used ethical factors, but that it is more common among the smaller foundations. Now that change is in the air in both the USA and Britain, it is likely that more trusts and larger trusts will respond to the challenges to invest more ethically. The huge pension funds of British Universities have already decided to take part, and take part more thoroughly than merely omitting tobacco shares, extending even to the trade in small arms. It will not be easy to achieve, because as early as 1932 for the first large Conference on Disarmament, the arms firms were paying agents to become disruptive elements in these meetings to make no progress possible. They continued acting in this way after the war and when Ruth and I were in Geneva 1980-1982, or so it was believed.

Since that time ethical investment has grown rapidly into a wide ethical movement, consumers have built up various practices such as 'Fair Trade' and Visa charity cards and shareholders have added negotiations with firms to the more usual practice of moving their funds. Robin Cook on becoming Secretary of State for Foreign Affairs even promised a more ethical foreign policy. It may not amount to much change in arms firms supplying arms to oppressive regimes, but it was clear where his sympathies lay. One wonders now whether those who make the most illegal weapons are trying to shift public interest away from themselves to the suppliers of small arms. What astonishes me are the old arguments that making weapons is needed to keep people in work, when it would be much better to have more nurses and teachers, and so the next question follows: 'What happens to the balance of payments in that event?' 'If necessary the nurses and teachers can work abroad, there is an unsatisfied demand for such skilled people. In addition if it led to a lowering of the value of the pound, that would increase exports of other kinds and reduce imports so as to reach a new balance.' The idea that every change puts someone out of work should always be questioned. The answer lies in the alternative ways in which the money is spent, some work involves much labour and some little. A chemical factory in Bristol depended on the part-time work of a single person, that kind of work is not labour intensive like a school, which employs many people, with its expenditure made up mainly of wages.

Society would dissolve in chaos if profit were the sole motive to consider when making decisions. Self-interest, selfishness and greed are capable of destroying whole civilisations, despite what some famous economists have argued. Those who live their lives on nobler principles are to be protected at all costs, and cherished as the light that leads the way. This is what the lady was thinking and saying as she removed our furniture in lieu of taxes, this was what brought the tears to her eyes as Ruth put her thoughts into words. This is what Mrs Thatcher never understood and never learnt at Somerville from her tutor, Dorothy Hodgkin. This is what is at the heart of the ethical movement. Furthermore the ethical movement is an essential attribute of democracy.

If there were fewer funds than there are at present, which are free of government control and of control by the large firms, which are often multinational themselves, the hopes of democrats for freedom from oppression, from war and exploitation would be less. Civilisation stands on three pillars, political power exercised by the government, economic power of the larger firms and what is coming to be called the civil power of the rest of which the grant-making trusts are coming to be a significant part. Personally I never saw it that way until recently. I imagined that the churches formed the third power, and certainly many of them deserve a place as part of the third pillar. Now as I read the proud words of the representatives of the Non-Governmental Organisations (NGO's), who attended their alternative conference at the UN in New York, I begin to understand how much the UN's Secretary General values their support that strengthens his arm against governments which are disloyal to the UN. On the principle of the separation of powers for the sake of democratic liberty I am strongly in favour of increasing the strength of the weakest of the three pillars by welcoming the very rich leaving their money to charity. It is particularly valuable in the USA and I envisage a time when the big global firms can be influenced by the massive fortunes created by their predecessors. To my surprise I had a visit from one of Rupert Murdoch's heirs who wished to know about the strategy of our little trust. He said that peace and the environment would be his two main fields. Barclays Bank doubles any funds collected for good causes by their employees, setting a useful precedent for others to follow. It almost makes me wish I had remained in that Bank, as my father had expected me to do.

Already the Government and the existing Trusts are hoping that there will be in the future more grant-making trusts with more money to spend. This form of privatisation is not open to the same objections as, for example, the privatisation of the railways in Britain. Anyone who sets up such a trust and gives it their own name will be likely to ensure that it has a good reputation for generous and enlightened grants. Their successors may not regard it with the same enthusiasm and this may well be an additional argument for trusts of a limited duration. Ideally, it could be argued, new problems really need trustees who have different values and assumptions but the present practices of creating self-perpetuating trusts makes no allowance for this. It is of interest that the Joseph Rowntree Charitable Foundation, which was founded from the Village Trust, has a provision, whereby alternate new trustees, are chosen by The Society of Friends.

Now and then I read in the papers about a publication by one of the three Rowntree Trusts and then I remember that Social Reform depends usually on some legislation or administrative changes but also on a change in values or attitudes. This leads one to feel that the public relations of charitable work are severely neglected because all funds seem to be needed for the basic work. It is clear when stated that prisoners who are released to make a fresh start, will benefit from an understanding public, as much as by an after-prison service. It is not enough to train mediators, it is necessary to create the atmosphere in which mediation can flourish. It is not easily done because the media pay more attention to social breakdown than to social build up. At least it is good to know that the grant-making trusts have organised themselves in the Association of Charitable Foundations (ACF). This apparently minor piece of organisation has the potential to become the agent with the power to keep global firms in order by helping form the third pillar.

As Stephen Burkeman has clarified in his illuminating paper, motives are always mixed, I plead guilty myself, but we try to do our best to start the new millennium as though it was going to be, according to the third meaning of the word, 'a period of happiness and benign government,'[49] when larger firms and wealthy people give so much to the needy that the worlds' major problems, if not being solved are on the way to being solved. It is worth trying, if attitudes and values are included in the change.

248

The work of grant-making trusts, like the function of churches and schools, has much to do with the quality of life. This attractive but elusive phrase deserves, perhaps more attention. In a sense it is the modern equivalent of 'truth, goodness and beauty,' and 'liberty, equality, and fraternity' but, being much more vague attracts less opposition when a trust mentions it among its aims. I attempted to change Shakespeare's words in the following way, having first considered Portia in *The Merchant of Venice* inviting Shylock to season Justice with Mercy:

Letting work become a form of service.
Illuminating travel with curiosity.
Deepening friendship with caring.
Trading with fairness.
Shopping, keeping charity in mind.
In business building with bricks of trust.
Enlivening social contacts with smiles and humour.
Treating children with tenderness.
Enhancing charity with selflessness.

These look odd for what they include and for what they omit, but they represent some thoughts of the moment and may encourage others to express their own thoughts about matching ordinary activities with ideals.

CHAPTER 15

Belfast in the Troubles

FROM A PERSONAL point of view 1975-1977 in Belfast came like a cold bath, refreshing after the event as the blood returned, but shocking to the senses at the first plunge. Ruth and I had never met so many people in the grip of hatred and fear. We had an easy time during the Second World War and apart from helping refugees, had not seen much of the causes and consequences of wars at first hand, so I sometimes felt handicapped when speaking or writing about it. Belfast helped us to fill the gap in our experience. We had often expressed sympathy with refugees of violence in Spain and Germany but often felt we lacked the right words and the right experiences.

After some skilled briefing at Friends House in Euston Road, we were sent by Quaker Peace and Service as Quaker representatives in a troubled area, we arrived in Belfast and were welcomed by our predecessors, John Whatley, and his wife, to complete our briefing. We were housed in the caretaker's bungalow built onto the back of the Friends Meeting House in Frederick Street, a couple of hundred yards north-east of the city centre. On the opposite side of the road were a long line of terraced houses, very small by modern standards, a warehouse used for repair of cars, a poultry food factory, and a very large department store built by the Co-operative Wholesale Society. On our side the corner was occupied by a large brick building, which served as a Youth Club. Until recently Protestants and Catholics had been equal in numbers, but owing to changes in population in the area there were few remaining Protestants. This introduced us to the difficulties involved in

250

The destruction, by burning, of cars and buses led to the prosperity of taxi drivers in Belfast during the troubles.

Soldiers in Belfast, 1972. Ruth and I admired the non-violence of such soldiers and thought that they might make good peacekeepers. The only time we had this treatment was when taking part in a march for peace with "The Peace People"

252

preventing the formation of ghettoes as the two groups sorted themselves out away from each other throughout the city.

Later I was to learn that boys from our area were unwilling to work in the shipyard partly because the journey there involved crossing a hundred yards of enemy territory! Next to the club building was a large car park with a sinister attendant who kept a suspicious eye on comings and goings. The Quaker Meeting House comes next and beyond it an empty bombed out area, which was occupied by the caravans of 'travellers' from the Republic of Ireland. On one occasion I went to visit them when their children had been throwing stones over the high wall and hitting our roof. 'Oh no!' came the reply, 'our children would never do a thing like that.' 'Well' I replied 'if you ever see any other children throwing stones over the wall, tell them that it is too dangerous.' On the spur of the moment I decided not to accuse them of lying, it is important to have friendly neighbours in troubled times.

The Whatleys left on a Monday. The following day a car drove up to the repair shop opposite, the foreman a Protestant was shot dead, the car drove away, a television crew arrived and I was left wondering whether John Whatley's departure had some connection with the event, whether there was some mysterious reason for Frederick Street being coloured red on a map of Belfast Centre, published in the Economist, which showed where most murders had been committed. I also wondered how long Ruth would stay if the violence was repeated, I should have understood her better after forty years of married life. She never questioned whether Belfast was the place for us to be, quickly got to know the housewives in the street and marvelled when they assured her that when a murder happened, they prayed not just for the victim and family but also for the murderer.

The level of violence was in fact lower than a television viewer in England might expect. In 1976 the average number of bombs used each day was only four. My first task in planning our work was to make an amateur systems analysis of the causes of the troubles, and the reasons for not settling the dispute in a law court. I found out some remarkable facts.

A Protestant and a Catholic Youth worker, who cooperated with each other very well, had gone to the USA to fund-raise. They told me that they were surprised to read in the Irish newspapers circulating widely throughout the country, advertisements offering prizes for every soldier and policeman killed in Northern Ireland. This is the seamy side of the freedom for which the USA is known. The dispute is triangular, the Protestants, or Loyalists forming one angle of the triangle, who made the mistakes of gerrymandering or relocating the boundary lines of electoral districts to benefit their party. The term comes from Massachusetts where Governor Gerry had produced one district in the early 1800's in the shape of a Salamander and the two names were combined. By this and similar devices they may be said to have provided their share of the troubles. Secondly the British Government has to take its share of the blame for the Black and Tans and other forms of official repression. The Catholics or Republicans form the third angle.

Lately the situation seems to have hardened into an almost unbreakable sequence of cause and effect, the Republicans or Catholics point out that most jobs are created by Protestants, who obviously prefer not to have on their payroll, people who might wish, or become coerced into using bombs. Funding for IRA organisers, or 'godfathers' as they were termed, was provided by demanding protection money from banks, shops, and offices. Skilled explosive experts who had served in the British army were said to have been employed. When accused of causing too much damage in Northern Ireland they switched their offensive to England in the hope of persuading voters to vote for peace at any price. The Protestants, caricatured by the so-called Reverent Ian Paisley, stiffened their opposition to negotiations with unrepentant murderers, as they considered them. The longer their situation lasted, the more it seemed impossible to change. When a Quaker building firm asked me if it was possible to build for those who had their homes burned down and those who were forced to leave, I had to admit that the activists on both sides would demand so much protection money that it was not practical to accept the offer, quite apart from the difficulty of finding safe places to build. I wish now that I had taken this opportunity to plead with the two sides. When I went to see the two groups of leaders of the paramilitaries, without any prompting from me, they remarked: 'There is one thing I am sure about, I don't want to see my son living as I have done.' There was no hint that they were prepared to do anything new to ensure it. They insisted that their opponents had to make a change. They had learned to be adamant and adamant they would remain no matter what the cost.

They may sound as though they were horrible people but they were pleasant, almost charming. They have warmth, which is exceptional, and many attractive virtues, for example the Irish enjoy the English language more than the English do. Their authors, poets, playwrights, and storytellers provide the evidence for that. When Professor Adam Curle was staying with us, he took a black taxi, one of those replacing the burnt out buses on the Falls Road (Catholic) or Shankill Road (Protestant). He was waiting in the taxi for it to fill up and by way of making conversation enquired of the taxi driver:

'How many passengers can you take?'

After some reflection, as though he was answering this question for the first time he replied:

'Well, six contagious or eight familiar.' Meaning side-by-side or using laps.

Most visitors to Ireland can cap such stories; my favourite from a Dublin friend was travelling in the south and coming to a level-crossing where one of the two gates was closed. After waiting longer than usual, he left his car and went to the shed to find the attendant and asked:

'What time is the train due and how is it that one gate is already open?'

'Ah well. Yes, there is a train from Dublin due, and I am half expecting it.'

This use of language is a sheer delight in times of peace but can be very mischievous in stirring up animosity. The slogan of Protestant areas 'No Pope here,' was softened by a Catholic adding the words 'Lucky old Pope.' A war of words may seem to be preferable to a shooting war and yet those defeated feel so resentful that it may lead to more bombing and killing. There are qualities in

255

Irish people, which fit them for leadership such as an irrational optimism and a preference for the stirring word rather than the truth, which gets them into all kinds of difficulties. More than their numbers appear to justify, they are to be found among the British Trade Union leaders and British Field Marshals. It may be that the English are to blame for the enjoyment of breaking rules; in particular government rules and regulations. A community worker told me he had been trying to persuade people to plant some flowers in their front gardens but there were no results. He thought rightly that this would compensate for the drab appearance of the town and be good for morale. Later the city with a similar thought decided on flowers for some traffic roundabouts and some good topsoil was dumped one day. He rubbed his eyes the next morning when he noticed the dumps had disappeared and realised that his advice had been taken in a way he had not intended.

Ruth and I were visiting the Irish Republic and were about to take seats in a non-smoking compartment. Ruth who was more interested than I was in avoiding the smoke and smell of cigarettes, commented on the quantity of stubs on the floor in this empty train. The stubs were so numerous that there was no gap between them bigger than the span of my fingers, so I asked her to wait a moment while I went to look in the smoking compartment. My theory was borne out. There were less than half as many stubs in there so we moved our luggage for the journey to Waterford and went on our way rejoicing.

Smoking is a trivial matter compared with more serious offences against law and order, such as the smuggling of weapons and the use of threats to obtain 'protection' money. It is sometimes difficult to keep the 'troubles' in perspective. The number of people killed and most likely the number of wounded compare favourably with those killed and wounded in road accidents. Moreover, for the soldiers it is safer to serve in Northern Ireland than in Germany or Britain because they are not allowed to drive when off duty in Ireland. What is difficult to believe is that it is the hatred and fear which consumes people, like a terrible disease, which is the price people pay for their unwillingness to change. Fear includes fear to leave the house empty, fear of a knock on the door in the night, anxiety about children, fear to use certain streets, of more riots, suspicion that some members of the family have joined an illegal organisation secretly. It is the contrary, the direct opposite of the 'Culture of Peace,' it is indeed a culture of war. By indulging in anger and hatred we strengthen the bars of our own prison. The quality of life goes down rapidly like a scree-runner sliding from point to point, towards the ultimate barbarism of social chaos. Whenever we are tempted to join in sharing anger we need to ask ourselves how can this strong feeling be turned to a constructive purpose?

My own reaction to this at the time was to write a book about the children in Northern Ireland and their schools. Like most books it remained unpublished but in the course of writing it I learned much of interest. I learned that any school, which desired to join the scheme, could have an additional teacher to visit the homes. Owing to the burning down and or bombing of houses many families doubled up to make room for more people and in any case it helps teachers to know the conditions in the homes. Sometimes the new teacher visited the homes herself; sometimes she taught the class while the regular class teacher visited. By these means it became possible not only to deal with individual children with more understanding but the class as a whole may benefit when a teacher learns from the parents of the fears and hopes of the children, on which lessons can be built.

It is possible that one or two of those who introduced the home teacher scheme may have been unwilling to talk about it for fear of being thought to be too revolutionary. Parents as well as teachers tend to be conservative in choosing teaching subjects and methods, otherwise the schools would not appear to be helping solve the problems of the previous decade. It cannot be said too often that, in educating future teachers in Universities, they will be in mid-career twenty years later, and that the children they will be teaching at that time will be in their mid-career thirty years later than that, making fifty years ahead, the appropriate target on which to set our sights.

That may be fifty years beyond certainty and the faint-hearted may give up the attempt. Others will look at the changes, which have occurred since 1950 and take that as a measure of what to expect. The growth in population is almost certain to continue, providing the violence associated with over-crowding. Control over our bodies and brains, is likely to be enhanced during that period, these will form the new frontier rather than space. The destruction of the environment may produce cooperation or conflict. This may depend in turn on the development of social education, as opposed to intellectual education. The world needs more Gandhis than Einsteins. Cloning could become a curse or a cure.

In addition to the Home Teachers there were other notable features of the educational system attempting to ease the conflict. The first school for mixed pupils was established. I remember hearing that vandals had damaged the buildings of Lagan College in the night and wondering whether it might prove impossible to persist. It not only survived but it has been replicated.

Another welcome factor was the development of Social Studies in both primary and secondary schools. One of these attempts, the Rowntree Charitable Trust funded. It was called 'The Schools Cultural Studies Project', and I was welcomed onto its Consultative Board. Under the guidance of a former Catholic nun, mixed groups of teachers developed the texts of a series of Social Studies books for the first four years of the Secondary Schools. Professor Malcolm Skilbeck, of the New University of Ulster had been a colleague of mine at Bristol and his interest in curricular reform encouraged him to originate the project to reveal some of the staffing and other problems, which face reformers. The Protestants and Catholics were able to study each other's cultures and, if all went well, to appreciate them; this was attempted by many gradual steps. Unless the difficulties are appreciated of all the participants, parents, children, teachers, and Principals, it is hard to gauge the obstacles to curricular reform, however much it is needed. Some concluded in despair that the attempt should never have been made, and teachers should be replaced by newcomers to the profession. When I attended a session of the mixed groups of teachers producing the texts line by line, it seemed that the new Ireland was being born before my eyes and that the teaching profession was proving to be it's best mid-wife. I was glad to be able to give some encouragement.

The troubles of Northern Ireland have been so fully reported that it would be inappropriate to add to them and it is time to pass on to the minor activities which we could undertake to justify the cost of Ruth and me staying there. In the early days of 1975 we were hesitant but gradually found our feet and did more. My very first action was to try to find Giovanni Guareschi, the author of the six or more books about Don Camillo, the Catholic priest who had tricks to play on his opponent the Communist mayor of the village in Italy, where they lived. The author had just the right sense of humour to help the Irish to laugh at themselves. Even hatred can be dispelled by humour. It was a great pity that he died in 1968, the year before the 'troubles' began. When another author attempted to copy his style, the book failed to make its mark, maybe it was too near the bone.

The next minor action was to entertain Waclaw Micuta, a Polish cavalry officer, who had spent his working life with the UN and his retirement on designing many different kinds of stoves to reduce fuel consumption in the Third World as one of several contributions to reducing fuel consumption. He is a Catholic and appalled by what was happening in Belfast. He would interrupt a meal and shout: 'This is not a religious quarrel' meaning that it was the old issue between the 'haves' and the 'have nots.' He is a man of action, never contenting himself with deciding what needed to be done. In Frederick Street he set off with Jonny to buy a wheelbarrow and tools to allow us to set an example in improving front gardens. When he added an axe to the tools, Jonny looked so doubtful about it that he asked him what was wrong with that. Jonny replied 'Dad will say it looks as though it's intended to be a weapon.' 'Alright' he replied 'No axe.' We used those tools to plant among other things a Philadelphus, the bush of brotherly love, just inside the front gate, of the meeting house. It was only later that I realised its other name is Mock Orange, orange being the colour of militant Protestantism. Guareschi would have appreciated the situation. I suspect there were some members of the Meeting who did not like it, but did not dare to say so! Whose leg were we pulling? Some of the Quakers were very strong Protestants!

Sometimes we seemed to be either just making friends or just waiting. At other times, days were not long enough. On one occasion I wrote a paper for the secretary of State for Northern Ireland Merlyn Rees at Stormont and was invited to go to see him there.

On entering I was twice requested to lay my guns on the table, a strange request for a Quaker to receive, but a useful reminder of the miserable life led by people in his position. For reasons of security he had been advised to send his son to boarding school and had chosen Leighton Park, being a member of the Labour Party, so it was very easy to talk with him. At the time there were moves to restore the self-government that had been terminated in 1972 but nothing came of them because the parties refused to sit down with people they called terrorists. The theme of my paper was that, although I could cite no precedents, legislation could be carried on by correspondence, indeed that there might be some benefits from avoiding the antagonism generated by debates in person. I was assured that my suggestions had been carefully considered before being rejected. Merlyn Rees seemed to be a wise, statesmanlike person and it seems a great pity that he is not an MP any longer.

On another occasion we met Airey Neave a Conservative MP concerned with Northern Ireland. He had been talking with the IRA, though this was officially denied. When he was a prisoner of war he had written an account of escaping from prison that he called 'They Have Their Exits'[50] after Shakespeare's lines in *As You Like It*:

> All the world's a stage,
> And all the men and women merely players;
> They have their exits and their entrances
> And one man in his time plays many parts.

He had been at a Nursery Class with Ruth and remarked that he had made such a nuisance of himself that as he confessed, he had been asked to leave. To which I could not restrain from adding 'They have their exits.' Poor man: he was killed by a car bomb at the House of Commons. I could never guess what the IRA had against him. They should have thanked him for daring to meet them.

We also made the acquaintance of Mr and Mrs Middleton. He had been seconded from the Foreign and Colonial Office to serve the Secretary of State. He was very friendly and in the course of conversation I discovered to my amazement that he had been a student at Saltley College, before I taught there. His wife was equally friendly and I was sorry that, for political reasons, I had to refuse their kind offer to stay with them during my convalescence; I had to be first and foremost a Quaker and British second, in the circumstances of Northern Ireland. We also had an offer from Denis and Monica Barritt; Denis was the author of *Orange and Green: Northern Ireland*,[51] that was used by the army to brief its soldiers, and Monica proved to be a very expert nurse. They convinced us that I would be better in the quiet of the countryside far away from Frederick Street. After pushing a car whose engine would not start, I had collapsed, feeling as though an elephant was sitting on my chest. An army patrol passing by had called an ambulance and I went into a hospital where eventually a Pakistani doctor diagnosed aortic valve trouble.

Two prominent members of the neutral Alliance Party came and prayed very suitably at my bedside as though I was preparing for the next life! This however was not to be, for the operation was a success. It consisted of replacing my valve with a plastic one from America, so that I can now justly claim to be partly American. I was moved to the Catholic hospital on the Falls Road. For the first time a bomb was found there. Until then hospitals had been regarded as a sanctuary free from the stress that other buildings had suffered. The excuse for this change was said to be due to the army using a room in the hospital as a storeroom. When I reported the news to Ruth she smiled in disbelief, because the medicine I was given produced such hallucinations that I could not believe my own eyes, let alone what I heard. On one occasion I had a visitor, dressed in black. I thought I knew that he was real because I could see him clearly and hear what he said. Eventually I admitted that I wanted to confirm his reality and sat up to poke him. He disappeared into thin air.

I wonder whether what seems to outsiders the turgid reasoning of the Irish, which helps them in telling and writing stories, is connected with the diet they eat. There may be trace elements in their soil, which gets into their food and results in them seeing things differently from other people, though to call it hallucination might be too strong. Is it better or worse when Bobby Sands starves himself to death instead of being hung? What do those who claim Home Rule for Ireland as a whole, say about Home Rule for

Northern Ireland? Does the same principle hold good for both? How much further evidence is required that violence is no more satisfying in the results obtained than non-violence? On one occasion when I was about to leave for England there was a strike in the ship-yards. Seeing a group of disgruntled strikers standing at the street corner I crossed the road and explained that I was going to England and would be likely to be asked about the reasons for the strike. 'What should I say?' I asked. All I got as a reply was 'We're on strike because they won't let us work.' He would add nothing to clarify this mysterious statement. I had the impression that he was too angry to speak. In his case his command of language had failed him.

It was my turn to feel that words failed me when attending a conference on the causes of violence, organised, if I understood correctly by Lord Peter Melchett in his official capacity as deputy to Merlyn Rees. The causes of war are much discussed by historians and others but I found it very refreshing to be looking at them from a new point of view; dealing with personal violence driven by poverty and anger as well as a desire for power, and considering whether women are different in respect of violence. All I had to contribute were my observations about diet and climate. The members of the conference wanted to talk about oppression and injustice as though aggression was always due to the wrongdoing of other people causing frustration. I would have liked to have persuaded them that that was only part of the issue. Years later I returned for a conference with the tempting title 'After Hatred' which was well conceived and executed except that no psychologist was invited to speak about the sublimation of hard feelings. The Truth Commission in South Africa has helped to make progress since that time by promising forgiveness to those who repent and make confessions.

Gerald Priestland, the BBC's expert on religious affairs would have wished to adapt the Truth Commission for Northern Ireland had he lived longer. When he stayed with us he was rather incommunicative, either because he was depressed by Belfast or he may already have been ailing from his fatal illness. He asked me whether I could take him to hear Ian Paisley preach. Paisley was in his usual form more rumbustious than ruminant, making a mockery of

Christianity. His 'church' building invites the congregation to worship the preacher more than anything else and Gerald delivered a whole programme about the experience on the radio. He never let me know he was planning this. I never saw him again until we met on a Quaker Committee to select a name to be put forward for the Nobel Peace Prize. The Committee has the right to do this because Quaker Peace and Service was awarded the prize in a previous year.

From our point of view the greatest event of our period in Belfast was the rise and convergence of the Peace People, the two Peace Women Mairead Corrigan (McGuire) and Betty Williams together with Ciaran McKeowen. The theme of their messages was that the time had come to make peace, that no one in their senses wanted to live the rest of their lives in fear of bombs. It was a Christian message in a city full of church-going people and that violence seldom brings justice. It was an emotional message that had a wide appeal, so wide that it seemed to be only the godfathers and the youngsters whose ideas about a united Ireland were firmly established, who would not accept it. Ciaran provided an authoritative promotion of the themes of non-violence, Betty Williams the crusty humour, and Mairead with her strong appeal to the emotions, aroused an enthusiastic response from their huge audiences such as is seldom seen in political life nowadays and it is seldom that such a trio cooperate so well. They led a procession from the Falls Road, to the Shankill Road and apart from a few stones thrown by ignorant children were received with open arms. Their achievements were remarkable. All the people who, being exasperated by the cruelty and extortions of the paramilitaries, had been waiting for something like this to happen, took the chance of showing where they stood by joining in the activities. They offered the young people still at school a chance to make a break with the past so that the groups of paramilitaries were severely threatened.

The paramilitaries waited for a mistake to be made and this took the form of journalists asking the two women what they were going to do with their Nobel Peace Prize money. Being unprepared for such a question they faltered and were mocked by the journalists and in due course by their readers. The support for them from that day onwards began to fail to some degree. Nevertheless much

263

of this good work of the Peace People among young people continues, even after twenty-five years. It was not because of a failure in strategy otherwise, the godfathers had seen their livelihood ebbing away and were glad to get back to what was normal for them.

One morning I was sitting in the Peace People's office chatting to journalists from *The Economist* and *Daily Telegraph* while we waited for interviews. I began to wonder what danger might arise if this new peace movement might come to be seen as an English initiative to bring the troubles to an end in the interest of business. A solution was soon found. An article had been written for the Peace People's paper to say that anyone whose life was in danger could apply for help at the office, but no one knew how help could be provided. There were a number of people who wished to give up setting bombs, or simply to leave the paramilitaries but did not dare face the revenge, which would follow. Others were suspected of providing information to the police. The lack of trust was widespread. I went back to Ruth and suggested to her that if other people were prepared to interview the applicants she could provide hospitality for those who were accepted, either in England or elsewhere. She quickly convened a committee of people who preferred to retain their anonymity and a satisfactory underground railway was established. Twenty-five years later I still hesitate to say how details were arranged, because the 'troubles' continue. My own job was to warn them that there were ears everywhere, especially in British public houses and that 'careless talk costs lives.' One man whom I well remember, who was very helpful with our washing up, was so rash as to return to his previous life. He was promptly murdered. There was such a pressure of work that I seldom stopped to ask applicants whether they were Catholics or Protestants. When we were able to count the number of each, they turned out to be very nearly equal, a satisfactory outcome.

There were some memorable people who came to us, such as the two men who could not face the future without their dog. Could the Peace People look after the dog until they settled and then send it to them by air, they wanted to know. Ruth undertook to send the dog, not knowing what she was taking upon herself. It was a large dog with a long tail and, as she discovered later, the regulations required a wooden box as long as the dog from its nose to the tip of its tail. She seemed to be too busy going about from the dog to the carpenter and the airport. At last the great day came for its departure in its costly wooden cage, and we half expected to hear no more about it, however in due course a cheque arrived together with a letter of thanks signed by 'The Dog.' Another couple, a man and his wife were in very special danger, according to the police, so much so that a police watch was kept over them in London for several months according to their very brave host and hostess, until they could be settled elsewhere, further away. A third case was a man who had been accused of being a police informer, in such a confused situation as in Belfast it is hard to tell who is serving whom; when there are informers informing on informers. He had been beaten, had his hair shaved off as a warning to others and threatened with his life. He was hardly in a fit state to be interviewed and the interviewer had so much pity for him that he had bought him a wig before seeing him safely onto a steamer. The question which arose later, was 'May the wig be charged to the Peace People?'

From time to time I sat down to ask myself whether we were doing what was expected of us by Quaker Peace and Service; I thought for some reason of the crossed swords fixed on the wall of Waclaw Micuta's living room. He was still a dashing cavalry officer at heart and a Catholic. It was hoped that he would become a willing neutral mediator, if ever such a person were needed. We were expected to see that he was sufficiently well informed. Was it reasonable to seek his help? The propaganda by both sides in Northern Ireland has been so successful that neither the so-called Protestants nor the so-called Catholics are capable of listening intently to each other so as to avoid misunderstandings; thus, the violence has continued.

My doubts were many. Helping people whose consciences told them to stop their crimes and leave the country were sometimes the very people who seemed to be greatly needed in Belfast. Maybe our peace tactics were right and our peace strategy wrong. Who is wise enough to judge; to set an example, of valuing people and therefore caring for them seemed right at the time. It may prepare the ground for making peace later, by providing an opportunity to demonstrate that we have goodwill and that we do not take one side and not the other.

The annual assembly of the Peace People was held in Enniskillen in County Fermanagh and we decided to attend. I never heard what speaker dropped out at the last moment but I was given an hour's notice to speak on how Quakers maintained their 'Peace Testimony' against war and violence over the period of more than three centuries since it was first proclaimed. That was a challenge I was glad to accept, and I did my best to describe how a culture of peace can be developed and passed on from generation to generation, among a small group of people separated to a large extent from the rest of society, both in Britain and the USA. They were helped in developing it by the savagery of the religious wars which preceded it and which appeared to contradict Jesus' teaching in which they were well versed. Before radio and television the influence of parents was paramount in the homes, Quaker boarding schools were set up for older children and also colleges in the USA. Thus by and large children were in harmony with this teaching at home. Meanwhile countless examples of Friends Meetings and of individual Friends, working and suffering for the cause of peace, provided the role models for the young as they dreamed their dreams in adolescence.

We also recognised that we had learned a great deal about how to work in a fog of not-knowing what was what and who was who. There is no compass as a guide, no beaten path to follow. When Adam Curle came and was invited to speak to the teachers of Belfast on education for international understanding he lectured on listening. The importance of listening was one of many things we learnt. Especially in early years it is wise to do more listening than speaking. By that means we heard some strange opinions. One Quaker from an outlying Meeting said 'I will not be surprised if on the day of judgement Ian Paisley is sitting at God's right hand.' His wife added 'You never expected to hear that in a Quaker family, did you?' That may have been a quaint eccentricity, a more significant remark was made by a supporter of the IRA who said he was a Marxist. He told Ruth 'I am confident that if only the Brits would leave, we Irishmen could get round a table with the likes of Ian Paisley and sort everything out.' Anger hardens opinions such as these so much that nothing can alter them. We know this in theory but meeting it in real life makes a very big difference. It may prove to be as difficult and as expensive to make peace as to make war. Hatred spreads as rapidly as Foot and Mouth disease. As so often happened Shakespeare coined the appropriate phrase. It might have been written for the Irish and their persistent 'troubles.'

It is the disease of not listening,
the malady of not marking, that I am troubled withal.
King Henry IV part 2, Act I, ii Shakespeare

Television has been a chief offender in inciting violence in society for I was keenly aware that the children, who were not already taking part in the violence in Ireland, were being conditioned to accept its inevitability. It boded ill for Ireland, when the demonstrations halted so as to allow time to go and see themselves on the TV news where the violence seemed much more realistic. I addressed my 4500-word paper on television violence, to the Annual Meeting of the National Confederation of Parent Teacher Associations, as their Founder and was reported on the BBC radio.

Among psychologists today there is less talk of friendship and more of modelling but the principle is the same. This unfortunate form of modelling was occurring as television became commonplace. Considering the contents of television programmes in the USA, and Britain may well be similar, it is unfortunate that the average adult has seen 18,000 deaths on television by the age of eighteen. The most cogent warning is the statistical growth in crimes with violence, over the period officially recognised when television came into wider use. 'Social Trends' provided these figures:

Crimes of Wounding and Assault Known to the Police
In England and Wales

1951	1961	1966	1971	1972	1973	1974
6,000	16,000	25,000	45,000	51,000	59,000	62,000

A change in television policy is clearly essential. Twice in television's history in England, once in 1956 and the second time some twenty years later when appearing on television programmes the Heads of Children's Television, have said to me in identical words, 'It is not our aim to have more children viewing but rather to give them ideas for other occupations.'

The figures were so interesting that I rang the man responsible for them to discuss the possible causes. He was not very communicative, but insisted the causes were not known! The years were, however, the years of the spread of television.

At that time Lady Plowden was the chairman of Independent Television and I had a great admiration of the report on Primary Education, which is named after her, and also by good fortune we had a mutual friend. Consequently I was able to go to see her about my paper. However she brought in an official who was unwilling to accept any doubts about the value of television and I came away empty-handed. At least I had the comfort of an American book[52] which appeared at that time and which made a broader attack on television. I do not believe that television can be abolished but I do believe it can be tamed. It is easy to make a case that there is a choice between leaving television as it is and the survival of the human race. It is said that guerrillas depend on television, cars, and arms in that order of importance, because winning popular support is essential to their aims.

When I described to Lady Plowden how the television gathers the little children for their special children's programmes and then follows them immediately with the worst of the news, they are creating the social chaos of the following decades. Guessing that she was proud of her Report, I thought she might wince, but there was no sign of it. What more could I do? Being no skilled campaigner, I turned to better opportunities elsewhere, while setting an example to parents by keeping no television set at home myself.

Although the operation to insert a new aortic valve, in the Victoria Hospital forced me to go slower in our second year so that there was less to report, it was not to be the end of our time with Quaker Peace and Service. There were three more years at Bristol University before offering our services again.

CHAPTER 16

Geneva and 'The Magic Formula'

WORKING FOR QUAKER Peace and Service is as varied as can be. Lady Plowden would have been surprised if she had visited us in Belfast and might have listened more carefully to what we had to say. One of the difficulties of being a Quaker is the feeling that one must be a very humble unimpressive person free from the tricks and devices that are used by advertisers and public relations experts and yet believing strongly in the good causes which deserve support. In this respect working in Geneva was similar. In other respects it was very different, no longer were we dealing with hostility and suspicion from those who wished to exacerbate the quarrel, everyone in Geneva whether diplomats or representatives of Non-Governmental Organisations (NGO's) tended to be on the same side and wished to be regarded favourably. They even made a social life too tempting. Historically the two cities are entirely different. Geneva was the base of the League of Nations, which preceded the United Nations. It is therefore associated with high ideals. Its buildings have the effect of inviting humanity not to despair, but to do better this following time now that the UN has replaced the League. It is significant that the new building, added on to the Palais des Nations, has a wider view across the lake of distant Mont Blanc. The League had a Euro-centric bias and a much smaller number of members, because the era of large empires was not terminated by that time. It is to be hoped that another fresh start following a Third World War will not be needed, but that the Constitution of the UN may be adapted to the new situation as it develops.

269

Here, in the back rows of the UN Human Rights Commission 1981 meeting, are the representatives of Non Governmental Organisations (NGOs)

The Irish nationalists argue that they also have high ideals, about the unity and freedom of the whole of Ireland, and they believe that the Protestants would accept a minority position, if given guarantees. This presents a challenge to any peace-builder.

In Geneva most of the UN officials and diplomats had already succeeded in making a grand life for themselves and were contented with their lot. The magnificent buildings where they worked, gave them a feeling of the importance of what they were doing. They are an extremely interesting group including those who had retired and remained in Geneva. Often I came across them when arranging the programme for a course. There was Ed Dommen an economist educated at Balliol College, his father was English, but he came to work for Nestlé's for the sake of mountain climbing. He has married into Roger Wilson's family and as a cousin, provided hospitality for us very willingly on many occasions. He is strongly Quaker, indeed he has written a book on Quakerism in French, in time for the showing of the Quaker Tapestry alongside the Bayeux Tapestry. His work until his retirement was in the UN conference on Trade and Development (UNCTAD) where he became the authority on the economies of small islands and landlocked territories, all of which are, from an economist's point of view, lands handicapped by difficulties of access by traders. He held a very unorthodox view of corruption, that it is sometimes a stabilising factor, if for example the bribes for the purchase of arms are used to maintain the influence of the Head of State, instead of being stored in Swiss bank accounts. Now that he is retired he has been busy setting up a European Peace Agency through the Quaker office in Brussels. He challenged me one day with the question 'Where had development been successful in the 'South' or Third World?' I had to admit that I could not think of a clear case. He continued 'Mauritius is a possible answer.' But that was because the expansion of the tourist trade was meant to set things moving. He takes the view now that a great spreading of the ethical movement can only reduce the extortion of the 'South' by the 'North'. This theory will recur in the following chapter dealing with Oxfam, because it is doubtful whether Oxfam has ever faced up to the possibility that there is no solution for poverty other than an ethical one.

271

Waclaw Micuta reappeared in our lives as he lives in Geneva, and has become a close friend. As soon as he retired from his UN work controlling the traffic in drugs, he commandeered, in his best cavalry officer's manner, the wide lawn on the south side of the Palais, from where you can look out over the lake. He insisted that no one was taking the shortage of energy sufficiently seriously in the 1970 period when it was already clear that coal and oil were soon going to be exhausted. 'Consequently' he continued 'I wanted to set up an exhibition of alternative sources of energy.' Wood stoves, solar power, working horses, waterpower, and windmills were all demonstrated. Thousands of people from all over the world, attending the UN conferences saw what was going on through the windows and visited.

Waclaw coaxed the wives of some officials into making cakes on some of the wood stoves. It was a huge success and should be repeated every ten years. Following this success he set to work in his very practical way to design so many different kinds of stove, mainly wood-burning that he seemed to have one for every set of circumstances. His book *Modern Stoves for All* was also published by Intermediate Technology Publications in a revised edition in 1985. Each year he used to come with a number of stoves to address the courses for Post-graduates at Quaker House and was always voted the best lecturer of their fortnight. He would tell the young people the amount of dry wood he had used to boil the water for the soup, for all the people in the course. He was lucky to have a topic that lent itself to demonstration and we were lucky to have our meal cooked for us! There appears to be an opening for the virtues of organic food to be taught in a similar way!

His patron was Prince Sadruddin Aga Khan, who wrote in the Foreword: about the 'problems threatening our very survival' and the need to 'take concrete steps to reverse trends that are already assuming disastrous proportions.' He knew about disasters from being the High Commissioner for Refugees, a part in which he was much appreciated by his staff. When he came to speak at Quaker House, it was when he had been short-listed for the post of UN Secretary General and I was glad to have the chance to wish him well. Ruth thought he was so well liked at the office of UNHCR,

Inventor, diplomat, and teacher, Waclaw Micuta is the most versatile man I know. Here he is pictured with his late wife, Janka.

the building by the edge of the lake, he would make a good job of the difficult post of UN Secretary General.

One of his staff, Djibril Diallo was recommended by Ruth as a speaker about refugees at one of our courses. After I had picked him up from a language course, I said to him 'I understand you are already a great linguist. What are you studying now?' He replied with dismissive modesty 'It's Arabic I am studying here. That will be my sixteenth language.' In response to my interest he explained that in Senegal he had taught in an Institute of African Languages, but he had also taught in a Secondary Modern School in Glasgow. He has now taken charge of the Public Relations Division of the UN Development Programme (UNDP) which finances the technical assistance provided by the various UN Agencies. If I ever make another visit to the UN in New York I will certainly visit him. He must be well aware of the greater acceptability of help from the UN than from bilateral aid, which has undertones of the imperialist past. I was so impressed by him that I would venture to hope that he would one day earn a place among the wise men of Africa, south of the Sahara, but perhaps Senegal is too far away.

Nelson Mandela. President 1994-1998 (South Africa).
Davidson Jabavu. Mandela's former teacher. Spokesman for Africans (South Africa).
Obafami Awolowo. Imprisoned and assassinated for political reasons (Nigeria).
Jomo Kenyatta. A student at Woodbrooke College. Visited by Lucy Cadbury when imprisoned. President 1964-1978 (Kenya).
Kenneth Kaunda. President. 1964-1991 (Zambia).
Julius Nyerere. President 1962-1965 (Tanzania).
Kofi Annan. UN Secretary General since 1997 (Ghana).

As political leaders they were known for their integrity, honesty, and wisdom. They were slow to take to violence, and many of them paid tribute to Gandhi. It is hard to think of a group of European leaders to equal them. It is also hard to believe that their lack of experience of governing turned out to be an advantage to them.

I was glad to meet Mr Muller who was Under Secretary General of the UN and author of several books about it. Such people are selected for their intellect and academic record and it is unusual for them to speak effectively to the hearts of young people in such a way as he did. He spoke of the splendour of the efforts of the UN to bring peace to a deeply troubled world every time he spoke. He highlighted the opportunities the future will bring, the progress already made. The fire of his enthusiasm stirred up the ideals of a younger generation, despite all the difficulties of international cooperation, which included the weariness of journalists as well as the hardened militarism commonly found in the armed forces.

To be a UN official or a diplomat attached to the UN is no easy task. Successes in keeping hope alive come seldom. On top of normal office stress there are language and cultural differences. When partners accompany their spouses they may have difficulty with the local language and become homesick for families and friends left behind at home. One couple I knew well, admitted that the best they could do was to remind each other from time to time that 'Home is where we are.'

When I happened to take the chance of discussing homelessness with the Soviet ambassador, he stated with good warmth that if Quakers could do something about this, it would be very welcome. They could arrange social outings for their own people but something more than this is needed. Unfortunately I was about to leave Geneva when this conversation took place; we were leaving sooner than we had hoped.

Finally we came across Monsieur Bertrand, prominent in suggesting reforms of the UN. Maurice Bertrand was head of the UN's Joint Inspection Unit and published a paper of 84 pages under the UN imprint[53] about UN reform. He was writing before the collapse of apartheid, before the fall of the Berlin wall and before the end of the Cold War. It is little wonder that he appears to be unduly pessimistic in some passages. Regarding development in the Third World he attributes its failure to the failure of the agencies (FAO, ILO, WHO, UNESCO etc) to coordinate their work adequately in such a way that the relevant Third World Ministries are confused by too many proposals for overlapping projects. To avoid this he proposed non-specialised technical assistance offices for regions. This criticism did not seem to apply in Ubon, where the ILO, WHO, FAO, and UNESCO cooperated readily to set up their training of community leaders with a wide variety of skills.

He also believed that such cooperation, bringing together people from different countries as students and as teachers would lead to the international understanding which forms a basis for peace. Indeed in his division of UN functions into peace and development he concentrated the two by stating that, given the constraints of negotiation, the UN is doing as much for peace as it can because with a light budget it is only allowed to:

Identify problems.

Provide the 'good offices' of the Secretary-General.

Pass resolutions in the Security Council.

Develop, with limited control of the media, a world consensus.

Improve techniques of conflict management.

This means that in his view the UN's functions were limited to decisions in a variety of different forms, and I am reminded of a little jingle from student days, with which we sought to prick the bubbles of the pomposity of some of us:

> If talk could set the world to rights,
> Its problems would not last two nights.

As work-campers we liked to think we were doing more than talk, or at least talking to better effect. I believe Maurice Bertrand would have understood that. He caused me to visit the UN Institute for Training and Research (UNITAR), which Roger Wilson and the Rowntree Charitable Trust had helped bring into existence. Training and Research are vital activities to counter the ageing of large bureaucracies. I got the impression that UNITAR had lost confidence in itself and was in need of the treatment that it was supposed to be offering to others, but this was only an impression and I was not in a good position to confirm it. It seems to me that the slogan of the UNESCO courier 'A Window on the World' might be applied to UNITAR. It implies that it is not enough to consider the internal creaks and groans by a careful listening to the complaints of colleagues but to look outwards envisioning a distant future when humanity has shown itself capable of adjusting to environmental changes and asking how did we get here and what follows next?

These are difficult tasks for bureaucrats and so, quite rightly, they have often been put out to people with lively minds such as Professor Johan Galtung. He lives with his Japanese wife just outside Geneva and Ed Dommen and I were lucky enough to have a monthly supper fixture with him. He has a delightful sense of humour. He went to a Seminary for training ministers and chose as his title 'The Future of God.' Nevertheless he was invited again. He addressed all the senior officers of the Belgium army and said 'You are making a great mistake. You should be asking for more money at this time of reductions, because you can now make a good case for Civilian Defence as an addition, rather than a substitute, for military defence.' His friends celebrated his fiftieth birthday by presenting him with a bibliography of his articles and book titles. It is a very thick volume indeed. As the father of peace research in Europe he confuses most of us by the sheer erudition of his work. I remember well his lecture for the founding of the Geneva International Peace Research Institute (GIPRI). 'If you approach peace as a geographical climatologist, you might find that the further north you travel the more peace you would expect to find, or if you approached it as a theologian you might find that Buddhists are the most peaceful of religious groups, but, now I look round the audience , I don't see many Eskimo Buddhists.' Later he came to his story of the man in space who was asked by his friends what does the earth seem like from up in space? The astronaut paused for a moment and said 'Like one of those huge ants nests which you see in the woods with everyone rushing to and fro, as busy as ants always are.' 'How do you mean busy?' He was asked, 'Busy with what?' The reply was sharp: 'Making insecticide, of course.'

In his book[54] Johan Galtung makes out a very strong case for a novel foreign policy:

Transarmament: from offensive to defensive defence.
    To avoid threatening others.
Non-alignment: to avoid being caught in the wars of others.
Inner strength: a measure of self-sufficiency.
Outer usefulness: e.g. Swiss banking.

His comments on these four points are as fresh as one has come to expect from him and he makes clear that he has never believed that it is sufficient to deal with a single cause of war, and that the whole peace movement is required to bring together enough power to make a lasting peace. Although he is used as a consultant by various UN bodies, he is also used by NGO's particularly when they want to re-plan their work.

Ruth and I were appointed as two of the five people to staff the Quaker House, an NGO of long standing because it began in the early days of the League of Nations. Earlier it consisted of one or two Friends working independently on promoting Quaker concerns about peace and refugees. They included my aunt Dr Hilda Clark and her friend and cousin Edith Pye, each of them distinguished for their relief work during and following the First World War. When later on I used to visit them in Street they said to me on more than one occasion that I should follow in the footsteps of Philip Noel Baker, who was a Cabinet Minister and the most persistent advocate of disarmament. I could never persuade them that I had not the talents to do so. In any case I never felt sure that disarmament brought about peace or whether peace leads to disarmament.

The Quakers have formed the Friends World Committee for Consultation (FWCC), so that it can be recognised by the UN with the privileges that entails, such as the right to attend committees and conferences and to circulate papers to their members. It is very seldom that an NGO representative is allowed to speak. The only occasion, which I can recall was when the very able lawyer, Nigel Rodley, who worked for Amnesty International, had more relevant information than anyone else.

Now, of course, there are two Quaker offices, one in Geneva, and one in New York. Geneva has half the work on the development of the Third World and half of following the debates on disarmament; the UNHCR is located in Geneva, UNICEF mainly in New York. All of them deal with Quaker concerns, as does the UN Commission for Human Rights. Ruth was allotted refugees and disasters as her work. I was invited to deal with the Brandt Report about help for the Third World. Our two colleagues handled disarmament and human rights. The third was a bright young man Simon Willis, whom I was asked to tutor. When I asked him about himself he told me that his last job had been as an au pair girl, for the four-year-old daughter of a Turkish couple! He got tired of reading her own books to her when she settled for sleep, so he

278

substituted his own copy of the philosopher Wittgenstein, she went to sleep just as quickly. His ancestors had been friends of Hegel. There was a great deal of laughter in these tutorials and yet we kept to the work he was doing, and to the reading of relevant books. On one occasion he reported on his role in the large meeting of disarmament NGO's. An Indian Marxist had succeeded in securing a ruling from the committee that no vote would be taken. Simon rose and held the floor to explain that for the report he was writing he needed a show of opinion: 'Please hold up your hand if you agree with the previous speaker.' Despite the Marxist's attempts to get this ruled out of order, he stuck to his point. Afterwards he was warmly congratulated by a Soviet representative, who said: 'Today is a good day, here is my badge, keep it as a souvenir.' It is my belief that the arms firms who from 1932 onwards have attempted to sow discord, had paid this so-called Marxist to be an obstructionist.'

Simon impressed me so much that I persuaded him to apply to Balliol College, Oxford. He duly obtained a first class degree in philosophy but then disappeared.

We worked in a handsome old house; when I first went to the desk to which I was allotted, I learned that it had been used temporarily by the campaign in favour of breast-feeding against Nestlé's deceitful advertising. I was pleased to hear that they had found a better place. The room served two other purposes, it was the library, and it was the dining and drawing room for meetings with diplomats and others. It had furniture and furnishings that appeared to fit their supposedly Victorian outlook on life. Whether they would suit or shock some of the cantankerous Quakers I know, I was not quite sure. The Quaker 'testimony' to simplicity is seldom discussed or elaborated. The periodical 'Living Lightly', which comes together with 'Positive News', implies that there is a job to do, but it is not Quakers who are taking a lead. Maybe this is due to some Quakers being very wealthy as well as others who are very poor, making a difficulty for anyone speaking about simple living, maybe it is the difficulty about using Oxfam's second hand clothes or managing without a car for going to a Meeting for Worship. At least it could be claimed that most Friends live well within their incomes and that releases funds for campaigning for peace and similar causes.

Another question, which might be raised about Quaker House, is the extent to which its people are authorities in the subjects they adopt. Is their knowledge of authors and people dealing with Human Rights and other ethical issues adequate? Ruth and I felt we knew more about Quakers and what they would wish us to do than we knew about our subjects. In Ruth's case she had read a few of the books written about refugees and had had a wide experience of dealing with Basque children escaping from the Spanish Civil War and of a wide selection of young and old escaping from Nazism from Germany and Austria. Sometimes she had dealt with individuals, sometimes hostels. Of sudden demands from disaster areas she had little knowledge.

For me it was a different matter. My work with UNESCO was barely helpful. It had helped me to understand the value that education may have in dealing with poverty, but it has to be a special kind of education, and the Brandt Report did not go into such details. I found no one who was interested in seeing the slides of Community Education. Interest lay with starting large and small village industries. Many of them got into financial difficulties, so Ed Dommen and I with a grant from a Geneva charity produced a handbook on running small development projects. It was translated into a number of other languages to enable more literate people to keep accounts and other records in such a way that others can get work and keep contracts with First World donors. Reading between the lines, anyone who studied it carefully, will realise that there are sensitivities to be considered if donations are received from the 'North.' There are too many unskilled donors as well as a lack of competent organisers in the 'South.' Part II in the book aims to encourage: 'open and trusting relations between the partners. Openness and trust are essential but cannot be achieved by formal reports alone. The intention of part II is to explain how to lighten the burden involved in the relations between the partners.' Perhaps we make the work sound too daunting, we have to remind ourselves that the poorest of the poor often do not get help because they cannot keep accounts and write reports.

It is doubtful whether the Quaker NGO is typical of others, because they vary widely from each other. The Red Cross is the largest and the most widely known. A friend of my daughter Candia, Louise Doswald-Beck has a very responsible job there, with the

International Red Cross. She was accepted through marrying a Swiss national. This is staffed by Swiss to maintain its neutrality. The other Red Cross/Red Crescent is the umbrella organisation for all the national ones. The International Red Cross is suffering badly during wars, a subject that I took the chance of discussing with Louise. The fact is that their emblem is given less respect and their employees killed or wounded, due to the ruthlessness of 'total' wars of the past century, where rules are no longer followed. Nor do guerrillas and terrorists keep to the rules of war, as the people of New York know.

Even if NGO's are narrowed down to those with an office in Geneva and having to be recognised by the UN, there must still be more than a hundred. Some are religious, notably the World Council for Churches, some are commercial and one wonders how they have gained recognition, some are powerful knowing more about abuses in a country than its diplomats themselves. Some are very old dating from the years before the League of Nations, such as the Anti-Slavery Society, some are very new, responding to new situations such as the Campaign Against Anti-personnel Mines. Many of them claimed to be promoting peace or human rights even though they are not normally viewed that way. Some would be so lacking in resources that they would only send a representative for a few sessions of one of the UN bodies, but would have no office in Geneva.

Since the time of Bertrand, the demand for reform of the UN has been growing from all quarters not just the NGO's. Richard Holbrooke the former US Ambassador to the UN has written[55] strongly about the Secretary-General's need for more influence, and more power for the Security Council, these needs arising from the expansion of the Department of Peace Keeping (DPKO). This latter is one of the many themes taken up by the UN Foundation set up by Ted Turner's gift of a billion dollars.

The representatives from the Guardian and the Times in Geneva were depressed about their situation. They complained that however important a conference at the UN might be, they had no chance of getting anything published, unless there was a disaster occurring, a crime committed or a dispute close to violence. When Kruschev took off his shoe and banged it on his UN desk to hammer some point, that was news, but when climate change was first discussed it was treated as a warning for the future and not for today. War propaganda makes news, peace propaganda seldom does. It might be thought a neglect of duty to provide peace-keeping forces, without any reliable news service to back them, but this is what happens at present. Early in the war in the Balkans a group of Yugoslavian journalists, claimed to be neutral, asked our little trust for financial help, to counter Serbian war propaganda. We first checked with the Peace-keepers that the English version would be useful to them. When they replied, they said that they often seemed to be working in the dark and they would be delighted to know more about what was happening near them, because, to a large extent they live in a fog.

In general many governments are so nationalist that they prefer to have minimum competition in providing news, in particular during wartime. UN Information Centres (UNIC), are confined to UN publications even in peacetime and are not allowed to embark on controversy.

Now that Information Technology has been greatly improved, the opportunities for peace propaganda are much greater, and should be seized by peace organisations, which may need to combine to meet the heavy costs. Capable and reliable translators of the rarer languages are difficult to find. It is therefore bound to be expensive and yet unlikely to be acceptable to governments. In such circumstances it is people like Ted Turner, George Soros, and Rupert Murdoch who are most likely to be able to act.

Another outcome from our two years in Geneva arose from a letter from my eldest brother Jan who was still working in the Herbarium at Nairobi. He was a keen observer of the politics of African States. Despite the ingenious step-by-step assumption of independent government by countries, which had previously been part of the British Empire, the difficulties of copying the British Constitution were apparent. It seemed in some cases that the only possible termination of misgovernment and corruption were military coups. Although the importance of fair play and accepting the rules in football and cricket were well understood the concepts had not affected politics through the laws and conventions, which form the British constitution. Elections were too often manipulated.

Bribery rose to the level of eighteenth century Britain. Moreover there was no reason to suppose that the British Constitution is the best example to follow.

The Swiss Constitution, Jan wrote, might be better for Switzerland because of its long history but it may also be more suitable for African countries. Switzerland has several different languages, it is divided between Catholics and Protestants and has rival cantons. He suggested that these difficulties correspond with the tribal and language difficulties in Africa. He went on to propose that I should find a writer with French, German, and fluent English to describe the aspects of the Swiss Constitution, hoping one of them would be African or familiar with Africa. After a prolonged attempt to find someone I abandoned the search and took on the job myself, hoping that the study of constitutions, which I made at Oxford would help me.

The book[56] met with initial success in the form of a prize from the Directory of Social Change, and a grant to send it to universities in the English speaking countries of the Third World, but never appealed to a wide public. Constitutions are regarded as inevitably dull it seems. Yet a theme that merits such a title deserves close attention. If a constitution encourages its politicians to set an example by living in a culture of peace rather than a culture of confrontation, it behoves the political scientists to take note of it because the politicians set the fashion for other people's way of life.[57] The Swiss have remained neutral in the two World Wars and escaped being overrun not so much on account of their military strength but by making themselves useful to neighbours. This theme is fully elaborated in the volume by Johan Galtung[58] already mentioned: It forms a starting point for those who believe international friendship should be a part of their peace programme. He cites the provision of secret banking services for the rulers of authoritarian states, who fear being driven out of their own countries, the services of the Red Cross and the facilities for holding international conferences as examples of the usefulness of the Swiss to their neighbours. He might well have added others such as the warm hospitality of their hotels towards people from abroad.

There are several aspects of Swiss government and its constitution, which make for basic peace. Paradoxically the army is one of them. Being a small country, men during their military service together often make lifelong friendships. When their full-time service is over they have to turn up for weekend refresher courses and though some find this a nuisance, many enjoy the open-air activities and renewing their friendships. Not having had a war, nor having any expectation of a war in the future, the military exercises are not taken too seriously I found. The only exception was their treatment of Conscientious Objectors. One such 'bad citizen' as they called them, married a distant relative of mine. He claimed to be of peasant origin, but when he returned to his alpine village after becoming sixty years of age when he became free to do so, he learned that by a strange set of circumstances he had become the Count. Ordinary objectors who remain are usually sent to prison where they are expected to go out to work during the week to pay for their incarceration at night and during weekends.

There are several features of the Swiss way of working their constitution that justify describing it as a cooperative form of democracy as opposed to the confrontational methods usually associated with the party system. In Britain the parties usually appear to be more concerned with scoring party points against their opponents, than with improving legislative proposals. In Switzerland in contrast, the parties agreed long ago to what is known as the 'Magic Formula,' by which all seven cabinet ministers have to be drawn from the four main political parties keeping in mind linguistic and religious considerations. This is in addition to the constitution requiring not more than one member to come from a single canton. This is only one example of the many complexities of Swiss government. It is easy to imagine that the army and business firms are also difficult to control. Following the principle of subsidiarity, which means driving down to the cantons and communes as much legislation as possible, it is intended to ease the situation, but it has curious results, which might test the patience of people elsewhere. Two examples suffice: teachers trained in one canton cannot teach even in a neighbouring canton without retraining and seatbelts for cars were compulsory in some cantons but not in others.

This part of cooperative democracy is something that the Swiss largely take for granted, and, as visitors do not readily notice it, it therefore receives insufficient attention. It consists partly of an expectation that a deal can always be made. People enter upon negotiations expecting that the other side will be reasonable people, not looking to striking a bargain unduly favourable to themselves, not competitive in a bad sense of the word, but giving the impression that they are good negotiators. The feeling of satisfaction in being a good negotiator is derived partly from the ability to see the point of view of others; partly from skill in spotting a new way of looking at the issue and partly from sheer friendliness. Business schools analyse this process in much greater detail, but the Swiss have developed their negotiating skills over generations, having been seldom in a position to dictate, and their style seems more natural.

The other features of the Constitution that tend to lead to peace include the referendum which can be used when many citizens disagree with proposed legislation and the 'initiative' which allows citizens to propose legislation. Ordinary legislation is based on bills introduced by the appropriate member of the Cabinet of seven. However these Ministers are as much civil servants as party politicians and, for example, do not resign when their bills are rejected. Some commentators accuse the Swiss of being dull and uninteresting especially in their political life, but this kind of dullness is surely what is needed. Peace and quietness go together in one way, in another way peace is what is needed for a full and vibrant life. As the English Buddhist Urgyen Sangharakshita makes clear with the title his book of aphorisms, when he suggests that *Peace is a Fire*.[59] Freedom from fear releases time and energy for all the best occupations. Certainly the members of the Assembly or Parliament do not shout at each other and jeer like British MP's. The position of President or Prime Minister is occupied by each of the seven Ministers in turn and so is much less likely to be a politician hungry for power.

To make such a complex system of government work smoothly requires the energetic cooperation of many good citizens and it might take a long time for another country to accept the spirit in which such a cooperation could work well. The Swiss themselves believe it takes several centuries to prepare the way for such a change and a threat from neighbours as an additional incentive. Personally I hope that the threat from the polluters of the environment is sufficient to force the adoption of a better system of government and it might not be necessary to commandeer a page of every newspaper and use the education system to teach cooperative democracy. However, when my Swiss friends hear this they reply: 'What about Uruguay? There they copied our Swiss Constitution, but when the president realised what little power he had, he called in the military, dismissed the Assembly, and established himself as a dictator. What do you say to that?'

This brings my account of Geneva and Switzerland to an unduly sad end. During my time there I had learned a great deal about the contribution a good constitution can make. I had learned about the difficulties of multilingual states, about the international civil service with its scope for idealists as well as its problems and added to my ideas about sustainable development.

CHAPTER 17

Oxfam and UNA: Cutting Conflict and Feeding the World

WHILE WORKING IN Geneva Ruth and I had a visit from Brian Walker, a very gifted man whom we had previously met in Belfast. There he had been a principal founder of the Alliance Party, which is neither exclusively Protestant nor Catholic. I asked him whether there was any chance of serving on the Oxfam Committee in view of my work on development at the Quaker Office. Now that I know how much competition there is for such voluntary work, I would have hesitated, but I assumed that Oxfam would not object to that degree of nepotism, my relatives having been heavily involved.

Oxfam began as a committee of the Oxford Quaker Meeting and adopted the name 'Oxford Committee for Famine Relief,' Mary Pask its first secretary was a hundred years old when I talked with her about it. She thought that the initiative came from some Oxford students, who were concerned at the accounts of the hunger in Greece during the Second World War. They thought Friends would be the most likely to be interested, and so early in 1942 the work began. It began badly. The request to send help had gone as far as Mr Churchill who had decided that the blockade could not be broken. He believed that the food would be seized by the German troops for their own purposes. Fortunately the matter was not allowed to drop. Professor Gilbert Murray, an exceptionally respected Professor of Greek was pressed by his wife, Lady Mary to approach his counterparts at Harvard University. His counterparts in their turn approached Eleanor Roosevelt, who spoke to her husband, President Franklin D. Roosevelt. After reflection,

287

President Roosevelt told Churchill that he should change his mind and allow food and medicine to be sent, so the first steamer went through the blockade.

It sounds like the Nursery Rhyme 'This is the house that Jack built,' but the change in policy was none the worse for that. In the meantime the Committee under the chairmanship of Dr Henry Gillett with my father as Treasurer and several other Friends helping had realised that Churchill might approve a rather different committee with an Anglican Canon taking the chair, Canon Milford. The name was soon changed to Oxfam. When I was in Greece in the nineteen eighties I collected some of the stories of the famine, of the rich and poor people dying as they struggled to find enough to eat in a country devastated by war. I heard stories such as a man in a very rich looking great-coat simply dropping dead as he walked along, and a mother with a baby on her lap sitting dead in a tram. No doubt this was simply the tip of the horrific iceberg of the war in famine stricken Greece.

I was writing at the time an account for Oxfam of Oxfam origins, to include the founders' family backgrounds to do with the terrible Irish Potato Famine, and of the Repeal of the Corn Laws, when 'Give us this day our daily bread' became a startling slogan and prepared the way for a minimal welfare state.

The Minute Book, a short school exercise book with minutes kept in pencil, has gone missing and was never seen by the historian of Oxfam. She rightly said that the first committee never intended to set up a permanent organisation, they owe precedents mainly for temporary campaigns, but even big international organisations like Oxfam have had small beginnings. Over the years Oxfam has been wisely guided, has grown year by year, and is often taken as an example of an organisation, which is well managed, being able to adapt to new circumstances in the Third World, clear in its aims to ease poverty world-wide and adroit in maintaining the freshness of its fund-raisers and the ingenuity of its campaigners. During my six years 1982-1988 on the Committee we attempted to distinguish between strategy and tactics, strategy to be laid down in Oxford. For example that grant makers should take into account the impact of the grants on the environment from soil conservation to money lending and the impact on women, who do much of the agricultural work in tropical countries.

The Committee was always conscious of the bottomless pit image of world poverty contrasting with the paucity of our funds. This led to some discussion whether our activities were too varied and too widespread throughout the world. Would it be better if Oxfam specialised in clean drinking water? To some extent this has been attempted for occasions when large camps of refugees are established. It is good to know that there are large plastic tanks for filtering or simply storing water with complementary equipment ready in a warehouse to be flown out to a disaster area, caused by an earthquake or floods. English people might well be pleased to hear such news. That is one kind of focus for the work. The other is territorial. We asked ourselves whether we would do better both in fundraising and in meeting needs if our part of Britain or the whole of Oxfam International made itself responsible for the work in a particular country. It might encourage holidaymakers to turn their long journeys to a practical use. The difficulties of mixing rich and poor might be too embarrassing or would a better under-standing result? In the USA the following story is sometimes told:

> A tourist on the coast of India began chatting to an Indian fish-erman who was sitting idly in the shade. Eventually the tourist to satisfy his curiosity asked:
>
> How is it you're not fishing today?
> I have caught enough fish, why should I catch more?
> You could sell some and make some money.
> What would I do with more money?
> You could buy a better net, or even a better boat.
> What would I do with a better net?
> You'd save time and catch more fish.
> If I saved time what would I do with it?
> Oh! you'd have time to enjoy yourself.
> That's just what I'm doing now isn't it?

The development agencies have to come to terms with the experts on how to live better on less. The world's resources are not sufficient for everyone to live like the rich but it is difficult to persuade anyone to accept a lower standard of living than they already have.

This story was not told in the Oxford meetings in my day but they convey the spirit of the discussions we held. On the sound principle advocated by Joseph Rowntree we tried to deal with causes whenever it seemed possible, the causes of poverty are so numerous that there is plenty to say! The causes of the choices of Christmas cards of the Committee being usually for cards, which would not sell well, were hard to identify and we laughed about that. Once we accepted plans for a seminar on campaigning and the staff arranged a session attended by the man responsible for the Campaign for Real Ale. A group of us who believed that fighting was a major cause of poverty held several meetings before the 'Cut Conflict Campaign' was launched with much help from Chris Barber the chairman at the time. By then the Charity Laws were starting to change due to a new interpretation allowing some campaigning in a field in which an organisation has developed some expertise. We had already had a lecture from a leading Charity Lawyer who concluded his exposition with 'It does appear to be true that the law is interpreted a little differently according to the views of the government in power.'

This did not protect Oxfam entirely. The New Internationalist for August 1991, lists some of the tricks and abuse used against Oxfam and Christian Aid in an article headed 'Mugging the Good Samaritans.' Dexter Tiranti asks 'How well-fed representatives of the establishment have the gall to hound agencies who are so patently working for the underprivileged, is beyond us. For every smear and every sneer will reduce the funds of the development agencies. And less funds will mean people will stay illiterate who might have read, will stay blind who might have seen, will remain jobless who might have worked, will remain thirsty who might have drunk clean water.' The Daily Telegraph and right-wing organisations in the USA are the chief offenders. Examples follow showing that right-wing bodies are allowed to be politically and controversially active but not left-wing bodies.

It takes strong leadership to oppose such concerted attacks and at the same time to deal with problems arising from the breakdown of law and order in parts of Africa. Decisions regarding putting the lives of staff at risk cannot be taken lightly, and there comes a time when it is necessary to withdraw. The Committee can seldom meet in emergency sessions to share the burdens born by the officers. On one occasion a panel of committee members decided to appoint as Deputy Director an army colonel. A group of staff made the mistake of leading a public protest saying that this was contrary to the Quaker pacifist traditions of Oxfam. Having confidence in the panel I rose to my feet and said 'I happen to be a Quaker pacifist myself' and thinking of General Smuts, Brigadier General Michael Harbottle, Waclaw Micuta and others, continued 'People who become army officers are of many different kinds. There are many good organisers among them; such as we need. I am happy to support our panel even though we may seem to be suborning her majesty's armed forces!' There was no laughter but perhaps they did not know the meaning of the word! David Jones proved to be an exceptionally good colleague.

On another occasion I was not so fortunate in making an intervention. The question was what could be done about grant making in South Africa while the government of Nationalist Party members were putting as many difficulties in our way as they could. Our chairman Joel Joffe, now Lord Joffe, had been one of Nelson Mandela's lawyers defending him from charges of political offences. He heard me say 'If we are blocked from making grants in South Africa now, let us establish a fund with the money we would have liked to use so that it accumulates and we would use it when the country has an African Government. We would make it widely known that we were expecting such an event to happen, though many people at that time believed it might not happen for fifty or more years. Educational psychologists know that expectation is very powerful so that it is the mark of good teachers that they expect their classes to do well. It is the mark of good researchers that they prevent expectations from damaging the results of their experiments. If we expect the government to change it will change sooner.' By the time of their meeting I was already known for what some people considered eccentric ideas and Joel simply said 'No: we couldn't do that.' He gave no explanation but I suppose a sufficient proportion of the funds were getting through to their intended destinations but he did not wish to let the South African government know how much, or put the recipients in danger. Joel Joffe always treated me with great respect and kindness when I approached him for contributions in support of peace organisations, on condition that he did not have to read any supporting papers!

One aspect of Oxfam's work disappointed me. There seemed little appreciation of the difficult role of the UN in helping developing countries. The UN has the advantage of being multinational and therefore having some degree of neutrality. On one occasion I was told in the Philippines 'We didn't invite you before, because it is always said that the English are race-conscious and we were not sure you'd want to come.' The UN teams have to take into account that on the one hand there may be deeper divisions among their members, which make misunderstandings within the teams more likely even though the relationships of the teams with the local people may be better.

It is unfortunate that the salaries paid to UN technical assistants are kept high in order to attract a high level of expertise and in so doing encourage a lifestyle, which may cut them off from local people and the workers in non-governmental agencies. This increases the friction when one organisation, often the UN, is chosen to act as lead agency, for example in a disaster area created by an earthquake, in order to make sure the work is well coordinated. I heard several times from Oxfam people that they liked working with 'Save the Children Fund' and several times that they did not like working with the UN. It would be hard to explain the difficulties of the UN team to the satisfaction of the Oxfam organisation. Large bureaucracies are sluggish, international large bureaucracies are inclined to be less united and cooperative, but the sooner the world has more experience of them the better, because only they can solve some of the problems of humanity. There would be no solution to global warming without the cooperation they promote. If nations could and would solve environmental and similar problems by themselves there would be no need for the UN. It is obvious that they cannot. Those dissatisfied with the UN should be learning how to improve it.

United Nations Association

The United Nations Association made an interesting contrast and comparison with Oxfam. It is supported by a very small grant by the Government. It has the leaders of the three main parties as its Presidents. Its image rises and falls with the image of the UN itself, but gets no financial support from the UN. It is therefore a very awkward organisation for which to fundraise and to manage. It is expected to deal with peacemaking since this is what the UN is properly expected to perform as its principle task. In addition to all other functions, that the UN undertakes, there are also UNESCO, the World Health Organisation, the International Labour Office, and the Food and Agriculture Organisation, to mention only a few. In an era when 'Small [seems to be] Beautiful' it is little wonder that it is denounced as being impossibly large.

Although I am sympathetic with those who praise small schools, small countries and small shops, I have always assumed that there are certain world problems, which can best be solved by world organisation, such as climate change, and the pollution of the seas and atmosphere. The shortage of oil is causing serious fighting at present in places as different as Iraq and Angola, pointing to the need for international law if peace is to prevail. It should be admitted that it is seldom agreed that international law is the cause of peace or vice versa. To me it seems likely that when the institutional and other conditions of peace are prepared in advance of its establishment that peace will not last long. I have often found that I have been so weak intellectually that I have been over-persuaded by the last book I have read, or the last person I have heard speak on the subject. What I could say in my own defence is that at any one time I could suggest priorities to enable a peace organisation to develop a strategy, and give good reasons for my choice.

My first contact with the national office of the UNA was in 1950-60 period. I was invited to chair the committee responsible for the social work of volunteers. There had been a dispute between the volunteers and the office, which arose from the failure to get the tools and funds to them when needed. As a work-camper my sympathies lay with the volunteers and I supported the two committee members who felt the situation so outrageous that they were resigning. Now that I think of disputes of this kind as an opportunity or a challenge I would have acted differently, as it was I resigned despite a very friendly interview with Nigel Nicholson of Sissinghurst Castle who was chairman of UNA at the time.

I kept in touch as an ordinary member of UNA, though I failed to notice how successfully the UN was promoting decolonisation, a process that might well have led to more fighting. I was beginning to learn that successes, particularly if they take the form of non-violence, are not regarded by journalists as newsworthy, a problem for which no solution has yet been found. In desperation I have argued that there are as many skills in negotiating as there are in football but one does not hear so much about them, even though they may be, as in Israel over the last decade, a matter of life or death. Diplomacy requires a diplomat to be in the right place at the right time, to be in good training, to put his team before himself and to use his head but not always in the same way. Morale is vital.

Unfortunately as years passed memories of the horrors of war faded and the fine slogans, such as 'Peace depends on the UN and you,' began to fade likewise. It takes a revered statesman to ensure that the lessons of war are well remembered and applied.

Bertrand Russell had written about a third generation world organisation, without explaining that the defects of old age, of which I am acutely aware in myself, can find compensations of some sort. He did this without claiming that the UN in Shakespearian terms is sans teeth (a rapid reaction force) sans eyes (an early warning system) sans taste[60] (discrimination regarding human rights) sans everything.

The UN and the UNA with it, should be regarded as being in their adolescence, making mistakes from time to time, but in need of a helping hand to show how much they can do as they alternate from despair to over confidence in their own capacity. At first I was surprised that UNA was spending much of its time and energy working for children in developing countries through UNICEF and for refugees through UNHCR. Eventually I recognised that this was a way of keeping going in straitened circumstances because it was allowed to keep a percentage of funds raised which could be used towards the cost of salaries. This explained the relative neglect of the peace activities of the UN, which were foremost in the minds of the public.

Having decided that I would see what could be done about this situation, I chose to try to get another film made and managed to persuade Oliver Postgate to use his talents in filmmaking. His excellence in this area had been revealed in his children's television programmes such as 'Bagpuss', 'Noggin the Nog', 'Ivor the Engine', and others. I asked him to make a film about the folly of nuclear weapons. It showed the futility of this scenario without actually frightening the children. It was shown on television in Australia but the BBC was not brave enough to show it in Britain, perhaps because the public were still regarding nuclear weapons as a protection instead of a danger.

The film's title was *Life on Earth – Perhaps*. His exceptional sense of humour remains undiminished by illness as is apparent in his autobiography *Seeing Things*.[61] He called the penultimate chapter 'Dementia' because it describes the crazy attempts to justify nuclear defence and the blast of emotional reaction to it. He published numerous equally cogent pamphlets on the subject. We invited him to come to Geneva to speak to diplomats and others in order to show them how strongly people felt. I have often wondered whether his insistence that nuclear bombs are not weapons puzzled them too much. In regard to his famous cartoon films for children he is completely disarming. He writes 'I am always delighted when people tell me how much they enjoy the films, but I am not being modest when I say I did not create that joy. The significant ingredients are everywhere, I was just the cook.' He would have enjoyed Mr Padolecchia's 'War Permit' sheet, which he wrote out of despair, and which appears in the next chapter.

Believing that the BBC would be equally lukewarm about the UN as they were about warning against the dangers of nuclear weapons, I wondered whether a book was needed to start a campaign, or whether educational work in schools would be more effective.

Eventually I came to the conclusion that an additional member at UNA was better as a way of raising the morale of other members of staff. At the time there was an all purpose director, a volunteer as a deputy director and a specialist in Human Rights, apart from administrators and secretaries. There was clearly a gap to be filled.

The UNA office is in a building in Whitehall of faded gentility, where my father-in-law had lodged in his youth. At that time it was ventilated to bring in air from outside, but today I am never sure whether it is better to keep air out. I think I would have become bad tempered if I had been working there. I had chosen UNA as the recipient of an additional worker because I did not wish to ask a university to house him and risk him becoming an academic. He had to be in a place but not attached to a particular party, nor promoting any controversial plans. I envisaged him staying long enough to get to know all the relevant people, such as journalists, Foreign Office officials and academics. I said this might require me to raise a higher salary to get a good person to stay, I was told sharply, 'You might have a strike on your hands if you do.'

Before the post could be created, a large sum had to be gathered. The fundraising began badly and it was not easy. The Rowntree Charitable Trust, although sympathetic towards the UN had a rule against contributing capital funds for long term projects. As this is the largest of the Quaker trusts and of the trusts giving for peace projects, this was a drawback. I had to create a list of sponsors for adding to the UNA letterhead.

I decided to name the post after my great grandfather John Bright, thinking that this would appeal to his descendants at Street, but it turned out that they knew very little about him. They did not know his great speech against the Crimean War, the speech, which was described by Michael Foot as the greatest peace speech of the century. Nor did they know that he was the only Cabinet Minister to resign on an issue such as the shelling of Alexandria by the navy. Some of them must have read G.M. Trevelyan's biography[62] but overlooked the author's assessment that, although Bright failed in his opposition to the Crimean War, the effects were so great that he wrote: 'It is otherwise probable that we should have fought for Austria against France in 1859, for the (US) slave owners against the North in 1861, or for Denmark against Germany in 1864 or for Turkey against Russia in 1878.'

There followed a period of letter writing to the hundred larger Quaker Meetings, to John Bright's relatives, to Quaker and other trusts. If I were to do a similar job again I would take much more trouble to get the wording right. I had to agree not to approach

UNA branches, because UNA depends on them for support for its own activities. It was interesting for a grant maker; such as I used to be, to find myself in the position of being the applicant for funds. I found the reference books published by the Directory of Social Change[63] particularly helpful. They give addresses, names of trustees, and some idea of the size of grants usually made or the total income of the donor trust. Frequently applicants for grants imagine that all they need is names and addresses, as a consequence many unsuitable applications are made by enthusiastic people whose enthusiasm, when properly channelled, is likely to be a major asset to society. I felt exceptionally grateful on receiving favourable replies. There was more to do, however, John Bright was MP for Birmingham after Manchester rejected him at the time of the Crimean War and both towns honoured him with statues.

It is difficult now for anyone to understand the importance of an orator before the era of the mass media, before radio and tele-vision, at a time when most people were illiterate, the two skills of speaking in public and in parliament were of the utmost impor-tance. One of his descendants at Street dismissed him as merely representing the interests of the middle class to which he belonged. I would have liked to have asked him whether he had ever read the 'Angel of Death speech.' It brought the House of Commons to an uneasy silence. After referring to MP's who had been killed he continued:

'The Angel of Death has been abroad throughout the land, you can almost hear the beating of his wings ... he takes his victims from the castle of the noble, the mansion of the wealthy, and the cottage of the poor and lowly, and it is on behalf of all these classes that I make this solemn appeal ... I would entreat the noble Lord [Palmerston, Prime Minister at the time] ... having become the director of the destinies of his country that he might seek the satisfaction that he had returned the sword into its scabbard – that at his word torrents of blood had ceased to flow, that he had restored tranquillity to Europe, and had saved this country from the indescribable calamities of war.'

He made such an impression on the House that Disraeli, soon to become Prime Minister, came over to him and sat beside him and said 'Bright, I would have given all that I ever had, to have

John Bright, my great grandfather, said speaking against the Crimean War 'I would not advise alliances with any nation. But I would cultivate friendship with all nations'.

Permission to use this illustration has been given by the Quaker Tapestry at Kendal. The Quaker Tapestry is a community textile of 77 embroidered panels made by 4,000 people from 15 countries. Further information can be obtained from: The Quaker Tapestry Exhibition Centre, Friends Meeting House, Stramongate, Kendal, Cumbria, LA9 4BH, England, UK.
Telephone and Fax: +44 (0)1539 722975
http://www.quaker-tapestry.co.uk   e-mail: info@quaker-tapestry.co.uk

298

made that speech you made just now.' Others heaped their compliments upon him. He amply earned a place in my book *Men Against War*. This would have, I thought, an interest for its many other Quaker truths.

In Birmingham the atmospheric pollution is so bad that the curator of the museum showed me how quickly marble statues deteriorate when erected out of doors and I had to admit that John Bright's was better kept inside. The street named after him was given a face lift, they expected me to wield a shovel for a photographer and drive a bulldozer, and when it was introduced to the John Bright Street Traders Association the Secretary turned up with a photo of a railway engine with the old man's name on it. He told of how when the 1914 war began, the railway company felt embarrassed by the name and so the engine received a new name!

The Anglican Cathedral was full to hear Donald Soper speak for peace and I followed him speaking for the UN's work. Maybe I undertook the harder task. Someone found in the large Reference Library a large kerchief with Bright's activities printed on it. I had them copied as a way of thanking the donors. The substantial financial help came from the many Cadbury Trusts. Sir Adrian Cadbury also helped by providing me with a list of people to invite to a Lord Mayor's Reception. This occasion led to a photograph in the Friend in which there happened to be a candelabra just behind my head. One of the wittier correspondents published a letter the following week to ask how it was that only Nicholas Gillett was wearing a halo.

I may have picked up a halo in Birmingham, but I did not pick up much else. I had not learned the principles of fundraising, which is rapidly becoming a new profession of skilled people who have to be trusted. Manchester proved more difficult, as I only had a contact with The Manchester Business School to start me off. Rochdale was worse. As it was John Bright's hometown there is a statue of him that we planned to have moved from a remote place in a park to the central square. A film director was confident he could get the moving of the statue on television news, but a powerful lobby against cotton factory owners had the decision reversed and did the best they could to break up our meeting. They can have understood very little about Bright's work to get manhood suffrage accepted in Parliament. I suspect that they did not know that the Bright Mills had been sold but the name kept for a number of years afterwards. Nor did they know that Punch made mock of John Bright from time to time, or they might have been more sympathetic.

I had to start to raise a sum large enough to cover the full cost of one additional person, without approaching the usual donors. I realised that I needed more skill in writing and in knowing whom I should approach. However, a total figure was reached to justify making an appointment. The post was advertised and among the short-listed applicants was one of the young post-graduates who had worked at the Geneva Quaker Centre. He was very highly recommended by Ed Dommen as the best trainee to fill the position.

We celebrated his appointment with a tea party at the Reform Club, which is still haunted so to say by the ghost of John Bright. In that strange place the newly appointed holder of the John Bright post, Sam Daws, spoke to the large gathering of his hopes for the UN and his work for it. Once he started work it was clear that he was born for the job. I told him at the end of his first year that he had accomplished ten times as much as I had expected. His brief was to promote the peace activities of the UN and he quickly established good relations with the Ministry of Defence officials concerned with UN Peacekeeping. After hearing him, they invited him to take a share in briefing future Peacekeepers on the work of the Security Council, of the Convention on Human Rights and the Geneva Conventions as well as some of the problems facing the UN. He carried this out so well that the invitation has been extended to his two successors. In connection with this he spent his first annual leave in the former Yugoslavia meeting the UN Peacekeepers and seeking their opinions about their difficult task.

His second official contact was with the section of the Foreign and Commonwealth Office (FCO), which deals with the UN. His knowledge gained while studying for his second degree at Kent University on Conflict Management as well as his grasp of the reforms suggested for the Security Council must have impressed them. One of the officials said to him, laughing, 'Sam, when I retire, may I become one of your volunteers?' When Sam, with his unusual modesty recounted this to me he added: 'To be one of the volunteers in the UN and Conflict Unit nowadays, you have to have a second degree in some peace studies and be computer literate! That's just to be a volunteer!'

Thirdly he attended meetings or conferences of many of the excessive number of peace organisations in London. I have sometimes wondered whether our opponents contrive to keep us fragmented in order to weaken the movement for peace. Fourthly he joined the British International Studies Association (UN Section) and brought out a directory for them so that academics could cooperate more effectively. Fifthly, having the wisdom to believe that man cannot live by bread and brain alone, he maintained his many Quaker connections, helped their peace work and kept open his resource for solving ethical problems with the help of Sunday Meetings for Worship.

When he left after three years to study for his doctorate at Oxford, he had a number of books in mind notably one on the Security Council, the subject of his thesis and he had already been adopted by the late Sydney Bailey to follow him in making available to diplomats up-to-date information on various UN institutions as well as a general guide.[64] In the course of a brief internship at the UN he made such an impression on the officials and diplomats that he was 'head-hunted' just a few weeks before completing his thesis and is now engaged in such tasks as accompanying Kofi Annan on his journeys to keep a written record of his conversations and using his special expertise regarding the Security Council. Sam reports ecstatically of working closely with the Secretary-General and of the good atmosphere at the UN top floors, despite often working fourteen hours a day, weekends included.

To me it is an enormous encouragement that all my efforts have come to fruition successfully. He is kind enough to me to say that without me he would not be there. I am a great believer in getting the right man in the right place and then adding strength to his arm. Just recently (April 2001) I have been able to send him at his request an intern as an editorial assistant and speechwriter.

The modest reforms needed by the UN are well set out in Sam Daws' *Memorandum on an Agenda for Peace*.[65] The need for a variety of reforms based on the difficulties encountered when the Security Council gives a mandate for action, are made abundantly clear. When violence begins to break out, prompt provision of funds and forces are needed and are seldom made available; national governments are quick to lay the blame on the UN. There is much support in theory for preventative action so as to nip violence in the bud. When the principle is accepted the next step will be a request for funds in advance.*

The second term of Kofi Annan as Secretary-General has provided an opportunity to make some progress. Now that several global firms have shown that they believe that peace is in their interest and that they need the help of the UN, there are additional reasons for hope. When we settled down for the seminar on which the *Memorandum* was based, I recall feeling that a new chapter of the peace movement was opening up before our eyes. These two references set out very clearly the points to bear in mind when advocating changes at the UN. Many other reports and books exist on the subject of UN reform.

* Sam Daws took up his new post as Director UNA UK on 6.9.04.

CHAPTER 18

Endings and New Beginnings

GOLDEN WEDDINGS SEEM to be out of fashion. Despite people living longer, and despite the need of children for a more stable family life, 'modern' people show less skill at seeking to make effective relationships. One afternoon two Chinese visitors were shown all the boys at Eton College playing games out of doors. It had been explained to them that the boys all lived at school. Their question was 'Whatever is wrong with so many homes?'

Our Golden Wedding began with an inspection of the golden daffodils, which I had planted in the front lawn for the occasion, when I could not be sure they would be in flower for the right day, April 20th, 1988. The children, led by Bevis I suspect, had arranged a party for a large number of our friends, in the Village Hall of Westbury on Trym, situated conveniently across the road from our house. Katy found one of her friends would do the catering, and David made the main speech. In short it was a splendid occasion.

We never guessed that in addition we would be presented with a 'book' with contributions from friends far and wide. It ran to a hundred and eighty pages and towards the end there is one, which gives the flavour of the whole book and yet is comprehensible to a stranger. It suggests that if you have children of your own you are very likely to be teased for writing your autobiography in old age. One publisher circulates advice to would-be authors, which includes the question: 'Are you famous? If not, what are you going to do about it?'

10 Ways on How to Survive as a Next Generation Gillett!

1. If Gandhi is held up as a marvellous example of a selfless leader – point out that he went around barefoot and thus didn't wear Clarks shoes.

2.   If you are encouraged to go on a work camp:
(a) To do good
(b) To form a cocoa drinking relationship with a member of the opposite sex, make sure you take up one respectable vice, e.g., have dinner with the future Queen of Holland.

3.   If you feel the heavy dose of chocolate ancestry – support research which proves that chocolate, sweets, etc., are the second biggest health hazard after smoking.

4.   If you were press-ganged into going on an Aldermaston march – a 50 mile + route march, join up with the march at Trafalgar Square, having slept in your clothes the previous night, and declare that you were up at the front with Bertrand Russell and Michael Foot.

5.   If you are given a copy of 'Parents Only (A.N.G.'s first attempt to get into print) take care not to read it until you have reached maturity, i.e., are at least a grandparent, great aunt, etc., when you will begin to appreciate that the characters mentioned therein are pure figments of the imagination.

6.   If you were taken camping to Wales or the Lake District in the wettest month of the year on a regular basis, never take another holiday in Britain, but return year after year to the sun drenched islands of Greece.

7.   If there are a lot of hints to get involved with the United Nations Association or with refugees, cut your losses and get married to a refugee from Vietnam.

8.   If the parent(s) go in for ancestor worship, ensure that they do one tour of duty in the East to see how it is done properly, with prayer mat, prayer wheel, small statue of Buddha, etc.

9.   If somebody tells you how marvellous your parents are, commiserate with him or her and say 'it does seem a terrible burden to bear and yet basically they are such nice people'.

10. Sausage picnics. To be on the safe side its best to turn up on Boxing Day for the family sausage picnic regardless of the weather.

Ruth had one of the grand children on her lap much of the time, but was already feeling a pain in her side, while looking her best in the photographs. She suffered more day by day and died of a mysterious liver complaint two months later. The wider family could not be given warning so as to say farewell and I would have liked

Sometimes constitutions have to be changed to save the state from violence.
"They call me a radical," said John Bright, "really I'm more conservative
than the conservatives". John Bright's statue is in the background at this
Charter 88 campaign event in Manchester.

to have told her how much I had enjoyed sharing the work with her in Belfast and Geneva. We had both assumed that she, the healthier of the two of us, would live longer. I would have liked to have persuaded her that my time was well spent for the future of our children, though she had the opinion that I was neglecting them, by going to meetings and conferences.

It was easy to agree that Ruth and I had been on a joint pilgrimage; it was somewhat less easy to identify ourselves with Quakers, who appeared to me to point in more than one direction, often turning back the more difficult decisions to be settled by our own consciences. Our pilgrimage only ended after more than fifty years together, when the six children joined us for her last hours in the Bristol Royal Infirmary. 'How are the mighty fallen in the midst of the pilgrimage!' I said to myself again and again, as I wished such people as Ruth could live forever. The world needs them.

With considerable difficulty I told the Quaker Meeting the story of the Bakbakiri Shrike of South Africa. It has a very well known call from which its name is derived – Bak Bak Bak – Bakiri, which is repeated many times. It was only relatively recently that it was realised that this was in fact a duet. The male, it is claimed, sings the first part of the call, and is followed by the female. However, if a female dies, the male adds her part and produces the whole call. The implication for me was clearly that I had to try to perform Ruth's role in addition to my own, but I found that changes of attitude do not occur easily just by wishing for them.

My Quaker resources brought brief moments of reassurance. Just like a water-diviner, when he no longer has ordinary perceptions of sight and sound, empties his mind to make a space for another kind of awareness, so my mind made a space for hope and help. I suppose that if I had made a regular time for such experiences I might have become not only a better person but a better peace maker, a better peace builder, or a doctor who could cure the disease of hatred. However, my pilgrimage led me to simpler, easier tasks, or so I believed.

Three encouragements happened to cheer me on my way during this disheartening period after the death of Ruth. It is to me always surprising when these happen. I had an enthusiastic letter from the John Runnings University, Seattle, Washington, with a handsome cheque, which was the prize for an eight page essay which I called 'USA and USSR Move Towards Each Other: A Study in Continental Drift.' It contained some twenty-four practical suggestions for improving relationships. The letter expressed support, and suggested improvements on the paper, and asked for my help in publicising the competition. A hundred and eighty nine entries had been received of which mine was given second prize. See Appendix 6.

The question has been raised by Peter van den Dungen of the Peace Studies Department at Bradford University, whether grant-making charities would do better to make more donations for such prizes, and less for projects. If the media were to pay more attention to the subject in question, it might well turn out that way. The Nobel Peace Prize Committee in Oslo believe in their success in drawing attention to the need to abolish war, now that weapons have become infinitely more dangerous.

On another occasion the Institute for Social Change awarded a prize for my book as previously mentioned, *The Swiss Constitution: Can it be Exported?* for the original ideas included in it. It was never very clear to me, which ideas were thought to be so sparkling with originality and I did not like to ask! I hope it was for the role schools can play in appreciating and supporting changes in a constitution.

Soon after starting to write this autobiography, the Gandhi Foundation astonished me by offering me the Gandhi Peace Award, and with the prize came a very thought-provoking statuette of Mahatma Gandhi standing on top of the world. As I commented at the presentation I might have refused it on Quaker grounds of simple living, had I not relished the thought of speaking to a meeting gathered to hear Bruce Kent give a memorial lecture. My acceptance speech was well received so has also been included. See Appendix 7.

The theme, which had also been included in the prize essay, was that disarmament keeps being postponed despite repeated failures, which indicate that other ways of promoting peace should be examined. Anyone coming fresh to the problem might note that the Channel for Britain and the Atlantic for the USA are sufficiently wide to discourage an enemy from invading and on top of this at

NO CULTURE
CAN SURVIVE
IF IT ATTEMPS TO BE
EXCLUSIVE.

MAHATMA GANDHI

KEINE KULTUR KANN ÜBERLEBEN

Gandhi demonstrated the potential of non-violence by leading the campaign for India's independence from Britain.

308

See appendix 7 for the text of my speech on receiving the Gandhi peace award.

present there are no serious enemies unless they be trading opponents such as Japan and Germany. These are only successful opponents because they waste less money on their military forces.

Encouraging though these three prizes were, they were nothing compared with the change in my personal life. After Ruth's death in 1988 I was discovering how bad I was at being on my own.

To my surprise, when visiting Mehr Fardoonji our old friend of more than twenty years standing, we both agreed that we would like to try to share each other's lives. So in 1990 I came to Oakcroft to get married to Mehr in the Quaker Meeting House in Chester. She is sixteen years younger than I am and we both wondered whether at this advanced age we were sufficiently adaptable to adjust to each other.

We each prided ourselves on being peaceful people, she, though vivacious and spontaneous is good at the forgiving and forgetting of reconciliation and I a quieter personality, less likely to get impatient in the first place. She had used Adam Curle's book, *Making Peace*[66] with her Workers Educational Association (WEA) students and I had used it in teacher training, being very anxious to ensure that teachers learn to put themselves in the shoes of their pupils, instead of losing patience with them. It seemed to us that, if anyone could make our partner happy, we could. More than thirteen years later we can say that it appears to be a peaceful household.

To compensate for my moving house, since market gardens cannot be moved, I was amply paid by the badgers and the birds, which thrive here. The bluebells, primroses, cowslips in large numbers, and those orchids of at least two varieties not to mention the improvements to the house which provide me with a sunny place to read and write, and an entrancing garden. We try to make one improvement each year.

Mehr comes from a Parsee family. The Zoroastrian religion was the earliest to be monotheistic. When the Muslims invaded Persia they persecuted them so much that many went by sea as refugees to India twelve hundred and fifty years ago. When they applied for asylum the Maharaja in Gujarat replied that the country was already full and demonstrated how full with a cup of milk. The leader of the Parsees added some sugar and said: 'See how the milk absorbs the sugar without a spill. Let us be your sugar.' On the strength of this they were allowed to remain. Some of them became the great

India became my country-in-law when I married Mehr Fardoonji.
She walked from village to village with Vinoba Bhave, a disciple of Gandhi,
in the Land Gift Movement known as Bhoodan

311

industrialists of India, like the Quakers in Britain, and, like the Quakers they tried to maintain their identity by arranging marriages within their community. Only now is the practice changing. Mehr herself lived in a large extended family, in which a form of social education happened automatically. At the age of seven her widowed mother brought her to Manchester with her brother. After studying at the London School of Economics she spent seven months travelling by land to India on her own. As she says about this journey, it was her mother that worried not herself.

Being a strong Gandhian, she soon joined Vinoba Bhave in walking from village to village in the 'Land Gift' or Bhoodan Movement to persuade larger landowners to provide some land for the landless. It was a great credit to India and especially to the Gandhians that four million acres were transferred in this way. Gandhi may have been assassinated, but his ideas persist. Since returning to England she set up the Organic Market Garden at Oakcroft forty years ago and has kept it going ever since, believing that it is the kind of work Gandhi would have approved. Since her mother died she has been returning to India from time to time, including those occasions when she has introduced me to her family and to my new country-in-law.

Returning to England and the garden after a visit to India gave me the chance to continue adjusting to my new home. For me joining Mehr meant big changes, the separation between where I was living in Bristol and Oakcroft amounts to three hours driving in the car from friends and family in Bristol, where I had spent twenty-five years. The move was well compensated by my being treated like the sugar in the milk by Mehr and her circle of friends. The opportunities to work as long as I wished on the light work of the market garden with its four green houses, cloches and cold frames, leaving me free to work at my desk in the mornings, gazing from time to time at A.E. Housman's hills.

> What are those blue remembered hills,
> What farms, what spires are those?
> That is the land of lost content,
> I see it shining plain,
> The happy highways where I went
> And cannot come again.

The past and the present have been very good to me, by allowing me to live in the countryside both in childhood and in old age. I could wish it for everyone. After my arrival at Oakcroft, before getting taken up with too much work in the garden, I decided to walk in a large circle around our home, benefiting from the footpaths of this dairying county, to get a sense of where I was to live and its surroundings. The radius of the circle averages some fifteen miles but as time passed I added to what I called our estate until it encompassed the towns of Chester, Wrexham, Llangollen, and Whitchurch. In all that distance I never met a farm labourer to speak to, because they were all isolated inside their tractor cabins. One farmer spoke at length, because he thought I was a fellow farmer, a fellow countryman, due to my guessing correctly the size of his flock of sheep.

This attempt to put down roots when I was already in my late seventies proved to be the right move; although my walking days are now over, I enjoy periods of quiet reflection in the garden and in the new wood at the bottom of our property. These trees have grown much taller than I expected to see in my lifetime from the time of the planting of the trees in 1998. It is difficult to express, except through poetry, the quiet satisfaction of living close to nature. It is related in some mysterious way to the thoughts, which arise in Quaker Meetings for Worship and are needed more and more as the pace of life in cities increases.

Mehr often mentions the impracticability of those who live in ivory towers. In this category she puts the people who live in the flat above our house, and me. We can have up to four people staying at one time, some of them coming through the WWOOF organisation, each working part time in lieu of rent. Some of them see smallholdings through the eyes of idealists and ask such questions as:

'Why don't you use your spare acre? Couldn't you do better if you produced more?'

'To do that I'd need more labour' Mehr replies with a smile.

'Where would that come from?' she asks and then adds, 'it is hard enough to find customers as it is. I'm always trying to balance labour, produce and markets or customers.'

'Can't you use more machinery and use it to save labour?' The persistent ones continue.

'No I'm really a Luddite at heart. I'd like to see more people living the good life, growing more of their own food and eating it fresh.'

Knowing she is on a sticky wicket, she may add:

'Physical work out of doors is good for everyone and in winter if the weather is bad, there is usually work to be done in the greenhouses. Don't you think people have grown a bit soft?'

Another facet of Mehr's opinions is the importance of skilled craft-work. She uses the word in a wide sense to include my poetry in addition to her own pottery and knitting. With William Morris she thinks more people could get acquainted with their own creativity. How can a person 'walk tall' with confidence, until they have designed and made something with skill? The custom of making presents is growing fast; preference could always be given to something that the giver has made with their own skills.

The people who come here sometimes want to learn gardening, others have been unemployed, some have been discharged from mental hospitals, others come from abroad to improve their English, others come to leave home, and some have simply no where else to go.

Almost all the previous points can be found somewhere in Gandhi's copious writing and in his practice, as he adhered strictly to the principles of practising what he preached. The following further list all have echoes in the way we live at Oakcroft.

'The beauty of self-help,' a wider concept than 'Do it yourself.'

A passion for vegetarianism or veganism.

Milk should be consumed only when illness makes it necessary.

'As a man eats, so shall he become.' (Indian proverb)

'Eat to live' writes Gandhi, 'Don't live to eat.' (Hard to follow. Mehr is a very skilled cook)

Untouchables must be welcome in the ashram.

Abuse is best not returned – it needs to be absorbed. (Now called part of the Culture of Peace)

'The little fleeting glimpses, therefore, that I have been able to have of truth can hardly convey an idea of the indescribable lustre of Truth.' (to which Gandhi attached his own special meaning.)

One further quote comes from Tagore, the friend of Gandhi, and links so well with the West and Oakcroft's people that it merits a place: 'The great problem is not one of poverty but of unhappiness. Man forgets that the divinity within him is revealed by the halo of happiness.'

It is little wonder that those who shed their unhappiness here, keep on coming to revisit us. We believe we catch some of the qualities of peace here during the varied jobs of a smallholding. We also catch a glimpse of social chaos, which the future threatens to bring, as I am reminded, as I write, by the news that water cannons are being used by police in the street riots of Belfast for the first time.

The seemingly all-conquering human race stands in wonder at the liveliness of a virus too small to see, (outbreak of Foot and Mouth) at the benefits of bacteria in the soil and at our methods of feeding the multitudinous microbes, which are as dependant on us, as we are on this 'organic' plot. Wonder characterises very young children as well as some very old people. While in our culture invention is admired, its sister activity wonder is regarded with suspicion as childishness or even ignorance. Creativity fits awkwardly into schools with their timetables, examinations, and discipline and yet it is the main criterion for civilization. The world needs creative diplomats and also statesmen rather than more politicians otherwise we are all in danger for lack of imagination.

My attention was drawn to a change in the charity laws enabling organisations to campaign, which have some expertise in their subject and are able and willing to present two or more points of view on contentious issues. Since my arrival at Oakcroft I have been impressed with Mark Lattimer's book *On Campaigning*, and believe that many of the organisations supported by the Polden-Puckham Charitable Trust could put some of its suggestions into practice. Being relatively free after retiring I was able to visit a number of them, and read the particulars of a much larger number, so that I became acquainted with a large section of the peace movement. I began to realise that it might be said that I knew them all superficially but was master of none.

The question haunted me, but I was also aware that as the leaders of the various organisations spoke about their plans and needs I was acquiring a certain expertise in campaigning for peace by asking such questions as 'what is the essence of the message? Who form your target audience? How can they best be approached and by whom?'

If the government in Britain fails to back the UN's alternative methods of defence and fails to follow the example of billionaires in the USA, it may still be possible to interest groups of millionaires in Britain. The question arises whether the many organisations of the UN can show that they are competent enough and prepared for a large expansion.

The Institute of Social Inventions has not been invited to break the logjam of ideas in which the peace movement has been caught. The need to identify the message a particular organisation seeks to deliver, and the appropriate target audiences to receive it, have already been mentioned. Target audiences may range from decision-shapers who may be few, to parents or trade unionists that will be many. On the various committees on which I have served, I have seldom noticed any agenda items derived from them, nor the adjusting of methods of publicity related to them. To take one example the Quaker Tapestry held in Kendal, drew on ideas of the famous Bayeux Tapestry, depicting the Norman invasion of Britain and show a history of Quakers and Quakerism. In its early stages, when I first heard about the tapestry, I wondered whether this was a good way of building on the leisure time of elderly Quakers and whether they should have been more actively involved in the peace movement. I was shown to be entirely wrong. It proved to be a novel way of strengthening Quaker's interest in their history including many ways of supporting peace, furthermore the groups, each in a different Meeting, enjoyed the give and take of cooperation in historical research, needlework and managing a group of children. The first book about it claims that more than 2000 people were involved with the work in eight different countries, and its success is shown by the invitation to take it to Bayeux and to the Houses of Parliament in London as well as countless other places.

It is easy to see how this very novel form of publicity, or outreach as Quakers prefer to call it, could be applied to the peace movement, or more specifically to parts of it such as the United Nations. It is always necessary to be on the look-out for new ways of reaching the public. Novelty is of the essence of good public relations. Another method is singing songs, if the targets are young, as in the Campaign for Nuclear Disarmament, on a march. Though the growth in the interest in the Internet may prove to be replacing people's previous love of singing. To get the feel of the many alternative ways of campaigning, I have made use of as many of the methods as I can. People are aware that another World War would risk bringing life on Earth to an end. The thoughts in this box below sum up efforts to prevent such a disaster; can they be improved?

GIVE US A BETTER UN

Goodwill and friendship greasing the wheels of diplomacy.
International law gaining the respect it deserves.
Visioning a more peaceful future, for hope's sake.
Educating for peace both young and old, girls and boys.

Understanding of all sides in disputes, to bridge gaps.
Security Council voting by size and contribution but no veto.

Agencies of UN knitted more closely together, for stronger
    teamwork.

Builders of peace follow the peace-keepers, as unarmed civilians.
Environmental issues wisely addressed.
Taming global firms' greed with fair trade campaigns.
Tobin taxes paid to the UN to avoid bringing "too little too late."
Early warning systems to anticipate and thus reduce violence.
Researching the conditions of peace, to follow Ted Turner's
    example.

Uniting against the threats of climate change.
Non-governmental organisations checking 'national interests.'

317

ONE DAY WE'RE BOUND TO EVOLVE A BETTER WAY OF SETTLING DISPUTES.

I use this Austin cartoon as a reminder to some of my correspondents of the increasing futility of war.

CHAPTER 19

The Conditions of Peace in a Time of Perpetual Change

IN THE COURSE OF my quest I have concluded that the conditions, which make future peace possible deserve more attention than the causes of war. Whereas the study of war and its causes instils pessimism by appearing to be overwhelming, the conditions of peace are so numerous that there is something everyone can do to create them. They lead to action and optimism. They are selected for their topical importance.

By ranking psychological conditions with political and economic, I have deliberately taken a leaf out of UNESCO's splendid dictum 'Since wars begin in the minds of men, in the minds of men the bulwarks of peace must be raised.' Anger, fear, hatred and greed for power, have psychological aspects so that there is no definitive way of listing them according to academic disciplines. However, psychological warfare or war propaganda has become far too well recognised to be omitted.

The Political Conditions of Peace

The United Nations can be strengthened by reforms. Reforms are of two kinds, those which require a change in the Constitution, and those which do not. People fail to understand that to reach an end of the long history of international cooperation to avoid war and establish peace, it is essential for all governments to realise that each country's main, national interest is to establish peace. The development of weapons makes it not just a good cause but also a

There is always more than one way of looking at it. When there is a dispute, mediators often find it hard to see things from more than one point of view. Perhaps they could learn from owls.

vital requirement to bring about Tennyson's vision in his poem *Locksley Hall*, which was written in the early eighteen forties.[67] After 'Peering in the future far as the human eye can see' he carries on:

> Till the war drum throbbed no longer, and the battle flags
>   were furl'd
> In the Parliament of Man, the Federation of the world.
> There the common sense of most shall hold a fretful realm
>   in awe.
> And the kindly earth shall slumber, lapt in universal law.

These lines were followed with his prediction of air warfare, but he does not make clear whether he foresaw its horrors leading to the 'Parliament of Man.'

In the past national governments have shown themselves to be strangely selfish and short-sighted when defining their own national interests, as though ignorant of the proverb 'United we stand, divided we fall.' They appear to have taught their citizens a narrow jingoism, or chauvinism instead of real citizenship, such as the world needs to tackle its global problems.

The politicians who are responsible for this interpretation of national interests are being challenged by the grouping of Non-Governmental Organisations which are demanding recognition for the help they give the UN for its varied projects and its general work such as peace-making. The Red Cross is the largest of these organisations but Oxfam, Amnesty International, a variety of religious groups and innumerable smaller ones have jointly a considerable influence. Jointly they are proposing that there should be a second international chamber in addition to the General Assembly, through which they could make their influence felt.

At the same time adding further to the high drama, some of the big global firms are beginning to understand that their interests lie in the same changes. Maybe the spreading ethical movement has influenced this development. As previously mentioned, I feel that certainly Ted Turner with his gift of a billion dollars to form the UN Foundation, and the additional strong support of the Bill Gates Foundation, have set an example to the very rich and strengthened the work and thus the reputation of the UN. If people such as these men believe in the UN to that extent, they must have good reasons

321

for their belief, and this will impress other people. I hope that I will live long enough to see some of the outcome. So far I have written for copies of the winter 2001 report for the UN Foundation and circulated a number of copies to key people. I have yet to draft a letter to accompany the report. This report includes an account of its 'sister organisation' the Better World Campaign, and as the report points out this 'helped to ensure that the USA paid its more than a billion dollars debt to the UN.' On the environment, support was provided for the Climate Change Framework and World Energy Assessment, to help ensure that action is soundly based. In regard to population issues it is pointed out that two-thirds of school aged children not attending school are girls, just as two thirds of world's illiterate adults are women.

The other main issues regarding peace are preventative action based on early warning and excessive supplies of small arms, which encourage people to use the arms to get their food. A point made in the latest document from the US Institute for Peace.

The abolition of the veto in the Security Council is, to many people, the major reform needed as a condition of peace. At some time the matter will become easier to raise. Already the US proportion of the budget is being reduced, nevertheless some modification, such as an agreement to stop using the veto, which would not involve a constitutional change, might be arranged, or a requirement that more than a single negative vote would be required before a decision is rejected. However governments are now unlikely to give up their power without gaining something in return, and the USA will not remain the single superpower forever. This suggests to me a long and complex campaign to extend the ethical movement to national governments and politicians.

There are many separate parts in the work of the Secretary-General and one of these is doing what he can to ensure some appropriate cooperation among the five principal organs of the UN; namely the General Assembly, the Security Council, the Secretariat, the Economic and Social Council, and the International Court of Justice (The World Court). The work of the Court has expanded enormously recently as governments have come to realise the immense advantages, when there is a dispute, of settling it by 'Going to Court, not War.' The pamphlet with this name is about to be revised and reprinted yet again and needs to be translated into yet more languages.

It suggests that acceptance of the World Court's compulsory jurisdiction is the mark of a civilised state, though only a third of states, including Britain, pass this test. There is an obvious need for changes, which no one is likely to initiate in its Department of Public Information far beyond what the pamphlet can do. We, at the World Court Project, are trying to find out what could be achieved by offering as interns young lawyers with some teaching experience or some interest in public relations, on the model of what is being done by those under Sam Daws' guidance.

Diplomacy provides another field in which improvements could be made. There is a tendency to suppose that the skills required are best acquired by what is termed in industry 'sitting next to Nelly' and reading a long list of books about the country to which one is to be attached. The UN points to some of the ways in which this can be changed. In the years I spent in Geneva among those charming diplomats at the UN, I was disappointed to find how little they knew about Dag Hammarskjöld's principle of 'keeping bridges open' between two countries in conflict, or of the UN pamphlet initiated by Waclaw Micuta with some help from Roger Wilson and myself on avoiding the mistakes liable to be made by anyone working in an unfamiliar culture.

Cultural differences often cause younger diplomats to make mistakes. I have already mentioned the Secretary of the Arab League who responded to my praise of the UN with the remark 'You have the UN. We have the Arab League.' In many countries there is a very strong distinction between guests and mere strangers, implying that two visits can be made more fruitful than a single one.

Spreading power is the very essence of democracy and democracy is a likely candidate for any list of the conditions of peace. Power is spread in the cooperative democracy of Switzerland in a number of ways. The Swiss rejected disbanding their army recently although they have not gone to war since the time of Napoleon's invasion. It is little wonder that though small it is a very prosperous country by most measures. Most countries have much to learn from Switzerland.

Mediation and conflict management have received much attention in the past fifty years, so that we know what to do thanks to the work of many brave and devoted people, with the result that we have only to apply the lessons taught. In similar ways much more understanding of the other aspects of non-violence has to be acquired. The financial costs of using new weapons and the risks of using them, whether we have in mind nuclear bombs or nuclear terrorism, should draw attention to the role of a change of heart, maybe a change of religion as worthy of consideration.

Professor Sir Michael Howard, paying a tribute to the Society of Friends, described in a speech about Peace Studies: 'their capacity to create peaceful situations arise very much from the kind of internal discipline which they impose upon themselves so that for the greater part, they are themselves the foci of tranquillity, which they spread out wherever they go.' I hope that for Peace Studies this whole question of inward peace will not be neglected, and its connection with the social aspect of peace-keeping and peace maintenance will be constantly stressed. As I have indicated the Buddhist monks with their smiling tranquillity, are more than equal to the Quakers in this respect.

Having arrived at the prehistoric stone circles of Avebury, very early one sunny morning in spring with Ruth, I noticed the benign aura created by these huge brooding boulders and they reminded me of a benign group of elderly Quakers sitting down worshipping together. Later, Scilla Elworthy of the Oxford Research Group laughed on hearing this story and developed this idea into a new kind of conference facilitator whose function it is to convey a sense of goodwill towards the aims and members of the conference. She once invited me to fill the role and I felt as though my dream of bridging the gap in peace work between Quakers, and official methods might be coming true.

It is also clear that peace does not occur independently but requires an active citizenship, organised in a great variety of organisations bringing pressure to bear on the government to follow wise policies, and preventing the vested interests from the pursuit of their selfish aims. The peace organisations will need better funding than they are getting at present from the government, from the wealthy and from skilled campaigning.

The second group of conditions might be termed psychological. Corruption by power has a place here as it has among the political conditions. Psychological warfare can be exposed to mitigate its efficacy and this can be done in schools and colleges. The ethical movement has to grow. It has grown recently, but never as fast as one could wish. A report recently came from a neighbour: he said he had been in Turkey with the British council and told me of the success in teaching about human rights, the due process of law, and the meaning of international law, to the police. The men that were met seemed to be resistant at first, and had been suspicious but saw the value by the end, may be on account of the need for Turkey to improve its ways in order to be accepted into the European Union. What was of special interest was that the work was covered by the funds voted for Robin Cook's ethical policy. This was a laughing matter at first by those who ridiculed the idea of an ethical foreign policy, but those who ridiculed this idea need to think again. If the ethical movement can spread as far as this, it must be possible to spread it into the boardrooms of the global firms, the majority of which stand to gain by maintaining the peace.

Violent news should be treated not as the normal expression of a violent society, but as a waste product barely fit for mention. The media survive like elephants by consuming their own dung. This is due to a faulty digestive system. When editors are using bad news they are using dung, a waste product and because they choose it, it's dung they get offered. Gresham's Law for currency applies to news that the bad drives out the good. It also applies to others who tamper with the truth, the spin-doctors, advertisers and even the more respectable experts in public relations.

A good mediator not only requires to learn more and more about what it would be like to stand in other peoples shoes, but has to teach the contestants to do the same, by teaching empathy and by getting close to people with varied backgrounds of experience. He must recognise that he is like King Canute, trying to defy the incoming tide. It is a tough assignment.

It is amusing to recall the story of the sandals that Gandhi made during his time in prison, for General Smuts. To the best of my belief that pair of sandals, though much appreciated by Smuts were passed on to my mother. They were kept for some years in a cupboard on the landing in our home in Banbury Road, Oxford. I found them there and used them, until they were worn out. So it is reasonable to ask whether literally wearing someone else's shoes, in this case a great man like Gandhi, somehow affects the way we live, did it for example influence me in any way to marry into the Gandhi movement?

Adapted from anonymous advice

If your children live among violence,
They grow to be violent,
If young children live with hostility,
They grow up to be hostile and fight.
But
If your children live with tolerance,
They grow to be patient.
If your children live with encouragement,
They grow to be confident.
If your children live with praise,
They grow up to appreciate.
If your children live with fairness,
They grow up understanding justice.
If your children live with security,
They grow up to have faith.
If your children live with acceptance and friendship,
They grow up finding love in the world.

All these psychological conditions of peace may sound to some ears to be wishful thinking and more like the fantasy of optimists but there is plenty of hard evidence for the claims, as may be judged by research papers listed in the bibliography edited by Åke Bjerstedt.[68] There are six hundred and sixty entries, almost all in English. Their large number indicates the growing importance of the subject. There is no shortage for briefing peace educators. They already have the tools needed and several attempts have been made to penetrate conflict areas with words of wisdom, but so far with little success. It is noticeable that when the conflicts are not about scarce resources ranging from oil and diamonds to water, they often

326

involve differences of language and culture. It looks likely that a coming new development in the peace movement will be in the use of many new developments in public relations, based on psychology.

The economic conditions of peace are already understood to a large extent and there is less scope for speculation. The level of corruption in the arms industry rises during arms races and attracts the interest of heads of state, who may already be corrupted by power.

Many countries suffer from severe poverty. One of the most successful ways to deal with this poverty that has been discovered are the Grameen banks of Muhammad Yunus.[69] These banks lend money with no interest whatsoever for those caught in a debt trap where they can never get clear of the interest on their personal loans. The figures are startling:

They lent 27 dollars spread between 42 women in 1976

They lent 2.3 billion dollars to people in 58 countries in 1998

In Bangladesh 12 million borrowers (94% women though it is a Muslim country) cover half the villages. This vigorous expansion all over the world has been achieved not by giving money to the poor but by lending to them from capital funds donated by large charities and official grants. It might be supposed that Bangladesh would be difficult because traditions include leaving money matters to men, and the women being largely illiterate, but Yunus was working in his own country and has unbounded enthusiasm. Other countries have different mixtures of advantages and disadvantages. The story of Muhammad Yunus reads like a thriller and reminded me of my own start in life.

Almost unnoticed a new principle for dealing with international problems has recently been introduced at the Kyoto Conference on pollution by carbon dioxide. The proposal was that a country should only be allowed to pollute up to the figure derived from the size of its population. Clean air was to be ranked with other scarce resources and eventually rationing might be necessary for all. Justice for all is seldom attained by the usual pricing mechanisms, mainly because the very poor are short of basic essentials and therefore in no position to demand a fair price for their products. This is the reason that rationing, by systems of permits for example, is also needed. The increase in the size of firms and other factors favour monopolies, making it increasingly necessary to check them. This was what caused the big demonstrations at Seattle and Genoa. Dr Padolecchia's early interest in alternatives to pricing controls arose in 1980 when he was working for the UN Industrial Development Organisation (UNIDO). I did not know him well enough to judge whether he was driven to humour by despair and ended up with the 'War Permit' so as to avoid disturbing his colleagues. His army colleagues were perhaps too sensitive to the interests of the global arms firms.

Unemployed younger men turning to violence is a risk which needs to be countered by providing more jobs. A radical response is the citizen's wage; according to this system part of everyone's income is covered by taxation, while the other part is paid by employers. As the number of people employed depends on what the employer has to pay, the employers will tend to employ more people when their additional cost declines. It is very likely that the best way to campaign on this is to strengthen the One Percent Group who want to have that small proportion of military expenditure to develop alternative ways of providing security.

Finally there is a group of issues, which are so varied and unexpected that they tend to be overlooked. Social inventions are one of them. Change grows faster and faster in the way we live and the more this happens the more we need to invent new ways of adjusting to it. One of these is education. It appears as though the more education people receive the more adaptable to new circumstances they become. In regard to this there is a noticeable difference between students at university and soldiers, though the gap between them appears to be reducing. There are, as yet no recognised ways of measuring such qualities. It was suggested some years ago that the average worker changes the nature of his work three times in the course of his lifetime.

In a consumer society such as exists at present, fashion changes a lot more often than that, especially where it suits producers of consumer items, giving additional reasons for the public to continue repeating their purchases. To anyone enjoying a peasant lifestyle both fashion and innovation are matters of regret and are barely

War Permit Application

1. Name of applying country _____.
2. Geographical location _____ (North, South, East, West)
3. First and last name of Head of State _____Age____Sex ____.
4. Population: Men _____.
                  Women _____.
                  Elderly persons (65 years and over)_____.
                  Children (under 13 years)_____.
                  Total _____.
5. Type of Government: Monarchy _____.
                        Republic_____.
                        Dictatorship_____.
                        Religious leadership_____.
                        Anarchy_____.
                        Others _____.
6. Proposed opponent(s)_____.
7. Expected casualties _____ _____Total
   _____Yours
   _____Theirs
8. Expected property damage: Yours_____.
                           Theirs_____.
9. Expected environmental damage_____.
10. Provisions to increase casualties but reduce property damage_____.
11. Provisions to increase property damage and reduce casualties _____.
12. Previous experience of war or internal conflicts
    _____.
13. Name of war _____Duration (years)_____.
14. Name of opponents _____Location_____.
15. Cause of war _____.
16. How did the war end _____.
17. Benefits to your country _____For other countries _____.
18. Have you paid your debts for this war? _____.
       What is the total amount of your obligations?_____.
19. List the amounts still owed _____.
20. List the names of creditors _____.
21. How do you reconcile the proposed war with the principles of
                    (a) Your religion _____.
                    (b) Your education _____.
                    (c) Your country's development _____.
                    (d) The charter of the United Nations _____.

*Answer in full, and forward to the President of the Security Council

S.P. Padolecchia, Geneva

distinguishable. In his book *Future Shock*,[70] Alvin Toffler has made very clear that, in view of inevitable change, society recognises the consequences of increasing the speed of change and prepares to become more adaptable. In my lifetime I have seen horses disappearing from the streets, the coming of the motorcar, the following of radio by television, the consequential shrinking of the apparent size of the world, the altered position of women. The ratio of children to the rest of the population has been dramatically reduced and the fear of the future looms larger. These are but a sample of the major changes, which have brought others in their train.

It is little wonder that we seem to suffer from what has been aptly described as 'future shock' or jet-lag. We can also feel sympathy with the chameleons, which for an experiment were moved rapidly from colour to colour until they became a sickly grey, a sign of some form of nervous breakdown.

The will to keep the peace was barely strong enough to withstand the Cuban Crisis. The whole human race depended on President Kennedy's wisdom on that occasion. It might turn out differently on another occasion with a different president in the White House. In the future nuclear weapons and the governments that control them will become increasingly unpopular.

How to escape the danger we are all facing is hard to say. We are in need of the kind of new ideas, which are produced by such people as the late Nicholas Albery, in *The Book of Inspirations: A Dictionary of Social Inventions*.[71] He has been mentioned previously as a specialist in new ideas. His ingenuity was creativeness at its best and I now regret that I did not take up his challenge to me to raise the funds for a series of brain storming sessions on how to abolish war. The latest Directory is well described by Brian Eno as 'about imagination'. It's also a book about the future, about how it could be different.' I find it both refreshing and stimulating. Once someone has read the brief accounts of experiments or dreams they can easily fall into this mode of thought themselves. It is, or may well become a condition of peace to have a proportion of lively minds in society. This volume will carry on his work after his untimely death and serves to introduce a couple who were working on similar lines.

Kenneth Boulding I came to know while I was still at school. I recall him helping me to choose a course to take when, or rather if, I found a place at Oxford. He spent his working life in the USA and came to be known in that country as 'The father of peace research.' Both he and his wife Elise involved themselves in future studies and she, as Secretary-General of the International Peace Research Campaign, did much to develop them as a teaching method for all ages, but especially for primary school age (5-11).

Elise Boulding's work among school children is widely known. The term she uses for it is 'Visioning the Future' and by that she means collecting and comparing children's ideas about what they would like to see come about in the future, forming a benign Utopia out of them and then posing the question: 'How can we get there from where we are at present? What obstacles would we find on the way? How can they be overcome?' This makes a perfect example of peace education. It has the great advantage of drawing from the children themselves, the substance of the lesson, it gives them time to digest the main points made, it maintains a positive attitude instead of enlarging children's fears; and finally, by assuming that democracy can be made to work effectively, it prepares people for active citizenship. I became convinced early on that studying possible futures is as valuable as the history of the past. The former leads to action based on optimism. Being aware that to understand the future one has to use history, she was developing a study of fears and hopes for the future of those who were going to be able to make it. Visioning the future in the following stages:

What might be happening thirty years later
What we might hope for after thirty years
What we might do to help it happen
How to overcome obstacles along the way

These topics in the hands of an average teacher and class would attract a lively response and help turn the often unspoken fears and pessimism into a positive or even optimistic view of life. The belief that there is nothing that can be done undermines democracy. Such is peace education at its best. This was my motive in writing my own previously mentioned *Utopia: Bristol in 2020*, when I was encouraging the teachers in my courses to give their children a hopeful future.

331

I am never sure whether it is possible to look for the surprises that the future brings and take them into account. I do not mean the personal astonishment such as meeting a Quaker in the middle of Beijing by sheer accident. What I do mean is the events in the world news that have affected the cause of world peace such as the achievement of Nelson Mandela in emerging from prison after twenty seven years, without bitterness, to lead his country as the first black president. The radio programmes being broadcast to former Yugoslavia from a ship in the Adriatic; or the attacks on New York and Washington. Surprises of this kind should prepare us for making our vision of the future include good surprises on that scale.

To counter this, it may well be supposed, a loyalty to roots in a home area and in a caring family, where some permanence is assured, may be a stabilising factor. An understanding of this by parents and schoolteachers leads to a certain amount of beneficial social engineering. This may take the form of refusing to move house from the extended family, of refusing to say 'Home is where we are.'

I have moved unwillingly from Oxford my hometown to Birmingham, to Bristol and finally to Cheshire, and I feel deeply that this was too much for the whole family and that I was guided by the wrong ideals. Those who work for international peace under-value the need for satisfying roots. After working for UNESCO I was invited to join a group of colleagues settling together in a group in a Commune in Switzerland. I am glad I refused to become a foreigner for the rest of my life. There is a sense in which nearly everyone is becoming a foreigner of some kind, of being an observer rather than a participant, part of the audience not one of the play-ers. As a citizen I feel sure of the value of our charitable trust into which I have put great effort, thanks to Bevis and the trustees. Though I sometimes feel partly alien through being a member of the Society of Friends, that feeling is amply compensated by the gratitude we feel for the use the recipients make of the grants they receive.

I do not wish to imply that good citizenship can be best expressed in terms of money. The opposite is the case. It just happened to be the way open to me. I hope that I have done more than that through writing and research.

In the light of what has been found out about the foundation of basic social attitudes during the years two to six, another condition of peace is that parents and teachers of younger children should be helped to do more about peace education. This does not have to mean formal teaching but rather an appreciation of opportunities to make the most of informal teaching as opportunities arise. This is well described in a book originating in New Zealand called *A Volcano in my Tummy*,[72] which deals with anger and is a help to both teachers and children. It is precisely this kind of publication I would have hoped to produce if I had become Director of the Nursery School Association. It involves parents as well as teachers and children, and play as well as work, philosophy as well as practice.

At present in Britain there is a move to increase the number of children in schools under the age of five. Such children cannot walk far to school and there is an opportunity to set up small schools, rather than use buses. The small schools are much more suitable than additions to large schools if the findings of the commission are believed.

The last condition of peace, to which I wish to draw attention, is an attitude of hope for the future. At present there is so much reporting of violence and other crimes by the media that children and indeed the average adult assumes that there will always be the danger of nuclear warfare. People also believe that violence was seldom more common than it is today and that there is very little to be done about this situation.

Conclusion

In bringing this story of doing and thinking to an end, I wish to assure you who have kept on reading as far as this, that I will persist as long as I can, doing what is suited to my fading strength. I believe that the serious matter of the fate of the earth can be improved by anyone willing to help. The question is not so much what good can one person do, the question is what problem cannot be eased by the work of a single group if the members each learn to use their talents. Fortunately military expenditure can be safely reduced in a way, which can reassure neighbouring countries, and the funds which are saved be diverted to the many needs of the environment. If the public knew more of the facts, they would hasten to take the chance to teach their children that this is what will give them a better chance of a good life. Mothers say they will do anything, for their babies but often they omit looking at the threatening future and so take no action.

Sometimes I wish that I were a prophet of the Old Testament and could summon the words to denounce the follies and short-sightedness of the human race and thunder the threats and scorn used to help the people of Israel to change their evil ways. Lucky were those who heard such warnings.

If I were a prophet, apart from the implications in the chapters of this book, I would draw attention to Costa Rica, the country lying between Nicaragua and Panama, which is the first country to disband its army. They say they cannot afford an army if they want a good educational system and health service. Additionally, they point out that they want a good education for their children and good health for all. Leonard Bird explains that 'Despite some border troubles, Costa Rica has demonstrated for more than fifty years that it benefits from having no army.'[73] England has better frontiers than Costa Rica and ample opportunity for turning neighbours into friends. Is it not wise enough to follow Costa Rica? Why should the whole world, as well as England, miss the benefit of international law and fail to reach a better stage in history? If the most military country in the world is not proof against terrorist attacks other forms of defence should be given a chance to show what they can achieve. On September 11th the Americans were given their warning, next time it may be nuclear explosions.

These are a few of the thoughts, which have come to me during my retirement at Oakcroft. Some of these ideas may chime with the thoughts of others for if not, the hopes for the future will be difficult to sustain. There are plenty of people of good will to help the wider peace movement, they have to be encouraged to study what most needs to be done, what best suits their skill and how best to enhance cooperation among the many organisations. When that happens we can watch the progress in our chosen fields. It is better to watch them than to watch football or race horses, and best of all to follow the example of Tennyson's Ulysses[74] later in life who said:

> ...'Come my friends,
> Tis not too late to seek a newer world. ...
> To sail beyond the sunset, and the baths
> Of all the western stars, until I die. ...
> Tho' much is taken, much abides; and tho'
> We are not now that strength which in old days
> Moved earth and heaven; that which we are, we are.

APPENDIX 1

ACTIVITIES PROMOTING PEACE
Referred to in Chapter 1

Teachers and sometimes parents

Enhancing social education especially in Nursery Schools and homes.

Applying 'learning by doing' to education for world citizenship and international understanding.

Promoting international friendship, pen friendship, and hospitality towards foreigners.

Explaining the temptations felt by those wielding power and explaining propaganda.

Teaching modern languages.

Individuals and Parents

Setting an example in loving (caring and compassion) and by feelings of fraternity (solidarity).

Understanding forgiveness, and reconciliation while regretting hatred, fear and revenge.

In general developing a culture of peace and non-violence.

Academics and Journalists

Appreciating the academic role of peace researchers in pointing to ways forward in peace work.

Managing conflicts.

Visioning a peaceful future.

Revolutionising the media so as to give more time and space to the promotion of peace.

Lawyers

Strengthening respect for international law
Demonstrating the many forms of mediation.
Considering current opinion about justice that may change from
one generation to the next.

Politicians

Expanding democracy in states and in the UN.
Creating early -warning systems about conflicts.
Exposing the motives and style of demagogues and secret service
agencies. Devising controls.

Business people

Controlling weapons, arms manufacture and trading, e.g. by
ethical investment.
Providing work for ex-combatants and grants for post-violence
development,
Advocating adequate funds for peace organisations especially for
the UN.

APPENDIX 2

A LETTER HOME FROM BAYAMBANG
Referred to in Chapter 9

UNESCO,
Bayambang,
Philippines
March 23rd 1955

Dear Family,

It is fun trying to convey to you some of the impressions of the work here so that you can imagine you are standing beside me looking at some of these places. Although the three days journey in Leyte, has been the most exciting I've had, it seems more difficult to describe. It's not so much people and places as the feeling of blue seas and gay flowers which remain with me. On this journey my two companions were Sancho Paulino, the Superintendent and Odon Perez from the training course at Bayambang. A Provincial Superintendent of schools in the P.I. is a unique person. He has been called a Satrap, but I would call him a Mandarin combining power and culture. Even the Provincial Governor who is nominally the head of the province looks up as a rule to the Superintendent. The latter has hundreds of teachers at his beck and call because for every one there is an unemployed teacher waiting for a place. Half the teachers lack security of tenure! If the head teachers are the philosopher kings of the barrios, the Superintendents are the philosopher kings of the Provinces. Nevertheless it would be quite wrong to think of him as a combination of royalty and teacher. If Princess Margaret gave up Townsend and married the Director of Education for Birmingham there would still be no Superintendent of schools. Although Leyte and Birmingham are equal in

338

population and in size of teaching staff and each is the largest school area outside the capital, the majesty of Sancho Paulino is lacking in Mr. Russell, the Director of Education in Birmingham. Both of them are wise men, Mr. Paulino is perhaps a little more widely experienced having worked for UNICEF for a year, but the great difference lies in the response of their 'subjects.' The people here are so aware of their problems and so anxious for his guidance that whatever he says goes. Just imagine what would happen if Jean came home with a message from Mr. Russell retailed by Mr. Lewis that she must put up on the gatepost a green notice with white letters showing her name and class and implying that if any waste-paper was lying about she didn't take proper pride in her home. How Ruth would snort.....

Unlike many of his colleagues, Paulino is uncorrupted by power and embarrassed me by pushing me forward all the time. The conventional introduction for a Superintendent when he is about to address a meeting is 'Our beloved and democratic superintendent.' It rang true in his case but often it is more in the nature of a prayer and a reminder.

There was no need for us to go into the remote parts of the island, for once I was satisfied not to be probing a little further and a little further, the seaside villages which look across the water to distant Cebu are so perfect that they are, as I told one barrio, 'somewhere very near paradise.' It is little wonder that even some of the teachers have never visited the Provincial Capital. One dancing partner who knew more than most English teachers about the United Nations confessed shyly that she had always wanted to meet an Englishman, because she had heard that we always have white hair and wondered whether it was true. If you live in paradise, there is little incentive to travel!

On our journey we passed not over the mountains to Baybay, which you will find on your map but by the northern route, which touches the sea on the northern coast and then turns inland. We were delayed and instead of reaching Palompon for lunch stopped at Cananga up in the hills. The teachers were just going to sit down to their fish and rice and we came like Harpies and ate it for them, while some more was cooked. Ways of doing things are strangely different.

Cananga is peculiar in its love of slogans, more than any place we saw. They were written in one of the Visayan dialects 'Work hard. Don't be afraid of life.' and 'Reading maketh a full man.'

After the meal we walked over to the new school building, which some parents were thatching. It is the third building the parents have paid for and built since the war, for Leyte is one of the worst places for typhoons. The long buildings hold up the wind until something must break. The men at work are often the poorest not being able to afford their share of the money. They come from their tiny thatched huts, no bigger than a caravan and fix the beautiful timber of the new school into place and one is forced to marvel at their faith in education. May the teachers be wiser than the Catholic priests who once held a similar position of power and prestige. They became such big landlords and so wealthy that they lost touch with their flocks.

We talked long and earnestly about windbreaks for schools. I couldn't get Paulino to agree that it was better to build classrooms in pairs so that there was a way of escape for the wind and so that in this country, where exact hearing is vital on account of the language problems, the classes should not disturb each other. However he was so enthusiastic about my suggestions of a complex windbreak of trees that he gave orders to 'carry out Mr. Gillett's plan' wherever we went. I have qualms lest the trees are the wrong variety and the wrong distance and blow down on buildings and maybe, on classes. A new sort of guillotine! Maybe that was why this was done on my suggestion not his. As I wrote before he is a wise and a modest man.

We left our luggage at Palompon and went straight off to visit tiny barrios along the coast. At Babang we looked at the Tilapia which had adapted themselves to salt water and then we walked across the road to the 'Social Hall.' A term, which must surely be a curiosity for those who study language for it had neither roof nor walls. It was a fine stretch of concrete with a basket ball goal at each end. On the far side was a raised platform for dramatics, and over the gateway the pergola had been elaborated into a musicians' gallery so that they could play free from the press of admirers when the concrete is used for dances. Maybe you think concrete not very suitable for dancing but Filipinos are so fond of dancing, they can dance on anything.

Both at Sapang and at Tinabilan the school gardens were a delight. There seems little need to teach boys to be gardeners where Nature herself is green-fingered, no, rainbow-fingered. Even the great trees shed their leaves and burst into flames of delightful colour. They call them Fire Trees. Though houses, rocks, everything is hidden in a luxuriant coat of green starred with red and yellow, this is enhanced by the Mangrove trees walking down across the beach and right into the sea like elderly bathers. Even among all this the school gardens stood out. Bright shells and corals marked the pathways, at one school the lanes of a 100 metres track were marked with flowers instead of chalk. A 'green house' is really green, a structure of latticed bamboo covered with hanging and climbing plants making a shady spot to sit. In the fishponds the white and red lotus flowers were in bloom, used for decorating at dances; their thick juicy stems are sometimes served as vegetables. Remembering Tennyson I looked at them half in delight, half fear and had myself tied to the mast!

Back at Palompon, a little port with a tiny pier which exports a lot of copra and a little furniture, we admired the newly planted Bermuda grass which lines the streets, behind it a line of flowers then a neat but variegated bamboo fence and then a riot of uncontrollable flowers, which clambered on each others shoulders up, up and almost into the houses. In the porches, in the windows, and hanging from the roofs the ferns and orchids leant out to meet them, balanced miraculously between gravity and the light. They asked me to write my impressions for the local paper and I wrote under the title of the 'Silent Serenade.' I ought perhaps to explain that serenading is an elaborate and well-established custom here. Those who can't play or sing may hire musicians to secure a betrothal.

There was a meeting that night at the school of two or three hundred parents and teachers. I spoke about UNESCO for the teachers and about my family for the parents until the lump in my throat grew too big and I had to change the subject.

We slept that night in the Home Economics building, there were more flowers in our room and even flowers embroidered on our pillows.

At Albuera there was again an evening meeting. The speakers stood at the top of the school steps with a light overhead and a microphone in front peering out at a vague sea of faces. The Mayor, an extremely stout man, had asked for something about the atom bomb. I suppose that is a reasonable request to make of a UNESCO specialist, but how anyone in such a paradise can bother about the morrow is a mystery to me and I couldn't bring myself to talk about the sentries at Pompeii, which is my usual recourse on such occasions. Instead I spoke about their hospitality to strangers, how they resemble their flowers, which lean out to greet the passer-by from their houses, how this needed to be developed in international relations.

A LETTER HOME
Referred to in Chapter 9

Mindanoa
Philippines
April 20th - 26th 1955

Dear Family,

The plans made were that we should not go forward to choose our campsite among the nine villages suggested but return to Iligan and take the road to Dansalan, the capital of the province two hours away. There we would talk with the authorities and take their advice on our site.

While waiting by a shop in Iligan where some of the campers, who had arrived earlier, had been housed, there was a sudden rumble of things falling in the house, people rushed out into the road from the buildings crying in their dialect 'God forbid' and the stationary car seemed to bounce over an imaginary bump. I imagined at first that someone was standing on the bumpers and jumping up and down. That was an earthquake of intensity 2. Intensity 8 experienced in some other places earlier, leaves no houses standing. We had already seen a crack across the road and when we motored to Dansalan there were many places barely cleared where there had been landslides of earth and boulders onto the road. This was after nineteen days from the first disaster. Everywhere there were houses shored up with bamboo, and corrugated iron shacks going up so that people don't have to risk living in their houses. The houses are very cheap light structures and are rebuilt normally after about twenty years, so that the fear of the people we saw impressed us more than their losses. You may remember the story of the children crossing themselves in fear when the gas in the science laboratory was first turned on and the account of the miraculous fire water. This helps in understanding an earthquake. One wealthy woman in a fine strong house found as she tried to escape that the door had been jammed by the tremors and she could not escape. She began shrieking and has been out of her mind ever since. Later on when she was convinced her house had evil intentions she burned it down completely. 'Questioning basic assumptions' is a phrase, which had taken on a new meaning for me. I've never before felt grateful for firm ground under my feet, it is so easy to take it for granted. It is hardly possible to explain how an earthquake shakes not only the houses but the people's minds however educated they may be.

As we climbed in the car by a zigzag road the signs of Moslems increased. There were two extraordinary corrugated iron mosques and then one with cupolas and gay colours. If I hadn't colour photographs to bring home you would hardly believe what bright colours they choose for their clothes. The men wear skirts and turn up and tuck the bottom into their belts for walking and working. Those who have been to Mecca wear white turbans but most of them manage to wear bright colours all over. There were more flowering trees than ever, especially the flaming Dabdab tree.

In Dansalan we went to see the Superintendent of schools and the Governor to make sure that our work was not overlapping with other agencies and to give us advice on where we should work. The Salvation Army and others were already at work. Two places were turned down because they were too inaccessible and we would have had to carry our load across a river. I always have more interest in out of the way places! The officials are worried about our safety in a land of knives and gruesome looking bolos and indeed two of the party were threatened in Manila harbour. However, it is much easier to be lazy and ignore such ideas. I think it's laziness rather than imitating William Penn! Other places didn't need new school buildings and so we agreed on Balimbing, where the school could be repaired.

Balimbing lies half way between Lake Lanao and the isthmus which divides Mindanao into two equal parts. Although it is low there are mountains all around.

We had a fine meal with the Superintendent who rang up his wife at 11.00am and said there will be six extra to lunch! Then we had a glimpse of the town and looked across the lake to where the great disaster was. An owner of a camera shop saw me looking for a good place for a photograph and took me into a cinema through the projection room and on to the roof. The Hollywood film droned on and contrasted strangely with the drama of the earthquake. As we came out I thought I would get some first hand news and began asking my companion. 'The paper said.....' he replied and had no further information because communications have been so interrupted.

After our business was complete, we all slept in or by, the good Mr. Picanal's house out in the country at Samburon. He and his family are sleeping in the hen house until the trouble is over. Some of us slept in the front garden and lay watching the fireflies, which looked like shooting stars.

The bathe at sunset with all these fine young people was a real delight. The sun had set behind the mountains of Zamboanga and the lights of Illigan began to twinkle.

The next day all our immense tents and hosts of suitcases and our 20 selves were loaded into a chartered bus for the long journey westwards along the coast. At two bridges we had to walk, for fear of them breaking. There were real signs of disasters, dozens of houses having toppled over and at least two churches. We didn't see the place where there are said to be two square miles of farmland permanently flooded by the sea. We turned inland and after a dusty, cramped ride arrived at Balimbing.

It took us all the afternoon to put up three marquees on the Bermuda grass besides the main school building which leans beyond repair, we thought, but has not collapsed yet. We had to wait until the next day to see round the little town. There might be as many houses as in Bournville but much smaller and huddled together. Now far more than half are either entirely destroyed, or leaning precariously or have fallen so to say on their feet, a fate which is not serious until the rainy season brings floods. It must have been at Whalley that I learned how to jack up corners of buildings which are drooping into soft ground and how to put a chain

345

from a tractor through the window of a barn to the far wall and pull the building upright, but there is no such equipment ready to hand here. All sorts of queer things happen, for example a roof may sink to the ground intact and form a safe camping out place, while a new house is built.

As we went on our tour of inspection with an American and two teachers as our guides, I noticed a crowd of one to two hundred people ahead. I asked what they were doing and received the reply, 'They knew you were coming this way.' When we came closer I had some doubts about the explanation and noticed that only one in four or five returned a smile much as you would expect from the traditional Englishman, but a great contrast to Pangasinan. We hadn't gone far beyond when I decided that it was too good a chance to miss so we returned and found them already gambling illegally with their cocks among the ruined houses. One of the teachers acted as interpreter for me and with tongue in cheek, I thanked him for welcoming us and told them about those of us who came from abroad and particularly the two Japanese in our party. The memory of the war is still fresh and these are rough people.

REVISED EDITION OF 'WHY IRAN ERUPTS'

First published in the *Sunday Times* on the 20th January 1980
Referred to in chapter 11

THERE ARE NO agreed theories to explain violence. In Britain crimes with violence have increased tenfold over a period of ten years, during the introduction of television, but in Iran the level which astonishes strangers had been high for centuries. Few journalists or social researchers have sought an explanation. The disease, for disease it should be called, affects town and country, old and young, men and women, rich and poor, and yet few demand to know the cause. It was the contrast with Thailand which forced it to my attention.

Iran, I found was still a country of countless villages at that time. The typical village contained houses of sun-baked bricks on a gravel-covered plain or steep mountainside, huddled close to each other for safety's sake. With drought, famine, and harsh landlords to face together, the inhabitants might be expected to form ideal communities, but in fact they are often torn by feuds lasting for generations and spreading a petty bitterness. Little children, when starting school, are told by their parents, which classmates they must not speak to, or join at playtime. Three-quarters of a large group of village teachers voted that their children knew perfectly well who were their enemies, but had difficulty in naming a friend. That changed my plans to gather some sociograms to compare. Even among the highly educated, such quarrels are passed on from generation to generation. They mention enemies with zest and rejoiced in their humiliations, like the psalmist who enjoyed making his enemies jealous by having a table set before him in their presence. Readers of the bible are familiar with this attitude because there are five times as many column inches referring to enemies as to friends in the Concordance of the Old Testament. The conditions of life on the edge of these deserts were akin, namely pastoral farming, scarcity of herbage, and water sources. No just place for women, who may pass on their frustrations to their children, and a religion, which promised ultimate victory over opponents. The Old Testament stories are as fierce as the teaching of Jesus is gentle. He turned moral principles upside down, instead of an eye for an eye, he taught, turning the other cheek; this was the great marvel in Galilee, but rather a stupid folly to the people of Jerusalem.

Violence in Iran and similar countries lacks the organised intensity of Nazis or nuclear violence, but it is widespread and reduces the dimensions within which life can be lived. Men who exist in a state of hatred or fear may be regarded as suffering from a special kind of mental handicap, like children who have never been loved. Economists, political scientists, as well as psychologists have their appropriate contributions to make to the study of this disease. It is evident in Iran that, over the centuries, it has been incorporated securely into the culture and has become self-perpetuating.

In my experience it is seldom asked whether there is a climatic or a dietetic factor at work, producing, a violent culture. Hot dry air may be possible to sustain, but it seems to irritate in some way. The value of negative ions is widely accepted and they may have more than mere comfort to justify them. Ionisers are installed in all lorries in Hungary and one may speculate that Heads of State might benefit more than from conventional air-conditioning.

In that case the political consequences might be considerable. Researchers would note that those who can afford to do so, instead of sitting in large pots of water, now use forms of air-conditioning, and like to sit by fountains or fast-flowing streams. Recently it has become possible to spend soothing holidays from Teheran by driving over the Elburz Mountains more than two thousand metres down to the Caspian Sea, which is well below sea level. There the holiday-makers from the harsher capital find themselves and their children calmer, while around them there lives a different kind of Iranian speaking the same language, coming from the same stock, but living on fish and rice, like the Thais, and behaving as gently as the others are fierce. One village was administered by a woman 'headman' a fact which people in Teheran could not believe. One man remarked to me 'In our country that could not be, the men would trample over her.'

The traffic in Teheran is one indicator of the prevailing culture. The taxi-drivers are blamed, rather unjustly I thought, for the psychological situation on the roads. In fact it is not only they who appear to take a delight in one-upmanship, in using for example a slight advantage to force another driver into abrupt braking. Every other driver is regarded as a potential opponent and from time to time this leads to amusing encounters.

On one such occasion, a colleague reported how two drivers came to a halt at a cross-roads in such a position that neither could go forward, one would have had to reverse. As this was out of the question for cultural reasons, they moved from abuse to fighting. A policeman began to walk towards them and being in great fear of arrest, they jumped back into their taxis to drive away. He, however, signalled to them to stop and wait for him. He ordered them to get out of their taxis, told them off and insisted that they kiss each other before leaving. I was told this was not a rare practice.

The squealing brakes, and the fast getaways from traffic lights are clear evidence, perhaps only to the sophisticated onlooker; a more obvious symptom is the large number of street brawls. On one occasion the son of a high government official was driving his father, his two sons, and myself. He found his way entirely blocked by a car parked in the middle of a narrow street. When the offending driver returned, a stream of abuse was soon followed by fisticuffs. His father's surprising comment was: 'He should not fight in front of his own children. I have often told my sons that they should not do that. I have only done that once when my daughter was insulted.'

The traffic and the number of brawls in the street are only two indicators of the level of violence. The anthropologist Margaret Mead has implied that the number of crying babies should be another. In Teheran mothers in buses and other public places are not ashamed to vent their pent up feelings on their babies and children. In the streets also may be seen violence between beggars over

349

their claim to stretches of pavement. It was rumoured that some of the begging children had legs broken to make them more effective at begging. Twice on building sites I saw workers striking each other with picks and shovels. A row was started by a mischievous American once, who used a tape recorder to copy the street call of a hawker selling lavender, and then replaying it to make the man think that he had a rival on his own territory. Walking on narrow pavements, there is frequently a clash of wills to determine who will give way and walk in the gutter. Working in committees apathy caused by frustration, alternates with periods when several people ignore the chairman by insisting on speaking simultaneously. Once a member walked out of the room in high dudgeon with his face pale and contorted with anger. At university the army was sent in to quell unruly students.

Before leaving Iran I was able to put my observations to a senior official in the Ministry of Education and gain his support, but it was difficult for him to influence research policy. Partly because no systematic research is done in such countries, nothing was taken up. It is more unfortunate that in Britain no research of this kind is taken up, and this despite the interest in developing social education. In addition to these observations about the culture of Iran, or rather the two cultures, if the Caspian is included, I gathered some information from other countries.

When working subsequently in Belfast I noticed the large amount of meat bought by average families. This was confirmed by an article in Blackwood's Magazine which pointed to a higher consumption of meat there than in any other part of the United Kingdom. In south India vegetarian restaurants are known as civil and where meat is available the term is military. In India generally there are more riots in the hot, dry period before the monsoon. In France the area noted for its hot dry wind is also noted for the men's fiery temper, during the period when the wind comes from the Sahara. In Israeli law courts it is possible for those charged with violent crimes to plead mitigating circumstances, laying the blame on the desert wind. It appears to me that more evidence about both the climate and the diet should be collected.

APPENDIX 5

PAGES FROM MY DIARY
Referred to in chapter 11

IRAN IS A LAND of poetry. In all Iran the thoughts of poets hang thickest about the gardens and cypresses of Shiraz. In late autumn the sun still shines warmly on the flat roofs in the valley but in the shade the air strikes a chill. There is nothing to do but move a chair to the borderline of sun and shade. So it is with the sunshine of the poets, to leave them for an instant is to enter a chill, Dickensian world of social problems and to get a grip on reality, it is necessary to see through the eyes of both Dickens and the poets.

The journey with my UNESCO colleagues took us on from Shiraz, which lies in the mountains in the south of Iran, to a tiny town of Fassa; and that evening owing to a chance encounter in the street we finished up in a meeting of officials at the municipal offices. This was no ordinary meeting, no one spoke in the dry, calculating voice of the civil servant, but there was an air of eagerness about the discussion and at the end of the long table were a number of young men in uniform. It was at the end of a day's work on how the various officials dealing with such matters as health and agriculture could help and be helped by the men in uniform. These young people, who maintained a certain reticence in front of their elders, formed part of the Army of Knowledge. Educated in the high school at Fassa for the most part, they had chosen to perform their national service not in the military camps but teaching in remote villages. For a period of fourteen months following four months training they were practising the high ideals worthy of the poets in surroundings which few but Dickens could adequately describe. The story goes that a young man once answered his worldly-wise father when accused of having his head in the clouds

351

– 'Certainly my feet will stay on the ground. How tall I grow is another matter.'

As there have been hitherto few schools in the outlying areas the first job of the teacher and his supervisor is to find a room and fix a blackboard. Not that their only task is classroom teaching, they are encouraged to work in the community looking at the needs of the villagers and acting accordingly, often calling on the help not only of the schoolchildren but of their parents. Hence the importance of the cooperation of all the local government officials. We came away that night with a list of schools to visit on the morrow.

Fassa is the kind of place, which may be summed up in a phrase – an adult evening class in literacy may be entirely filled with shepherd boys. Its fine trees and spacious streets contrasted oddly with the barren country round about which had been suffering from a disastrous three-year drought. As we motored out in the cool of the morning it seemed a long way from one village to the next and the difficulties of the road emphasised the loneliness faced by these town boys in their pioneering task. They are men who have completed twelve years schooling and to do that it is almost essential to live in a town, consequently they are often more at ease in a cinema than behind a plough. No doubt this enhances the difficulty of gaining the confidence of the villagers but it did not show among the men we met.

The first of them was living in the gatehouse of the mud-walled village where you could lean out of the window and look down on the backs of the white donkeys coming in laden from the fields. The classroom was in the adjoining room and there a crowd of fathers gathered in the doorway to hear their children being tested in reading and writing. Although the Army of Knowledge schools had only been open seven months it was extraordinary how much had been learned. If a child is the right age, has a strong wish to learn and has suitable books, literacy may be acquired in the space of a few weeks.

Literacy however, is not enough. Most of the parents of the school children had an unquestioning belief in mere literacy and from this there will be a reaction one day, unless newspapers and libraries of entertaining and useful books reach these remote places.

At the second school, the school wall surrounded a fine vegetable garden and some discussion was held about the best way for the children to read and write about the preparation of the soil, the planting of the seed and the progress of their personal plants.

It was said by Napoleon that an army marches on its stomach, the saying is equally true of the Army of Knowledge and progress will certainly be slow unless the education of the children shows economic results by increasing the food supply, improving cooking, introducing new handicrafts and so on.

The third village looked entirely different. Instead of hiding within a high wall it lay open to all comers and in front of each house stood a black tent. These were the tribesmen who had lost or sold all their flocks of sheep and black goats in the drought and had, therefore, no longer any reason for keeping on the move, so they had settled down by the side of a good stream and were establishing an irrigation system while waiting for better times. The teacher had made excellent contacts with them and showed us into the dark one-roomed mud houses where a low fire threw a little light on the faces of the old people and children crouching round it for their evening meal. There are about two million people in Iran who either move continuously with their flocks or who migrate twice a year as farmers move in Switzerland or elsewhere. The severe cold of winter and the fierce heat of summer make the move well worthwhile, quite apart from the need to find fresh pastures and new supplies of fuel. Suiting an education to their needs is a fascinating problem for educationalists and in the Tribal Training College in Shiraz, an institution unique in all the world, the curriculum includes the care of tents, animal husbandry, and astronomy, on account of the heat, their people travel by night and need the stars to guide them. A year later I was invited by UNESCO to set up a similar college for students going to teach in portable schools in Libya, but I was not free at the time.

As yet, however, the Army of Knowledge has not touched the tribesmen but has concentrated on the poorest people of the permanent villages, and the next day in the village near Jarhom we saw vividly what poverty due to drought can mean. In a tiny stone-built school, where nothing but the rock and stone were in sight, our interpreter asked the class what they would eat with their bread for

353

their meal that day – one meal a day being normal practice. There was an awkward silence because no one knew what the question could mean, children began to look round to see what the others were thinking. At last, the embarrassment was broken by a boy who raised his hand with hesitation. 'Water' he said, and all were at ease again. Although it is a sheep area and sheep are kept for their milk as well as for their wool and meat, less than half the class had ever tasted milk, because owing to poverty the milk was turned into cheese and sold. Unless the teacher is resourceful, establishing a school in such a place seems like giving a stone when asked for bread.

This, however, is not what the local people think. The education officer at the town of Lar sighed almost bitterly, 'An earthquake destroyed our secondary school so no one completed the twelfth grade and we have no Army of Knowledge.' We slept that night in an empty classroom of the handsome new secondary school. The next day we went on through a volcanic area where huge craters had blown out layer upon layer of ash, later sculptured by heavy rain and contorted into improbable shapes, of purple, white and brown. After eight hours of such driving, without seeing a village or more than half a dozen cars, we stopped at a teahouse and sat on the low carpet-covered benches in the whitewashed doorway.

The gnarled old man shuffled to and fro pushing more sticks under the kettle and arranging the cups. 'I had fifteen hundred sheep and goats' he said 'before the drought, now I've only four hundred, but despite hard times my twelve children need a teacher. Some of us in this village joined together to pay for one and he lives here in our house. I promised that even if we have nothing to eat with our bread, he will always have something. He has only four years of schooling himself and he is lame in both legs but...' Then followed the same story to be heard everywhere, reading like bread is the key to everything, worth any sacrifice, the only hope for the future. I was reminded of another old man in a much more prosperous part of the country who stood on a hill looking across the river to the site of the new school. The late afternoon sun touched his turban with gold and there was a gleam in his eye. 'I know what you mean,' he remarked 'about the symbolism of our new young teacher finding us a new spring of water. As I watch layer on layer of bricks rising up to form our new school building, I feel that this is our way of worshipping God.'

We left the teahouse and dropped thousands of feet to the great new road leading to the port of Bandar Abbas. The romance of its trading history in the early days of the Portuguese empire is not sufficient to compensate for the climate. Until recently officials used to perform their duties sitting in large jars of water. The young men from Teheran posted in villages in the Army of Knowledge felt the same way about it. The climate is such that a shelter of branches topped with a mat against the sun is all that is needed but it is too much of a change from a Tehran living room complete with its television set. Food was hard to buy and one man remarked wryly – 'Prison in Teheran must be better than this.'

Moving northwards through pouring rain, the first in years, we reached Sirjan and went out to see a school built with the help of a gift of American wheat distributed according to the hours each man had worked. It was a fine building with a handsome vaulted roof in brick, which contrasted with the humble shelters partially excavated in the ground, serving as houses in the most poverty-stricken part of the country. The teacher had gone away and the school was closed as it was Friday, but the children thronged round and were proud to show us how much they had learned, by writing the answers to our questions in the sand.

From Kerman we motored out a long way in order to visit an Army of Knowledge village, which had been awarded a UNESCO radio set for being one of the best in the whole province. With strong backing from the village elders the teacher had organised the building of a length of new road as well as the construction of the school. He had planned the use of the village water supply so as to separate drinking from washing, but by far the most remarkable achievement was the founding of a cooperative shop. Two hundred people had bought shares to finance the original purchases. Dozens of articles from potatoes and biscuits to combs and matches were on sale under the care of a young boy who attended an Adult Education class to improve his arithmetic.

At the school the teacher had displays of different kinds of stones, seeds and coins for use in teaching. Outside stood a tent,

355

which is loaded up on a donkey when the school goes on a field-trip. On being asked whether he wished to continue teaching when his fourteen months would be finished he replied 'Yes, if I can teach in the same village.'

In many of the Army of Knowledge Schools there are a few girls, despite the facts that prejudice against girls education dies hard and the village industry of carpet-making employs girls from the age of seven. In time it will be realised that progress in nutrition, health and education comes slowly unless women as well as men are open to new ideas.

Yazd is a town where the people build houses with a room below ground level where they hide from the summer heat. For our visit it was snowing and bitterly cold despite sheepskin waistcoats. In that area eighty Army of Knowledge teachers are organising the building of eighty new schools, which is an astonishing achievement considering that the funds have to be coaxed from the pockets of the villagers.

The Isfahan Army of Knowledge is known for its success in getting the teachers into good contact with the children. No organisation, no building is a substitute for this outstanding quality which is the real essence of education. It was significant that the official felt seriously cut off from the two hundred and ten teachers for whom he is responsible. A quarter of them work beyond the reach of jeeps; he had persuaded the radio station to give him time on the air each day to talk to them, but he has as yet no funds to provide them with sets.

As the Army of Knowledge grows from three thousand in 1963 to seven thousand in 1964 this problem of communication will become more and more acute. At least one teacher was eaten by wolves this last hard winter though he was walking only half a mile to post a letter. There is a limit to what a young man with four months' training can do, but if his supervisor can visit every week and he has newspapers, books and technical advice when he needs them, he can solve many of the rural problems of Iran. Certainly we felt that for the men themselves, the tackling of a man-sized job formed a perfect education, better in many ways than a course at University, and as every country has its remote areas this scheme of the Shah is likely to spread.

356

USA AND USSR MOVE TOWARDS EACH OTHER: A STUDY IN CONTINENTAL DRIFT
Referred to in chapter 18

IT CANNOT BE affirmed too often that enemy countries can become friendly countries. Bigoted nationalism is, at times, consumed by its own fires. A Frenchman in the period between the wars did not have to be a chauvinist to keep on his desk a gilt cock mounted on a miniature German helmet, stark hatred was assumed to be normal and inventive, and yet seventy years later the French are as close to the Germans as they are to the Italians or English. This spread of trust is not a sensational process like the flaring up of fear and hatred after a riot, it does not figure in the headlines of newspapers, like mercy 'it droppeth as the gentle rain from heaven.' It tends to be overlooked by historians just as they often omit the slow almost invisible growth of democracy, or the disappearance of corruption. There are, consequently, few guides to point out the way. This needs to be made good by writing case studies of countries which have turned enemies into allies if not friends.

The past has much to offer in the lives of the great peacemakers, the men against war, from William Penn dealing with Indians, to Mahatma Gandhi with the British. It is not true that no fresh ideas are derived from past successes, the novelty lies in the adaptation of old ideas to new situations. Biographies of such peacemakers as Ashoka and Ceresole should be more available.

These fresh ideas fall into a number of groups of which the political comes first to mind. Many approaches are tried by diplomats and politicians, the peace-making and peace-keeping of the

UN is well documented but more attention needs to be given to developing certain methods. For example Dag Hammarskjöld was accustomed to advise that <u>an exploration of common interests</u> should be undertaken. In the case of the USA and the USSR there are many more such interests than are at first apparent. The oilfields of the Near East are seen by pessimists as a source of conflict but by optimists as an opportunity for co-operation. Oil may be the first important natural resource to be exhausted. The OPEC countries would be in an unprecedented position if, as is possible the oil elsewhere is exhausted before an alternative fuel for aeroplanes is discovered. <u>An agreement reached peacefully for an equitable sharing of the last oil</u> would be in the best interest of both powers. The influence of OPEC might be decisive in bringing this about, thus ending the temptation to both parties to establish military bases in the region. Just as Nixon made a new relationship with China by using the USSR as a bogey, so a President might establish a new relationship with the USSR by using the oil shortage as a bogey. First the shape of the beast, of a world without oil, would be drawn more clearly. If OPEC countries were willing to help by using their amassed wealth the next step might be to initiate new forms of competition in aiding developing countries comparable with the three steel mills built in India by the Russians, the Chinese, and the British.

In the course of such negotiations the diplomats would be able to get better acquainted with the reciprocal attitudes among statesmen and populace. It was very revealing that Brezhnev on returning home from a conference exclaimed with astonishment on the radio: 'They're just as afraid of us as we are of them!' The <u>'controlled communication' exercises,</u> associated with the name of the Australian diplomat and academic John Burton, <u>need to be applied to the USA – USSR</u> relationship much more fully, so that the Americans know what the Russians think the Americans think about the Russians and vice versa. He sets up study seminars composed of academics capable of interpreting to the two groups of diplomats representing the two conflicting countries, the feelings, which they are led to express. In this way misunderstandings can be cleared up and this may lead on to a more constructive approach to conflicting interests. The Russians are at present severely hampered by their ignorance of the outside world; as is revealed when their exhibits are shown at international exhibitions. By sheer size they tend to frighten rather than win approval. It is also to be noticed in their handling of diplomacy.

Fortunately the United Nations exists and in its buildings, Soviet and American officials and diplomats rub shoulders. Despite the tendency of the two great powers to ignore it, the UN remains the best hope for peace. There is always talk of reform but more needs to be done; the headquarters, which were located in New York to ensure US participation should now be moved away to a non-aligned country. This would prevent Asian students saying that the UN is 'An American organisation for fighting communism. United Nations and United States both begin with the same name don't they?' If the USA offered to part with the UN it is possible that the USSR would agree to its reform in a package deal. An institute such as the UN and indeed the constitution of a nation state should be reviewed every fifty years in order to adapt it to new circumstances. A loyalty to the UN comparable with the excessive loyalty to nation states needs to be developed. A small step towards it could be made by the awarding of a prize each year to the country which has done the most for the UN. A short-list of diplomats would be drawn up to state their countries achievements on television; each would be briefed with Angell's scale of National Support for World Order, but strict adherence to this would not be expected. In this way new aspects of the subject would be revealed each year. And the determination would grow to raise the USA from its rather low present place on the scale.

Canada has made a significant gesture by reducing armaments in accordance with the UN conference decision, and it spends much of the funds saved on assistance to developing countries. Unfortunately this good news is not widely known. It would appear to be desirable to produce a pamphlet about it in Russian and English and circulate it widely in government circles. The only relevant publication, however, edited outside the USSR but circulating within it is the UNESCO Courier. Its articles occasionally cover information such as that about Canada.

As time passes and nuclear bombs proliferate, the two powers have a common interest in keeping them in their own hands.

Already it is conceivable that either country might be hit by a bomb coming from terrorists in a minor country and would mistake it for an attack by the other major power. If governments have failed to recognise their common interests, a much wider public has failed to realise the nature of the policy of piling up bombs and armaments for deterrence. It is not possible to deter bullies in the schoolyard by issuing all pupils with revolvers; it ensures disaster. The nature of the international situation needs to be explained by similes such as this. In short the skills of the public relations and advertising experts have not yet been directed to the main problem of the day. 'Too much armour, too little brain, died out' runs the caption beneath the picture of the scaly dinosaurs of primeval times. Posting a toy dinosaur suitably inscribed to each of the main participants, who include the presidents of arms firms and television companies should be a first step; cities could be encouraged to erect statues of dinosaurs with the same inscription. At present the arms manufacturers continue making money with the prospect of subsequent annihilation as a result of their own work. Those politicians who claim that bombs are only to be used as a deterrent should be invited to send their sons to study in the capital city of the opposing country.

It is becoming increasingly obvious that only politicians with an excessive hunger for power reach the top in most modern countries and that the very quality which brought them success, makes them unsuited for international negotiations. In their desire for high office, moreover, they stoop to acting as demagogues, who play on the fears and hatred of their vast television audiences. It holds for democracies, military dictatorships and socialist countries alike. The hereditary principle looks harmless by comparison and yet has its own drawbacks. Citizens must learn to recognise when they are being manipulated and when they should reject a plausible speaker.

Political scientists could be invited to study alternatives to this selection of the unfit. A similar enterprise should be undertaken regarding non-military forms of defence. In Sweden such a conference attracted official financial backing but the topic has still received too little attention. It is obvious that a country can be overcome by internal collapse as well as by direct attack, by drugs as well as by poison gas but it is less obvious that the bravery of the

Norwegian teachers, who refused to teach Nazi doctrine even when a third had been punished by death, has many parallels.

Until international law is strengthened by a supportive public opinion it will be necessary to accustom governments to the use of mediators. They are difficult to find. They must be drawn from non-aligned countries, have some experience of the work, be familiar with cross-cultural studies, good at relevant languages, ready to listen sympathetically, having already acquired the status which commands respect and finally they must be available at short notice. A major Foundation would render a great service by accumulating a few such people in the wings, ready to play their part if and when the situation demanded it.

A common objection to mediators is that they expect contestants to listen and then do nothing, to sit on their bayonets, in Bismarck's phrase. A compensating activity allowing faces to be saved is often helpful. Thus Thailand, having lost its case at the International Court at the Hague for ownership of the temples of Khao Phra Wihan, challenged Cambodia to a basketball match. Mediators in the case of the USSR and the USA would keep in mind the possibilities of cooperating over the law of the sea-bed or maintenance of forests to stabilise the quantity of carbon dioxide in the atmosphere. The threat of future ecological disasters is the common enemy against whom the aggressiveness, of Soviets and Americans alike, must be redirected. The giants might be described more vividly, their methods of defence studied, and an attack concerted.

The economic and financial aspects are as important as the political. Arms expenditure can be redirected to aid development in the Third World thus reassuring employees. Eventually the peace budget would equal the defence budget. It was said that reaching the moon was a question of dollars; maybe the same can be said of reaching the heart of Moscow.

There are also many internal uses for the large sums released. They are not only needed for the retraining and redeployment of arms workers but for countering the xenophobic tendencies of the news media which are always prone to use fear to hold the attention of readers and viewers. It seems to be desirable to establish an

<u>information service for the press</u> and to provide a background to items of conflict and violence ensuring that no serious report would be complete without an opinion from the prestigious institute drawing on the help of its panel of advisers.

On the cultural side <u>an exercise consisting of stepping into their shoes</u> would be timely. At present there is little preparation in schools and colleges for the pitfalls of adult life. It is essential <u>to warn citizens</u> that just as they are deceived by advertisers into mismanaging their expenditure so they are deceived by those who whip up an unwarranted fear of an enemy in order to get expenditure on arms approved by Congress. Indeed Americans have been so free from external attack that they have difficulty in glimpsing what lies at the back of minds in the USSR. The Napoleonic War, the Crimean War, three invasions in the six years following 1914 and finally the war with Hitler's force which caused the deaths of twenty million Russians have created an expectation of further disasters and a distrust of the west. These run so deep that they are difficult to plumb. It is certainly worth taking great trouble to catch the feelings of the Russians. For some it might be achieved by <u>learning how to listen</u> or <u>by role playing</u> and sensing it at the individual level by having strangers coming to the house and picnicking without leave in the yard, so that the owner of the house can study in himself the strong feelings which are aroused when territorial rights are infringed. This is the kind of exercise which could be worked out in detail in a school of Peace Studies.

More mention is made of Americans understanding Russians than vice versa because it is at present difficult to involve the Soviet government. However, Americans need to know that a bargain could therefore be reached about textbook reform. The blanket of secrecy in the USSR is of such long standing and so complete that ignorance is enhanced or even cultivated. Something needs to be written on secrecy in government and its effects. The fact that nearly four million Soviet citizens travelled outside the USSR in 1978 as tourists, should be turned to advantage.

Other significant examples of Russian culture are their humour and their proverbs. A proverb can be found to justify or illuminate a new idea or course of behaviour just as a puritan family finds a biblical text. It is part of the ritual thinking of a peasant society.

The books of the Russian proverbs need to be used both to explain Russian thinking and to strengthen Russian confidence, in strangers and potential enemies. The tale of the Turnip, for example, has assumed proverbial status, huge cut-outs of a team which eventually pulled up the vast turnip are to be seen in shops and schools and the lesson they teach is cooperation. It awaits application to the international scene. A first step might be the publication of a book consisting of annotated proverbs.

In both countries the importance attached to children is very great; peacemakers could build on it by relating it carefully to the future such as to the husbanding of resources and making this an exercise in cooperation, perhaps based on the UNEP in Nairobi. For example, the children of today will need all possible help in prolonging the use of timber and oil, during the next century.

Passing from culture in the sociologist's sense to that of the fine arts, it may be noticed that music has already been used as an international language, musical tastes differ, but there are areas of common interest. The extension of these should be attempted. All approaches which are at present too difficult in view of the iron curtain of secrecy may be reconsidered as activities for the non-aligned countries. Indians, for example, are relatively welcome in Moscow and as students and travellers are capable of making contact with the Soviet peoples. Such people can help brief the voice of America and the BBC, so that they do not misunderstand their audience. Until better times come friendship may be made at second hand.

Spreading goodwill in small circles of society is not enough to counteract the vast influence of the military-industrial complex, a very widespread campaign has to be organised. In schools Russian can be learned, and friendships encouraged by the twinning of schools, as soon as détente permits. Classes should be able to accumulate comparative material so as to be examined on it; thus bringing the task into the basic school work rather than leaving it on the fringe. Television, like school education, is a powerful force working at present, alas, towards an increase in violent attitudes and violent behaviour. It has been claimed in defence by the television authorities that they ended the war in Vietnam. A challenge should be issued to them to end the cold war likewise. At present the average American has seen eighteen thousand acts of violence on the screen by the age of eighteen. The increase in crimes with violence suggests that this may be leading to an ungovernable society prone to risks of desperate war; it should be ended by a <u>system of monitoring</u> the programmes such as parents are demanding.

Finally there must be a search for creative thinkers. <u>De Bono's 'Lateral Thinking'</u> is relevant not only to the discovery of new ideas, but to their implementation. Often conferences, articles, books, radio or television programmes, campaigning for new legislation or further research come to mind as the best way to proceed, but there is much more to it than this. There should always be a place for actions appropriate to the particular matter in hand, whether it be enabling electors to recognise power-hungry politicians or expanding the teaching of Russian. <u>A systems analysis has to be made</u>, a study of the forces at work to show the obstacles, which have to be overcome, and the supports which have to be strengthened. It is always important <u>to cultivate the ground</u> in which, one day friendship will flourish. Hatred and fear seldom end abruptly; they are diffused slowly over a long period. Even the longest journey begins with one step.

PEACE MOVEMENTS: A FRESH LOOK
OCTOBER 18TH 1999
Referred to in chapter 18

IT IS A VERY GREAT honour to be treated like this by the Gandhi Foundation. It is much more than I deserve. You have only to look round this room to see distinguished people who are much more deserving than I am. We can all rejoice that there are many people capable of making an effective contribution to the ever-growing peace movement. I might well have excused myself from accepting this threat to my proper feeling of self-unimportance, if I had not been anticipating the pleasure of addressing you for some twenty minutes tonight.

The first message which l have to bring is that for a century there has been a failure to mitigate, let alone abolish, wars and weapons and it is therefore timely and reasonable to make radical changes in the way we make decisions about our own policy and methods.

To begin with l would like to engage the help of some insects to explain what I mean. You may be able to recognise your colleagues or even yourself, as I proceed. Many years ago a member of this meeting sent me on an assignment, to the Lebanon. I spent some time there in contemplating the famous processionary cater-pillars, those engaging little creatures that contrive to move from place to place by following head to tail in a chain. That is to say all except the leader, which is selected by some process I do not under-stand. The leader and its followers are strangely lacking in what might be termed common sense, because if they are arranged in an unbroken circle round the lip of a bowl, they do not know what to do. Not a single caterpillar dares to save itself and all the others by breaking ranks and leading them in a different direction. They will continue marching in their circle until they begin to drop off in complete exhaustion. Thus they form the perfect warning to all those suffering from convention in thought and behaviour, even more eloquent than the prophets of doom of the Old Testament. They constitute a dire threat to anyone who destroys society by refusing to change when change is needed, to anyone who does not value lateral thinking.

In using another story of insects I hope to show how widely our brainstorming might spread. It was more than a century ago that a very senior cavalry officer decided that the New Forest would make a very pleasant place for manoeuvres. He got some local people to ride round with him to survey the terrain. Needless to say the local people were unwilling to lose the use of the area. When the party came to a halt, unnoticed by the officer, a box was opened surreptitiously and out flew a number of a particularly virulent species of horsefly in a hungry condition. The effect on the horses was almost immediate. They bucked and reared so wildly that the army officer was unhorsed. With tongues in cheeks the local people made apologies for their local scourge. To cut a long story short the New Forest was declared unsuitable for manoeuvres. There may be more ways than one to rout an army. This story might be of interest to those concerned with civil defence.

Before leaving insects in a search for some lateral thoughts regarding wars and weapons, peace, mediation and reconciliation, we might look at the culture of bees. They are remarkable, social animals, which deserve more study. It is well known that they can direct each other to sources of honey with the utmost skill. The equivalent message among ourselves would be something like this: 'Go south-west by south for as far as half a gallon of petrol will take you and then look for a flower with such and such a smell.' Humans would not do well with those directions, but the bees do remarkably well. However bees also have their failures. I went out into the garden one day and found that a war was going on between two colonies. A square yard in front of one hive was so densely covered with corpses that the grass was scarcely visible between them; many of them were twinned in a fatal embrace, as they tried to kill each other. It seemed like a cruel skit on human beings. You may want to know what had happened. Bees do not often behave like this. Unfortunately I had left the doors of a weak colony wide open and when robbers from a neighbouring hive found that they could get past the sentries at the door, the fight for honey stores began. The rich were robbing the poor. They paid a heavy price for having no effective police force, nor any equivalent of international law. Many of them had laid down their lives for their colony.

It should be explained that, although bees look alike, each colony has its own smell. When beekeepers wish to join two weak hives together they have to take this into account. One method is to dust all the bees with flour, before putting them together. By the time they have finished cleaning themselves the two smells have blended into one. Alternatively they may be separated by a double thickness of newspaper and by the time they have chewed through that, the blending and pacifying have been accomplished. It may well be the nearest many newspapers ever get to peace-making! If you have been following closely you may have spotted that there is a time among bees when their wars come to an end and the question may well be posed who gave the signals, backed up by the further questions, whether there is a case here for gene manipulation and how far does violence derive from genes. The Seville Statement on Violence, which UNESCO has adopted, is not quite clear on this.

In attempting to apply the principles of lateral thinking myself, I came to some tentative conclusions that were of sufficient interest to be published in the *Sunday Times*.

While working for UNESCO in Iran, I noticed how much the culture of peacefulness by the Caspian Sea contrasted with the vigorous, sometimes violent way of life six thousand feet higher up in Teheran. The first has a humid climate and the negative ions from the waves of the sea and a diet of fish and rice like that of the gentle Buddhists in south-east Asia. The second has a hotter drier climate, being on the edge of the desert where the diet is based on meat and wheat. With other supporting evidence I made out a case for a research project.

The person in our field who exemplifies lateral thinking extremely well is Professor Johan Galtung. He has rightly been called the father of peace research in Europe. In addressing the inaugural meeting of the Geneva International Peace Research Institute, he said, 'If you look at peace to select the most promising religion, you might easily conclude that Buddhism ranked highest among world religions, and if you looked at it as a geographer you might judge that distance from the equator was significant. But looking round this hall 1 do not see many Eskimo Buddhists.' Similarly he astonished the top brass of the Belgian army by telling them that they should not accept cuts in their budget, but should demand an increase to provide for civilian defence from an army of occupation. He has recently been in England to take a lead in the training or retraining of journalists as peace correspondents.

Relatively new peace activities other than training peace correspondents are based on the assumption that we have been barking up the wrong tree in the peace movement and must plan our long-term strategy afresh. Here are some of the newer forms of peace work:

Cultivating the culture of peace e.g. in homes, schools, prisons and parliament. Making more use of the ideas involved in Truth Commissions. Expanding the ethical movement from investment to other areas. Establishing radio for troubled areas to counter war propaganda. Strengthening the UN to be more independent of narrow national interests.

Visioning peace. What would a peaceful world be like? By what steps can it be won?

Improving the quality and quantity of funding for peace organisations and individuals.

Fund-raising is an essential part of campaigning such as the peace movement and, as I have been involved in it for a long time, I am proposing to spend the last minutes commenting on it.

There are many ways of raising funds other than from charitable trusts, but this is where I have some varied experience, of large trusts and small, of making appeals to them as well as making grants in response to appeals. Trustees often seem to be rather remote and inaccessible people who are fond of secrecy. It is as well to remember that they are usually trying to do a full-time job as well as the unpaid work for their trust and may therefore fear being buttonholed to hear about a forthcoming appeal.

Ideally a trustee would not make decisions on the basis of information in the Sunday papers, but would work in what might seem a rather narrow field, but would become something of an expert who keeps up with the reading, attends an occasional conference and knows some of the leaders in the subject. Such a person is, of course, a rarity. The typical trustee is too often an elderly man, rather conventional, having some difficulty in keeping up with the implications of inflation and with a suspicion of peace as being controversial, political and apt to be on the wrong side of the charity laws. Even the experts say that these laws are hard to interpret especially in regard to peace. This is one of the reasons that peace remains under-funded. The evidence for this is plentiful; the administrators of trusts report that they get good appeals, which are rejected for lack of funds, the UN & Conflict Office at UNA reported that the minimum qualifications for an unpaid volunteer have become a second degree in some aspect of international affairs and computer literacy. This means that the people are available, the work is, of course, of great importance and it only remains to find the funds to bring the two together.

You will be glad to know that this problem was identified some time ago and there is a reasonable hope that a new trust, drawing on new sources, will be making grants for peace work. If all goes well, there will be a subsidiary for helping so-called non-charitable organisations of which CND and the International Peace Brigade are examples.

This month at home we had a visitor who remarked that she could not see what she could do about peace as an individual. She felt powerless. When she left I wrote down two dozen things which such a person might undertake by using her skills or acquiring some new ones and posted the list to her. I believe most of you could do the same.

THE ADVANTAGES OF COMMUNITY SCHOOLS JANUARY 1978 REVISED OCTOBER 1979

THE HUB SCHOOL or community school has spokes radiating influences from the centre to the circumference of its catchment area and vice versa. There are many kinds of school called community school, but here it is intended to mean a school which both serves as a community or social centre used by individuals, clubs and societies for classes and recreational activities, and also serves as a centre from which groups, usually of children, go out to study and serve the community and its environment. In short the external relations of the school are complex, as it both gives and receives, there is a going out and a coming in. It is an appropriate response to Ivan Illich[75] who in 'De-schooling Society' mocks the complexity and ineffectiveness of ordinary schools. It may be asked how many British schools satisfy all the criteria and the answer is few or none, but over the decades the movement has been in the direction of expanding social education and making educated communities as well as educated pupils the central aim of the schools.

To weigh up the value of such a transformation of an ordinary teaching life requires an examination of the many claims made on behalf of these new methods:

1. Lessons which seem 'relevant' to pupils, parents and teachers
2. Democratic Citizenship based on learning by doing
3. A Sense of Purpose
4. Roots and Territory
5. Accommodating Change

6. Dual Use of Buildings
7. Schools based on ecology.

1. Lessons which seem relevant

In the first place community education can provide clearer lessons for the children because in every subject cogent illustrations can be drawn from the locality thus building new knowledge and understanding on the existing experience of the children. This is normally carried out in geography when a comparison is made between the local river and, say, the Rhine, but the community school teacher is more likely to know who of the local inhabitants has travelled down the Rhine, whether they can be persuaded to talk about it and how to interview them in front of a class.

It is rather less usual for the French teacher to know the number of French people within reach and make use of them, or for the woodwork master to know how many woodwork tools are available to the children at home. By using such local resources and teaching through the help of the environment, lessons become clearer and more interesting and they also become more effective by enlisting the support of parents. Parents are often interested themselves in local people and places and are more likely in a community school to show interest and give encouragement to work done at school and to homework. It is precisely parental interest and encouragement which have been shown to be of special importance in children's success at school, but this depends on them being convinced that the values of the school are worthy of support. Douglas[76] is one among several who have indicated that teaching methods need to change so as to take account of what has been discovered. Already schools are using grandparents' memories to make social history seem more real.

Steel and Taylor[77] have extended this idea into a substantial part of a primary history syllabus. Teachers are beginning to plan their lessons so that they flow over into leisure time for at least the more enthusiastic pupils and sometimes involve their families in such a way that a process of indirect adult education occurs.

2. Democratic citizenship

It is unlikely that many children become better citizens by listening to teachers talking about the obligations involved in democracy, or even about the people who have helped develop it through the centuries, unless this is part of a wider programme of activities. It is relatively easy to teach facts but hard to change attitudes and behaviour because children start school with many fundamental attitudes already shaped. Children are more likely to learn by copying an adult or another child whom they accept as a model; they choose teachers to some extent, as suitable models to be copied. They are also more likely to learn on the principle of learning by doing, so the key subject in a community school is social studies in which local studies forms a large part. The children study the needs, problems or opportunities of their school's catchment area and take some action as a result. In the course of this they may acquire a belief that people like themselves can take initiatives, that it is not always necessary to wait for the county or national authorities to act, that the authorities can sometimes be persuaded, that most issues have many aspects and several sides should be heard, that there is a time to make use of consultants or experts and that a group usually needs to operate through a committee.

The teacher's role is to steer his class away from controversial political issues to the innumerable other issues such as accident black- spots, adventure playgrounds, the care of the very old and the care of the very young.

One of the objections raised to such work is that the organisation of practical work is time consuming. There is no need whatever to assume that community education in general or local studies in particular should place more work on busy teachers.

Eventually it will be realised that it is worth paying for the extra teachers required. Soon there will be a marked drop in the number of secondary school pupils following the drop in the number of primary school children. The teaching profession can well claim that it has something to offer beyond normal teaching, something which will be seen and appreciated by the general public and ratepayers. As usual education authorities differ in their policies but a recent estimate of the number of secondary pupils undertaking regular, voluntary community service was a hundred thousand. This is too valuable an asset to be lost on account of lack of skilled guidance. An additional member of staff for organising the work in secondary schools could be provided for the cost of a destroyer and might do more for the defence of the British way of life.

3. A sense of purpose

A common criticism of people today, and especially of young people, is that they have little sense of purpose and that many become apathetic.

They feel frustrated at the sheer impossibility of copying their 'models' seen on television programmes, money until recently has come easily, they have got what money can buy and they cannot see beyond it. This kind of criticism by the old of the young has always been made, the question is whether it is more justifiable nowadays. In any case there is so much to be done to make the unexciting suburbs where most people live, the places they could become. They are an invitation to the young and also to those who have the patience to work through the slow but effective process of democratic persuasion, to plan campaigns. Once a person feels that his place is getting better, especially if he has had a hand in it himself, he begins to feel an enhanced loyalty for it, and an enthusiasm to go further. He has put down real and lasting roots. In some communities they put up a board showing the projects to be accomplished such as the establishment of a festival, the planting of trees and the building of a playground. This may lead on to the young people going to international workcamps abroad where they pick up fresh ideas about what can be accomplished. If the older people are wise they relish the spirited efforts of the young and protect them from the discouragement created by cynics and unsympathetic officials. The question is sometimes posed whether the moving spirits in community schools are the staff, the children or members of the public including parents. The answer clearly is that it is a judicious mixture of them all, the pupils learning to seek advice in promoting projects based on their own ideas and thus preparing for the age of leisure which is approaching with its shared employment, longer holidays and unemployment.

4. Roots and Territory

When a peerage is created the new peer adopts a place of which he is the lord. This honour is attributed to few but everyone needs to put down roots and to feel that they belong somewhere. Migrant tribes who appear to wander often have, in their own eyes at least, grazing rights in their winter and summer quarters; gipsies likewise return to favourite camping sites and when strangers move towards their caravans they are well aware that with the help of their dogs a magic circle of ownership extends beyond the door of the caravan. This is much more true of ordinary people who resent trespassers in their gardens and show by the fences and gates they erect the strength of their feeling for their property. Young people who grow apart from their original family during adolescence but have not yet set up homes of their own are the section of the population which is least able to feel a sense of ownership and belonging. This accounts, in part, for the alienation which is liable to set in at this time of life. The community school finds a role for them as the prime movers in community development with a loyalty which extends to the neighbourhood as a place to be improved. They learn how to amplify their connections with people and institutions round about them.

It is possible for a school catchment area to grow too inward-looking, too aggressive towards its neighbours, or too proud to learn from outside consultants and visitors, but the usual complaint is that there is no real community at all and the first task of the community school is to help bring one into being. Privacy has been carried to such a point that already most households consist of one or two people; the more that people are isolated in their homes the more they need to extend their feeling of territoriality beyond their homes to the neighbourhood. The bees make a special kind of glue called propolis is to protect their societies; the word comes from Greek meaning the bounds or defences of the city. People also use the propolis of social interaction to glue their societies together and defend them from invasions from outside. Sociologists in the past have directed more attention towards the divisions in society, although the positive bonds or propolis are also important.

5. Accommodating Change

Paradoxically the same institution favours roots together with accommodation to change. The same community service, for example, may enhance local loyalty and also meet a new need. The pace of social change is increasing rapidly. Motor cars and television have transformed the framework within which schools have operated in this century, just as tape libraries in place of many books and learning drugs may transform it in the next. It is, however, normal for schools to address themselves to the problems of a past generation when their teachers were young. One of the accepted justifications for altering the curriculum is the recognition of new social needs. Educationists can join with town planners in saying "Tell us your social problems and then we can start work". They may be seen as needs by parents, pupils, teachers or by visitors unfamiliar with the locality but able to make comparisons with their own. Some problems are outside the scope of the school but most have implications either for the curriculum or for extra-curricular activities, particularly for the planning of community service. Although Toffler[78] has enlarged on the mental and even physical difficulties of adapting to changes, less has been written about the difficulties of hiding from them, of continuing a routine way of life long after the reasons which gave rise to the routine have ceased to exist. Some older teachers consider that more routine is needed as an anchor during a period of increasing change and so they point to the administrative complications of schools with, as they say, more than one job to do. There is no attraction for them in institutionalising change by the annual surveys conducted by the Social Studies departments. The average age of teachers is rising, and will continue to rise thus introducing a rigidity into the educational system, schools with pupils who will be in mid-career thirty five years hence have a special need to resist this rigidity, community education is one of the ways of doing so.

6. Dual use of buildings

The argument against dual use is that the complexity of the institutions lays too much strain on the staff, who often work voluntarily or with extra pay during the evenings. From the beginning it was realised that some teachers would work in the evenings and take time off during the day. There is often less stress in a community school because it is working with the homes and not against them.

The cost of allowing capital equipment to lie idle is so great that very many school buildings are used in the evenings in addition to their normal daytime use. The growth in adult education necessitates the use of classrooms and halls so it would be surprising if the schools were not expected to help in this way. Often the contrast between the new buildings and those the adults remember from their childhood is so marked that they are made aware that education is not what it used to be. Dual use is often merely a convenience; it does not necessarily constitute a community school nor does it imply community education, it may even lock up the energies of teachers by involving them in evening teaching and discourage them from undertaking the more adventurous task of surveying local needs and acting on their surveys, but it does encourage the public to think of the school in new ways. It requires a revolution in thought to conceive an institution of a completely new kind and Henry Morris helped in this respect by devising the new term Village College and abolishing the old term 'headmaster' in favour of 'warden'. Some of the recent changes which justify consideration in many secondary schools are the increase in unemployed school leavers, the growth of travel abroad, the rebuilding of towns which leaves few spaces for informal play, the newly recognized importance of parents in education, the continuing growth in viewing television and the 10 per cent increase over twenty years in crimes with violence.

7. School based on ecology

To sum up the community school accords with the principle underlying ecology that many things are best understood in their setting whether they are plants, animals or institutions such as schools. To shut out the environment from the school by banning visits and visitors is like locking the library, it defeats the purpose for which the school exists. The community is indeed a textbook, an essential learning aid, and each one unique to its own school, its full significance grasped by comparison with others. There is a time for silence, there is a place for hermits but no school, even one concerned narrowly with passing on the heritage from the past can afford to accept the blinkered windows of the ivory tower. Ultimately the success of a school can be assessed in the homes of its pupils, an inspector does not necessarily have to visit the school itself. Where a school staff is hesitating about a change of policy it is possible for one or two departments to make a start by enlarging their aims to include all the people in the area. Despite the possibility of starting in a small way, the concept involves a substantial change in education which is only likely to become acceptable when the full significance of the choice between a rather isolated private life, and existence in a circle of friendly neighbours is appreciated. The issue may be seen to lie between selfishness and co-operation or between freedom, and fraternity (friendship). In the past two centuries much has been made of liberty and later of equality, but the third part of the slogan of the French Revolution has seldom been considered.

APPENDIX 9

BOOK LIST

Abelson, Reed: Charities' Investing: Left Hand, Meet Right. The New York Times Archives. June 2000

Albery, N. et al (eds) The Book of Social Inspirations: A Dictionary of Social Inventions. Institute of Social Inventions, London, 2000

Anheier, Helmut: Can Culture, Market and State Relate? London School of Economics Magazine Vol.12 No 1, December 2000

Bailey, Sydney .D. & Sam Daws. The United Nations – A Concise Political Guide. 3rd edition, 1995, Macmillan

Barritt, D., Orange and Green. Northern Friends Peace Bd. 1972

Bertrand, Maurice. Some Reflections on the United Nations. Geneva, 1985, JIU/REP/85/9

Bird, Leonard, Costa Rica: The Unarmed Democracy, Sheppard Press, London, 1984

Bjerstedt, Åke. (ed) Peace/War: Issues from a Psychological Perspective. 1993, Department of Education and Psychology Research, school of Education. Malmo, Sweden.

Busby, Chris. The Wings of Death: Nuclear Pollution and Human Health, Green Audit Books, Aberystwyth, 1995

Curle, A., Making Peace. London: Tavistock 1971

Charity, Kate, A Many-Sided Man. John Bellows of Gloucester 1831-1902. York: Sessions (1993)

Daws, Sam. Memorandum on An Agenda For Peace: The Expanding Role of the UN and the Implications for UK Policy. UNA, London, 1993. (p.38)

Douglas, J.W.B. The Home and the School, MacGibbon and Kee, London, 1964

Easwaran, E. , A Man to Match His Mountains (London: Random House., 1984).

Einstein, Albert. Out of My Later Years, Philosophy Library, New York, 1950.

Ferguson, J., The Politics of Love: The New Testament and Non-Violent Revolution, Cambridge, 1982

Forrester, Susan, ed., Peace and Security:A Funding Guide for Independent Groups. Directory of Social Change, London, 1998

Galtung, J., There are Alternatives – Four Roads to Peace and Security, Spokesman, 1984.

Gilbreth F.B., Cheaper By the Dozen, Heinemann, 1949

Gillett, A. N, Parents Only, 1953 Island Press.

Gillett, Nicholas, Men Against War, Victor Gollancz, London 1965

Gillett, Nicholas., The Swiss Constitution: Can it be Exported. YES Publications, Bristol, 1989

Goleman, D., Emotional Intelligence: Why It Can Matter More Than IQ, Bloomsbury, London, 1996.

Grangeon, Y. and Haller, C. The Coûme Across the Years (Tran: Stubbs, C.R.)

Greenwood, J.O. Quaker Encounters –Volume I – Friends and Relief, Sessions of York, 1975

Hancock, W.K., Four Studies of War and Peace in this Century, Cambridge University Press, 1961

Hancock, W.K., Smuts Volume I and II, Cambridge University Press, 1962 and 1968

Healey, D. The Time of My Life Michale Joseph, 1989

Housman, A: A Shropshire Lad. K. Paul, Trench, Treubner, 1896

Howard, Michael: The Causes of War in The Causes of War and Other Essays. London, Temple Smith, 1983.

Huizinga, J. Homo Ludens: A study of the play element in culture. Boston: The Beacon Press

Illich, Ivan Deschooling Society, Harmondsworth: Penguin 1973.

Keynes, J.M., The Economic Consequences of the Peace, 1919

Lattimer, M., On Campaigning: Second edition, 2000, Directory of Social Change

Lloyd, W.B. Waging Peace: The Swiss Experience. London, 1958, Methuen.

MacGrath, M. The art of teaching peacefully: Improving behavior and reducing conflict in the classroom. D. Fulton, London, 1998. .

MacMurray, John, Freedom in the Modern World, London, Faber and Faber, 1932

Mander, Gerry. Four Arguments for the Elimination of Television. 1977, Quill

McLean, D.: Nature's second sun: Leaves from a teacher's log. William Heinemann Ltd. 1954.

Miller, A., For Your Own Good – Hidden Cruelty in Child-rearing and The Roots of Violence Virago, London, 1984

Neave, A., They Have Their Exits. Pen & Sword, 2002

Pawley, M, The Private Future: Causes & Consequences of Community Collapse in the West,. Thames & Hudson 1973

Poster, C., & Kruger, eds. Community Education in the Western World. Routledge, London and New York, 1990

Poster, C., A., & Zimmer., eds. Community Education in the Third World, 1992.

Postgate, Oliver. Seeing Things: An Autobiography, Sidgwick and Jackson (Macmillan) London, 2000, p.442

Ruskin, J Unto This Last Smith, Elder & Co., 1862

Sangharakshita, U., Peace is a Fire, Windhorse Publications, 1995

Schumacher, Fritz, Small is Beautiful: Economics as if People Mattered. Blond and Briggs Ltd. 1973

Sellar, W C & Yeatman, R J, 1066 and all that, Methuen, 1931

Shakespeare, William. As You Like It. II. vii

Smuts, J.C., The League of Nations: A Practical Suggestion, Hodder and Stoughton, London, 1918, pp.71

Southey, Robert: 'After Blenheim', c.1800

Smuts, J., Holism and Evolution,. MacMillan. 1927

Sun Tzu, The Art of War, Translated by Lionel Giles, Stackpole 1944.

Tennyson, A., The World's Classics III: Poems of Alfred, Lord Tennyson: A Selection, Oxford University Press, 1901

Toffler, Alvin. Future Shock, Bantam Books, New York, 1970

Trevelyan, G.M., The Life of John Bright. Constable, London, 1913

Various Authors, Quaker Faith and Practice, Warwick, 1995

West, Ranyard., Conscience and Society, Methuen, London, 1942

Whitehouse, E & Pudney, W., A Volcano in my Tummy: Helping Children to Handle Anger, New Society Publishers, Canada, 1996.

Yunus, Mohammed with Alan Jolis. Banker to the Poor: The Autobiography of Mohammed Yunus, Founder of the Grameen Bank. Aurum Press, London,1998

Notes

1. John Ferguson, The Politics of Love: The New Testament and Non-Violent Revolution, Cambridge, 1982.
2. Various Authors, Quaker Faith and Practice, Warwick, 1995.
3. Various Authors, Quaker Faith and Practice, Warwick, 1995.
4. W C Sellar & R J Yeatman, 1066 and all that, Methuen, 1931.
5. Southey, Robert, 'After Blenheim', c1800.
6. Sun Tzu, The Art of War, Translated by Lionel Giles, Stackpole 1944.
7. Einstein, Albert. Out of My Later Years, Philosophy Library, New York, 1950.
8. Howard, Michael: *The Causes of War* in *The Causes of War and Other Essays*. London, Temple Smith, 1983.
9. Schumacher, Fritz, *Small is Beautiful: Economics as if People Mattered*. Blond and Briggs Ltd. 1973.
10. MacMurray, John, *Freedom in the Modern World*, London, Faber and Faber, 1932.
11. His remains were found eighty years later preserved by snow and ice.
12. Douglas, J.W.B. The Home and the School, MacGibbon and Kee, London, 1964.
13 Hancock, W.K., *Smuts Volume I and II*, Cambridge University Press, 1962 and 1968.
14. Smuts, J.C., *The League of Nations: A Practical Suggestion*, Hodder and Stoughton, London, 1918, pp.71.
15. Keynes, J.M., *The Economic Consequences of the Peace*, 1919.
16. Hancock, W.K., *Four Studies of War and Peace in this Century*, Cambridge University Press, 1961.
17. Smuts, J., *Holism and Evolution,*. MacMillan. 1927.

18. Quoted by W. K. Hancock in his two volume official biography of Smuts. Cambridge University Press, 1962 and 1968.
19. *Julius Caesar* III.i.1.
20. MacMurray, J. *Freedom in the Modern World*, Faber and Faber Limited, 1932.
21. West, Ranyard., *Conscience and Society*, Methuen, London, 1942.
22. Ruskin, J *Unto This Last* Smith, Elder & Co., 1862.
23. Greenwood, J.O. *Quaker Encounters - Volume I - Friends and Relief*, Sessions of York, 1975.
24. Grangeon, Y. and Haller, C. *The Coûme Across the Years* (Tran: Stubbs, C.R.).
25. Healey, D. *The Time of My Life* Michale Joseph, 1989.
26. Miller, A., *For Your Own Good - Hidden Cruelty in Child-rearing and The Roots of Violence* Virago, London, 1984.
27. The Diggers of the 17th Century were a community like the Bruderhof.
28. Pawley, M., *The Private Future: Causes & Consequences of Community Collapse in the West,*. Thames & Hudson 1973.
29. Charity, Kate, A Many-Sided Man. John Bellows of Gloucester 1831-1902. York: Sessions (1993).
30. Gillett, A. N., *Parents Only,* 1953 Island Press.
31. Gilbreth F.B., Cheaper By the Dozen, Heinemann, 1949.
32. A description of this incident can be found in the next chapter.
33. Douglas, J.W.B. The Home and the School, MacGibbon and Kee, London, 1964.
34. Gillett, Nicholas., *The Swiss Constitution: Can it be Exported.* YES Publications, Bristol, 1989.
35. Illich, Ivan Deschooling Society, Harmondsworth: Penguin 1973.
36. Easwaran, E., *A Man to Match His Mountains* (London: Random House., 1984).
37. Housman, AE: *A Shropshire Lad.* K. Paul, Trench, Treubner, 1896.
38. Gillett, Nicholas, Men Against War, Victor Gollancz, London 1965.
39. This book remains in an unpublished format December 2004.

40. Poster, C., & Kruger, eds. *Community Education in the Western World*. Routledge, London and New York, 1990, and Poster, C., A., & Zimmer., eds. *Community Education in the Third World* in 1992.

41. McLean, D.: *Nature's second sun: Leaves from a teacher's log*. William Heinemann Ltd. 1954.

42. Huizinga, J. Homo Ludens: A study of the play element in culture. Boston: The Beacon Press.

43. Goleman, D., Emotional Intelligence*: Why It Can Matter More Than IQ*, Bloomsbury, London, 1996.

44. MacGrath, M. The art of teaching peacefully: Improving behavior and reducing conflict in the classroom. D. Fulton, London, 1998.

45. Lattimer, M., On Campaigning: Second edition, 2000, Directory of Social Change.

46. Busby, Chris. *The Wings of Death: Nuclear Pollution and Human Health*, Green Audit Books, Aberystwyth, 1995.

47. Anheier, Helmut: Can Culture, Market and State Relate? London School of Economics Magazine Vol.12 No 1, December 2000.

48. Abelson, Reed: Charities' Investing: Left Hand, Meet Right. The New York Times, Archives. June 2000.

49. Jill Ratner of Oakland, California.

50. Neave, A., *They Have Their Exits*. Pen & Sword, 2002.

51. Barritt, D., *Orange and Green*. Northern Friends Peace Bd. 1972.

52. Mander, Gerry. *Four Arguments for the Elimination of Television*. 1977, Quill.

53. Bertrand, Maurice. *Some Reflections on the United Nations*. Geneva, 1985, JIU/REP/85/9.

54. Galtung, J., *There are Alternatives - Four Roads to Peace and Security*, Spokesman, 1984.

55. Richard Holbrooke explains that 'In addition to coordinating all programmes and activities of the UN (Including) its specialised agencies, he (the Secretary-General) should have the ability to make resource management decisions and reallocate personal Funds.' Cited in UN 2000, The UN's Millennium Summit New York 6-8 September 2000.

56. Gillett, Nicholas, *The Swiss Constitution: Can it be Exported.* YES Publications, Bristol, 1989.

57. Lloyd, W.B. Waging Peace: The Swiss Experience. London, 1958, Methuen.

58. Galtung, J., *There are Alternatives - Four Roads to Peace and Security,* Spokesman, 1984.

59. Sangharakshita, U., *Peace is a Fire,* Windhorse Publications, 1995.

60. Shakespeare, William. *As You Like It.* II. vii.

61. Postgate, Oliver. *Seeing Things: An Autobiography,* Sidgwick and Jackson (Macmillan) London, 2000, p.442.

62. Trevelyan, G.M., *The Life of John Bright.* Constable, London, 1913.

63. Forrester, Susan, ed., *Peace and Security:A Funding Guide for Independent Groups.* Directory of Social Change, London, 1998.

64. Bailey, Sydney .D. & Sam Daws. *The United Nations - A Concise Political Guide.* 3rd edition, 1995, Macmillan.

65. Daws, Sam. *Memorandum on An Agenda For Peace: The Expanding Role of the UN and the Implications for UK Policy.* UNA, London, 1993. (p.38).

66. Curle, A., Making Peace. London: Tavistock 1971.

67. Tennyson, A., The World's Classics III: Poems of Alfred, Lord Tennyson: A Selection, Oxford University Press, 1901.

68. Bjerstedt, Åke. (ed) Peace/War: Issues from a Psychological Perspective. 1993, Department of Education and Psychology Research, school of Education. Malmo, Sweden.

69. Yunus, Mohammed with Alan Jolis. Banker to the Poor: The Autobiography of Mohammed Yunus, Founder of the Grameen Bank. Aurum Press, London, 1998.

70. Toffler, Alvin. *Future Shock,* Bantam Books, New York, 1970.

71. Albery, N. et al (eds) *The Book of Social Inspirations: A Dictionary of Social Inventions.* Institute of Social Inventions, London, 2000.

72. Whitehouse, E & Pudney, W., *A Volcano in my Tummy: Helping Children to Handle Anger,* New Society Publishers, Canada, 1996.

73. Bird, Leonard, *Costa Rica: The Unarmed Democracy*, Sheppard Press, London, 1984.
74. Tennyson, A., The World's Classics III: Poems of Alfred, Lord Tennyson: A Selection, Oxford University Press, 1901.
75. Illich, I.D. De-schooling Society. Calder and Boyars. 1971.
76. Douglas, J.W.B. The Home and the School. MacGibbon & Kee. 1964.
77. Steel, D.J. & Taylor, L. Family History in Schools. Phillimore 1973.
78. Toffler, A. Future Shock. Penguin 1975.

Index

Brockington, David, 222
Bruderhof Camp, The, 79
Brynmawr in 1931, 70
Buddhism, 159
Building acoustics, 190
Burkeman, Stephen, 248
Cadbury, George, 86, 201
Cadbury, Henry, 87, 91
Campaign Against Anti-
    personnel Mines, 281
Campaigner, 207
Campaigning for peace, 316
Canute, King, 325
Car size, 176
Carpets, 180
Caspian Sea, 367
Centre for Civil Society, 245
Ceresole, Pierre, 69
CEWC, 193
Chakravarty, Amiya, 59
Change of heart, 15
Chauvinism, 321
Cheaper by the Dozen, 101
Chernobyl, 225
Chief of police, 161
Child art, 136
Child psychology, 195
Children in Northern Ireland,
    257
Children, the, 94
Chile, 93
China, 358
Churchill, 108
Circle of friends, 312
Circulated, 197
Citizens, 114
Citizenship, 138, 199, 214
Civil power, 247
Class sizes, 89
Climatic factor, 348
Colour bar, 35
Colour slides, 169
Communist Party, 14
Community, 138

Community Education, 199,
    202, 228
Community life, 80
Community Schools, 159, 192,
    370
Compensating activity, 361
Condover, 139
Conference on literacy, 190
Conferences
Peace in the Minds of Men, 194
Conflict between Moros and
    Christi, 156
Conflict management, 186
Conscience, 2, 4, 67, 73
Cook, Robin, 325
Cooperative democracy, 323
Cooperative form of democracy,
    284
Cooperative games, 96
Corrigan (McGuire), Mairead,
    263
Corruption, 271
Council for Education in World
    Citizenship, 205
Counterparts, 166
Crabbs Cross, 74
Creativeness, 128, 135, 138
Creativity, 131
Crucifix, 93
Cultural differences, 323
Culture of bees, 366
Culture of Peace, 2, 7, 14, 101,
    166, 266
Curiosity, 219
Curle, Adam, 266
Curriculum, 198
Cyril Poster, 202
Dalton Plan, 206
David, aged two, 53
Daws, Sam, 300
de Bunsen, Bernard, 30
Democracy, 13
Democratic, 113
Democratic citizenship, 371